LL 60

ECONOMIC HISTORY SERIES, No. XV

MANCHESTER MERCHANTS
AND FOREIGN TRADE
1850-1939

MANCHESTER MERCHANTS
AND FOREIGN TRADE
VOL. II.   1850-1939

BY

ARTHUR REDFORD

Professor of Economic History in the University of Manchester

ASSISTED BY

BRIAN W. CLAPP, B.A.

MANCHESTER UNIVERSITY PRESS

Published by the University of Manchester at
THE UNIVERSITY PRESS
316-324 OXFORD ROAD
MANCHESTER, 13
1956

08549885

L000318345

03057060

PRINTED IN GREAT BRITAIN AT
THE UNIVERSITY PRESS
ABERDEEN

FOREWORD

by SIR RAYMOND STREAT, C.B.E.

THE part played by industrial and commercial organisations in political and economic affairs is of great importance to our entire society. One of their principal functions has always been to represent to government the desires and needs of the particular section of the industrial or commercial community which they happen to represent in connection with internal legislation and external relationships. Sometimes political parties, either at the instance of commercial organisations or for social or political reasons, initiate legislation which affects the conditions under which industry and trade can be carried on. On such occasions the trade organisations represent the views of their members for or against proposed legislation or in favour of amendments which will in their judgment make the proposals more workable or more advantageous. In regard to problems of overseas trade, developments calling for representations by trade organisations may arise on the initiative of the home government who, for example, may change their tariff policy or embark on negotiations with the governments of other countries. On the other hand, foreign governments may introduce measures which have the consequence of altering the terms under which British goods may enter their territories.

In the nature of things the officers and officials of trade associations react from month to month to all such circumstances as they arise. They organise their deputations to the seat of government, they publish their views in the newspapers, they consult with their members to make sure that what they are recommending is supported by the current facts relating to industry and trade and is fully in accord with the opinions and wishes of their constituents. Often enough the issues of today are found in practice to be different from those of yesterday: no sooner is one question settled than another arises to demand attention, and the trade associations are too busy to stand back from their preoccupations of the hour and reflect upon the changing trends of opinion and policy which their representations and arguments are constantly influencing in one direction or the other.

It is, therefore, of peculiar interest to the business man and those interested in the activities of trade associations when the academic historian studies the records of their activities over a substantial period of years, trying to discern and define the changing trends of opinion and how they came to develop as they did. The historian might try to set the transactions of any individual trade association against the general historical record relating to the same periods or, more simply, in any one piece of work, he might limit himself to a study and a survey of the individual trade organisation's records, leaving it to others or himself in another work to relate all this to events on a wider scene. Obviously there is something to be said for the merits of both these lines of approach. Professor Redford has chosen to focus his attention closely on the records of the Manchester Chamber of Commerce. As a result, Manchester business men will find it immensely interesting to study in the longer perspective of history their own decisions and actions, and those of their predecessors, as formulated under the pressure of current events. Some decisions will seem better than others, no doubt, for hindsight is a simpler process than foresight, but the comparison between opinions at the time and subsequent events will be instructive.

Business men elsewhere may be interested to find how active their Manchester brethren have been through such a long period of years in influencing national policies, particularly in the field of import duties at home and abroad. The student of history who often traces the emergence and development of new or changed policies through the records of Parliament and the biographies of statesmen will, I imagine, be very pleased to have access to a survey of the same course of events seen through the eyes of a deeply-involved section of the trading community.

I am not sure that in trade policies history really repeats itself or that any of us who today are grappling with current problems of trade policy will find the answers to our conundrums from the records of our predecessors. We may get a rather wry sense of consolation from the proof these pages will afford that the difficulties with which we have to contend, and the obstacles we encounter, are nothing new in principle though the details of today's arguments are different from those of yesterday. Perspective should give greater depth to judgment, even if it may not point specifically to the right answer.

For all these reasons I am much gratified to be afforded the privilege of commending this book to business men and students. It would be an excellent thing, from many points of view, if other trade organisations could follow the example of the Manchester Chamber of Commerce and make their records available to the Department of Economic History in one of the Universities.

PREFACE

WORK on this book has been spread over too many years. The first suggestion that I should study the records of the Manchester Chamber of Commerce came from Mr. (now Sir) Raymond Streat, so long ago as 1928. To make a preliminary exploration of the material I organised a team of six senior undergraduates, who co-operated among themselves in working through the earlier Proceedings of the Chamber. The members of the team used their notes as raw material in preparing academic theses, which I then used as a guide to my own study of the records ; the resultant volume, entitled *Manchester Merchants and Foreign Trade, 1794-1858*, was published in 1934.

By that time a fresh team of undergraduate students had already begun work on the later records of the Chamber, and it was planned to write a further volume covering the second half of the nineteenth century. The nine members of this new team were Constance Mills, H. Inch, H. Oddy, A. Duckworth, Beryl Price, Muriel Arnett, Jessie Mercer, C. A. Firth, and J. Croft. They wrote their theses in 1934-35, and I began on the second stage of the work. In the summer of 1935, however, the Corporation of Manchester asked me to write a full-length work on the administrative development of the town, to commemorate the centenary of Manchester's municipal charter, which was granted in 1838. *The History of Local Government in Manchester* was published (in three volumes) in 1939-40 ; but it was not possible for me to resume work on the records of the Chamber of Commerce during the next few years. Even when the war was over the work did not get beyond the note-taking and card-indexing stage, until Mr. Brian Clapp came to Manchester as my research assistant in 1950. For four years he collaborated very closely with me at every stage in the preparation of the present volume : note-taking, indexing, drafting, and revising. He carried my study of the records forward from the year 1910, and was therefore especially responsible for the substance of the later chapters of the book ; the Appendix on the membership of the Manchester Chamber of Commerce

was entirely his own work, and he voluntarily undertook
the drafting of the index. That the book is at last ready
for publication must be ascribed largely to Mr. Clapp's mental
energy and youthful zeal ; nevertheless, on all points relating to the constructional framework of the volume, all
questions of literary style, and all matters of fact I have
had the last word and must bear the sole responsibility for
any faults.

The main purpose of the work, as a whole, has been to
analyse the problems which have troubled the business men
of Manchester during the last century and a half, and to
trace the development of commercial opinion. In the earlier
volume the growth and triumph of the Free Trade movement
was the central theme, though the volume left for later discussion the Anglo-French Commercial Treaty of 1860, with
which (according to Gladstone) " the movement in favour
of free trade reached its zenith ". The present volume
carries the story forward to the eve of the Second World
War, and finds its natural dividing point at the beginning
of the First World War in 1914. The earlier part of the
volume (Chapters I-XIV) describes the fluctuating but
generally prosperous fortunes of Manchester under Free
Trade. The later chapters (XV-XXIII) are concerned with
the grievous setbacks and chequered trading conditions of
our own generation. In these later chapters questions are
discussed which will be in the memory of many Manchester
business men still actively engaged in the cotton industry
and trade. They may find what appear to them to be mis-
takes of fact or errors of judgment ; the wrong points may
have been emphasised and the important points missed.
Such short-comings should be attributed to ignorance rather
than to carelessness or conscious bias.

If some parts of the book seem to exaggerate the influence
of the Manchester merchants upon national policy, this
defect may be charitably excused as arising partly from local
patriotism but mainly from the limitations of the documentary
material used. All such records as those of the Chamber
of Commerce are tantalisingly incomplete ; they only sum-
marise discussions which took place at meetings of the
Chamber, or of the Board of Directors, or of one of the
Sections, omitting what was discussed elsewhere or talked
about privately without being brought before any formal
meeting. At their best, such records can only reflect the

special point of view of the Manchester merchants; they do not form any adequate basis for a general survey of the forces moulding British commercial policy and governing the course of overseas trade. Nevertheless, the world-wide range of the export trade in cotton goods has confronted successive generations of Manchester men with questions of international scope, and the commercial opinions reflected in the records of the Chamber of Commerce have often been of more than local or regional interest. On many occasions the Manchester merchants have given a lead which the country has followed, for good or ill.

The Directors of the Manchester Chamber of Commerce have left us entirely free to write the book in our own way and according to our own conception of historical truth; they have also shown great generosity and public spirit by agreeing to bear part of the expenses of publication. We owe a special debt of gratitude to them and to the present Secretary of the Chamber, Mr. James Ainsley, who has clarified many technical points and has given us much special information. Sir Raymond Streat read the typescript of the present volume and suggested many amendments, especially in Part II; his close personal knowledge of the questions which were being discussed in Manchester during the 'twenties and 'thirties has enabled him to save us from several blunders. We are very grateful to him for help and encouragement extending now over a quarter-century; we hope that he will soon add to his many public services by publishing his private memoirs of the period.

Several of my academic colleagues have given unselfish and invaluable help in the final preparation of the book for publication. Professor Ely Devons, Dr. T. S. Willan, Dr. W. H. Chaloner, Mr. A. E. Musson and Dr. E. R. R. Green have all shared in the hard labour of proof-reading, and have made special contributions from their widely-varied fields of learning. To members of the staff of the Manchester Central Library I have been indebted for expert and enthusiastic help throughout almost the whole of my working lifetime; it might be ungracious to single out individual members for special mention, and therefore I hope that they will allow me to thank them collectively. Lastly, I wish to thank Mr. T. L. Jones, the Secretary of the Manchester University Press, for his watchful care and unfailing patience in overcoming the many technical difficulties encountered during the protracted process of publication. I am deeply grateful to all my friends and colleagues for their help ; I wish that I could do as much for them as they have done for me.

ARTHUR REDFORD.

CONTENTS

PART II

WAR, DEPRESSION, AND NEW PROBLEMS

NOTE ON SOURCES

THIS book, like its predecessor *Manchester Merchants and Foreign Trade, 1794-1858*, is based mainly on the records of the Manchester Chamber of Commerce. These records fall into two classes, the unprinted and the printed. Of the unprinted records, by far the most important are the Proceedings of the Board of Directors of the Manchester Chamber of Commerce, cited in the earlier book as " Proceedings of the Manchester Chamber of Commerce ", and here as " Proceedings ". The Proceedings, handwritten to 1894 and in typescript from then on, cover the years 1849-1925 in eleven very bulky volumes ; from 1926, the Proceedings of the Board of Directors have been bound separately each year. Except in the years 1904-20, when Walter Speakman was secretary of the Manchester Chamber of Commerce, the Proceedings give a full account of the debates and decisions of the Board of Directors, and are the principal source for this book. Under Walter Speakman the Proceedings are much more concise and much less informative ; luckily, the deficiency can be made good from other sources. Other manuscript records of the Chamber exist, but have not been of much use for this book. There are no outgoing manuscript letters, but a few letters from the Board of Trade and the Foreign Office survive for the years 1855-65 ; they contain very little material not incorporated in the Proceedings. At points where the Proceedings are not as full as could be wished it has been possible to consult the minutes of the Chamber's committees and sections. Until 1889, the minutes of committees were written into the same volume as the Proceedings ; but with the establishment of standing committees and the development since 1889 of sections for particular trades, committee and sectional minutes have been preserved separately. Except for the manuscript letters, all these records down to the year 1937 are now deposited in the Manchester Central Reference Library.

Printed sources were a valuable supplement to the unprinted records. The Manchester Chamber of Commerce possesses a bound series of its printed Annual Reports for the years 1821-89. These Annual Reports include verbatim accounts of the proceedings at the annual general meetings of members, cited in this volume as " Annual Meeting ". The reports for the years 1854-58 are missing, but the loss can be made good from Manchester newspapers, which printed the Annual Reports in full. For the years 1880-89, the Chamber circulated to its members with the Annual Report a long printed appendix containing the text of memorials and the most important correspondence, inward and outward, of the previous year. This valuable source has been cited as " Letter ", or " Memorial ", followed by the date. The appendix to the Annual Report developed into a monthly journal in 1890, when the Chamber of Commerce began to publish its *Monthly Record*. The *Monthly Record* contains the Annual Reports of the Chamber and of its sections, together with an account of Board meetings and much of the Chamber's correspondence, besides other information of interest to Manchester business men, especially textile exporters. Until 1920, the *Monthly Record* printed long extracts from the Chamber's correspondence, and gave a full report of the meetings of the Board of Directors ; for the years 1904-20, when the Proceedings are disappointingly brief, the *Monthly Record* is the best source for the history of the Manchester Chamber of Commerce. After 1920, the *Monthly Record* is much more reticent ; but as the Proceedings again become fuller under the secretaryship of Mr. (now Sir) Raymond Streat, there is no shortage of material for the history of the Chamber between the wars.

INTRODUCTION

MANCHESTER IN THE EIGHTEEN-FIFTIES

By the middle years of the nineteenth century Manchester was a great city and a regional metropolis. Since the incorporation of 1838 the population of the municipal borough had increased from 180,000 to over 300,000 ; this large population was crowded into an area less than one-sixth of the area of the modern city. The civic charter of 1853 was of merely formal significance ; in everything except the name, Manchester had already assumed the status of a city, and was quite willing to accept Disraeli's assurance that " Manchester is as great a human exploit as Athens ". The Corporation had already taken over the powers and functions of the several bodies of Police Commissioners previously operating in the various townships of the borough ; it had also bought out the manorial rights of the Mosleys and extinguished the Court Leet. The Manchester General Improvement Act of 1851 had transferred the management of the highways from the highway surveyors of the townships to the Borough Council ; the borough had also secured a separate Commission of the Peace and a separate Court of Quarter Sessions.

The gasworks developed by the Manchester Police Commissioners had been taken over in 1843, and had greatly strengthened the financial position of the municipality ; even in the intense commercial distress of 1847, the municipal credit of Manchester had remained unchallenged. An investment in the bonds of the Corporation of Manchester was recognised to be " quite as safe as in the public funds ; it is less subject to fluctuation, and will incur less expense of management." It was in 1847 that the first Manchester Corporation Waterworks Act allowed the municipality to buy the property of the old Manchester and Salford Waterworks Company, and to begin the construction of the Longdendale reservoirs. The scheme became fully operative in 1851, and by that time water from Longdendale was available for use in Manchester. In all the circumstances, this was probably the most spectacular achievement of the new municipality ; the Longdendale reservoirs contributed more than any other work of that generation to make Manchester a clean and healthy city.

This " classic type of modern manufacturing town " had never been merely the barracks of an industry ; long before the middle of the century it had begun to develop an urbane cultural tradition which was notably strengthened during the 1850's. The Manchester Grammar School had been keeping a sharp edge on Mancunian brains for three centuries ; Cheetham's Hospital and Library might claim to be the oldest Blue Coat School and the oldest surviving public free library in England. The Manchester Royal Infirmary had been serving the community for a century, and had become the focus of an elaborate system of medical institutions. The Manchester Literary and Philosophical Society had been active for about three-quarters of a century ; the Manchester Statistical Society was older than the Royal Statistical Society. The Royal Manchester Institution " for the Promotion of Literature, Science and the Arts ", had built in Mosley Street the Art Gallery, designed by Sir Charles Barry, which still remains the chief art gallery of the city. The Manchester Natural History Society had established the museum which later became (and remains) the Manchester Museum, administered by the University. The Manchester Royal Medical College, founded in 1824, might claim to be the first and best provincial school of medicine and surgery.

Round these substantial and dignified institutions appropriate to a great city there had grown up the lighter amenities of political and social clubs, circulating and subscription libraries, theatres, and concert halls, as well as some working-class educational and social institutions. The two most prominent clubs were the somewhat exclusive Union Club and the more democratic Athenaeum ; among the libraries were the Manchester Subscription Library at the Exchange, and the Portico in Mosley Street. The chief theatres were the Theatre Royal in Fountain Street and the Queen's in York Street ; there were also several public Concert Rooms, in addition to those attached to many of the public houses patronised by the working classes. For the serious-minded working men there was the Manchester Mechanics' Institution, which was eventually to develop into the Manchester College of Technology, now affiliated to the University. Opportunities for outdoor recreation were not so plentiful as they should have been ; nevertheless, by the middle of the century Manchester had opened three fine public parks (one of them in Salford), for the enjoyment of those townspeople who were not active enough to reach " the beautifully undulating country between the valley of the Irk and Cheetham Hill " or " the fine valley of the Irwell, with its verdant meadows ".

During the 1850's urbane culture advanced with rapid strides. Manchester seems to have been the first town to set up a free public library under Ewart's Act of 1850, though it is true that Salford and Warrington had already taken action under an earlier statute of 1845. Manchester's first municipal library was opened in 1852 at the Owenite " Hall of Science " in Campfield, and was from the beginning divided into a Reference Library and a free Lending Library ; before the end of the decade several branch libraries had been started, in spite of formidable legal and financial difficulties. While the Public Free Library was arranging its first collection of books in Campfield, Owens College opened its doors to students for the first time in Quay Street, not far away. For some time the existence of the College was decidedly precarious and its survival uncertain. In 1852 it had only sixty-two students and an annual income of £3,240 ; there were then three full-time and three part-time professors. By 1857 (a year of commercial crisis) the day students had dwindled to thirty-three, and even the *Manchester Guardian* thought that the College had been " a mortifying failure ". Within a few years, however, the tide had turned and the number of day students was well over a hundred ; from these small beginnings there was to emerge the Victoria University of Manchester, which in 1950 had nearly six thousand students and an annual income of over a million pounds.

The fine arts in Manchester were slow in coming to maturity. Benjamin Haydon " found Manchester in a dreadful condition as to art " ; Ruskin " perceived that Manchester could produce no good art and no good literature ". Nevertheless, the exhibition of the Art Treasures of the United Kingdom, which was held in 1857, must have given an important stimulus to the local appreciation of art ; about 1,336,800 persons visited the exhibition, and Ruskin lectured on " The Political Economy of Art ". The exhibition was also an important landmark in local musical history ; Charles Hallé was in charge of the musical arrangements, and the Hallé Concerts have been a glory of Manchester life ever since that time. A less famous consequence of the Art Treasures Exhibition

was the settlement of the Manchester Cricket Club at Old
Trafford. Previously the club had played on a pitch in the
Botanical Gardens, Stretford Road; this was commandeered
for the purposes of the Exhibition of 1857, and a fresh start
had to be made at the Old Trafford ground, which was ultimately to achieve world-wide renown for its perfect turf and
its imperfect weather.

" Civilisation had begun slowly to raise its head above
the smoke "; but the smoke remained, and thickened with
the continued expansion of industry. The prosperity of Manchester did not depend on cotton alone; nevertheless, cotton
was unquestionably the main industry of the town and of the
surrounding region. The cotton industry of the world was
growing rapidly, and the machine products of the industrialised
countries of Europe and North America were ousting the hand-
produced cotton goods of most other countries. The British
cotton industry accounted for about a half of the cotton
consumption of the industrialised countries; this meant, in
effect, about a half of the cotton consumed by the cotton
factories of the world. Cotton yarns and piece goods accounted for nearly a half of Britain's visible exports. In the
1850's the Lancashire cotton industry, with its outliers in
Cheshire and North Derbyshire, comprised about three-
quarters of the whole cotton industry of Britain; this remains
broadly true whether the proportion is stated as a percentage
of the steam power employed, or the spindles, or the power-
looms, or the number of factories, or the number of factory
workers. Lancashire was the home of the most important
cotton industry in the world; and of the Lancashire cotton
industry Manchester was indisputably the centre.

Although Manchester was chiefly important as the centre
of the Lancashire cotton industry, there were many other
considerable manufactures in the town. Its silk factories
rivalled those of Macclesfield and Norwich; the town also
had outliers of the woollen and worsted trades, and even of the
linen industry. There were extensive works for bleaching,
dyeing, printing, and engraving, paper mills, saw mills, hat
factories, rubber works, soapworks, glassworks, breweries,
collieries, and chemical works. Engineering was very important, especially the manufacture of stationary steam-
engines, railway rolling-stock, textile machinery, and machine
tools. Sir Joseph Whitworth, whose armament and precision
instrument works had been established in Chorlton Street

since 1833, was a pioneer of the machine tool industry ; his method of " standardising screws, screw threads, and other mechanical essentials ", was soon widely used.   Three railway companies had their locomotive workshops at Manchester : the Manchester, Sheffield, and Lincolnshire at Gorton, the London and North Western at Longsight, the Lancashire and Yorkshire at Newton Heath.   The firm of Beyer and Peacock began in 1854 to make locomotives for both the home and the export trade.   Galloways, who built the first Manchester locomotive in 1831, were by the 1850's already beginning to develop their later speciality of boiler making.   One of the best known names in the engineering history of Victorian Manchester was that of William Fairbairn ; his Ancoats works for the building of bridges, steam engines, and boilers was still active in the middle years of the century, and was carried on by his sons after 1853.

The abundant local supplies of coal encouraged the development of important chemical industries, which were already well established in and round Manchester by the middle of the century.   The next two decades were crowded with chemical discoveries which transformed the dyestuffs industry and widened the markets for Lancashire textile goods.   In 1848 Edward Schunck, at Kersal, laid the scientific foundation for the later commercial production of artificial alizarine from a coal-tar derivative.   Manchester had been a pioneer in the gas industry, and the distillation of gas-tar was already established on a commercial scale.   The firm of Hardman and Holden, of Miles Platting, was using gasworks' waste in the production of sulphocyanides ; this firm was the first to manufacture artificial alizarine after the German patents had expired.   In 1856 Perkin discovered Mauveine, the first coal-tar dye ; within a few years Aniline Black had been followed by Aniline Yellow, Manchester Yellow, and Manchester Brown, later called Bismarck Brown.   By that time heavy chemical manufactures were moving from Manchester to Merseyside ; but Grace, Calvert, and Lowe were producing carbolic acid from coal-tar at their factory near the Bradford Road Colliery, and according to Ludwig Mond there were ten soda factories in the neighbourhood of Manchester.

It would be misleading to concentrate attention exclusively upon the industrial activity of the town.   By the 1850's Manchester was primarily important as a commercial centre, the focus of a vast urban network of which such towns as

Ashton-under-Lyne, Bolton, Bury, Hyde, Oldham, Rochdale, and Stockport were the manufacturing parts. The centre of the city was becoming congested with offices and warehouses ; the factories (and the middle-class dwelling houses) were being pushed farther out. The typical business men of Manchester were becoming merchants rather than manufacturers, though the manufacturers in the surrounding towns often had their offices in Manchester, attended the Manchester Exchange, and were members of the Manchester Chamber of Commerce. As the commercial centre of a mighty industrial region, Manchester reflected in its history the triumphs and vicissitudes of a most unsettled generation. The commercial crises of 1847 and 1857 were quite as disturbing and perplexing as those of 1825 and 1836 ; the Manchester business men of the 'forties and 'fifties " cannot for long have been free from the fear of commercial collapse lurking behind each temporary revival of trade ". It was against this background of unstable industrial and commercial expansion that Free Trade struggled towards its crowning triumph of 1860.[1]

[1] For the developments outlined in this introductory chapter, see A. Redford, *The History of Local Government in Manchester*, Vol. II (1940), Chaps. XX and XXI ; A. Redford, *Manchester Merchants and Foreign Trade, 1794-1858* (1934), Chap. XVII ; *Manchester Guardian*, 26th and 27th March 1953, especially the articles by P. B. Dingle, Derek Senior, H. B. Charlton, W. H. Chaloner, R. Robson, P. K. Standring, Lawrence Haward, H. D. Davies, and Charles Nowell.

PART I

THE AGE OF FREE TRADE, 1850-1914

CHAPTER I

THE CLIMAX OF FREE TRADE, 1846-1860

" When Peel fell in 1846 ", wrote Sir John Clapham, " the free trade programme was in the ascendant, but there had been few clean cuts." Nearly all raw materials had been freed of import duties, the most notable exception being timber, which still bore considerable duties with preferences for the Empire. Though there remained only a registration duty of one shilling a quarter on corn, many other foods were still taxed, including butter, cheese, hams, tongues, and cured fish ; there were imperial preferences on sugar and coffee, that on sugar being as high as a penny a pound. The only important class of manufactures still protected was silk, some silk goods bearing specific duties, the rest paying 15 per cent. *ad valorem*.[1] In the struggle which had thus " disposed of effective protection to the staples of agriculture, the extractive industries and nearly all manufactures ",[2] the Manchester merchants had been well to the fore. But they were by no means satisfied with the fact that Parliament had substantially granted their demands ; the belief in free trade had become a dogma which would have to be carried out to the letter before the Manchester merchants would rest contented.

The years of good trade which followed the repeal of the Corn Laws fortified the Manchester merchants in their strong beliefs. In 1851 Thomas Bazley, President of the Chamber, described the previous year as

characterised by steadiness in all the operations connected with trade and commerce. Our people on every hand [he said] have been well employed ; abundance of labour and of food we have seen in every direction ; and upon the whole we have had as much national and commercial prosperity as the country may have witnessed at any former time.[3]

This happy state of affairs was contrasted sharply with the

---

[1] J. H. Clapham, *Economic History of Modern Britain*, Vol. I, pp. 497 ff.
[2] *Ibid.*, Vol. II, p. 1.
[3] *Manchester Examiner and Times*, 12th February 1851.

course of events on the Continent, where since 1848 the most important countries had been in a state

either of actual convulsion or of doubtful tranquility . . . and yet during that period have the exports and imports of Great Britain attained a magnitude at once astounding and gratifying. . . . The sound condition of the people of this country, as shown by the trade returns, proves that what is known by the name of reciprocity among nations is in reference to commercial pursuits a phantom or a snare.[1]

The Navigation Laws were still, in 1846, an obstacle to the spread of free trade ; it is true that by negotiating treaties of reciprocity the government had whittled away the scope of the Laws, but for Manchester merchants this was not enough : the Laws might be harmless at the moment, but while they remained on the statute-book they were a potential danger and a standing challenge to all free-traders. As early as 1841 the Manchester Chamber of Commerce had included the Navigation Laws in the general condemnation of protective duties contained in their *Report on the Injurious Effects of the Restrictions on Trade.*[2] More urgent questions, notably the Corn Laws, later distracted the Chamber's attention from restrictions on shipping, and it was not until 1848 that the Navigation Laws came in for serious criticism. In that year the Chamber addressed the first of a series of petitions to Parliament praying for the repeal of the Laws ;[3] after the agitation had come to its successful conclusion in 1849 the Board of Directors noted with satisfaction that the Chamber had been " the first of all public bodies to call for this salutary course of policy . . . and that the opinions of those who were averse to the change have softened down more quickly than on any other large questions ".[4] In 1853, this time at the request of the Newcastle Chamber of Commerce, the Manchester merchants petitioned for the removal of all restrictions on foreign vessels in the British coasting trade, condemning the mistaken caution which had exempted the coasting trade from the repeal of the Navigation Laws in 1849, and the particularly injurious effects which the remaining restrictions were having on our relations with the United States.[5] The coasting trade was thrown open as

---

[1] Annual Report for 1851, p. 23.
[2] For this report see A. Redford, *Manchester Merchants and Foreign Trade, 1794-1858*, pp. 152-3.
[3] Proceedings, 29th March 1849.   [4] Annual Report for 1849, p. 7.
[5] Proceedings, 30th June 1853, and Annual Report for 1853, p. 11.

desired, for by 1853 the opposition to free trade had grown very feeble : the chief obstacle was no longer the protests of affected trades but the government's need for revenue. The Manchester merchants did not realise at the time how slight was the support still given to Protection. The return of a Conservative government in 1852 aroused the sharpest anxiety ; without any very good reason, the Chamber of Commerce jumped to the conclusion that the Corn Laws were about to be reimposed. A special public meeting was called to protest against any reversal of the policy of Free Trade, which was " diffusing happiness by spreading employment on every side, and elevating the moral character of the people by diminishing poverty and crime ".[1] The Chamber disclaimed any intention to interfere in party politics, but showed unconcealed satisfaction when Lord Derby's government was defeated at the polls in 1852. This defeat, it was held, ensured that " whatever opposition the needful extension of unrestricted commerce may yet meet with, no party in the state will hereafter advocate a return to a protective policy ".[2]

Throughout the 'fifties, the Manchester merchants kept up their attack on the few remaining protective duties and on the differential duties affecting the importation of imperial and French wines. The reasons for concentrating the attack on these duties were twofold : in the first place, few other substantial duties remained ; in the second place, wines and silk goods were staple French products whose exclusion from the British market was believed to hamper the growth of British exports to France. The agitation against the wine and silk duties began a curious phase in the history of Manchester policy, based on a belief that persisted in the face of all the evidence for over thirty years that France could be induced to allow free imports and could therefore become a large market for Manchester goods. But by linking lower duties on foreign goods with the hope of lower duties abroad, the Manchester Chamber laid itself open to the charge of advocating the exploded doctrine of reciprocity. This charge it took some pains to deny: " British taxation should have reference to British interests only ". Britain's example, it was maintained, would encourage France, and through her the other countries of Europe, to adopt "improved principles of taxation ".[3] No other form of pressure would be consistent with free trade principles.

[1] Annual Report for 1852, p. 12.   [2] Ibid., p. 13.
[3] Proceedings, 10th October 1852.

The Manchester Chamber of Commerce first broached the
question of the wine duties to Lord Derby's ministry in October
1852. Since the removal of the preferential duties on Empire
coffee in 1851,[1] reform of the tariff had been at a standstill
and the Chamber felt that a fresh advance was overdue.[2]
While recognising that the Chancellor of the Exchequer
might not be able to abolish all the differential duties that still
disfigured the tariff, the Chamber urged that he should reduce
the wine duties by about four-fifths. In this, Manchester
was not alone : in February 1853 a deputation from the London
Association for the Reduction of the Duties on Foreign Wines
visited Manchester to enlist support for the campaign.[3]
The arguments brought forward were applauded as enthusias-
tically as if they had never been heard before, and it was a
great disappointment that Mr. Gladstone's otherwise admirable
budget of 1853 did not touch the wine duties.[4]   In a budget
which swept away so many protective duties it was perhaps
hardly surprising that the Chancellor refused to sacrifice any
of the £3,000,000 raised by the wine duties.   It may be that
the Manchester merchants tacitly recognised this fact, since
interest in the question waned when it became clear that
Mr. Gladstone was not willing to amend his budget to meet
Manchester's demands.   When important cabinet ministers
visited Manchester—Mr. Gladstone, at the end of 1853,
Lord Palmerston in 1856—the Chamber of Commerce took
the opportunity of reminding them that the wine duties were
very heavy and discriminated against European wines ;[5]
but such sporadic action was taken more to keep the flag
flying than with any serious hope that immediate relief
would be granted.   In the end the country had to wait until
1860 for the equalisation of the wine duties, and the change
when it came took the form not of a unilateral renunciation
but of a clause in a commercial treaty.   Reciprocity might
be an exploded doctrine, but Manchester merchants were
practical men, and rightly acted on the principle that in-
consistency in a good cause is sometimes justifiable.

The attack on the silk duties followed a very similar
course.   The Chamber of Commerce had mentioned them
unfavourably in its *Report on the Injurious Effects of the*

[1] For the coffee duties see Redford, *op. cit.*, pp. 144-7.
[2] Annual Report for 1852, p. 8.   [3] Proceedings, 24th February 1853.
[4] *Ibid.*, 28th April 1853.
[5] *Ibid.*, 6th October 1853 and 3rd November 1856.

Restrictions on Trade (1841), but had not pressed the matter at that time. The question was revived in 1852 as part of the campaign to show Europe by encouragement and example that free trade paid ; as with the wine duties, the Chamber hoped that lower duties would have their most beneficial repercussions in France.[1] In 1853, moved by the buoyant revenue of 1852-53 and by " a further examination into the actual conditions of the silk manufacturing trade ", Manchester went further and demanded the " total and immediate abrogation of duty on imported silk manufactures ".[2] Surprisingly enough, twenty-seven of the principal Manchester silk manufacturing firms also favoured free trade in silk ; they argued that the effect of the 15 per cent. duty on imported silk goods was " to create an impression in the markets of the world that England is unable to compete with the Continental Manufacturer ".[3] They therefore asked to be stripped of their privileges, " not partially and gradually but totally and immediately ". Mr. Gladstone refused, however, to go beyond the slight changes he had already announced in his Budget speech ; [4] to have repealed the duties entirely would have cost him £240,000. He did promise to consider the matter again later.[5]

Relying on this promise, the Chamber of Commerce prepared a memorial renewing the demand for free trade in silk goods. " Freed from protection, the Throwsters of silk have prospered beyond all precedent ", according to this memorial, while the manufacturer of broad silk had languished in depression.[6] But the time was not auspicious ; Turkey and Russia were already at war, and before the end of the month Great Britain and France had joined Turkey. In these circumstances Mr. Gladstone could plausibly plead " the disturbed aspect of European politics " as his reason for not complying with Manchester's request.[7]

Having failed in eighteen months of fairly continuous agitation to repeal the silk duties or to reduce the wine duties, the Manchester Chamber of Commerce turned away from the reform of the British tariff. The Manchester merchants had not lost any of their enthusiasm for free trade, and willingly sent a representative to a Free Trade Congress

[1] Proceedings, 7th October 1852.   [2] *Ibid.*, 14th April 1853.   [3] *Ibid.*
[4] For the very complicated details, see *Customs Tariff of the U.K.*, Cmd. 8706 of 1897.   [5] Proceedings, 26th May 1853.
[6] *Ibid.*, 8th March 1854.   [7] *Ibid.*, 22nd March 1854.

at Brussels in 1856 ; [1] but other matters, such as the reform
of the Government of India, and the currency laws, were of
more pressing importance. Not until 1860 did interest in the
tariff question revive, and then the Manchester Chamber of
Commerce acted in response to outside events ; it did not
initiate the movement which swept away the remnants of protective tariffs in England, though it gave powerful support while
the changes were proceeding.

Secret and unofficial negotiations for an Anglo-French
treaty of commerce had begun in October 1859, between
Michel Chevalier, the leader of the free trade party in
France, and Richard Cobden, the hero of the English free
traders.[2] The negotiations began in London but were soon
transferred to Paris, where at the end of the year Cobden
was given the status of an official representative of the
British Government. The secret and conspiratorial atmosphere so dear to the Emperor of the French continued to
surround the negotiations almost until the signature of the
treaty on the 23rd January 1860.[3] But as soon as the
Manchester Chamber of Commerce understood the terms of the
treaty—which included the abolition of all British duties on
imported silks, and steep reductions in the wine duties—it
lent the weight of its authority to the cause. It congratulated
the House of Commons on the comprehensiveness of Mr.
Gladstone's budget, which incorporated the measures necessary
to bring the treaty into effect. This Budget, declared the
Manchester Chamber of Commerce, was

a sound fiscal, industrial and commercial measure which will
confer great benefit on the entire community and be the means of
giving increased energy to those principles of free trade to the
adoption of which by this Country . . . may be traced much of the
prosperity and happiness at present enjoyed by all classes.

The Chamber voted its cordial thanks to Richard Cobden,
M.P., " for his voluntary and patriotic exertions in negotiating
the recent treaty with France ".[4]

Cobden's exertions were not at an end yet, however, and
the Manchester Chamber's had hardly begun. Article XIII
of the treaty provided that the French duties on imported
goods should be converted from *ad valorem* to specific duties

---

[1] Proceedings, 24th June, 10th September and 23rd October 1856.
[2] A. Dunham, *Anglo-French Treaty of Commerce of 1860* (1930), pp. 52-3.
[3] *Ibid.*, pp. 72-3 and pp. 83-4.   [4] Proceedings, 13th February 1860.

equivalent to not more than 30 per cent. ; the prices on which
the duties were to be based would be the average price of the
six months preceding the signature of the treaty. A mixed
Anglo-French Commission was to decide what the duties should
be.[1] When it was realised that the treaty contained such a
provision the Manchester merchants were quick to voice their
disapproval ; they resolved that conversion of *ad valorem* into
specific duties " would be impracticable so far as regards the
manufactures of this district ", and appointed a deputation
to wait upon the Chancellor of the Exchequer and the President of the Board of Trade.[2] Later a further deputation
pressed their views on the President of the Board of Trade and
Richard Cobden, who " did not at first appear to see the difficulties with which the [specific] system was surrounded " ;
but " before the interview terminated, Mr. Cobden's
opinion had undergone considerable modification". To modify
Cobden's opinion was one thing ; but to get the French to
reopen negotiations on the terms of an agreed and signed
treaty was quite another. In any case the Chamber of
Commerce, though resolved to press for the *ad valorem*
principle to the utmost, was willing to co-operate in the
work of framing a practicable scale of duties and to assist
Cobden with technical advice at the proper time.[3] The
Manchester delegation which was to advise Cobden on the
cotton clauses of the revised French tariff eventually left for
Paris in September ; the delegation had instructions not to
commit the Chamber " to any opinion as to the rate of duties
which ought to be imposed by the French Government on
English manufactures ".[4]

In Paris the delegation optimistically began by urging
the case for *ad valorem* duties, but met with a blank refusal.
The delegation, which included representatives of the Glasgow
Chamber of Commerce, then settled down to the work it was
meant to do—the valuation and classification of cotton goods
for inclusion in the tariff. At the outset the delegates had to
convince the mixed Commission that the classification proposed by the French expert was altogether too complicated.
Although the Frenchman stuck to his scheme " with all the
tenacity of an Inventor " the British delegates finally secured
its rejection by the mixed Commission. In its place they

[1] Dunham, *op. cit.*, pp. 100-1.　　[2] Proceedings, 23rd February 1860.
[3] *Ibid.*, 26th April 1860.
[4] *Ibid.*, 16th July and 21st September 1860.

prepared a simpler scheme for Cobden to submit to the Commission, but even then the difficulties were by no means at an end. At one stage in the negotiations Cobden and Slagg, the Manchester Chamber's chief expert, were driven to conclude " that it would be better simply to say that if they refused *ad valorem* (for certain classes of goods) we had nothing to propose ".[1]   The Convention embodying the new tariff was eventually signed on the 16th November 1860.[2]

At a special general meeting in December, the Manchester Chamber of Commerce recorded its confidence in the great value of the treaty, though the detailed schedules did not give full satisfaction.

The difficulties in attempting the classification of printed goods, and every class of fancy woven fabrics, have been practically acknowledged in the Tariff by the admission of many kinds of such goods at an *ad valorem* duty ; but it will be found that in the case of Yarns, cotton woollen and linen, in plain cotton and linen fabrics, in Fustians and Velvets, a complicated scale of specific duties has been adopted.   The Directors regret that the very simple form (*ad valorem* duties) suggested by them was not accepted.

Apart from the complication of the specific duties, the Chamber had objected because of

the unfairness of calculating them upon the medium prices ruling during the six months preceding the ratification of the Treaty, as a fair average would not be arrived at, prices having been higher during that period than at any time during the previous ten years.[3]

As it happened, the cotton famine soon drove prices far above the 1859 level, to which they did not return until the end of the 'sixties.   The Manchester merchants could not have known that the protectionist French would be so soon hoist with their own petard.

Despite this lucky accident, there was no spectacular increase in the volume of cotton goods exported to France, which remained one of Lancashire's smaller markets.   For all that, the Manchester Chamber of Commerce was well satisfied with the results of the treaty :

The exports of cotton goods to France, which in 1858 amounted to £279,918, had in 1867 reached £1,659,433.   It was not a losing business to send seven times the value of cotton goods into France that we did in 1858. . . . The imports from France to this country

[1] Proceedings, 5th November 1860.   [2] Dunham, *op. cit.*, p. 139.
[3] Proceedings, 19th December 1860.

had increased from £13,000,000 in 1858 to £34,000,000 in 1867 and the value of our exports from £9,000,000 to £23,000,000 so that the increase was about equal on both sides.[1]

When the treaty was signed Mr. Henry Ashworth, a Bolton cotton spinner and a Director of the Manchester Chamber,

rejoiced at the state of things it indicated . . . for after forty years of business he had never had a French Merchant's name in his ledger, and he should like to have many there in his lifetime.[2]

Whether many French merchants' names ever did appear in Mr. Ashworth's ledger may be doubted, but that there were some is highly probable. " The dawn of free trade principles in France ",[3] and Mr. Gladstone's budget in 1860, had less practical effect than is traditionally assigned to them, but they made a splendid coping-stone to the free trade edifice.

[1] Annual Meeting, 1st February 1869.
[2] Annual Meeting, reported in *Manchester Guardian*, 31st January 1860.
[3] Annual Report for 1859, p. 14.

CHAPTER II

THE CHAMBER OF COMMERCE AND THE COTTON FAMINE, 1861-1866

THE American Civil War did not descend like a bolt from the blue upon the Lancashire cotton industry. There had long been anxiety at the industry's dependence on a single source of supply, an anxiety which led in 1857 to the formation of the Cotton Supply Association.[1] The Manchester Chamber of Commerce did not lose interest in the question of raw cotton supplies after this event, but it did surrender to the Cotton Supply Association the detailed work of stimulating cotton growing in various parts of the world. The many letters that poured in, telling of hopeful developments or prospects in Brazil, Natal, West Africa, or Australia, were passed on to the new body ; the supply of cotton seed and gins to willing planters ceased to be part of the Chamber's duties. Relieved of the troublesome details, the Chamber could concentrate its energies on the major question, the development of cotton growing in India. This was a matter not of seeds, gins, and technical advice, but of radical reforms in the economic structure of India that could only be effected with the aid of the British and Indian Governments. This aid the Manchester merchants sought to enlist.

By the beginning of 1861, a clash between the northern and southern states of the American Union appeared inevitable. At the Chamber's annual meeting the President, Edmund Potter, expressed the general alarm :

There could perhaps be no internal revolution or commotion in any state in the world that could have endangered our commercial prosperity so much as the American one. . . . Any internal commotion must lessen the supply of cotton. This prospect then is very appalling. . . . Our main hope if America fails to any great extent depends upon India for cotton.[2]

The Manchester Chamber of Commerce hastily convened a meeting with other interested bodies, including the Glasgow,

---

[1] For the Chamber's early interest in cotton supply, see Redford, *op. cit.*, Chap. XVI.
[2] Annual Meeting, 21st January 1861.

Bradford, and Sheffield Chambers and the Liverpool China and East India Association. To this meeting the Manchester delegates submitted a memorandum and a series of resolutions which laid down a comprehensive policy for the development of India as a market for manufactured goods and a source of raw cotton. The memorandum argued that even allowing for the cost of the Indian Mutiny the deficit on the Indian budget was excessive, having led to a suspension of necessary public works, including roads, railways, canals, and irrigation :

With a country capable of consuming manufactures and of exporting produce on a scale that would, by the ordinary operation of trade, put an end to deficiency of revenue, there exists from want of public works little power of improvement and the country remains undeveloped.

The main obstacle to larger exports of Indian cotton " lies in the defective and expensive mode of transport ", though admittedly American cotton was of better quality. The memorandum went on to attack the Indian import and export duties, which were " already checking the progress of trade by fostering native manufactures under a false system of protective duties ".[1] The resolutions based on the memorandum called for a loan, backed if necessary by an imperial guarantee, to finance public works ; they urged the reduction of the import duties and the reform of the Indian law of contract and the land tenure system to encourage the investment of European capital. As the stocks of American cotton dwindled in 1862 and 1863, the Chamber of Commerce put more and more emphasis on the reform of Indian law and land tenure, and the question of import duties faded into the background. Manchester, however, found itself advocating more radical reforms than the government was willing to adopt. Sir Charles Wood, the Secretary of State for India, refused to raise the suggested loan of £30,000,000 or £40,000,000, " as the money could only be obtained at a ruinous rate " ; but the construction of railways had not been stopped, and would continue as rapidly as Indian finances allowed. Military and general expenditure was being steadily reduced, and the import duties would be cut " as soon as circumstances permitted ".[2]

[1] Proceedings, 30th January 1861.
[2] Ibid., 27th February 1861. Later in the year the import duties on cotton yarns were reduced from 10 per cent. to 5 per cent.

India's financial problem, the Chamber believed, might be solved by the sale of the 500,000 square miles of waste lands in India, which could be devoted to cotton growing. The Hon. S. Laing, Finance Member of the Viceroy's Council, pointed out, however, that " waste lands generally lay in one place and population in another "—a difficulty that improved communications might fairly soon be able to remedy, since within two years a complete system of railways would be open throughout India.[1] At the time, the Chamber did not press the matter, for the shortage of cotton was still prospective, not actual ; the American Civil War had lasted only six months and the Federal government had not had time to organise an effective blockade of the southern ports.   In 1861 imports of raw cotton remained at a high level—1,261 million lb.— of which by far the greater part came from the southern United States.

It was not until 1862 that the effects of the American blockade made themselves felt.   In the early part of the year, indeed, the stagnation of trade was attributed as much to " want of markets as to want of cotton ".[2]   But by July the temporary effects of a falling-off in demand had been submerged in the greater disaster of the " impending failure of the supply of cotton, which must speedily result in the entire stoppage of the factories throughout this district ".[3]   Faced with this calamity, the Manchester Chamber of Commerce reiterated its belief that the salvation of the cotton trade lay in the development of Indian production by means of public works, and denounced plans which had proposed that

the Government should become the merchant and carriers of the raw cotton. . . . Any such proposals [it was maintained] are utterly at variance with true trading principles and amount to a direct renunciation of the law of supply and demand ; constituting an interference that would paralyse private enterprise, and creating instead a species of protection in its worst form by giving a bounty from the public purse for the production of an inferior article.[4]

The Manchester merchants urged the British Government to remove the two main obstacles to the settlement of Europeans in India, namely : " The refusal of the Indian Government to grant a secure and permanent tenure of land upon definite and equitable terms, to any proposed purchaser ", and secondly

[1] Proceedings, 18th September 1861.
[2] Annual Meeting, 30th January 1862.
[3] Proceedings, 8th July 1862.   [4] Ibid., 16th July 1862.

" the absence of any effective law for the enforcement of contracts ". The Government of India had in 1861 adopted a satisfactory scheme for the disposal of waste lands, but after nine months the scheme was " suspended and practically rescinded by the Secretary of State ", and the contracts of sale repudiated.[1] Lord Palmerston, who received the deputation which presented the case, stoutly upheld the policy of his Secretary of State and in a vigorous reply to the Chamber's complaints enquired why Manchester spinners even in the middle of the cotton famine were allowing Indian cotton to leave the country to be spun in Continental mills.[2]

Imports of raw cotton in 1862 amounted to only 533 million lb.—less than half the imports of 1861, and (as it proved) the lowest quantity to arrive throughout the famine. The distress in Lancashire was very great, but as one Director of the Chamber of Commerce remarked, " It was not charity they wanted, but cotton ", and this the India Office seemed unwilling to help Lancashire to get. The Home Government's decision to stop the sale of waste lands caused deep resentment :

the change that was made a few years back in the Government of India [it was declared] was a sham and a delusion. The old Board was abolished and its worst, most bigoted and conceited members were taken to form the new Board.[3]

Despite their unfavourable opinion of the India Office, the Manchester merchants continued to hope for reforms in India; and to put pressure on the government they tried, without much success, to enlist the support of members of parliament, including the leader of the Opposition, Lord Stanley. The persistent efforts of the Chamber of Commerce led to two long debates in the House of Commons within two months. In both debates[4] Sir Charles Wood came under heavy fire from the Lancashire spokesmen chiefly for his refusal to support the Viceroy's scheme for the sale of waste lands. He

displayed much official dexterity in warding off the attacks made upon his Indian policy ; but it is to be regretted that he did not attempt any explanation of his reason for having subverted the

---

[1] Proceedings, 29th October 1862.   [2]*Ibid.*, 1st December 1862.
[3] Annual Meeting, reported in *Manchester Guardian*, 27th January 1863.
[4] *Hansard's Parliamentary Debates*, 3rd series, Vol. 170, col. 1610 ff. and Vol. 172, col. 178 ff. : H.C., 12th May and 3rd July 1863.

measures of Lord Canning.   Nor did he venture to notice the unsatisfactory state of the law of contract . . . without which it is vain to expect material progress. . . .[1]

Having failed to change the government's policy about waste lands, the Chamber of Commerce attacked another question—the reform of the Indian currency.   India had long been notorious as a country that exported much and imported little, the difference being met by a drain of silver from the West.   During the cotton famine the export of Indian cotton rose considerably and its value rose even more.[2]   The drain of bullion to the East became more pronounced than ever and one Director of the Chamber was moved to ask at the annual meeting :

How are we to continue to pay in specie for the cotton now coming from India, seeing the effect already produced in the money market by the absorption of our precious metals ?[3]

The Manchester merchants took only a short while to decide on their policy about the Indian currency, in sharp contrast to what happened in later years, when the controversies over the respective merits of bimetallism and monometallism were to engage the earnest attention of the Chamber over long periods.   By March 1864 a memorial had been drafted and submitted to Sir Charles Wood.   It declared that the existing silver currency was inadequate to the increasing trade of India.   In the past year the aggregate trade of the three Presidencies had amounted to £106,000,000, and was still increasing ;   the balance of trade was largely in favour of India, which was probably absorbing silver faster than the rest of the world could produce it.   The memorial added that a silver currency was difficult and expensive to transport and suffered heavily from wear and tear.   The Chamber therefore concluded that the reintroduction of a gold currency had become absolutely necessary and that an extension of the paper currency based on a metallic standard would also be desirable.[4]   On this occasion the India Office viewed the policy of the Manchester merchants with more favour, and at

[1] Proceedings, 8th July 1863.
[2] The average price of Middling Orleans rose from 8d. in January 1861, to 24d. per lb. in January 1865 : see W. O. Henderson, *Lancashire Cotton Famine* (1934), pp. 122-3.   The price of other growths would rise in sympathy.
[3] *Manchester Guardian*, 26th January 1864.
[4] Proceedings, 23rd March, 1864.

the end of the year directed that the British sovereign and half-sovereign should be received at all Indian treasuries at the rate of 10 and 5 silver rupees respectively.[1]

By then the resistance of the Confederate armies was rapidly coming to an end, though reconquest of the Southern States did not automatically bring with it a renewed flow of raw cotton to Lancashire. Nevertheless, the worst of the shortage was over by 1865, as the following table of imports of raw cotton shows :

IMPORTS OF RAW COTTON [2]

	(*million lb.*)
1861	1,261
1862	533
1863	690
1864	896
1865	966
1866	1,354

Even in 1864, the position had been growing easier : " When the American War broke out ", the President of the Chamber of Commerce reported,

our industry suffered to the extent of losing about five days' work a week for want of raw material, the supplies from all other sources amounting to one day's work in a week. Now the supply has been so far extended that last year (1863) cotton had been received equal to a supply of three days' work a week, and there was reason to hope that in the coming year it would amount to a supply for four and a half days per week.[3]

But at the next annual meeting the President had to admit to disappointment. In 1864 Lancashire had consumed only half the quantity of cotton consumed in 1860, which was admittedly a record year ; but he calculated that employment had not fallen in the same ratio owing to the poor quality of Indian cotton, which demanded more labour in its manufacture.[4]

As we have seen, the Manchester Chamber of Commerce had had little success in getting its Indian policy put into

[1] In 1870 the silver rupee became again the only form of legal tender : see V. Anstey, *Economic Development of India* (1936), p. 410.
[2] W. O. Henderson, *op. cit.*, p. 50.
[3] *Manchester Guardian*, 26th January 1864.
[4] *Ibid.*, 31st January 1865.

effect, though it had undoubtedly been right in believing
that Lancashire should look to India for the greater part
of its supplies during the famine.   Imports of Indian cotton
rose steadily, though less rapidly than many had hoped,
throughout the period of the American Civil War.   From
a level of 560,000 bales in 1860 they rose to 1,400,000 bales
in 1863 and 1,850,000 bales in 1866.[1]   But, as the President ruefully remarked : " We must attribute the advantage
gained not to any change of policy, but to the magic effect of
price." [2]

Though the Manchester Chamber of Commerce looked to
India to provide the bulk of the raw cotton during the American Civil War, other possible sources of supply were not
neglected.   Unlike India, however, the other cotton-growing
areas were outside the British Empire and could be spurred
on only by indirect methods and occasionally by diplomatic
pressure.   One such instance was the Portuguese Empire
which had lands in Africa suitable for cotton growing.
Even before the cotton shortage had become acute, the
Directors of the Chamber memorialised Lord John Russell,
the Foreign Secretary,

pointing out the advantages that would attend the extension of
the cultivation of cotton in the empire of Brazil and also in the
Portuguese settlements in Africa, and praying his Lordship to
urge the matter upon the attention of the respective governments.

It was later reported that the wishes of the Manchester
merchants had been carried out, and had borne fruit at least
to the extent that the Portuguese Government had " offered
large premiums with a view to promoting the cultivation of
cotton in their African settlements ".[3]

By 1864 the cotton growers of Egypt had given an agree-
ably surprising response to Lancashire's needs.   From a
paltry 100,000 bales in 1861, Egypt had increased her exports
to England by 1863 to 250,000 bales, quite apart from her
contribution to the European cotton industry.[4]   So valuable
had Egypt become as a source of supply that great alarm
was felt when the cutting of the Suez Canal threatened to
interfere with the development of the cotton crop by with-

[1] W. O. Henderson, *op. cit.*, p. 41.
[2] *Manchester Guardian*, 26th January 1864.
[3] Annual Report for 1861, p. 8.
[4] *Manchester Guardian*, 26th January 1864.

drawing labour from other work. A deputation called at the Foreign Office to protest that the Viceroy of Egypt had " begun to monopolise not only the railway but also the means of transport by water to the interior, taking by force Nile boats, lighters, weighers, porters, etc.". The Foreign Office undertook to raise the matter with the Viceroy, at the same time assuring the deputation that the system of forced labour would soon be abandoned.[1]

The end of the American Civil War did not immediately restore to Lancashire its previous sources of supply, nor was Lancashire at that moment willing to put all its eggs back into one basket. By the beginning of 1866 " Lancashire had returned to something like its old state of prosperity. It still, however, was below its condition before the American War ".[2] The Manchester Chamber of Commerce had still not given up hope of a great increase in the quantity of cotton to be imported from India, though the quality was very poor ; it was expected that, unless there was some drastic improvement, " Indian cotton would cease to be used the moment an abundant supply of American cotton could be obtained ".[3] One further effort was made to increase the Indian supply when later in 1866 a deputation urged the new Secretary of State for India, Earl de Grey, to encourage the sale of waste lands, reform the currency and the law of contract, and carry out a bold programme of public works.[4] No startling change of policy followed these renewed representations, however, and with the recovery of American supplies and fading memories of the famine, Lancashire became once more reconciled to its dependence on a single source of supply. In 1872 the work of the Cotton Supply Association came to an end, its records being transferred to the Manchester Chamber of Commerce.[5] After 1866 the price of raw cotton fell fairly quickly from the great heights of the famine years to the more reasonable levels of the 1850's. Indeed, in the last quarter of the nineteenth century, prices reached lower levels than ever before or since.[6] In these circumstances the Manchester Chamber of Commerce saw no reason to concern itself with the supply of raw cotton. Only with the change in the terms

[1] Proceedings, 9th March 1864.
[2] Manchester Guardian, 25th January 1866.
[3] Annual Meeting, 29th January 1866.
[4] Proceedings, 19th March 1866.   [5] Ibid., 1st August 1872.
[6] See Economic History Review, 2nd series, Vol. IV (1951), p. 72, for a convenient summary of raw cotton prices from 1790 to 1945.

3

of trade that occurred about 1900 did the price of raw cotton begin to move upward again, and as it did so, raw cotton supplies resumed their former place in the discussions of the Manchester merchants.[1]

[1] From 1872 to 1900 almost the only raw cotton question to come before the Chamber was the adulteration of Indian cotton. The Bombay Cotton Frauds Act of 1863 had been passed in an attempt to prevent adulteration, and until 1873 Manchester was " in favour of maintaining all those legal checks against fraud which are now in operation ". (Proceedings, 6th Nov., 1873.) With the improved organisation in the trade it came to be felt that a special law was unnecessary and in 1877 the Chamber petitioned for its repeal. (*Ibid.*, 30th May 1877.)

CHAPTER III

MANCHESTER AND INDIA: (i) FROM THE MUTINY
TO THE REPEAL OF THE IMPORT DUTIES
IN 1882

THE nineteenth-century business man is nowadays often
made to appear as a complacent optimist who took Britain's
industrial supremacy for granted. He could without much
trouble make a fortune in almost any of the national industries; in particular, the Lancashire cotton industry offered a
most promising field for his enterprise, because it had the
natural advantages of a damp climate as well as easy access
to its raw materials and to its Asiatic markets, the chief of
which was India. The Manchester man is often looked upon
as the most complacent representative of the complacent
Victorian age. Yet the picture is overdrawn : it is true that
the Lancashire cotton industry was immensely proud of its
great achievements, and was complacent enough to challenge
all comers to meet it in the world's markets on equal terms ;
but always at the back of their minds the leaders of the
industry knew that the price of prosperity was unceasing
vigilance. An industry based on the export trade had to
take great care that its markets were kept open by low tariffs
and expanded by improved communications. This was the
task of the shipping merchants organised in the Manchester
Chamber of Commerce ; to no other market did they devote
as much anxious attention as to India.

Throughout our period, India was the largest market for
Manchester goods, measured either by volume or by value.
To no other market has Manchester ever dispatched 1,000
million yards of cloth in a single year, or any quantity
approaching that figure ; but from the early 1870's to 1930
the exports of piece goods to India never fell below 1,000
million yards, and for most of that period were far above it.
Even in 1850, when the total export of cloth was only 1,300
million yards, almost a quarter of that total went to India ;
in later years Lancashire became increasingly dependent on
Indian demand, and from 1880 to the outbreak of the First

21

World War no less than 40 per cent. of Lancashire's piece
goods exported went to the Indian market.

PIECE GOODS EXPORTS, 1850-1913 [1]

(million yards)

	Total	India
1850	1,358	314
1860	2,776	825
1870	3,253	923
1880	4,496	1,813
1890	5,124	2,190
1900	5,034	2,019
1913	7,075	3,000

Statistics of cloth exports by volume tend to exaggerate
the importance of the Indian market since they exclude
the important yarn export trade which was directed largely
to Europe, and they do not allow for value. The highest
quality finished goods found their best markets in Europe
and the Americas ; and a high proportion of the grey cloth
with its low average value went to India. Nevertheless,
with all these qualifications, the Lancashire cotton trade
leaned heavily on the Indian peasant and could not afford
to lose control of the Indian market.

We have seen in the previous chapter that during the
cotton famine, and for a short while afterwards, the Manchester
Chamber of Commerce looked on India primarily as a supplier
of raw materials. This was a temporary aberration (caused
by the American Civil War) from the normal Manchester point
of view, which saw India through the eyes of the shipping
merchant, not the cotton-broker or spinner. Before 1861
and after 1865 the Chamber advocated policies which were
intended to secure and expand the market for cotton goods
in India ; often these policies led incidentally to the development of India's natural resources, and indeed without such
development the Indian peasant would not have had the
money with which to buy Lancashire goods; nevertheless,
since the Chamber of Commerce represented exporters rather

[1] Sources: 1850-1900: Cmd. 1761 of 1903 (British and Foreign Trade
and Industrial Conditions). 1913: Annual Statement of the Trade of the
United Kingdom.
Note: The figures for India in Cmd. 1761 relate to "The British East
Indies ", but in fact exports to Malaya were quite small. Burma from its
annexation until 1936 was part of the Indian Empire proper and is
included in the Indian statistics of 1913.

than importers, it always put more emphasis on India as a market than on India as a producer of raw materials.

The Indian Mutiny left behind it, among other things, a new constitution and a budgetary deficit. Between 1858 and the outbreak of the American Civil War, the Manchester Chamber of Commerce spent much of its time seeking to reform the constitution and mitigate the evil effects of the deficit. The Manchester merchants had never had a good opinion of the East India Company,[1] and readily approved of the transfer of power from the Company to the Crown in 1858.[2] But the Chamber of Commerce objected to some of the details of the constitutional settlement, and in particular protested against the proposed Council which was to share with the Secretary of State responsibility for the affairs of India in this country. The Chamber denounced the Council as " unconstitutional in principle and highly dangerous in practice, since it would tend to relieve the Secretary of State from the due responsibilities of his office ".[3] The Chamber's fear was that the new India Council would be packed with the members of the old Board of Control, and that the obstructive tactics of the East India Company would thus be perpetuated. During the cotton famine the Chamber believed that its worst fears had been realised,[4] but in fact the India Council never exercised the powers nominally entrusted to it and in 1869 it was reduced to the status of an advisory body.

The Mutiny left the Government of India with an unbalanced budget. Low specific import duties [5] had long been a standard means of raising revenue ; they had not in any way hindered Manchester's trade with India, which in 1859 was " wonderfully prosperous ". As the President of the Manchester Chamber remarked, an " amazing and unparalleled increase " had taken place in the Indian trade during the past two years ; but, he added, it had been accompanied by an enormous amount of new loans, increasing the debt from £60,000,000 to £100,000,000, and " as mercantile men they ought to wish for a regular, systematic, and safe

---

[1] See Redford, op. cit., Chaps. IX and XIV.
[2] Proceedings, 8th April 1858.   [3] Ibid., 21st April 1858.
[4] See above, Chap. II, p. 15.
[5] Equivalent to 5 per cent. on British cotton piece-goods and 3½ per cent. on British yarns ; double duty was levied on foreign cottons : see R. Dutt, Economic History of India in the Victorian Age (1904), pp. 157 and 401.

trade, not liable to such an amount of fluctuation ".[1] The
Manchester merchants believed that a balanced budget was
the first step towards this desirable end ; therefore they did
not oppose the low import duties, though they considered
that it would be " highly impolitic on the part of the Indian
Government to raise permanent revenue by increased duties
on imports and manufactured goods ".[2] Rather the government should raise fresh revenue by the consolidation of the
debt, the establishment of note-issuing banks, the sale of
waste lands, and the promotion of public works. Any new
taxes should be on real and personal property, not on imports
and exports.[3]

The new finance member of the Viceroy's Council,[4] to
whom these recommendations were addressed, soon found that
he would have to sacrifice his free-trade principles to India's
pressing need for revenue ; he promptly doubled the import
duties on British goods, thus ending the preference they had
enjoyed. At the same time the Indian Custom House undertook a revaluation which, by taking the extraordinary prices
of 1859 as a basis, instead of averaging over 1857-59, would
considerably increase the duty to be paid.[5] These measures
were naturally unwelcome to the Manchester merchants, who
resolved that

The import duties of India . . . are now excessive . . . any
further advance is alike impolitic and unsound in principle and
would have a tendency to restrict operations to the manifest
injury of commerce as well as of revenue.[6]

To give added weight to their representations the Directors
of the Chamber of Commerce called a special general meeting,
which endorsed the measures already taken to safeguard the
trade of Lancashire. " These heavy duties will amount [it
was asserted] to a positive prohibition on some classes of
cotton goods and yarns." The burden of the new valuations
would fall with especial severity on the common makes of
cloth, which came into most direct competition with native
manufactures.[7] What made the high duties and high
valuations especially hard to bear was that by the middle of

[1] *Manchester Guardian*, 6th October 1859.
[2] Proceedings, 12th May 1859.
[3] *Manchester Guardian*, 6th October 1859.
[4] James Wilson, formerly editor of *The Economist*.
[5] *Manchester Guardian*, 31st January 1860.
[6] Proceedings, 19th March 1860.   [7] *Ibid.*, 22nd May 1860.

1860 the boom in cotton exports was showing signs of coming to an end ; as prices fell, duties levied on the basis of the high prices ruling in 1859 became increasingly irksome.[1] Throughout the rest of 1860, the Manchester merchants were active in organising deputations and petitions to ministers and in corresponding with the Chambers of Commerce at Glasgow, Leeds, and Liverpool for some relief from the Indian duties. The government refused to reduce the rate of duty, but Manchester's efforts did not go entirely without reward, for the Annual Report of the Chamber for 1860 recorded that :

A new tariff, applicable to the ports of India, had been received in which the valuations had been readjusted and the *ad valorem* principle largely recognised ; but the duty still continues at 10 per cent.—a rate which the Board still deprecate as strongly as ever.

In 1861 the duties on yarn were reduced from 10 to 5 per cent. but this (though satisfactory so far as it went) did not go far enough for Manchester's liking ; early in 1862 a further deputation pressed the government to relieve the Lancashire cotton industry from this heavy burden :

The cost of conveying the raw material to England and carrying it back to India in the manufactured state amounted, including all charges, to 26 per cent. of its value ; and it was impossible that any industry could contend against such odds, when heavy protective duties were added.[2]

By this time the Manchester merchants were losing patience with the whole idea of revenue import duties, which they had formerly accepted as a necessary step to the restoration of Indian finances.   In March 1862, when the duty on yarns was further reduced to 3½ per cent. and the duty on manufactured goods to 5 per cent., they looked forward to the ultimate abolition of all such imposts, " the equilibrium between the revenue and the expenditure of our Eastern Empire being now, as we trust, nearly restored ".[3]   However, as we have already seen, their attention at this point was diverted to the question of cotton growing in India ; the duties, if not forgotten, were no longer a main subject of agitation. After a sporadic revival of interest in them in 1864 and again in 1866,[4] they received no mention in the records of the Chamber of Commerce

---

[1] Proceedings, 18th June 1860.   [2] *Ibid.*, 27th January 1862.
[3] *Ibid.*, 13th March 1862.
[4] *Ibid.*, 15th June 1864, and 19th March 1866.

for several years ; indeed the President in 1867 went so far
as to say that : " Perhaps at no time for twenty years had the
Chamber met having fewer grievances to complain of in regard
to India."[1]

Indian import duties have from 1858 almost to the present
time been the greatest menace (at least in the opinion of the
Manchester Chamber) to Lancashire's trade with India.
Less interest attaches to the history of Manchester's relations
with India in periods when import duties were not a burning
question.   Yet such periods have been quite long ; there was
a distinct lull in the controversy from 1867 to 1874, and again
in the twenty years after the imposition of a countervailing
excise duty in 1895.   Except at these quiet times, Manchester's
policy towards India reflected the general belief of Manchester
merchants that protective duties threatened the whole economic basis of the Lancashire cotton industry.   With no great
object to pursue in the late 'sixties and early 'seventies the
Manchester Chamber of Commerce contented itself with
urging upon the India Office various desirable reforms that
had long been part of the Chamber's programme, such as
irrigation, canals, railways, and schools of agriculture.[2]

After the financial crisis of 1866, the Chamber renewed
its pressure for a gold currency in India, attributing the crisis
to the drain of silver to India that had followed heavy imports
of Indian cotton ; a gold currency, it was believed, would
overcome the difficulties caused by the Indian habit of hoarding
silver and would correct the unfavourable balance of trade
with India.[3]   Concern for the cotton trade also lay behind
Manchester's view on Indian taxation : the Chamber of
Commerce preferred that reductions of taxation should take
the form of a lower salt tax, which would benefit the poorer
classes—the chief consumers of cotton goods ; the income
tax was held to be a fair source of revenue.[4]   The Manchester
merchants naturally felt that Indian merchants and industrialists ought to bear a weight of taxation comparable with that of
their English competitors.

When the Government of India was transferred in 1858
from the East India Company to the Crown, the Manchester
Chamber had done its best to put the responsibility for

---

[1] Annual Meeting, 28th January 1867.
[2] See, for example, *Manchester Guardian*, 28th October 1868, 3rd
August 1869, and 30th January 1872.
[3] Proceedings, 25th March 1868.   [4] *Ibid.*, 19th October 1870.

Indian policy squarely on the shoulders of the Secretary of State, and strongly disapproved of the condominium between Secretary and Council which was then established. By 1868 the Manchester merchants had changed their opinion; if there was to be an Indian Council, at least it ought to include representatives of commercial interests.[1] An opportunity soon occurred to get this view put into practice; the government introduced a bill to alter the status of the India Council. In conjunction with the Liverpool Chamber of Commerce, the Manchester merchants petitioned for the more effectual representation of commerce on the Council,[2] but were put off with a promise that when some of the present members of the Council retired the government would not forget the wishes of the mercantile community.[3] Despite this assurance, the government continued to fill vacancies on the Council with scant regard to commercial opinion: the appointment of Sir Henry Maine, the eminent jurist, and Sir Louis Mallet, a high official of the Board of Trade, evoked a complaint that the government had broken its word; when told that the India Council had no power, Manchester retorted that in that case the Council should be abolished.[4] Further protests in 1874 to the new Conservative government bore more fruit.[5] Mr. Andrew Cassels, a former Director of the Chamber of Commerce, and one of its experts on India, was appointed to the Council and thus " at length the claims of commerce obtained practical recognition ".[6]

In 1874 the Indian import duties on cotton goods still stood at 5 per cent. and on yarn at $3\frac{1}{2}$ per cent.; but the official values on which the duties were levied had been fixed before the effects of the cotton famine had worn off, and the subsequent decline in raw cotton prices made the true incidence of the tax rather higher. Thus the protection granted to the Indian cotton industry was greater than would appear at first sight. Moved by these considerations, the Manchester Chamber of Commerce began a campaign early in 1874 which after eight years of pressure by memorial, petition, and deputation eventually secured the repeal of the obnoxious duties in 1882. The first shot fired in this new campaign was a

[1] Proceedings, 10th February and 4th March 1869.
[2] Ibid., 25th August 1869.   [3] Ibid., 25th May 1870.
[4] Ibid., 29th November and 27th December 1871; Manchester Guardian, 30th January 1872.
[5] Proceedings, 15th February, 9th and 25th March 1874.
[6] Annual Report for 1874, pp. 6-7.

memorial to the Prime Minister, W. E. Gladstone, which gives a reasoned and useful summary of Lancashire's case :

The Memorial of the Manchester Chamber of Commerce respectfully sheweth

. . . That a fiscal duty of 3½ per cent. on yarn and 5 per cent. on cloth is now levied in India on the importation of British Cotton Manufactures assessed on tariff rates fixed many years ago when values ruled much higher than they do now, so that the duties thus levied actually amount to about 4 per cent. on the present prices of yarns in India, and nearly 6 per cent. on cloth. . . . That the tax is now found to be absolutely prohibitory to the trade in yarn and cloth of the low-priced sorts and your Memorialists are informed that it is proposed to import Egyptian and American raw cotton into India (no duty being charged thereon) to manufacture the finer yarn and cloth which will thus compete with goods received from England on which duty is levied ;

That a protected trade in Cotton Manufacture is now consequently springing up in British India and an unsound commerce is being fostered in that country which will, sooner or later, cause embarrassment and distress to the native capitalists and workmen ;

That the levying of such duties, when their effect is to afford protection to one portion of Her Majesty's subjects in India to the disadvantage of another portion in England with whom they are brought into competition in trade is inconsistent with the commercial policy of this country and subversive of the soundest principles of political economy and free trade ;

That just in proportion as the protective duty stimulates the erection of Cotton Factories in India, it defeats the primary object of the tax as a source of revenue, by encouraging the production of Goods in India to the exclusion of British Manufactures on which alone the impost is levied ;

That the inevitable tendency of any trade nursed and fostered by protection is to divert capital and labour from the natural channels into which they would more beneficially be turned ;

That the said duties are increasing the cost to the native population—or at least to the poorest of the people—of their articles of clothing, and thereby interfering with the health, comfort and general well-being of the Queen's Indian subjects.

Your Memorialists therefore pray that having regard to the reasons set forth above, an early consideration may be given to the subject of the duties now levied on Yarns and Manufactured Goods on import into India, with a view to their abolition.

Manchester 29th January 1874.[1]

The Indian cotton industry which had called forth this protest was by no means a large one:

[1] Annual Report for 1873, pp. 15-17.

Before the duty was raised to 10 per cent.—that is up to 1859—there were in the Presidency of Bombay two cotton mills, built in 1853 and 1854, and the ill-success attending them was such as to deter others from following the precedent ; but during the three years in which the 10 per cent. was levied seven or eight more mills were erected and now (1874) there were in and about Bombay upwards of twenty cotton mills. . . .

As the import duties on cotton goods provided a mere £800,000 out of the Indian revenue of £50,000,000, the Manchester merchants felt that some economy in the home charges of Indian Government and in the " large salaries " of the British officials in India would easily offset the loss of customs revenue. The proposal for a countervailing excise duty on locally produced cloth (which one of the Manchester newspapers had supported) was rejected by the Chamber of Commerce on the grounds that

Gentlemen here wishing to be relieved themselves of a burden would not . . . ask the Government to place a burden upon their fellow-subjects in India, who, when building their mills, had no ground whatever for expecting that an excise duty would be levied upon their productions.[1]

A deputation which pressed these views upon Lord Salisbury, the new Secretary of State for India, received the stock reply : " There can be no question that in point of principle you are right. This duty is not one that can be defended in theory." In practice, however, the financial exigencies of the Indian Government gave Lord Salisbury a strong enough case against repeal, and the deputation came away empty-handed.[2] The Chamber of Commerce was not deterred. It set up a standing committee on the duties, and circularised British and Indian Chambers of Commerce in order to mobilise opinion on its side. In this it met with fair success in that only the Madras Chamber opposed the repeal of the duties ; the Bombay merchants, and Chambers of Commerce in Britain, supported Manchester's policy.[3] The first fruits of the persistent agitation were dispatches from Lord Salisbury to the Viceroy, dated 15th July and 11th November 1875, instructing the Indian Government to make provision for repeal not after " an indefinite period

[1] Annual Meeting, 2nd February 1874.
[2] Proceedings, 9th November 1874.
[3] Ibid., 9th and 25th November and 23rd December 1874, and 8th February and 31st March 1875.

but . . . within a fixed term of years ".[1] Lord Salisbury's
action came under attack in both Houses of Parliament in
1876, thus giving the Chamber of Commerce an opportunity
to educate Lancashire M.P.s in the merits of the question.[2]
In 1877 Hugh Birley and Jacob Bright (both of them Members
for Manchester, and both prominent in the Lancashire cotton
industry) moved

That in the opinion of this House, the duties now levied upon
Cotton Manufactures imported into India, being protective in
their nature, are contrary to sound commercial policy and ought
to be repealed without delay.

To the already familiar arguments Jacob Bright added another
which would be heard again and again in future controversy :

It would perhaps be said that although the export of coarse goods
to India had very much declined, the export of the finer fabrics
had very much increased.   This was true.   In shirtings we had
had a great increase of exports to India ; but the manufacturers
in India having succeeded so well in making the coarser fabrics . . .
had now begun, we were told successfully, to manufacture the
finer fabrics.   If this went on long enough we should find that there
would in time be the same falling off in the finer as there had been
in the coarser fabrics. . . . The security of our commerce should
not be treated with indifference by a House which represented a
people millions of whom lived by the exchange of their products
with other countries.[3]

At the insistence of the government an amendment was added
providing for repeal only " so soon as the finances of India will
permit ".   With the sting thus removed the resolution passed
without a division.   Government and Parliament had both
recognised the justice of Manchester's case in principle ;
the harder task of converting words into deeds remained.

The Government of India decided to repeal the duties
by instalments.   Early in 1878 goods made from yarns of
coarser count than 30's were exempted from the duties ;
this concession was, however, hedged round with so many
qualifications that the " only goods that are to be admitted
free are T cloths under 18 reeds, Jeans, Domestics, Sheetings
and Drills ". This partial exemption, the Manchester
merchants complained, " has naturally awakened a strong

---

[1] *Annual Register*, 1876, p. 88.   [2] Proceedings, 19th April 1876.
[3] *Hansard*, 3rd series, Vol. 235, cols. 1091 and 1093 : H. C., 10th July
1877.

feeling of impatience especially in presence of the depression of the trade of this district ".[1]   In March 1879, the Indian Government, acting on the advice of a committee of customs officials, extended the exemption to all goods made of yarn of 30's count and under.   The Manchester Chamber of Commerce

acknowledged with pleasure the expressed intention of the Government to afford relief to the cotton industry engaged in the Indian trade, and hoped that some benefit would result from the change of tariff just made, but deeply regretted that the duties on cotton manufactures imported into India were to be continued, to the great detriment of the consumers of cotton goods in India and of injury to the cotton industry of Lancashire. . . .

If as is only too probable the abrogation of the duty on the coarser counts stimulates in India the creation of means for the production of finer counts we shall ere long have the battle to fight once again, and we therefore look to the total repeal of these duties as the only fair and final solution of the question.[2]

The exemption of some but not all cotton goods from the duties soon gave rise to disputes between merchants and customs collectors on what were and what were not dutiable goods.   While not condoning deliberate attempts to defraud the customs, the Manchester Chamber felt that in many instances the collectors of customs were interpreting the rules too harshly ; but the only satisfactory solution of the problem would be " total and early abolition " of the duties.[3]   Not until the spring of 1882 did the Indian finances permit this final step to be taken.   The Chamber of Commerce promptly recorded its pleasure at the favourable turn of events :

The general prosperity of which the favourable financial position is evidence is matter for sincere congratulations, and it is felt that in dealing with the surplus by removing all import duties except those on wines and a few other articles, and thus leaving capital and labour to find their natural and consequently most productive field, and giving relief to the poor by lessening the cost of clothing as well as by lowering the salt tax, the Indian Government has adopted measures which are best calculated to advance the well-being of the people, to extend their commercial intercourse with their fellow-subjects in England, and to promote the prosperity of both.[4]

[1] Letter of 27th March 1878 to Secretary of State for India, quoted in Annual Report for 1878, p. 6.
[2] Proceedings, 26th March and 8th October 1879.
[3] Annual Report for 1880, p. 7.   [4] Proceedings, 13th March 1882.

CHAPTER IV

MANCHESTER AND INDIA : (ii) THE GREAT DEPRESSION AND THE RETURN OF PROSPERITY

THE Manchester merchants were not content merely to keep their share of a static market by opposing import duties. They wished to enlarge the Indian market for cotton goods to match the growing productive power of the Lancashire mills, and one of the surest means of doing this was by opening further areas of India to economic penetration by building railways. When trade was growing rapidly, as it was in the 'seventies and after 1900, the need for public expenditure on railways was not obvious ; but in a crisis such as the cotton famine, or in years of stagnant trade such as the period from the early 'eighties to the end of the century, the Manchester Chamber of Commerce naturally cast about for new outlets for Lancashire cloth, and saw that railways were the key to a fuller exploitation of the Indian market. It would not be true, however, to explain the policy of the Manchester merchants only in terms of fluctuations in the export trade ; the Chamber of Commerce was ready to express its point of view whenever public discussion turned towards India. Such an opportunity occurred in the late 'seventies. The early Indian railways had all been built by private companies working with a government guarantee of a minimum return on capital of between $4\frac{1}{2}$ and 5 per cent. But for many years the railways had earned less than their guaranteed minimum, thus involving the Indian Government in considerable loss. In 1870, therefore, the government decided to undertake railway building on its own account, and in constructing the new lines to abandon the old broad gauge of 5 feet 6 inches in favour of the narrow metre gauge.[1] Under this system the mileage of track rose from 5,000 in 1871 to nearly 10,000 in 1880.[2] Nevertheless, the use of the narrow gauge had its defects ; it complicated the transit of goods when they had

[1] V. Anstey, *Economic Development of India* (1936), p. 132.
[2] R. Dutt, *Economic History of India in the Victorian Age* (1904), p. 548.

to travel on both the private and the state-owned lines, and it could not stand the heavy strain put upon the railway system during famines or frontier wars. In 1880, after the inadequacies of the railway system had been laid bare in the terrible famine of 1877, the government reverted to its original policy of construction by private companies with a government guarantee.[1]

In the discussions which preceded this decision the Manchester Chamber of Commerce took its full share. It had already opposed the use of the metre gauge on more than one occasion, pointing out the needless breaks in transit it would cause.[2] It also opposed the return to the private construction of railways, believing that if India had not been "sucked dry" by enormous military expenditure the railways would pay.[3] When it was suggested that " mercantile gentlemen— and those connected with the Chamber of Commerce particularly—should themselves undertake the construction of public works and railways by private capital ", the Chamber had a ready answer. Mr. George Lord delivered judgement as an expert on Indian affairs :

When they looked at the low rate of interest at which the Indian Government was able to borrow money, namely at $3\frac{1}{2}$ per cent., without involving the Imperial Government in any responsibility, and when they saw that many of the railways and public works were earning a profit over and above the 5 per cent. guaranteed by the Government, they could see that there was every inducement to the Government to spend money in opening up the country, whereas the private individuals in this country had not the confidence necessary to do the work. Nor could the works be carried out so readily by private individuals as by the Government, as the Government owned a large portion of the land in India.[4]

In the 'eighties a further 8,000 miles of track was added to India's railways,[5] but the Manchester Chamber of Commerce was by no means satisfied with this rate of progress. In 1887 it began to take an interest in a proposed Karachi–Delhi railway ; the development of Karachi, which had a good harbour and was two days' steaming nearer Aden than was Bombay, would obviously be advantageous to Lancashire.[6]

[1] V. Anstey, loc. cit.
[2] Proceedings, 5th August 1877 and 26th March 1879.
[3] Ibid., 25th July 1879 ; Manchester Guardian, 26th July 1879.
[4] Annual Meeting, 7th February 1881.   [5] R. Dutt, loc. cit.
[6] Proceedings, 28th September 1887.

In 1889, before bombarding the India Office with a new series of memorials and deputations, the Chamber of Commerce prepared its case by getting three experts at different times to address the members on the subject of Indian railways. The Indian Government persisted, however, in relying as much as possible on private construction for all but the strategic and famine railways, and the Directors of the Manchester Chamber had to record sorrowfully, in the Annual Report for 1889, " their conviction that a vast and profitable field was yet open for fresh railways, and that the Government of India could not be merely a spectator in this matter ".

The Manchester merchants continued to take an interest in Indian railways until the end of the century. At various times they put forward suggestions to raise capital in India for state construction,[1] and to use the narrow gauge for feeder lines.[2] After the end of the century, however, their interest became intermittent. By 1900 India had 25,000 miles of railways, and all the trunk lines had been laid down. Whatever contribution railways could make to the expansion of Lancashire's trade with India had been made already. As far as the Manchester Chamber of Commerce was concerned the subject was exhausted.

One of the reasons why the Indian Government was always falling foul of the Manchester Chamber of Commerce was the depreciation of silver. The large Indian debt held in Britain, and the pensions and bills for stores that the Indian Government had to meet in London, were even at the best of times a strain on Indian finances, and with the fall in silver prices after 1873 the strain became severe. In large part this financial difficulty explains the need for import duties and the delays in building railways that gave the Manchester merchants so much anxiety. It might be expected, therefore, that the silver question would receive earnest and prolonged attention in Manchester. Indian difficulties, however, were never attributed to this one cause alone ; problems were dealt with as they arose, and the depreciation of silver did not seem to contemporary opinion in Manchester to be as important as it does in retrospect. Nevertheless, the problem was taken quite seriously by the Manchester merchants when (rather belatedly) they realised its urgency.

[1] Proceedings, 29th December 1892 ; *Monthly Record*, January 1893.
[2] *Ibid.*, February 1894.

The fall in the price of silver began in 1874, but did not attract the attention of the Manchester Chamber of Commerce until 1876, when the Calcutta Chamber appealed to Manchester to support measures for restoring the gold value of the rupee.[1] To this appeal Manchester turned a deaf ear : " Artificial expedients for a readjustment of the value of silver " were bound to fail. " Adjustment could only be sufficiently supplied by the natural laws governing supply and demand."[2] The next assault on Manchester orthodoxy came from the Liverpool Chamber of Commerce, which was urging that Britain should adopt a bimetallic system. Manchester was not convinced by the arguments put forward in two lengthy debates.[3] The Board of the Chamber was of opinion

that the existing system of English currency, with Gold as standard and unlimited legal tender and with a subordinate and limited coinage of Silver and Copper as token money, is best adapted to the necessities and conveniences of the country and should therefore be continued. No Act of Parliament or Convention of Nations can prevent changes in the conditions of production or the action of demand and supply.

The Chamber went on to rebut the most important part of the bimetallists' case—that the existing system hampered trade with the silver-using East.

The temporary inconvenience to buyers of exchange in silver-using countries, being an exaggerated form of an ordinary incident of trade, should be met by the usual remedies through terms of contract, and in any case the removal of such temporary inconvenience would be too dearly purchased by any measure which would destroy the simplicity and stability of our national currency.[4]

At that time Manchester merchants could afford to make light of the depreciation of silver, since the Indian import duties had not been repealed and were very generally believed to explain, when taken together with the effects of drought and famine,[5] the depression in Indian trade. With the repeal of the duties on cotton goods in 1882, this explanation fell to the ground. When depression came round again in 1884 there were many Manchester merchants who saw in the depreciation of silver the prime cause of their difficulties in the Indian and Far Eastern markets.

[1] Proceedings, 19th July 1876. [2] Annual Report for 1876, p. 14.
[3] Proceedings, 6th March and 3rd April 1879.
[4] Ibid., 28th March 1879. [5] Annual Report for 1878, p. 17.

4

In 1885 opinion at Manchester had become sufficiently
divided for the Chamber of Commerce to ask for an official
inquiry into the silver question, either by a Select Committee
or by the Royal Commission on the Depression of Trade.
This was a change from the attitude of the Manchester merchants in 1881, when they had opposed the sending of a
delegation to a monetary conference at Paris ;[1] but even in
1885 their request for an inquiry was made " without committing the Chamber to any opinion on the question of
bimetallism ".[2]   In 1886 a Royal Commission was appointed
to inquire into " the relative values of the precious metals ",[3]
but by then the bimetallists in Manchester were thoroughly
alarmed at the course of events in the Far East, and in 1887
the Chamber of Commerce instituted its own inquiry into
the silver question.   In form the inquiry was into the growth
of the Bombay spinning industry, the terms of reference
being :

That in view of the very rapid increase of cotton spinning in India
and the exports of yarn therefrom more especially to China and
Japan, while at the same time there has been a very serious check
to the growth of Lancashire yarn exports to these countries, the
Directors be requested to examine and report to a special meeting
of the Chamber as to the causes and circumstances which have
thus enabled Bombay spinners to supersede those of Lancashire.[4]

In fact, however, the sponsor of the inquiry (Mr. J. C.
Fielden, a Manchester manufacturer) believed that the cause
of Bombay's success was the depreciation of silver.[5] " The
whole of our costs ", he told the Board of Directors, who
constituted the committee of inquiry,

are affected by exchange.   When we sell a bale of piece goods or
yarns, every item that we have paid for is affected by the variation
in exchange . . . which is the crux of the whole matter.   When
we import cotton from Bombay [6] we gain because of the increased
purchasing power of our money, as compared with theirs, upon
the cotton.   But this advantage is exactly reversed when we ship

[1] Proceedings, 24th March 1881.   [2] Ibid., 28th July 1885.
[3] The Royal Commission reported in 1888.
[4] Proceedings, 31st October 1887.
[5] The Chamber published the Evidence and Reports in 1888, under the
title Bombay and Lancashire Cotton Spinning Inquiry.
[6] The coarse yarns which were meeting Indian competition were spun
from Indian cotton, or from Indian and American cotton mixed.   (Ibid.,
qq. 192 and 521.)

the yarn there. We gain an advantage in the buying and lose it in the selling, and in addition upon all the charges that have been incurred by the cotton while in our hands—whether spinning charges, or charges for transport, or commission, or charges upon whatever, in fact, we have done to the cotton after shipping from Bombay. I say, according to these figures it is proved beyond all doubt that this competition is a competition only possible upon the basis of low exchange with this country.[1]

In endeavouring to sustain or refute this contention the various witnesses produced a mass of evidence on the relative costs of production in Oldham and Bombay, but without bringing the Board of Directors to a unanimous conclusion. Eventually the monometallists signed a majority report in these terms :

The principal circumstance that has favoured the rapid increase of mills in India and enabled them to a great extent to supply China and Japan with yarns is their geographical position, which today gives them an advantage of at least $\frac{3}{4}d.$ per pound on the portion of their output that is shipped to China and Japan and $1\frac{3}{8}d.$ to $\frac{7}{8}d.$ per pound on what is consumed in India itself. This is an estimate of the nett advantage to the Indian spinner, arising from his proximity to the cotton fields on the one hand and to the consuming markets on the other, after allowing for his extra outlay for machinery and consequently enhanced interest and depreciation, as well as greater expenditure in such items as imported coals, stores, etc.

The majority did not deny that the depreciation of silver had benefited the Indian spinner by as much as a halfpenny per pound of yarn ; but they held that as freight rates had fallen by a much larger amount since 1873 (when the rupee was at par), the Bombay spinner's advantage from silver depreciation had been more than counterbalanced.[2]

The minority report laid stress on the obverse of this argument. The report admitted that in 1887 the geographical advantage in favour of Bombay amounted to $1\cdot03d.$ per pound of yarn, but pointed out that owing to the fall in freights the geographical advantage was now less than half what it had been in 1873. " It appears that the geographical advantage enjoyed by the Bombay spinner has been lessening while his power to compete with Lancashire has been increasing." It therefore followed that Bombay's undoubted

---

[1] *Bombay and Lancashire Cotton Spinning Inquiry*, qq. 43 and 44.
[2] *Ibid.*, pp. 356-9.

success in Far Eastern markets had some other cause, and this cause the minority found " in the great fall in Eastern exchange since 1873 ". This they believed was worth nearly one penny a pound to the Bombay spinner.[1] However, even if this estimate is a better one than that accepted in the majority report, the Bombay spinner was still relatively no better off than in 1873, so that it is hard to know why the minority should have seen in the depreciation of silver " the principal cause which has enabled Bombay spinners to supersede those of Lancashire in exporting yarn to China and Japan ".[2] Whatever the merits of their reasoning, the minority had the satisfaction of knowing that among the members of the Chamber of Commerce their report was held to be the more accurate account of the facts, for at a special members' meeting the minority report was approved and adopted by sixty-four votes to fifty-two.[3] At the time this decision had no effect on policy since the reports did not go beyond fact-finding. For the next three years, despite requests to attend conferences with Chambers of Commerce in Lancashire and elsewhere,[4] the Board of Directors refused to commit itself to an opinion on this " difficult " subject.

In 1889 and 1890 the Indian trade was prospering, but the returns for 1891 showed that the export of piece goods to India had fallen by 200 million yards or nearly 10 per cent. In these circumstances, Manchester merchants more easily believed that the silver question might be the cause of their profitless condition. In April 1892 a group of them asked the Chamber of Commerce to declare that

The unsatisfactory conditions of trade which have existed for so long without there being any prospect of alleviation in the future are largely caused by circumstances connected with the frequent and violent fluctuations in exchange with India, China, and other silver-using countries, and this Chamber is of the opinion that the Government should take immediate steps to promote an agreement on a broad international basis in order to secure a stable par of exchange between gold and silver moneys.[5]

After prolonged debates spread over three days, this resolution was carried by a narrow majority of eight votes out of

[1] *Bombay and Lancashire Cotton Spinning Inquiry*, pp. 360-7.
[2] *Ibid.*, p. 366.
[3] The Chamber had a membership of about 1,000.
[4] Proceedings, 29th April and 18th November 1891.
[5] *Ibid.*, 13th April 1892.

three hundred votes cast.[1] The monometallists, not content with this decision, demanded a poll of the members. Over eight hundred votes were cast, but by a remarkable coincidence the majority in favour of the resolution was unchanged.[2] The Board of Directors therefore forwarded this expression of the members' opinion to the government, but took no further steps towards a bimetallist policy.[3]

The Manchester merchants would not willingly countenance a departure from the gold standard for England ; neither would they agree that India could usefully abandon its silver standard. Thirty years before, in their enthusiasm for the rapid development of Indian resources, Manchester merchants had hoped for the introduction of English monetary and banking institutions into India. But when in 1893 the Indian mints were closed to the free coinage of silver, the Manchester Chamber of Commerce did not welcome the step, holding that

an alteration in the existing currency laws of India, either in the direction of closing the mints to the free coinage of silver or attempting to establish a gold standard, is to be deprecated as certain to disappoint the expectations of those who advocate the change, as being fraught with the possibilities of serious economic loss and political danger, and as undesirable looking either to the recent financial history of India and to the steadily improving condition of the people, or to India's commercial relations with Europe, the Straits Settlements, China, and the Far East.[4]

In elaboration of these views the Board made it clear that their objection to the gold-exchange standard was primarily the old one that had led them to oppose bimetallic policies : " A gold standard without gold has thus been introduced into India, and an artificial value given to the rupee." To tamper with the laws of supply and demand in this way would do no good : it would depress the price of silver still further and this in turn would lead to dissatisfaction among those natives who hoarded silver bullion ; and the fall in the gold price of Indian exports that would result from the stabilising of the exchange would impoverish Indian producers and so diminish the yield of the land tax. Thus a measure designed

[1] Reports in the *Manchester Guardian*, 14th and 28th April and 4th May 1892. A verbatim report of the debates was also published, entitled *International Bimetallism.*
[2] *Ibid.*, p. 88.   [3] *Monthly Record*, May 1892.
[4] Proceedings, 14th June 1893.

to ease the strain on the revenues of the Indian Government
would have exactly the opposite effect.[1]

The establishment of a gold-exchange standard did not
immediately restore Indian finances to a sound condition.
In the fiscal year 1893-94, there was a deficit of £2,000,000 [2]
which was met, provisionally, by the imposition of import
duties of 5 per cent. on a wide range of goods, excluding
cottons. The Manchester merchants foresaw that renewed
duties on cotton yarns and piece goods could not be warded
off for long, and were ready with an alternative. Bimetallism
in the abstract had secured only a very narrow majority
of adherents in Manchester, but bimetallism as an antidote
to Indian import duties was much more popular. The
members carried " by a large majority " [3] a resolution

That in the opinion of this Chamber the necessity for raising
additional revenue in India arises solely from the losses in exchange
which the Government of India sustains annually on its sterling
payments, and as the adoption by the Home Government of the
policy of International Bimetallism, which the Indian Government
has urged upon it for more than twelve years, would establish
a steady Par of Exchange between silver and gold and thus obviate
the necessity for any import duties, this Chamber strongly urges
this policy upon the British Government and Parliament so as to
effectually remove the exchange difficulties between England and
India.

In support of this policy a prominent Oldham cotton spinner [4]
declared :

I look upon the reimposition of the cotton duties as inevitable
unless there is a speedy rise in exchange. At the same time I
believe these duties would inflict a serious blow on a harassed
industry—an industry of the greatest importance to this country.
In this Chamber which was the birthplace of Free Trade we protest,
and we do right to protest, against the reimposition of these
duties. But our protests must seem selfish to the rest of the country
and they are not likely to avail unless we can show some way out
of the present difficulties of Indian finance. The fixing of a par
of exchange would remove these difficulties.[5]

This desperate expedient failed. In December the Indian

[1] *Monthly Record*, June 1893.
[2] R. Dutt, *Economic History of India in the Victorian Age*, p. 538.
[3] *Monthly Record*, November 1894.
[4] Ald. A. Emmott, later Lord Emmott.
[5] *Indian Import Duties and International Bimetallism* (1894). Verbatim
report of the debate in the Manchester Chamber of Commerce, 5th
November 1894.

Government put a 5 per cent. duty on imported cotton yarns and goods, and to avoid the charge of Protectionism imposed a countervailing excise duty on Indian yarns above 20's counts. The Manchester Chamber of Commerce had announced in advance that it would feel " bound to protest against the policy of such duties as an injurious interference with trade, even though a countervailing effective excise duty should be placed upon similar goods in India ".[1] Nevertheless, the Chamber tacitly accepted the need for customs and excise duties on cotton goods and concentrated all its influence on getting the excise extended to all Indian yarns. The exemption of 20's and under, it held,

will operate as a distinct protection to the spinners and dyers of a large quantity of coloured yarn now produced in India and therefore—contrary to the principle of Free Trade professed by this country—unfairly interfere with or wholly destroy the trade of a large number of English and Scottish spinners and dyers. . . . This Chamber has no desire to see checked the expansion of the Indian mill industry resulting from geographical and natural advantages, but it does . . . protest against the development being artificially stimulated.[2]

The protest eventually bore fruit, for in 1896 the excise and import duties on all yarns, imported and Indian, were withdrawn, and a duty of $3\frac{1}{2}$ per cent. was imposed on all imported piece goods and on all Indian piece goods woven on power-looms. In this settlement the Manchester merchants reluctantly acquiesced as being " the solution of present difficulties least open to objection so long as revenue must be raised from these duties " ; but " the duties are bad in principle and are injurious alike to the interest of the Indian people and to the British manufacturing industry ". [3]

The 1888 inquiry into Bombay spinning had incidentally drawn attention to the bad working conditions and long hours of work in Indian mills. Evidence had been given by English owners and managers of Bombay mills that a seventy-hour week with no regular breaks for meals was usual, and that mills ran for thirteen days out of every fourteen.[4] At one mill in 1887, eighty hours were worked every week and the

[1] Proceedings, 13th June 1894. This was a board resolution but the members endorsed it at the meeting on the 5th November.
[2] Letter printed in *Monthly Record*, February 1895.
[3] Annual Report for 1896, p. 1.
[4] *Bombay and Lancashire Cotton Spinning Inquiry*, qq. 106, 113, 289-90.

mill only stopped for twenty-one days in the whole year.[1] There had been agitation in Lancashire in the 'seventies and 'eighties for some control on the hours of labour in Indian mills, and an ineffective Act had been passed in 1881,[2] but in this movement the Manchester Chamber of Commerce had taken no active part.   After the inquiry of 1888, however, Mr. Fielden moved and carried a resolution :

that in view of the excessive hours of labour now worked in the Cotton Mills of British India, this Chamber recommends that the provisions of the British Factory Acts, so far as they relate to the employment of women, young persons, and children, should be at once extended so as to apply to and include the Textile Factories of British India.[3]

During the course of the debate, Mr. Fielden had to contend with the opposition of members who feared that Indian opinion might misconstrue Manchester's motives.   It may be that the Board of Directors shared this fear, since they did not pursue the question with any vigour.   They declined to take part in a deputation to the India Office which the Blackburn and Oldham Chambers were organising.[4]   In 1890 action was again deferred until the Manchester Chamber had had time to consult the Bombay and Bengal Chambers of Commerce ; [5] and in 1891 the Manchester Chamber acquiesced in the Government of India's new Factory Act, which fell a long way short of English standards.[6]

The later nineteenth century had been an anxious time for Manchester merchants.   By 1880 Lancashire had a century-old tradition of expanding foreign trade; but the last twenty years of the nineteenth century saw very little further expansion. Exports did continue to grow, but at a much diminished rate ; and nowhere was this relative stagnation more noticeable than in the trade with India.   In the decade 1881-90 exports of cotton piece goods to India averaged just under 2,000 million yards each year ; in the decade 1891-1900 the corresponding figure was a little under 2,100 million yards.[7] These relatively gloomy results gave urgency to the activities of the Manchester Chamber of Commerce at this period. After the end of the century the gloom lifted ; prices were

[1] *Bombay and Lancashire Cotton Spinning Inquiry*, q. 472.   (Evidence of James Cocker, a Bombay mill manager.)
[2] V. Anstey, *op. cit.*, pp. 296-7.   [3] Proceedings, 5th November 1888.
[4] *Ibid.*, 24th April 1889.   [5] *Manchester Guardian*, 1st July 1890.
[6] Proceedings, 30th September 1891.   [7] Cmd. 1761 of 1903, p. 444.

rising once more, and with them exports (measured by yards as well as by pounds sterling) began to grow again at the old rate. Trade reached a record height in 1907 but 1911 was even better, and exports in the last two full years of peace reached still greater heights. In each of the five years 1909-13 India imported over 2,600 million yards of piece goods, nearly all from Britain.[1] In this period of expansion British merchants had no excuse for querulous complaint. No major governmental policies had to be questioned ; the Chamber of Commerce concerned itself almost exclusively with technical questions such as arbitration and the terms of contracts between English and Indian merchants. One last attempt was made in 1903 to secure the repeal of the duties and excise on piece goods, but the Government of India stood firm and the question was allowed to drop.[2]

Disputes over terms of contract in the Indian market usually concerned problems arising from the late delivery of goods. The structure of the Lancashire cotton industry, with its horizontal divisions, complicated this inevitably complex question. The merchant could blame the printer, the printer the manufacturer, and the manufacturer the spinner, for unpunctual delivery of goods in India ; the European and native merchants in India did their best to fix the responsibility on Manchester shippers and they naturally enough tried to shoulder it off on to someone else.

The problem first became serious during the boom year of 1899. Five Indian Chambers of Commerce wrote to the Manchester Chamber in February 1900 pointing out the serious consequences to Indian importers and to bazaar dealers when Manchester failed to deliver goods to time. In a rising market customers were unwilling to exercise their undoubted right to cancel the contract.[3] The protest caused some discussion in Lancashire, and all sections of the industry were quick to blame other people. There was general agreement that stricter definition of delivery dates in contracts would obviate most of the difficulties ; but while every section was willing to impose stern conditions on its supplier, none was willing to be tied down to firm dates itself.[4]

[1] V. Anstey, op. cit., p. 535.
[2] Proceedings, 13th May and 17th June 1903.
[3] Ibid., 14th and 21st February and 7th March 1900 ; Monthly Record, March 1900.
[4] Proceedings, 13th June and 18th July 1900.

The Indian Chambers of Commerce returned to the charge in 1905, and the Manchester Chamber gave to a small committee the arduous task of consulting all the Lancashire interests involved and preparing a model contract. This took two years, and copies of the draft scheme were not in the hands of the Indian Chambers until July 1907. " It had been impossible to hurry the procedure where mutual agreement was so essential and individual considerations so various." [1] Delay did not produce the hoped-for unanimity, however, for only the merchants and manufacturers (not the spinners or the printers) agreed to the terms finally submitted to the Indian Chambers. Briefly, the proposed contract suggested moderate penalties for avoidable late delivery in a rising market ; in a falling market the buyer was " sufficiently met by cancelment ". To the Indian Chambers, who were anxious to secure prompt delivery, not compensation for delay, this scheme was quite unacceptable.[2] As the European merchants in India had failed to get satisfaction from the Manchester shippers, the native dealers (led by the powerful Bombay Native Piece Goods Merchants' Association) took matters into their own hands. By the middle of 1909 they had forced the Manchester merchants to agree to their terms, which were much severer than those proposed by Manchester in the first place.

The chief object gained by the native traders is that time-contract goods shipped after due date will in future become liable to a penalty allowance varying from $1\frac{1}{2}$ per cent. *ad valorem* to $7\frac{1}{2}$ per cent. according to the length of overdue time. Late goods may be cancelled at buyer's option without allowance and the same applies to goods delayed by non-preventable causes such as floods, fires, strikes, lock-outs, war or tempest.[3]

The Manchester merchants soon came to regret this last concession, for the great strikes of carters and railwaymen in 1911 made late delivery very common. The Calcutta merchants allowed a month's grace when goods were delayed by *force majeure*,[4] but the Bombay Native Piece Goods Merchants' Association steadfastly refused to follow their example.[5] Under sustained pressure the Delhi Chamber of Commerce permitted the insertion of a strike clause modelled on the one in force at Calcutta, and were held to their promise,

---

[1] Annual Report for 1906.   [2] *Monthly Record*, January 1908.
[3] *Ibid.*, July 1909.   [4] *Ibid.*, November 1911.
[5] *Ibid.*, November 1911 and August 1912.

although the Delhi Hindustani Mercantile Association did its best to upset the agreement.[1] Thus with some difficulty the Manchester merchants recovered some of the ground lost in 1909.

While counter-attacking on one flank, Manchester merchants had to defend themselves from assault in the rear, for if the merchants wanted the protection that a strike clause could give so did the manufacturers who supplied them. As early as May 1911 the Cotton Spinners' and Manufacturers' Association had asked for discussions on this point, but had been rebuffed. They tried again in 1912, threatening to enter into no more contracts after the beginning of 1913 unless the Chamber of Commerce conceded a strike clause. After long negotiations the manufacturers obliged the merchants to agree to grant them the Calcutta terms, *i.e.* one month's grace when goods were unavoidably delayed;[2] but the agreement was short-lived. At the end of January 1913, the Chamber took the opportunity to withdraw its support from the clause when manufacturers did not accept it " with the unanimity required to make it effective ".[3]

In these last years of high prosperity Indian nationalism had not yet become a force that Manchester had to fear. A boycott of Manchester goods in 1905, in protest against the partition of Bengal, did not prevent a rise in exports to that area.[4] On the other hand, Manchester's distrust of native merchants may well have wounded Indian susceptibilities and so prejudiced the future ; for example, in 1909 the Chamber of Commerce protested against the practice whereby Indian partnerships adopted European trading names, and suggested as a remedy the compulsory registration of partnerships in India.[5] A more serious dispute broke out in 1911 between the Bombay Native Piece Goods Merchants' Association and the Manchester merchants ; the Indian merchants asked that in future native as well as European umpires might be appointed when arbitration had failed to settle a dispute, but to this Manchester would not agree.[6] The Bombay Association next approached the Bombay Chamber of Commerce (which represented European merchants), but met with another refusal ; the Bombay Chamber's resistance was

[1] Annual Report for 1913 ; *Monthly Record*, February and June 1914.
[2] Annual Report for 1912. [3] *Monthly Record*, February 1913.
[4] *Annual Statement of the Trade of the United Kingdom for 1905.*
[5] Proceedings, 8th September 1909.
[6] *Monthly Record*, August and September 1911.

reinforced by "the practically unanimous view of all [Manchester] merchants engaged in the Bombay trade ".[1] Despite this support the Bombay Chamber had to give way in the end, and the Manchester merchants had no choice but to accept the position.[2]

Though careless of Indian feelings, the Manchester merchants and spinners had not forgotten their earlier dread of the Indian cotton mills. At the annual meeting in 1909 the President of the Manchester Chamber pointed to the rapid growth of Indian mill production—a 25 per cent. increase in the number of looms in two years—and argued that if England adopted Protection, "naturally and logically the millowners in India would demand protection . . . and . . . such a claim could not be resisted on any principle of equity ".[3] Even in 1913, the fabulous year in which piece goods exports to India topped 3,000 million yards for the first and last time, the President of the Chamber was asking what would happen if Indian demand fell off. He answered the question himself in an optimistic vein : West Africa, the Sudan, China, the Balkans, and Asia Minor, "so far hardly developed", would absorb Lancashire's production; in addition Lancashire would concentrate on the finer finished goods.[4] This was a shrewd prophecy based on already discernible trends ; what nobody foresaw was the rate at which Indian demand was to fall off.

[1] *Monthly Record*, May and June 1913.
[2] *Ibid.*, August and October 1913.
[3] *Ibid.*, February 1909.   [4] *Ibid.*, July 1913.

CHAPTER V

EUROPEAN TARIFFS FROM THE COBDEN TREATY TO THE FIRST WORLD WAR

THE markets which give most trouble are not necessarily the most important ; an illustration of this may be drawn from the history of Manchester's trade with European countries after 1860. There had been a time, no farther distant than 1820, when Europe (excluding Turkey) had taken half the British export of cotton piece goods. But by 1860 Europe imported only 10 per cent. and by 1900 only 6 per cent. of Lancashire's vast export of cotton goods. However, a relative decline in those days of rapidly expanding world trade was quite consistent with a greater volume of trade, as the following table shows :

EXPORT OF COTTON PIECE GOODS TO EUROPE[1]

	(million yards)	per cent. of total
1820	128	51
1860	300	11
1870	295	9
1880	365	8
1890	348	7
1900	292	6
1913	430	6

As Europe took the finest quality of Lancashire goods, a comparison of volumes does less than justice to the trade ; and though relatively small the quantities of goods involved were quite large enough to explain the keen interest Manchester took in the European markets. This, however, does not fully explain the course of Manchester policy, since the largest markets for Lancashire cotton goods were Holland and Germany, whereas the Manchester merchants fixed their eyes on France. The problems of French trade attracted most attention partly because French commercial policy

[1] Cmd. 1761 of 1903, p. 444, and for 1913 the Annual Statement of Trade.

was the least liberal in Europe, at least after the fall of the
Second Empire, but partly also because the opening of the
French market in 1860 had symbolised (in the eyes of the
Manchester merchants) the triumph of Free Trade. French
defection from the cause would stultify the Cobden Treaty,
and shatter the hopes of the Cobdenites that economic
liberalism would spread from France to the rest of Europe.

The Cobden Treaty marked the opening of a brief period
during which European tariffs were lower on the whole than
at any time before or since. The commercial treaties which
embodied these tariff changes usually included a most-
favoured-nation clause extending any privileges contained in
the treaty to all other countries with which a most-favoured-
nation treaty had been concluded. Thanks to the operation
of this system the benefits of low duties were extended to most
of the countries of Europe, and it became an important part
of Manchester policy to insist that Britain should have a most-
favoured-nation agreement with as many countries as possible.
This was the more necessary as by 1860 Britain's bargaining
position had deteriorated so much that she could get no
concessions from any country except by means of the most-
favoured-nation clause. In 1861 Belgium and France
concluded a commercial treaty from the benefits of which
Great Britain was virtually excluded because there was no
most-favoured-nation clause in her treaty with Belgium.
The Manchester Chamber of Commerce denounced the existing
tariff as " illiberal and restrictive in its effects on the import of
British produce and manufactures ", and as an " unbecoming
and ungrateful " act on the part of the Belgian Government.
A memorial to Lord John Russell, the Foreign Secretary,
asked him to " induce Belgium to adopt a more liberal
commercial policy towards this country, and to admit our
merchandise on terms as favourable as those granted to any
other country ".[1] In July 1862 Britain and Belgium signed
a most-favoured-nation commercial treaty,[2] and this particular
hindrance to trade was removed.

The Manchester merchants felt a similar anxiety for their
trade with the Zollverein and with Italy. In 1861-62,
while Franco-German negotiations were going on for a
commercial treaty, Manchester asked for an assurance that
the British representatives at Berlin would observe " the

[1] Proceedings, 15th July 1861.
[2] C. J. Fuchs, *Trade Policy of Great Britain since 1860* (1905), p. 29.

utmost vigilance " in securing most-favoured-nation treatment for British exports.[1] Lower duties were also needed :

Before the establishment of the Zollverein [it was declared]
our dealings had been so extensive as to have induced many
German merchants to settle in the manufacturing districts of
Lancashire and Yorkshire. . . . The imposition of specific duties
had, however, acted so prejudicially on our commercial intercourse
with the German states that the trade in manufactured goods had
been almost annihilated. The value of our total annual exports
thither did not amount to a greater sum than was formerly exported
by a single firm.[2]

This was quite untrue, but there was some reason for alarm
at that time because of bad trade and the impending threat
of a cotton famine. Despite the assurances of the President
of the Board of Trade, it was not until 1865 that the Zollverein
and Britain signed a commercial treaty by which Germany
extended to the British the concessions won by the French in
1862.[3] The Manchester merchants had also urged the government to secure most-favoured-nation treatment from Italy,
and this was done by a treaty of 1863.[4]

" Since the conclusion of our Treaty with the Emperor
of the French ", noted the Annual Report for 1862, " a more
liberal spirit has been manifested by continental nations
with respect to their commercial legislation." Austria
was a regrettable exception to this rule. Not until 1864
did the Manchester merchants begin to hope that Austria too
might fall in with the general trend towards freer trade.
In July of that year the Chamber of Commerce received a
confidential letter from the Foreign Office giving reasons why
a change in Austrian fiscal policy might be expected : the
Austrian Government favoured a degree of free trade and had
the support of the merchants of Pesth and Trieste, but the
trading community generally was " strongly protectionist ".
The Manchester merchants were advised that an unofficial
delegation might do some good, but in the end it was felt that
the embarrassment which the visit might cause to the Austrian
Government would outweigh the advantages of informal
discussions with Austrian traders.[5] When, early in 1865,
the Austrian Government took the plunge and proposed the

[1] Proceedings, 5th August 1861.   [2] Ibid., 26th February 1862.
[3] Fuchs, op. cit., p. 30.
[4] Proceedings, 26th February 1862, and Fuchs, loc. cit.
[5] Proceedings, 20th July, 17th August, and 14th September 1864.

appointment of an International Commission of Austrian and English members to examine the commercial relations of the two countries, the Foreign Office invited the co-operation of the Manchester Chamber. This was readily granted, but the mixed Commission held few sittings and a commercial treaty was signed in December before the Manchester merchants had had a proper hearing.[1]

This treaty followed the precedent set in 1860 by providing for maximum specific duties of 25 per cent. (to be reduced to 20 per cent. in 1870), such duties to be based on the prices ruling in 1865. As in 1860, the Manchester merchants were dissatisfied with the base period chosen for establishing the prices of cotton goods,

inasmuch as the prices calculated on the average of the last three months would rule from 2 to 300 per cent. above the averages of the three years immediately preceding the American Civil War ; it would be much fairer to take the prices fixed by the French treaty as a guide. . . .[2]

Alternatively Manchester suggested that a fair adjustment would be to deduct 40 per cent. from the abnormal 1865 prices of raw cotton. Neither suggestion was adopted, though the Austrians did make some concessions to the view that the 1865 prices were unrepresentative.[3] The new tariff did not give complete satisfaction, but it did grant a " considerable abatement " of duties on most branches of Lancashire goods.[4]

By the end of the 'sixties the liberalising movement on the Continent had worked itself out. Tariffs did not begin to rise again at once, but they had stopped falling. Manchester merchants found that to ask for further concessions was no longer to push at an open door ; rather they had to be vigilant to preserve such privileges as they had already won. The new situation showed itself most clearly in commercial relations with France, where the Cobden treaty was due for renewal in 1870. The Manchester merchants remained for some time unaware of the change in the European climate of opinion ; recognising that the treaty of 1860 had proved " highly beneficial to the commerce and general prosperity of the two nations ", they expressed the hope that some very

[1] Proceedings, 22nd February, 28th June, and 22nd November 1865.
[2] Ibid., 3rd January 1866.   [3] Ibid., 24th April and 1st August 1866.
Annual Report for 1867, p. 11.

high duties remaining in the French tariff would be reduced when the treaty came up for revision.[1] These hopes came to nothing. Before the revision of the treaty had gone very far, the Second Empire fell and France began looking round for new sources of revenue to meet her heavy post-war expenses, notably the indemnity to the German Empire. As public opinion in France had never wholeheartedly supported the treaty of 1860, higher tariffs were an obvious means of raising money. The French proposals (which took the form of taxes on imported raw materials, and " compensatory " duties on imported manufactures) moved the Manchester Chamber to express its deep regret that " with the beneficent result of the free trade policy of this country before their eyes, the French Government should think it necessary or desirable to fetter the interchange of commerce with other nations ". The Chamber therefore most earnestly recommended the British Government " not to be a party to any transaction which will have the effect of undoing in the slightest degree the good work done by that eminent statesman, the late Richard Cobden ".[2]

This declaration of resistance did not prevent Manchester from making detailed representations to the Commission which was sitting in Paris to determine the new tariff. Indeed, the Chamber's representatives maintained that " by combating the claims and assertions of the French protective classes " they had advanced the free-trade cause in both England and France.[3] As it happened, the French Government, the Commission, and the Manchester Chamber of Commerce had all laboured in vain ; the French National Assembly refused to accept the proposed duties on raw materials, the government fell, and the treaty of 1860 was extended until 1877, with provision for automatic renewal thereafter unless denounced.[4] The Manchester Chamber complacently noted that " the principles of international trade are now more widely appreciated amongst the French people ".[5]

By 1876 the question of the treaty, due to be renewed in the following year, was again agitating the Manchester merchants. They published a manifesto setting forth the mutual benefits that the treaty of 1860 had brought to both

[1] Proceedings, 6th January 1869.   [2] Ibid., 13th October 1871.
[3] Report of the Chamber's Deputation to Paris, printed with the Annual Report for 1872.
[4] Fuchs, op. cit., p. 43.   [5] Annual Report for 1873, p. 11.

5

52 MANCHESTER MERCHANTS AND FOREIGN TRADE

countries ; but this met with a very mixed reception in France, where Chambers of Commerce replied in terms " distinguished by a leaven of Protectionism and a qualified approval of Free Trade, or in so far only as it affected their special interests ".[1] Manchester thought that the Cobden treaty, particularly in the provisions concerning cotton goods, had not moved far enough in the direction of free trade ; exports of cotton goods and yarns to France were still in 1875 valued at no more than £2,250,000, a vast percentage increase over pre-treaty days, but a trivial proportion of the total Lancashire export trade.[2] The Manchester merchants therefore argued that the French Government ought not to be inquiring into Lancashire's costs of production with a view to imposing a protective tariff ; nevertheless the Chamber of Commerce co-operated in supplying the information required.[3]

Negotiations for the new treaty began in March 1877.[4] Manchester urged that a 5 per cent. duty at the most would be enough to equate the British and French costs in the cotton trade, but that the existing duties were much higher than that—as indeed the French intended. The specific duties which in 1860 had been worked out as the equivalent of 15 per cent ad valorem were by 1877 in some cases equal to 20 or 30 per cent. owing to the fall of prices.[5] The Chamber of Commerce objected to these " high and protective rates " very strongly, and without committing itself to any detailed proposals urged the Foreign Office in general terms to get as many concessions as possible. At the same time the Chamber of Commerce supported the French demand that the British duties on wine should be lowered, not as part of a bargain but because the wine duty was an " example of the impolicy of an assessment on the specific system " against which Manchester had long since set its face.[6] But neither the British nor the French Government was willing to take Manchester's advice, and the negotiations broke down. At the end of 1878 the French Government denounced the treaty of 1873 (which itself was virtually a copy of the Cobden treaty) in order to free itself to make a new tariff. This took longer than was expected, and the treaty of 1873 had

[1] Annual Report for 1876, pp. 10-11.
[2] Ibid., and Address to the Chambers of Commerce and to the People of France.
[3] Proceedings, 31st January and 2nd February 1877.
[4] Dunham, op. cit., p. 336.   [5] Proceedings, 22nd March 1877.
[6] Ibid., and Annual Report for 1877, p. 6.

to be renewed from time to time until the new tariff was ready.

Meanwhile negotiations had been resumed in June 1880 for a new commercial treaty. It soon became clear that the new agreement would be less favourable to Manchester than the old, and " having regard to the distinctly protective nature of the new general tariff and to the little value which the French Government evidently places upon friendly commercial relations with Great Britain ", the Chamber of Commerce urged the British Government to abandon the attempt to renew the treaty.[1] The Chamber continued to give technical advice to the British negotiators who were discussing details of the new tariff in Paris,[2] but as in 1872 British and French interests could not be reconciled. In February 1882 the attempt was finally abandoned and the treaty replaced by a simple most-favoured-nation agreement which was to last for ten years.[3] With this settlement the Manchester merchants were well content, and in retrospect were inclined to think that

they were no worse off without the treaty than they had been under the disadvantageous treaty they had previously been working under. So far as they could see there was growing up in France a free-trade spirit which left to itself would in the course of a very short time lead to a reduction of the duties on many articles.[4]

Maturer consideration would modify this optimistic forecast, but in fact the new French tariff was by no means excessive, representing an advance of 24 per cent. on the rates previously in force. Not until 1892 did the French turn decisively towards high protection.[5]

The Anglo-French treaty of 1860 had an incidental effect on our relations with Spain and Portugal that was overlooked at the time but later caused some anxiety in Manchester. Before 1860 a high uniform duty had been levied in Britain on all imported wines, an arrangement that penalised the light and cheap wines of France and favoured the heavy wines of Spain and Portugal; by the treaty of 1860, Britain undertook to recast her wine duties according to the alcoholic content of the wines, thus effectively ending the concealed

---

[1] Proceedings, 27th April 1881.   [2] Ibid., 2nd and 29th June 1881.
[3] Dunham, op. cit., pp. 348-9.   [4] Annual Meeting, 5th February 1883.
[5] J. H. Clapham, Economic Development of France and Germany, 1815-1914 (4th edn. 1945), pp. 262-4.

preference to Spain and Portugal that had long been a part
of British fiscal policy. For some years no ill consequence
followed from this change of policy, but in 1867 a Franco-
Portuguese commercial treaty reduced many Portuguese
duties on French goods without extending like benefits to
Britain. Manchester therefore urged the government to
negotiate a most-favoured-nation treaty with Portugal, and to
admit the strong Portuguese wines at a lower rate of duty,
" as on this basis would rest our sole influence in obtaining
concessions for our imports ".[1] Nothing came of this attempt,
and in 1869-70, when the Spanish tariff was being revised, the
Manchester merchants renewed their appeal for lower wine
duties, with no greater success than before.[2]

In 1877 Spain introduced a new tariff with two sets of
duties, the higher of which fell on Britain, to whom Spain
denied most-favoured-nation treatment. The Manchester
Chamber of Commerce took a serious view of this development, " which would transfer to Germany and to Switzerland
and Belgium a trade in which they were our closest competitors ".[3] The Spanish Government's grievance over the wine
duties, it was felt, ought to be sympathetically considered by
Britain ; on the other hand, an attempt to conciliate Spain
by suppressing smuggling from Gibraltar was not considered
worthy of support. In the name of "freedom of trade " the
Manchester merchants opposed the vexatious restrictions
which, they alleged, were to be imposed solely in the interests
of the Spanish revenue.[4] Negotiations between Spain and
Britain dragged on fitfully for several years, the Manchester
merchants continuing to defend the special status of Gibraltar
but remaining otherwise favourable to Spanish claims. When
at last in 1886 Britain revised her wine duties in order to
admit strong Spanish wines at the lowest rate, and Spain
granted Britain most-favoured-nation treatment, " a sensible
increase in the trade " between the two countries quickly
took place, thus justifying the Manchester merchants'
persistent interest in the Spanish market.[5]

The Manchester merchants were not slow to detect the
trend towards protection that set in at the end of the 'seventies.
Even in 1878, a year before the traditional dating of the change

[1] Proceedings, 25th September 1867, and Annual Report for 1867, p. 13.
[2] Proceedings, 20th October 1869 and 30th March 1870.
[3] Annual Report for 1877, p. 12.   [4] Ibid., pp. 7-8.
[5] Ibid., 1886, p. 12.

in European fiscal policies, the Chamber of Commerce had warned Lord Derby " that the Governments of the Continent were unduly influenced by those interested in obtaining protection for their manufactures ".[1] However, Manchester trade had not as yet suffered unduly ; even as late as 1886 European tariff barriers were probably lower than they had been before the Cobden Treaty.[2] The return to protection in Germany, Manchester's largest European market, passed almost unnoticed. German tariff policy received so little attention, indeed, that if the records of the Chamber of Commerce were the only source of information it would seem as if Lancashire's export trade to Germany was negligible : whereas in fact Germany was a much better customer than either France or Spain, to whom the Manchester Chamber gave so much attention. Austrian policy, too, gave satisfaction in Manchester, particularly after 1890 when Germany took the lead in reducing Central European tariff barriers. An Austro-German commercial treaty reduced Austrian duties on cotton piece goods by amounts varying between 6 and 16 per cent., and thanks to the most-favoured-nation clause Lancashire shared in the benefits.[3] The other treaties negotiated by Germany at this time were also in welcome contrast to the high protective policy of France and the United States ; Manchester was pleased to note that these treaties, " although not designed to extend the foreign trade of the United Kingdom ", would undoubtedly " have a beneficial effect in that direction ".[4]

Though Austrian tariff policy did not become aggressively nationalist, the rates levied on imports were by no means as moderate as Manchester merchants would have wished ; certainly they were much higher than the 8 per cent. levied in the Ottoman Empire. Therefore, when Austria virtually annexed Bosnia and Herzegovina, in 1878, Manchester merchants rightly feared that the change from the Turkish to the Austrian tariff would restrict trade. The Foreign Office willingly conveyed their protests to the Austrian Government, but without avail ; in 1880 the Austrian tariff was applied to Bosnia-Herzegovina.[5]

Over a long period, Manchester made persistent attempts

---

[1] Annual Report for 1878, p. 9.
[2] T. H. Farrer, *Free Trade versus Fair Trade* (1904 edn.), p. 92.
[3] *Monthly Record*, December 1890.　　　[4] Annual Report for 1891.
[5] Proceedings, 30th June and 28th July 1880.

to save its trade from harm during the decay of the Ottoman Empire. A treaty of 1861 had fixed the import duties of the Ottoman Empire (including Rumania) at 8 per cent.,[1] and whenever a new state was carved out of the moribund Empire the Manchester Chamber of Commerce tried hard to limit the tariffs of the successor states to the old level. When Rumania, an independent state since 1861, negotiated a commercial treaty with Austria in 1876, Manchester protested that under the Anglo-Turkish treaty of 1861 Rumania had no right to make commercial treaties at all.[2] The protest went unheeded, but a request for most-favoured-nation treatment was granted.[3] Similarly when an Anglo-Bulgarian commercial treaty was being negotiated in 1889 the Chamber supported the Foreign Office demand for the traditional 8 per cent. duty and no more ;[4] eight years later Manchester merchants were still insisting on the same point.[5] When, as a result of the First Balkan War in 1912, Turkey lost almost the whole of her European possessions, Manchester merchants adopted a slightly less aggressive attitude ; they no longer stipulated that the liberated territories should retain the old Turkish tariff, but they did urge the Foreign Office to secure a guarantee of the "open door", a variant of the most-favoured-nation clause usually reserved for colonial peoples.[6]

After the lapsing of the Cobden treaty in 1882, Manchester merchants abandoned their attempt to convert the French to the gospel of free trade. The best that could be hoped for was to prevent a further deterioration in commercial relations, but the Méline tariff of 1892 dashed even this faint hope, and Manchester had to acknowledge the triumph of " extreme Protectionism " in France.[7] As a result of the new tariff Lancashire's exports to France fell off sharply : piece-goods exports to France which had averaged 42 million yards per annum for the decade 1882-91 dropped to an average of 18 million yards in the years 1902-07 ; yarn exports declined even more sharply. In the ordinary course of events Manchester would have had to accept this adverse trend without complaint, but in view of the *entente cordiale* the Chamber of Commerce thought that where economic argument had failed

[1] Fuchs, *op. cit.*, p. 33.   [2] *Manchester Guardian*, 1st August 1876.
[3] Proceedings, 28th June 1876, and Fuchs, *op. cit.*, p. 61.
[4] Proceedings, 29th July and 25th September 1889.
[5] *Monthly Record*, March 1897.
[6] Proceedings, 11th December 1912.   [7] Annual Report for 1891.

political pressure might succeed.[1]   As Manchester could not persuade the Association of British Chambers of Commerce to accept this view, it was unlikely that either the Foreign Office or the French Government would show much enthusiasm for it.   In fact, the French tariff on certain classes of cotton goods rose steeply in 1909.[2]

Germany treated Manchester goods much more liberally, even after the expiry of the Central European commercial treaties in 1902 and the remaking of the German tariff on more restrictive lines.   The new tariff raised the duties on cotton piece goods by 50 per cent., but left unchanged the duties on yarn ; [3] this was an important concession, since Germany was one of Manchester's best yarn markets.   The German colonies remained open to Manchester goods, in contrast to the French colonies where the once-open door had been partly closed in the 'nineties.   If Germany had become a serious competitor in Manchester's overseas markets, the Manchester Chamber of Commerce might have had less friendly feelings towards her in the years before the First World War ; but although it was believed that Germany was the main threat to Manchester's domination of the world trade in cotton goods,[4] the danger was not yet serious.   It was therefore easy for Manchester merchants to speak of the commercial interdependence of the two nations,

which must always go far to check any serious interruption of our friendship. . . . Rivals in world commerce we must necessarily be, . . . but commercial rivalry should be no more a barrier to amity between nations than it is between individuals. . . .[5]

We frankly admit and admire the wonderful industrial progress made in Germany in the past forty years, and it is only reasonable that she should want outlets for her expanding trade, and her place in the sun.[6]

These sentiments may have been partly an indication of the Manchester merchants' quiet confidence in their un-challenged supremacy over the cotton trade ; but there was surely also a width of outlook which reflected the cosmopolitan character of the city.   The Manchester business

[1] *Monthly Record*, September 1908.
[2] Proceedings, 15th February 1909, and Annual Report for 1909.
[3] Clapham, *op. cit.*, p. 321.
[4] The President at the Half-Yearly Meeting of the Manchester Chamber of Commerce, 23rd July 1913 ; *Monthly Record*, July 1913.
[5] *Ibid.*, November 1909.   [6] *Ibid.*, February 1912.

community included many foreigners—Germans, Greeks, Armenians—and many Englishmen who still bore names that testified to their foreign origin. Without any self-consciousness, the Manchester Chamber of Commerce in 1913 could ask the Hamburg merchants to co-operate in resisting the monopolistic concessions that Lever Bros. were trying to secure in Liberia.[1] Sixty years before this time Richard Cobden had dreamed of international peace as a consequence of free trade ; though Manchester in the early twentieth century was not pacifist, something of the dream remained.

[1] *Monthly Record*, February 1913.

CHAPTER VI

THE AFRICAN TRADE

By the end of the nineteenth century the export of cotton piece goods was in the hands of Manchester shipping merchants who bought cloth, had it finished on commission, and despatched it overseas in response to firm orders. These merchants, who were the largest group in the Manchester Chamber of Commerce, rarely imported goods into England ; the raw materials and food paid for by the export of cotton goods were imported by a different body of merchants who generally operated from Liverpool rather than Manchester. The only Manchester merchants who handled imported goods on a large scale were the cotton merchants, who had their own trade organisation—the Manchester Cotton Association, and the food importers who were organised as the Produce Section of the Manchester Chamber of Commerce. The main lines of organisation at the end of the century are thus quite clear ; what remains uncertain is how far back this division of function goes. There is little direct evidence on the point, but indirectly the records of the Manchester Chamber of Commerce suggest that the export shipping merchants had never been much concerned with importing ; if they had been, the Chamber would have paid more attention to the problems of particular importing trades. In actual fact, the Chamber confined itself to the particular problems of the export trade in cotton goods. Its hostility to the Corn Laws, timber duties, and other restrictions on trade arose from its general policy and did not merely reflect the interests of such importing merchants as belonged to the Chamber.

There was, however, one group of export shipping merchants who imported as well ; these were the West African merchants, who exported piece goods and imported West African produce[1]—rubber, palm oil, groundnuts, and raw cotton. It seems likely that in other parts of Africa, also, Manchester merchants may at times have done a two-way

---

[1] *Monthly Record*, May 1913 : the President, introducing Sir Frederick Lugard, Governor of North and South Nigeria, who was to give an address to the Chamber.

trade. Some of the earliest references to trade in Africa are to its importance as a source of raw materials and food rather than as a market. At the end of 1860 Moorish commissioners arrived in England to negotiate a loan ; the Chamber of Commerce was urged to use the visit to get a reduction of the Moroccan export tax on grain, but this it declined to do.[1] Instead, it made the more general request that the Foreign Office should influence the Emperor of Morocco to adopt " a more enlightened commercial policy ".[2] The export taxes on grain were still giving trouble thirty years later.[3]

In the middle of the nineteenth century Africa was not an important market for Manchester goods ; in 1856 it accounted for no more than 3 per cent. by value and 5 per cent. by volume of the export of cotton goods ; the only considerable African markets were Egypt, which took 50 million yards, and the West Coast and the Cape, which took about 20 million yards each.[4] As long as this small trade went on undisturbed, the Manchester merchants had little reason to put any special pressure on the government ; when they did act, it was generally in response to outside pressure. In 1860, for instance, the Church Missionary Society asked the Chamber of Commerce to ask the government for " encouragement and support to our Commercial Intercourse with Africa ", and a memorial was despatched to this effect.[5] In the same year, after being reminded of " the innumerable products " that Africa could supply, the Manchester merchants asked the government to continue its support for McGregor Laird's exploration of the Niger ;[6] but in 1864, when the Governor of Lagos himself complained that tribal warfare was interfering with trade and asked the Chamber to put pressure on the government, the subject aroused so little interest that nothing was done.[7]

By 1870 the trade of Lagos was growing rapidly ; imports had increased since 1866 from £262,000 to £515,000.[8] With more at stake, the Manchester merchants subsequently took more interest in the state of the hinterland and the policy of the colonial government. The Governor of Sierra Leone,

---

[1] Proceedings, 10th and 17th December 1860.
[2] Ibid., 7th and 18th January 1861.
[3] See for example, ibid., 18th November 1891.
[4] T. Ellison, A Handbook of the Cotton Trade (1858), App., Table C.
[5] Proceedings, 1st and 8th February 1860.
[6] Annual Meeting, 30th January 1860, and Annual Report for 1860, pp. 7-8.
[7] Proceedings, 10th September 1864.   [8] Ibid., 29th January 1873.

they complained, had interfered with the administration of Lagos and so provoked the natives to close the main road from Lagos to the interior ; while not supporting demands for the construction of new roads and the annexation of more territory, the Chamber of Commerce did ask the Colonial Office to reform the West African administrative system.[1] As in India, administrative reform meant, in the eyes of the merchants, better representation of their views on the legislative councils ; the government agreed, but pointed out that the main difficulty was to find merchants who were willing to serve.[2] Gambia was a case in point ; when the solitary mercantile representative retired from the council in 1875, a successor could not be found.[3]

Though not anxious to add to Britain's African Empire, Manchester merchants were not prepared to lose ground that had already been won. When in 1870 the Colonial Office opened negotiations with a view to ceding Gambia to France, " great anxiety " was expressed by the Manchester merchants, who were " averse from the transfer of their persons and property from the protection of the British Government to that of a foreign power ".[4] By memorial and petition the Chamber of Commerce protested against the transfer. Both the British and the French merchants in Gambia were said to be opposed to the change ; the natives had already uttered violent threats against their prospective new masters, and the change from English to French law would certainly cause confusion.[5] This protest had less effect than the Franco-Prussian War in bringing the negotiations to an end. They were resumed in 1874, but vigorous opposition from Manchester and a hostile debate in the House of Lords in 1876 killed the scheme.[6]

African trade on the whole pursued an uneventful course, as far as Manchester was concerned, until about 1880. After 1880, on the other hand, the problems of trade with Africa (particularly West Africa) demanded constant attention from the Chamber of Commerce. This was not because West Africa had yet become a large market for Manchester goods ; Egypt and the north coast ports took two yards of cloth for every one exported to the rest of Africa ; indeed, in 1883 the total value of cotton goods exported to Africa

---

[1] Proceedings, 26th February and 29th April 1873.
[2] Ibid., 28th May 1873.   [3] Ibid., 29th September 1875.
[4] Annual Report for 1870, pp. 12-13. [5] Proceedings, 20th July 1870.
[6] Ibid., 29th September and 24th November 1875 ; Manchester Guardian, 2nd May 1876.

amounted to only £4,500,000 or about 6 per cent. of the total value of the cotton export trade.[1] In 1856 it had been 3 per cent. of a much smaller total. The reason for the change in Manchester's attitude must therefore be sought not in the intrinsic importance of West Africa but in the growing European desire to develop new markets there.

By 1880 there were British settlements in the Gambia, Sierra Leone, Lagos, and on the Gold Coast ; the French had a foothold at Senegal, and on the coast to the north of the Congo River ; Germany had no colonies yet, but was soon to seize the Cameroons and a long strip of coast-line in south-west Africa ; King Leopold of the Belgians was busily developing his enormous private estate on the Upper Congo ; and Portugal, who had long been established in Angola to the south of the Congo, was thinking of reasserting her claim to all the territory between 5° 12' and 8° south, a claim that would have given her control of both banks of the Congo River. The Portuguese took this step largely because they were afraid that the explorations of De Brazza on behalf of the French would extend the French possessions at least as far as the north side of the estuary of the Congo. Without British support, however, the Portuguese claim could hardly hope to succeed ; in 1882, therefore, the Portuguese formally asked Great Britain to recognise their extensive claims on the West African coast.[2]

The Manchester Chamber of Commerce soon got wind of this move, and vigorously protested against any attempt to " interrupt the progress of British commerce in that part of West Africa ". It was pointed out that as recently as 1853 Portuguese pretensions had been resisted by the British Government ; the native chief was quite capable of maintaining order and the slave trade had been put down. Though exact calculations of the value of Lancashire's trade with the Congo were not possible, since many Lancashire cotton goods were exported to West Africa by way of Holland and France, yet " Lancashire has so large a share of this trade, both direct and indirect, that it views with anxiety any attempt to put restrictions on it ". Not only existing British trade but also the prospect of future trade with the " vast tribes inhabiting the interior of Africa " would be placed in jeopardy if Portugal were allowed to cut off King Leopold's access to

---

[1] T. Ellison, The Cotton Trade of Great Britain (1886), p. 161.
[2] S. E. Crowe, The Berlin West African Conference (1942), p. 16.

the sea. Though most unwilling that Portugal should lay its dead hand on the territories round the mouth of the Congo, the Manchester merchants felt that the " nature of African commerce does call for protection and fostering attention " from the government ; more frequent visits by British officials to the various trading stations would do good.[1] The Chamber of Commerce later elaborated and extended this proposal. The British consul at Loanda, in Angola, nominally protected British interests on the neutral coast-line that lay north of the Congo between the Portuguese and French possessions, but the distances were too great for him to exercise any effective influence. The Chamber suggested the appointment of a consular agent specially for this disputed territory ; it also asked that the government should permanently station a gunboat there at the disposal of the consular agent.[2]

If the Manchester merchants hoped that a British consul and a gunboat would make Portuguese annexations up to 5° 12' south unnecessary they were disappointed. While the government was quite willing to appoint a consul, it would not spend the £30,000 necessary to keep a gunboat near the Congo unless the merchants footed the bill, and this they were not prepared to do.[3] As negotiations with Portugal still dragged on, the Chamber of Commerce had to renew its earlier direct protest against disturbance of the existing situation. It now confined its argument to the question of import duties. It contended that as neither duties nor taxes were at that time being levied, "even the most liberal terms [of annexation], if those terms were short of absolute Free Trade and freedom from taxation, would be very disadvantageous to an important branch of British trade ".[4] But the Chamber's insistence on the " absolute neutrality of the district of the River Congo " went unheeded ; the most that the government would concede was that Parliament would be able to express an opinion before the treaty was ratified.[5] After further delays the Anglo-Portuguese treaty, recognising Portuguese claims to the coast between 5° 12' south and 8° south and fixing the maximum customs duties at 10 per cent., was signed in February 1884.[6] The fixing of a maximum duty, and provisions for equal and

[1] Letter of 30th May 1881 to the Foreign Office.
[2] Memorial of 13th November 1882 to the Foreign Office.
[3] Proceedings, 27th and 29th November 1882.
[4] Memorial of 12th March 1883 to the Foreign Office.
[5] *Hansard*, 3rd series, Vol. 277, col. 1284 ff. : H.C., 3rd April 1883.
[6] S. E. Crowe, *op. cit.*, pp. 16 and 23.

most-favoured-nation treatment for Britain, did not pacify the Manchester merchants ; they protested that, because of the obsolete valuation on which the duties were based, the nominal 10 per cent. duty might well work out in practice at 30 per cent. or more, and they were not reassured when the Foreign Office undertook to have the valuations revised. This, however, was a question of minor importance ; the principle of free access to the Congo remained the basis of Manchester's opposition to the treaty.[1]

It seems unlikely that this opposition could have prevented ratification of the treaty, which the government confidently expected Parliament to approve, had not the European Powers also voiced their displeasure.[2] By the end of June 1884 the British Government had recognised that the treaty was unacceptable to the Powers, and had told Portugal that it would not be ratified. Instead, on the joint invitation of France and Germany, a conference of the Powers was to be held at Berlin at the end of the year to bring some order into the " Scramble for Africa " and to secure freedom of trade in the annexed regions.

Meanwhile H. M. Stanley, the African explorer and the spokesman for King Leopold's International Association of the Congo, had addressed a well-attended meeting in Manchester at which he had painted in glowing colours the commercial prospects of the Congo Basin, improved as they were by the Association's deliberate refusal to levy customs duties in its territory. Originally the Manchester merchants had opposed the establishment of any European Power at the mouth of the Congo, but Stanley's eloquence won them over to full support of the Association's claims. The Board of Directors of the Manchester Chamber unanimously resolved that :

Our commercial interests and the freedom of trade and navigation will be best secured by the entire jurisdiction of the whole of the Congo River and of the adjacent littoral being entrusted in perpetuity to the free and independent State now being founded by the International Association under the auspices of H.M. the King of the Belgians.[3]

It was not likely that Portugal and France would tolerate so

---

[1] Letter of 5th March 1884 to Chambers of Commerce and M.P.s ; letters of 6th and 26th March 1884 to the Foreign Office.
[2] S. E. Crowe, *op. cit.*, pp. 25-6.   [3] Proceedings, 29th October 1884.

wide an extension of the Congo Free State ; nevertheless the Chamber of Commerce urged the Foreign Office to support Leopold's claims at the forthcoming Berlin Conference.[1]

Though the settlement reached at the conference did not meet Manchester's wishes in every detail, none of its provisions seriously infringed Manchester's interests. The clause limiting the period of free trade in the Congo Basin to twenty years had come under fire from the Manchester merchants, who denounced the limitation as " imperilling the proposed free state and rendering the future interests of British trade with the Congo highly precarious ".[2] But when it became clear that French opposition would prevent a guarantee of perpetual free trade, the Chamber of Commerce gracefully accepted the twenty-year period. Similarly, although the Congo Free State did not get both banks of the Congo, its access to the sea was well assured when it gained possession of the north or right bank as far inland as Manyanga, an acquisition which included the fine harbour of Banana at the mouth of the Congo. The Manchester merchants had high hopes that " on the establishment of railway and steam communication between the Upper and Lower River a large trade will be gradually developed and the industries of this district will derive there-from considerable benefits ".[3] A small trade with the Belgian Congo did grow up in time, but it never rivalled in importance the trade with British West Africa, especially the territories that later became the colony of Nigeria.

The Manchester merchants had more than once expressed a poor opinion of the administration of the British West African settlements ; in 1884 these complaints were renewed. Not long before, there had been reports that the French were preparing to sail up the Niger and annex Onitsha, only two hundred miles from the coast ; the Manchester Chamber felt that if Britain was to retain its hold on that part of Africa the colonial and consular services would have to be expanded. The value of British trade with the West Coast of Africa was estimated at £3,000,000 in 1882, yet the government spent only £1,000 on the consular service there; the much smaller markets of Morocco and Tripoli received far more generous treatment.[4] When the Foreign Office stipulated that if the merchants wanted more consuls they would have to pay for

[1] Letter of 5th November 1884 to the Foreign Office.
[2] Ibid., 12th December 1884 to the Foreign Office.
[3] Annual Report for 1884, p. 8.   [4] Proceedings, 4th April 1884.

them by a tonnage tax on British vessels trading with West Africa, the Chamber of Commerce indignantly protested that British interests in West Africa were of a national character and ought to be safeguarded out of the national revenue.[1] Though by no means satisfied with the government's attitude to the problems of trade in West Africa, Manchester merchants preferred British rule to any other; they wholeheartedly supported the government in its refusal to put the Niger River under the control of an international commission. That would be suitable enough for the Congo, but where British authority had been established for many years, as it had been on the Lower Niger, it would be wrong " to place a trade now exclusively British under international control ".[2]

With the establishment in 1884 of a British protectorate over the coastal strip between Lagos and the German colony in the Cameroons, the seizure of the coast-line of West Africa by European powers was practically complete.   Inland, however, boundaries were still undefined and prospects of conflict were considerable.   In 1888, the Liverpool Chamber of Commerce warned Manchester of French encroachments at Abeokuta, not far from Lagos, and the London Chamber sought Manchester's co-operation in urging the British and French Governments to delimit their spheres of influence in West and North West Africa.   The Manchester merchants willingly fell in with this suggestion and recommended the Colonial Office to negotiate " an amicable settlement of boundaries and an exchange of their several territories in those regions ".[3] An Anglo-French agreement settling these disputes was eventually reached in 1890.   Nevertheless, the Manchester merchants continued to keep a close watch on French activities, which seemed to be particularly aggressive on the borders of Sierra Leone.   In 1891 the Chamber of Commerce disputed the French claim to the inland town of Faranah, whose loss would inflict " serious injury upon British commerce with Sierra Leone " ; but further information made it clear that Faranah, being north of the tenth parallel of latitude, did rightly fall to France.[4]   Though the Manchester merchants would not have objected to the extension of British political control in the hinterland, they deplored " the conclusion by

[1] Proceedings, 15th February 1884.
[2] Letter of 23rd October 1884 to the Foreign Office.
[3] Proceedings, 25th July and 28th November 1888.
[4] *Monthly Record*, October and December 1891.

French agents of treaties with the rulers of territory hitherto exempt from European control ". The preservation of free commercial intercourse with the interior was regarded by the Chamber of Commerce as of vital importance to the interests of the West African colonies.[1] Had France shown more willingness to maintain the open door, the Manchester merchants would probably have complained as little of her expansion as they did of Germany's.

Having disgusted Manchester merchants with the high Méline tariff of 1892, the French still further blackened their reputation by imposing imperial preferences on those of their colonies not bound to free trade under the Congo treaties of 1885. After the conquest of Madagascar in 1896, they swept aside a most-favoured-nation treaty that the Queen of Madagascar had made with Britain in 1865 and imposed high duties on foreign imports, allowing their own goods to enter duty-free. As Britain had enjoyed almost half the total trade of Madagascar before the annexation, the Manchester merchants took a grave view of French behaviour ; but the only concession that could be wrung from the French was that the minimum French tariff should be applied to the goods most widely used in the island, including cotton textiles.[2] In Tunis, also, the French declined after 1897 to continue most-favoured-nation treatment of British goods ; Tunis had been a French possession since 1881, but it was not until 1897 that France took advantage of a revision of the tariff to allow her own goods free entry while foreign goods paid 5 per cent.[3] In West Africa, where French military expeditions had encroached on lands awarded to Britain in the agreement of 1890, long negotiations were needed in 1897 and 1898 before the French could be induced to restore even a part of the territory they had seized.[4] The Manchester merchants were well content, however, with less than complete restoration, since the terms of the Convention of 1898 included a thirty-year guarantee of equal treatment for British and French nationals in the West African colonies. A favourable economic agreement more than compensated for a few minor territorial concessions.[5]

---

[1] Letter of 29th February 1892 to the Colonial Office.

[2] *Monthly Record*, March 1896.

[3] Annual Report for 1896 ; *Monthly Record*, September, October, and December 1897. It must be admitted, however, that this was a lower rate of duty than had previously been charged.

[4] R. C. K. Ensor, *England 1870-1914* (1936), p. 243.

[5] *State Papers 1898-1899*, Vol. 91, p. 47 ; *Monthly Record*, July 1898.

6

This single act of grace did not remove suspicion of French policy from the minds of Manchester merchants. The *entente cordiale* of 1904 had provided that, while France should have a free hand politically in Morocco, most-favoured-nation treatment should be guaranteed to British trade for thirty years. By 1900 Morocco had become an important market for Lancashire piece goods, taking nearly 50 million yards of cloth as against only 16 million yards in 1880.[1] A thirty-year guarantee did not satisfy Manchester merchants, who took advantage of the Algeciras Conference of 1905-6 to ask that the guarantee of the open door should be made perpetual. They were probably not surprised when this was refused, though they still hoped to secure the withdrawal of the thirty-year limit.[2]

The Manchester merchants had always been sceptical of the benefits they could hope to receive in their trade with French colonies, but of the Belgian Congo they had at first the highest hopes. They were soon disillusioned. The free trade that King Leopold had promised in 1884 never materialised, for the administration and commerce of whole districts were handed over to monopolistic companies. Even in the boom year of 1913 the Belgian Congo imported less than seven million yards of Lancashire cloth. The Manchester merchants bore this disappointment in silence until the transfer of the Congo from Leopold to the Belgian state was mooted in 1907. The proposed change, it was felt,

afforded an opportunity for His Majesty's Government to insist that no interference with the right of free trade, accorded by the Berlin Treaty, shall be permitted to continue under any arrangement which may be made for the future administration of the Congo Free State.[3]

Sir Edward Grey was " entirely in sympathy " with this view,[4] but Manchester was still impatiently awaiting the promised reforms in 1911, two years after the transfer of power to the Belgian State.[5] In fact, the reforms did not take place until 1913.

In its relations with French and Belgian colonies the Manchester Chamber of Commerce could not say all that

---

[1] *Annual Statement of Trade*, 1880 and 1900.
[2] Proceedings, 21st June 1905, and Annual Report for 1905, pp. 4-5.
[3] Letter of 20th November 1907 to the Foreign Office.
[4] Proceedings, 10th March 1909.   [5] *Ibid.*, 22nd February 1911.

it would have liked to say. It was in no position to tell the French or Belgian Governments that they were not building railways fast enough, or that their river transport services were grossly inadequate and too expensive. The policy of the Manchester merchants on such questions may best be studied in relation to the British colonies, and in particular to those on the West African coast—the Gambia, Sierra Leone, the Gold Coast, and the territories that in 1913 were united to form the colony of Nigeria. In some respects the problems of West Africa in 1885 were similar to those of India in 1860. Both had only recently been brought under direct British control; both lacked railways; both were populous and fertile, promising large markets and plentiful supplies of raw materials to the enterprising merchant; in neither had the government's performance satisfied the Manchester Chamber of Commerce. It is not surprising, therefore, that the policies advocated by the Manchester merchants for British West Africa should have a familiar ring about them.

The first need was for better government. In 1885, perhaps because of the falling off in West African trade during that year, the tribesmen were particularly hostile, and the Chamber more than once had to call the attention of the Colonial Office to the need for firmer administration and better protection for merchants. In the delta of the Niger and Benue rivers, which had been proclaimed a British protectorate in 1884, no settled government had been established more than twelve months later. " The defenceless state of the country ", complained the Chamber of Commerce, " creates considerable anxiety in the minds of the mercantile and industrial communities of this country, and retards the further development of trade." [1] There was even less excuse for the " disastrous condition of affairs in the Gambia ", which had been an established colony for many years; according to their own account, Gambia merchants had lost 25 per cent. on their invested capital in the previous two or three years. In English of unwonted vigour the Manchester merchants suggested that since taxation and protection go together

the colonial authorities should either give protection to Her Majesty's subjects or should celebrate the demise of their authority and power by the removal of all duties and all official impediments and restrictions on the Gambia river.[2]

[1] Letter of 16th September 1885.   [2] Letter of 13th October 1885.

Disturbances continued in 1886-87. The Colonial Office excused itself in part by pointing out that able administrators would not go to West Africa, " except for a short time and with promotion in prospect " ; but it did undertake to send Sir Samuel Rowe, the Governor-in-Chief, on a special mission to the Gambia, and to persuade the Admiralty to show the flag more often on the river.[1] In Lagos, raids by the King of Dahomey and a fourteen years war between tribes in the interior provoked a further spate of complaints in 1891.[2]

Law and order alone did not satisfy the Manchester merchants. By an accident of history the present colony of Nigeria was for long divided into three parts (Lagos Colony, the Oil Rivers Protectorate, and the territory of the Royal Niger Chartered Company) each with its own laws and fiscal system. Manchester was urging as early as 1895 that this irrational division should be ended, at least as far as tariffs were concerned ; in 1896 the Chamber of Commerce put forward the more ambitious demand for complete fusion of the three colonies, but this was not achieved for a long time. When the Royal Niger Company lost its charter in 1899 its territory and the Oil Rivers Protectorate were reorganised as North and South Nigeria. South Nigeria absorbed Lagos in 1906, but North and South Nigeria remained separate colonies until 1913.[3]

A further administrative change that the Manchester merchants pressed upon the Colonial Office, from 1898 onwards, harked back to earlier disputes over the composition of the Indian Council in London. In 1898 the Manchester and Liverpool Chambers of Commerce jointly urged the need for an official advisory West African Committee with mercantile representatives.[4] Nearly seven years passed before the Colonial Office agreed to the establishment of any such body, despite persistent agitation from merchants in London, Liverpool, and Manchester. Even when established, the committee had no official status ; it merely served to convey the views of the merchant community to the Colonial Office, which did not necessarily consult the committee before initiating new policies.[5] Probably the right to correspond direct with the

[1] Letter of 12th January 1887.
[2] Proceedings, 25th March and 29th May 1891.
[3] Sir Alan Pim, *Economic History of Tropical Africa* (1940), p. 56.
[4] *Monthly Record*, July and October 1898.
[5] Proceedings, 5th November 1902, 16th March 1904 ; Annual Report for 1905, p. 9.

Governors of the West African colonies, conceded in 1903, proved more valuable to Manchester merchants.[1]

Once a colonial government had been set up, and some security for life and property achieved, as was the case by the early 'nineties, the way was open for more extensive development of West African resources. The Manchester Chamber of Commerce favoured railway development as a means to this end. In 1895 not a single railway was working in British West Africa, although the Colonial Office had been considering plans since 1892.[2] The Manchester merchants feared that the French would succeed in diverting the caravans to the French ports :

If railways were laid into the interior the existing trade would be at once attracted to the cheapest route and thus run through British and not French territory. . . . It should not be forgotten that the native trader bought goods in the same market where he sold his produce. . . . New railways would mean the building up of a new trade.[3]

As in India, the Manchester merchants preferred public to private construction of railways, but since the lines might not be profitable at first, they advised the use of a narrow 2 ft. 6 in. gauge both on the Gold Coast and in Sierra Leone.[4] The Chamber of Commerce had always held that in backward areas it was the government's duty to foster the development of transport, but its most forthright statement of this principle was not made until 1917 when it declared :

The provision of cheap transport is a primary duty of the Government in the general interest of the development of the Colony [Nigeria] and this duty extends to river and railway services.[5]

It was a principle that the Chamber had been acting on for sixty years.

Railway building in Africa continued to interest the Manchester merchants for several years, but by 1905 their attention was shifting to the question of freight rates, the chief railway lines being by then in operation. If the railways were to capture the traffic formerly carried by men or by camels, freight rates would have to fall sharply. On the

[1] *Monthly Record*, March 1903.
[2] Annual Report for 1895, p. 9.   [3] *Monthly Record*, June 1895.
[4] *Ibid.*, October 1894 ; Annual Report of the Africa Section for 1896 ; *Monthly Record*, July 1898, August 1899, February 1900, and February 1901.
[5] Letter of 11th May 1917 to the Governor of Nigeria.

Gold Coast the railway was charging nearly £13 a ton for carrying cotton goods 165 miles from Sekondi to Kumasi ; even if freight were halved, traffic might not be wholly diverted to the railways.[1] Later the rates for cotton goods were reduced from 1s. 10d. to 1s. 3d. per ton-mile, and passenger rates from 5d. to 4d. a mile.[2] " The very high rates " on the Lagos railway also caused dissatisfaction ; the Chamber of Commerce urged " that in the case of traffic which has yet to be wholly developed and displaced from its former grooves, the policy of very low rates should be adopted ".[3]

In Manchester's view the government's responsibilities included river as well as rail transport.   When the government tried to evade this obligation by proposing to grant a monopoly to a group of merchants trading up the Cross River in Southern Nigeria, the Manchester and Liverpool Chambers of Commerce protested strongly.   They suggested either a government steamship service on the river, or a subsidy to a private company ;   neither would cost the government more than four or five thousand pounds.   The government yielded to this argument and established its own service.[4]   When in 1913 the government proposed to transfer the service to a private merchant, Manchester scented the old danger of monopoly : " Private enterprise generally means that the owners of the service make use of their position to prevent the opening up of trade routes by other people " ;   only transfer to a steamship company would guarantee equal treatment of all merchants.[5]   In 1909 the Chamber of Commerce had occasion to complain of the inefficient river service on the Niger ;   a transfer of responsibility from the North to the South Nigerian Government would best solve the difficulty, but the Chamber was not unwilling for a private company with " an adequate subsidy " to undertake the work.[6]

Increased trade put a great strain on the primitive harbour facilities of the West African ports.   As early as 1900 the Manchester merchants were urging the Colonial Office to improve the harbour at Accra, where goods were being loaded and shipped on board steamers lying at anchor in the open

[1] Proceedings, 9th December 1903, and letter of 22nd December to the Colonial Office.
[2] Monthly Record, June 1905.   [3] Ibid., August 1907.
[4] Ibid., January and April 1904 ; Annual Report for 1904, p. 10.
[5] Letter of 15th December 1913 to the Colonial Office ; Annual Report for 1913.
[6] Letter of 8th November 1909 to the Colonial Office.

sea.[1] Facilities at Accra were still inadequate in 1909, when the Chamber asked for a longer breakwater.[2] Lagos, the chief port of Nigeria, the largest and most populous British colony in West Africa, likewise failed to develop as rapidly as its trade required. After complaints, the Colonial Office promised in 1907 to extend the Iddo wharf at Lagos " without avoidable delay ".[3] In 1916, a year of feverish planning for post-war development, the Manchester merchants fixed their gaze on a more distant horizon :

Lagos is the natural doorway to a vast hinterland of West Africa. For North and South Nigeria, with their great possibilities of development, Lagos is the port, and it may confidently be asserted that its importance at present is no measure of the greatness to which it will grow in the future. For these reasons the Chamber urge that a far-sighted policy [of port development] shall be adopted forthwith and energetically pursued. . . .[4]

At first sight sanitary questions would appear to be irrelevant to the work of a Chamber of Commerce ; but if a Chamber can reasonably demand that a colonial government shall protect merchants from death at the hands of turbulent tribesmen, it can equally well expect colonial governments to save merchants from death by disease. This at any rate was the view held in Manchester, where merchants took a keen interest in the sanitary problems of the notoriously unhealthy West African colonies. In the 'nineties the West African ports had neither water supply nor sewage systems. The Manchester merchants not only demanded that the colonial government should organise such services, but also that it should provide doctors for the trading community. The Colonial Office held, however, that it was no part of its duties to guarantee medical attendance on payment of a fee, except for Europeans in the government service.[5] Early in the twentieth century Freetown and Lagos did get pure water supplies, and Freetown had the luxury of a modern drainage system.[6] Even in 1909, however, the proposed £200,000 waterworks of Accra—" a great desideratum for many years " —had not been completed.[7]

[1] Monthly Record, June 1900.
[2] Ibid., June and August 1909.
[3] Ibid., November and December 1907.
[4] Letter of 20th December 1916 in Monthly Record, January 1917.
[5] Ibid., December 1899 and March 1901.
[6] Ibid., November and December 1902.   [7] Ibid., September 1909.

Sanitary improvements cost money, which in backward countries can most easily be raised by customs duties ; but the only commodity which the Manchester merchants would willingly allow to be taxed was spirits.   In 1893 they suggested that the authorities in West Africa might well raise the duties on spirits and use the extra revenue to lower the 10 per cent. duty on other commodities, including cotton textiles.[1]   A revision of the tariff of Southern Nigeria in 1908 provoked general complaint, not so much against the rate of duty levied as about the stringent regulations which went with it.   They followed the same lines as the Canadian tariff, which was entirely inapplicable to West Africa, "where there are no similar industries to foster and protect".[2]   When the customs regulations were altered again in 1911 the Chamber of Commerce protested against such "frequent changes, which are very upsetting and detrimental to trade".[3]

Equally offensive to Manchester merchants were the internal tolls levied by native chieftains on goods passing through their territory.   A Manchester proposal that extra taxation should be levied at the Customs House at Lagos, and the proceeds handed over as a subsidy, was rejected by the chieftains.   The only assurances Manchester could get were that tolls should not be increased without the consent of the Secretary of State, and that goods in transit through the province of Ibadan to Northern Nigeria should not be chargeable.[4]   In 1906 Manchester made further protests against internal tolls, levied this time in North Nigeria and by Ashanti tribesmen on the Gold Coast.

The imposition of any tolls or taxes after goods have once cleared the Customs House is bound to act as a restraint on trade, and must have the effect of retaining Northern Nigeria in its present undeveloped condition.[5]

However, as long as the Colonial Office delegated local authority to native chieftains, there was little hope that internal tolls would disappear.

Despite these obstacles, trade with British West Africa grew apace.   Between 1880 and 1913 exports of cotton piece goods to Sierra Leone, the Gold Coast, and Gambia did not greatly increase, rising only from 35 million to 50 million

---

[1] *Monthly Record*, February 1893   [2] *Ibid.*, April 1908.
[3] *Ibid.*, March 1911.   [4] *Ibid.*, May, June, and July 1903.
[5] *Ibid.*, May 1906.

yards. The trade of Nigeria, which was not large enough to be separately enumerated in 1880, amounted to nearly 100 million yards in 1913. British West Africa as a whole, which in 1880 took about 40 million yards of Lancashire cloth, in 1913 took 145 million yards ; this was less than was taken by Egypt (always Lancashire's largest African market) but far more than was taken by French West Africa or Morocco (each with 60 million yards), South Africa (with 68 million), or the Congo Free State with a mere 7 million yards.[1] The African markets, which had taken 5 per cent. by volume of the British export of piece goods in 1856, still took less than 6 per cent. in 1880, but by 1913 their share had risen to more than 9 per cent.

In itself this development of the export trade was satisfactory enough, but it was not all ; for since Manchester merchants were importing African produce as well as exporting Lancashire cloth, the Manchester Chamber of Commerce for once stood guardian over part of the British import trade. Many of the measures which it recommended for the development of West Africa, such as railways, river steamers, harbours, and sanitary reforms, helped the export of West African produce quite as much as the trade in cotton goods. In some matters, however, the Manchester Chamber was acting solely in the interests of its members' business in African produce.

The trade in rubber gave the Chamber a good deal of trouble. In the early days of the trade the Africans, either through carelessness or through fraud, supplied the merchants with rubber mixed with other substances. The Manchester merchants believed that adulteration would end if means could be devised to enforce the Lagos Produce Adulteration Ordinance, but the Governor of Lagos preferred to leave the purchasers some responsibility for the quality of the rubber they bought. Within a few years the merchants had taken to examining the rubber before purchase, with the result that adulteration had noticeably declined.[2] Overtapping of rubber trees was a more serious threat to the trade. In Sierra Leone, where the Africans had no plantations but tapped wild rubber trees, the government was anxious to prevent careless exploitation of the country's natural wealth, and proposed certain restrictions such as a system of licences and a

---

[1] *Annual Statements of Trade.*
[2] *Monthly Record,* February and August 1897.

ban on tapping by non-residents.   The Manchester merchants,
while paying lip-service to the need for conservation, were in
practice opposed to such authoritative interference, preferring
" to see the native at perfect liberty to collect his rubber
where he would, provided always that he did not destroy or
in any way injure the tree or prejudice its productiveness ".[1]
They were especially hostile to the licence system ; they
maintained that the fee proposed for North Nigeria was too
high, and that in any case " the whole system of licences is
. . . wrong ".   In Sierra Leone they recommended a purely
nominal licence fee,[2] which would presumably have had no
restrictive effect whatsoever.   If the Manchester merchants
were thus hostile to the licence system, it was natural that
they should be even more hostile to the imposition of export
taxes.   Their opposition to the Moroccan grain duties has
already been noticed ; a proposal to tax Gold Coast rubber at
$1\frac{1}{2}d.$ per lb., and mahogany at 10s. a log, met with equally
firm opposition :

The policy of the government should in the Chamber's opinion
be to encourage the natives to grow produce for exportation. . . .
What is proposed is a considerable handicap to their endeavours."[3]

In 1909 the Gold Coast Government began to supply the
Africans with information about the current prices for produce
in the British market.   The Manchester merchants protested,
not only that the prices supplied omitted transport costs
and were frequently out of date, but also that the practice
was " an interference—somewhat hard to justify—with the
free play of economic forces ".   The Colonial Office declined,
however, to " admit that there was anything unfair in affording
the natives some independent means of judging the value of
their products ".[4]   When in 1917 the Gold Coast authorities
went a step further and began to advise the natives on the
likely course of future prices, the Manchester merchants,
by then reconciled to the publication of prices current,
protested again.[5]   In the rising market of 1917 they had need
to protect themselves against higher prices, but within a few
years the world-wide agricultural depression was to add considerably to the bargaining strength of the buyer of West
African produce.

[1] *Monthly Record,* March 1906 and February 1909.
[2] *Ibid.,* August and October 1906.
[3] Letter of 17th July 1911 to the Colonial Office.
[4] *Monthly Record,* May 1909.   [5] *Ibid.,* October 1917.

In the last quarter of the nineteenth century raw cotton had been cheap and abundant. The Manchester merchants had abandoned their efforts to develop India as a source of raw cotton for Lancashire, which in 1900 was as dependent as ever on American supplies. About the end of the century prices began to rise again. At first the Manchester merchants attributed the higher prices to a poor American crop, to speculation, and to rumour; [1] but when the rise went on they began to detect more permanent reasons for the change, such as the competing demands of the rapidly expanding American industry, and a shortage of plantation labour as negroes drifted to the towns. [2] Lancashire began to scour the world again for new sources of supply.

As in the 1850's and 1860's the Manchester Chamber of Commerce had left the detailed work of stimulating the growth of cotton to the specially created Cotton Supply Association, so after 1900 it gave moral support to the British Cotton Growing Association and only took positive action on matters of great moment. But whereas the Chamber had looked in 1860 to India for supplies of raw cotton, in 1900 Africa (and particularly British West Africa) seemed to offer most promise of a rapid expansion of cotton supplies. The Manchester merchants had already formed and expressed strong views on the inadequate railways of West Africa; the shortage of cotton caused them to renew their demands. It was generally believed by them, and on this point they had the support of Sir Frederick Lugard, the Governor, that North Nigeria offered most scope for the introduction of the cotton plant. They suggested that the Exchequer should finance the improvement of transport facilities in North Nigeria, as a preliminary step to the large-scale cultivation of cotton there; [3] but it was not until 1907 that the government decided to extend the railway from Baro on the Niger to Zaria and Kano. For this favourable decision credit was due chiefly to Winston Churchill and the British Cotton Growing Association. [4] Next to West Africa, the Sudan was believed to be the most likely source of fresh supplies of raw cotton ; in 1910 the Manchester merchants urged the government " to take immediate steps for pushing on the development of

---

[1] *Monthly Record*, August and November 1902.
[2] *Ibid.*, December 1903 and August 1904.
[3] *Ibid.*, October and December 1903.
[4] Annual Report for 1907 (Africa Section).

cotton growing " there.[1]   Nevertheless, the development of cotton growing in the Empire remained sluggish ; in 1912, 85 per cent. by weight of Lancashire's supplies still came from the United States; Egypt supplied nearly all the rest.[2]

[1] *Monthly Record,* October 1910.
[2] *Working Party Report : Cotton* (1946), p. 24.

CHAPTER VII

TRADE WITH THE EAST

IN the hot and populous countries of the East, Manchester had a ready-made market for its cottons, so long as economic and political conditions remained favourable. Economically, the eastern countries were as yet untouched by the development of modern industry ; Chinese and Turkish hand-loom weavers could offer no effective resistance to the competition of Lancashire's power looms. Nevertheless, this economic backwardness was not all gain to Manchester ; internal tolls, and taxes on goods in transit over national frontiers, hindered the rapid growth of trade, as did also the lack of railways and (in China) a chaotic currency. In the same way, the political weakness of the East had its advantages and disadvantages. Throughout the period, the whole region was politically subject in one degree or another to Europe. The Dutch East Indies and the Philippines were European colonies ; the Ottoman Empire, fearful of Russia, had to put itself under the protection first of Britain and then of Germany, who used their political influence to keep tariffs low ; China had even less control of her customs, which were collected for her by Europeans and could not be raised without the consent of the Great Powers. In Turkey, China, and Persia, and also until 1899 in Japan, British merchants enjoyed the further privilege of extra-territoriality ; they were subject not to the local courts but to a European jurisdiction specially established to try Europeans according to European law. The chief drawback arising from the political weakness of the East was the threat from Russia, an expanding Power with an illiberal tariff policy ; areas absorbed by Russia would almost certainly cease to be expanding markets for Lancashire cotton goods.

The course of Manchester's trade with the East shows that the advantages of dealing with weak and backward countries far outweighed the disadvantages. Although the volume of eastern trade was enormous, the Manchester Chamber of Commerce needed to devote relatively little time to these markets ; the affairs of Europe demanded far greater effort for a far smaller reward.

79

EXPORTS OF COTTON PIECE GOODS TO EASTERN
COUNTRIES, 1856, 1880, AND 1913 [1] (MILLION YARDS)

	1856	*1880*	*1913*
Turkey	229 [2]	383	360
Persia	—	15	40
China [3]	113	448	716
Dutch East Indies	39	77	304
Japan	—	61	50
The Philippines	31	51	17
Siam	—	—	42
Indo-China	—	—	2
Total	412	1,035	1,531
Percentage of Total Exports	20·6	23·0	22·1

The most notable points that this table brings out are the vast
growth of the trade with China and the Dutch East Indies
and the ominous [4] failure to develop a large market in Japan.
Turkey proved a remarkably buoyant market considering her
heavy losses of territory in Europe, but by 1880 exports to
Turkey had reached their peak ; they tended to fall in the last
two decades of the century, and did not fully recover until
1913.

In most countries the Manchester merchants feared high
tariffs and little else. In China, however, where the tariff
was controlled by European Powers, who could be trusted
not to raise it unduly, it was the proliferation of internal
tolls which constituted the most serious hindrance to trade.
Likin, as the Chinese called these tolls, had been first levied in
1853 and in 1861 they were extended to the whole country. As
the central government exercised very little supervision over
the likin collectors, the tolls often exceeded the legal maximum
fixed at 2½ per cent. in the Treaty of Tientsin of 1858 ; tolls
amounting to 50, 60, or even 90 per cent. were not unknown.[5]
In 1868, when negotiations were taking place for a revision of

[1] T. Ellison, *Handbook of the Cotton Trade* (1858), App. C. (for 1856) ;
Annual Statements of Trade (for 1880 and 1913).
  [2] Includes Rumania.   [3] Includes Hongkong.
  [4] The omens were not noticed at the time.
  [5] H. B. Morse, *The Trade and Administration of the Chinese Empire*
(1908), pp. 106 and 109 ; *Manchester Guardian*, 28th October 1869.

the treaty, the Manchester Chamber of Commerce insisted that no new convention would be satisfactory that did not limit likin to 2½ per cent. and did not allow British subjects to trade and settle up-country.[1] When the new convention came up for discussion in 1870 it did not, in the Chamber's opinion, contain strong enough guarantees that local officials would cease their exactions ; indeed, " its provisions would impose additional and vexatious restraints on trade ". The Chamber, in agreement with other commercial associations in this country and in China, therefore opposed the ratification of the convention, which the Foreign Office reluctantly abandoned.[2] The Chefoo Convention signed in 1876 was more to the Manchester Chamber's liking : as it provided for the opening of " four new ports, six new landing places, and two large provinces to British commerce ", Manchester merchants desired that it should be ratified in its entirety.[3]

In the cause of freer internal trade the Manchester merchants were even willing to accept higher customs duties. When Li Hung Chang, the great Chinese statesman, visited England in 1896 he brought with him proposals for a higher tariff, the proceeds of which would be used to abolish likin and develop Chinese railways. Provided these conditions became part of the agreement, the Manchester Chamber had no objection to a " reasonable increase " in the Chinese tariff ; and in this opinion the London and Hongkong Chambers of Commerce concurred.[4] But nothing came of Li Hung Chang's visit ; only after the Powers had burdened China with a heavy indemnity as punishment for the Boxer Rising did China's need for extra revenue make a higher tariff essential. An international commission met in Shanghai in 1901 to revise the 5 per cent. tariff of 1858 which, owing to the depreciation of silver, no longer bore much relation to a true 5 per cent. *ad valorem* tariff. At the same time the British Government proposed, with the consent of the Manchester Chamber of Commerce, that China should abolish likin in return for a surcharge on imports equivalent to a further 7½ per cent. *ad valorem*. The Chinese, after holding out for a 10 per cent. surcharge, eventually agreed to the British proposal, but owing to the opposition of other Powers it

---

[1] Proceedings, 27th May 1868.
[2] *Ibid.*, 12th January and 17th February 1870 ; Annual Report for 1870, p. 5.   [3] Proceedings, 28th and 30th November 1877.
[4] *Monthly Record*, July 1896.

never came into force.[1]   Instead, the international commission confined itself to a revision of the book of rates based on 1897-99 prices.   As these were considerably lower than prices ruling in 1902, the Manchester merchants felt, with some reason, that the new tariff was not unfavourable to merchants.[2]

Although the new tariff rates gave satisfaction, Manchester merchants did not cease to take an interest in Chinese affairs. When in 1906 Sir Robert Hart, the Inspector General of the Chinese Maritime Customs, was subordinated by imperial decree to two Chinese officials, the Manchester Chamber of Commerce quickly protested.   It regarded the decree " as a measure calculated to affect very seriously British prestige in China, and to diminish materially the security and confidence of all foreign traders in that country." [3]   However, as the Foreign Office pointed out, the change was one of form rather than of substance ; [4] the level of the tariff and its administration remained firmly under European control. When Sir Robert Hart retired in 1910 the Manchester merchants again feared the consequences, but with as little reason as before.[5]

By the Convention of Balta Liman of 1838 the Turkish tariff had been fixed at the low level of 5 per cent.   Britain and Turkey renewed the Convention from time to time, and it did not finally expire until 1861, when the Turkish tariff rose to 8 per cent. Despite the great importance of the Turkish market this change went unnoticed in Manchester, where Turkish fiscal policy rarely gave cause for complaint.   In 1878, as a result of the recent war with Russia, Turkey proposed an addition to her import duties for revenue purposes, but after protests from Britain the project was abandoned.[6] In 1883 the British Government did agree to a Turkish proposal for higher duties, and incurred a rebuke from the Manchester Chamber of Commerce for doing so ; [7] however, for reasons which remain obscure, the Turks dropped their proposal and the 8 per cent. *ad valorem* duty continued to be levied until 1907.   In that year Turkey raised her duties to 11 per cent. *ad valorem* and, as in 1861, the Manchester

[1] S. F. Wright, *China's Struggle for Tariff Autonomy* (1938), pp. 372 and 374.
[2] *Monthly Record*, October and November 1902.
[3] *Ibid.*, September 1906.   [4] Proceedings, 26th September 1906.
[5] *Monthly Record*, April and July 1910.
[6] Annual Report for 1878, p. 10.
[7] Letter of 22nd August 1883 to the Foreign Office.

merchants acquiesced in this increase, being content to ensure
that the new rates of duty did not affect goods already in
transit to Turkey.[1] In 1914 the Chamber accepted without
protest a further rise to 15 per cent. in the Turkish tariff.[2]

Though a much less important market than Turkey,
Japan took up at least as much of the Chamber's time. At
first Manchester merchants looked on Japan as a potential
source of raw materials, particularly silk and tea. As a
modest trade in cottons began to grow up, attention shifted
from Japan's export taxes to her import duties. In 1881
Japan proposed to replace the low tariff of 1866 by higher
duties, which on cottons would range between 12 and 20 per
cent. The Manchester Chamber of Commerce expressed its
regret at this proposal, " conceived as it seems in a spirit of
protection ", and added that it would be

most desirable that Her Majesty's Government should also press
for the inclusion of English officials on the Commission of Customs
of Japan, in accordance with the system now prevailing in China.[3]

The Japanese would probably have taken no notice of this
latter suggestion even if the Foreign Office had forwarded it ;
but British protests may have had some moderating influence,
since even in 1898 the Japanese tariff was still only 5 per cent.
It was doubled in the following year.[4] In that same year
(1899) British merchants lost their extra-territorial privileges
in Japan. Earlier the Manchester merchants had opposed
the abrogation of extra-territoriality on the ground that

the time has not yet arrived when questions with regard to rights
arising between subjects and citizens of foreign powers can safely
be left to the jurisdiction of Japanese tribunals.[5]

But by 1899 Manchester was prepared to acquiesce in the
change. In 1910, on the expiry of the Anglo-Japanese treaty
of commerce of 1899, Japan again proposed to double her
duties on cotton goods ; a deputation from Manchester and
London put the case against such a heavy increase to the
Foreign Secretary, Sir Edward Grey. Thanks to the Anglo-
Japanese alliance of 1902, the Foreign Office was able to
achieve " a very considerable measure of success " in its

[1] *Monthly Record*, March and July 1906, and July 1907.
[2] Proceedings, 18th March 1914.
[3] Letter of 9th September 1881 to the Foreign Office.
[4] *Monthly Record*, May and July 1898.
[5] *Ibid.*, October 1890.

7

efforts to keep Japanese duties to a minimum. When the new commercial treaty was signed in 1911 the Manchester merchants warmly congratulated the Foreign Office on the modifications it had secured in the new tariff.[1]

By various forms of political pressure Britain might manage to keep tariffs low in China, Turkey, and Japan; no such methods were of avail in the colonies of other European Powers. Fortunately for Manchester, Holland pursued a liberal commercial policy. After 1872 the Dutch East Indies were thrown open on equal terms to the trade of the whole world; and they remained an open market until the early nineteen-thirties. The Philippines, on the other hand, belonged first to Spain and then to the United States, both of which countries pursued highly protective policies. In 1891 Spain doubled the duties on British cottons exported to the Philippines, and this action combined with the onset of a depression to halve the value of the cottons exported to that market in 1891.[2] When the Philippines changed hands in 1898, the United States undertook to maintain most-favoured-nation treatment for ten years, but when this period expired the Philippines were absorbed into the customs system of the United States, despite strenuous protests by the Manchester merchants made through the British ambassador at Washington.[3] As a result of these successive blows, the export of British piece goods to the Philippines had shrunk by 1913 to one-third of what it had been in 1880.

After her defeat in the Crimean War, Russia had turned away from expansion in Europe to expansion in Central Asia, where she was unlikely to come into immediate conflict with British interests. When in 1877 war again broke out between Russia and Turkey, opinion in Manchester, as in the rest of Britain, was divided : some thought that, if

Constantinople should fall into the hands of a country like Russia, whose policy undoubtedly for a hundred years had been protective and repulsive to Commerce, such an event would be a loss to us of a very important market ;[4]

others doubted very much if it was the business of a commercial country even to hint remotely at the desirability of waging war in order to preserve a city or country because it

---

[1] *Monthly Record*, November 1910 and May 1911.
[2] Annual Report for 1891, and *Monthly Record*, April 1892.
[3] *Ibid.*, March and September 1908, and July 1909.
[4] The President at the Annual Meeting, 5th February 1877.

happened to be more free-trade than some other country.[1]
This latter view was at the time the more popular one in
Manchester. In December 1877, when the Turkish defences
had collapsed and Constantinople seemed likely to fall into
Russian hands, the Chamber of Commerce forwarded a
memorial to the pacific Foreign Secretary, Lord Derby,

approving the policy he had pursued and earnestly praying that at
this momentous crisis the endeavours of Her Majesty's Government would be directed to the preservation of a strict neutrality
on the part of this country.[2]

The more active foreign policy pursued after the resignation
of Lord Derby did not meet with much approval in Manchester:
as a commercial body the Chamber of Commerce eschewed
politics as far as possible, but the use of the Suez Canal to
transport troops from India to Malta was considered to
involve important questions of trade. To infringe the
neutrality of the Canal in this way might set a bad
precedent, " considering the extreme facility with which the
navigation could be obstructed ". Unless the governments
of the world agreed to neutralise the Canal in time of war,
trade might be endangered in any war in which Egypt took
part.[3]

Indignation at Turkish misrule of her European subjects
had in 1877 and 1878 prevented Manchester from following
the natural policy of hostility to Russian expansion. No such
difficulty arose at the end of the century when Russia began
to encroach on northern China. After the seizure of Port
Arthur and the strengthening of Russian control over Man-
churia, the Manchester merchants (advised by the Shanghai
branch of the China Association) urged the Foreign Office
to take a firm stand against the threatened dismemberment
of China; in particular, Manchester advocated " the policy of
open markets throughout China for all nations ", and the need
for co-operation with other commercial powers, notably
the United States and Germany.[4] Unlike other British
Chambers of Commerce, however, Manchester did not support
the proposal that Britain should secure a railway concession
from the Burmese frontier to the Yangtse to counterbalance
concessions made to France and Russia.[5]

[1] Jacob Bright, M.P., ibid.   [2] Annual Report for 1877, p. 15.
[3] Proceedings, 29th May 1878.   [4] Ibid., 27th April 1898.
[5] Ibid., 20th July 1898.

The insistence of Britain, Germany, and the United States on the open door temporarily checked Russian ambitions, which were eventually thwarted by the armed forces of Japan in 1905. Manchester merchants soon found, however, that the respite would not last long; foiled in the Far East, Russia turned her attention to Persia, a smaller but still valuable outlet for Manchester piece goods. As early as 1902 the Chamber of Commerce had feared that Russian influence would be used to manipulate the Persian tariff to Manchester's disadvantage; [1] later, when brigands were infesting the roads, Russia had an excellent pretext for intervention. In 1909 the Manchester merchants urged the Foreign Office to organise a police force for the troubled area ; this should be financed, if Persia could not pay, by a toll on native and foreign merchants. The Foreign Office, tied by the Anglo-Russian Convention of 1907, refused to act.[2] The Russians, however, felt no such inhibitions in their sphere of influence in Northern Persia. In 1912 Cossacks were escorting Russian cotton goods to Ispahan, " while Manchester goods were lying indefinitely at Bushire and Ahwaz without prospect of protection to their destination ".[3] Meanwhile, Russia had been putting pressure on the Persian Government at Teheran, causing acute anxiety in Manchester ; if the British Government could not make Russia keep to the letter and spirit of the 1907 Convention, the Manchester merchants considered that Britain should retaliate by policing the roads most important to British trade.[4] The Foreign Secretary refused to act on this advice. He agreed that policing of the roads would not be costly, but it

might lead in the future to a really vast addition to the burdens of Empire ; you have to ask yourself whether for a trade in a particular place it is really good business to incur what may be a large increase in national expenditure.[5]

High tariffs and Russian imperialism threatened existing trade ; other obstacles, such as export taxes, a chaotic Chinese currency, and the absence of railways, prevented its further development. As in India and Africa, Manchester

---

[1] Proceedings, 9th April 1902 ; Monthly Record, June 1902.
[2] Proceedings, 8th September 1909, and 14th February 1910.
[3] Ibid., 4th September and 9th October 1912.
[4] Ibid., 14th December 1911.
[5] Sir Edward Grey at a Chamber of Commerce banquet : Monthly Record, February 1914.

had a policy to overcome these difficulties. Recognising that Lancashire's export trade could not flourish unless its customers could export freely also, Manchester merchants opposed all suggestions for higher export taxes, as for example on Japanese tea and silk in 1868.[1] They even went so far as to oppose an export tax on Persian opium, on the ground that any injury to Persian export trade would lessen the consumption of Lancashire piece goods in Persia.[2] In China the incredible confusion of the currency, and of the weights and measures, drew from the Manchester merchants, particularly in the early years of the twentieth century, a stream of prescriptions for reform. In 1907 the Chamber commended to the Chinese the virtues of the English system of weights and measures, but without effect.[3] With the willing co-operation of the British Government, Manchester merchants also urged the need for currency reform, which was indeed long overdue. The unit of currency was not a coin but a weight : " In China every one of the hundreds of commercial centres not only has its own tael-weight, but in many cases has several standards side by side." [4] However, the Chinese seemed to be content with this chaotic system, and repeated reminders from the British Government of the advantages of a uniform currency went unheeded.[5]

Because so little of the East came within the British Empire, the Manchester merchants had in this quarter few chances to advocate their favourite policy for opening up new markets—railway building. Only in the most general terms could they recommend railways to the Chinese Government, as in an address to the retiring Chinese Minister in London :

We are only too sensible that the consumption of Lancashire goods in the Chinese dominions is capable of almost indefinite increase and we consequently look forward with great interest to the contemplated railway service which your Excellency's Government is reported to be about to establish, feeling confident that with further railway . . . facilities, the mercantile interest of the two countries must be vastly increased.[6]

But if the Chamber of Commerce would not approach the Chinese Government directly, it could and did expect the

---

[1] Proceedings, 30th December 1868.
[2] Monthly Record, September 1901.　　　　[3] Ibid., December 1907.
[4] H. B. Morse, Trade of the Chinese Empire (1908), p. 145.
[5] Monthly Record, June 1905 ; Proceedings, 8th September 1909.
[6] Annual Report for 1886, App. p. 47.

British Government to open the way to China's backdoor, the south-western provinces of Szechuan and Yunnan, which bordered on north-eastern Burma.

Britain had annexed Lower Burma in 1852, and was in friendly relations with the King of Upper Burma whose possessions stretched north from Pegu to the Chinese border. In 1860 the Manchester Chamber of Commerce made the first of many approaches on the subject of routes to Western China. It asked that the British Commissioner at Peking should negotiate " for the opening up of the western portion of the Chinese Empire by means of communications from the British possession in Pegu ", and for the city of Esmok to be made an open inland mart. With the co-operation of the King of Burma, the British Government should build roads northward as far as the Chinese border.[1] In 1863, despite the cotton famine, the Manchester merchants were still busy looking for fresh outlets for their goods. A further memorial to the Prime Minister suggested that the treaty of friendship recently signed with the King of Burma afforded a good opportunity to develop the road to western China ; the Government of India should forthwith undertake the preliminary survey needed.[2] The Indian Government must have been unwilling to assume this responsibility, for the Chamber of Commerce itself contributed £50 to the expenses of Capt. H. Sprye who was pioneering the new route.[3] After further prodding from Manchester, Liverpool, and Huddersfield, the Indian Government did begin to survey various possible routes to western China, but it abandoned the work when civil war broke out between the King of Burma and his sons.[4]

After these setbacks interest in the route waned for some years, but revived in the early 'eighties when a British engineer reported very favourably on the prospects of a railway from Rangoon through the Shan states to Kianghung in Yunnan.[5] The Manchester merchants welcomed the annexation of Upper Burma in 1886, as promising " much encouragement to the opening up of trade " even if the long-awaited railway was not built.[6] Surveying work for a railway from Mandalay to the Chinese frontier was still going on in 1892,[7] but despite

[1] Proceedings, 6th July 1860.   [2] Ibid., 17th June 1863.
[3] Ibid., 16th December 1863.
[4] Ibid., 15th August 1866, 27th November 1867, and 28th June 1871.
[5] Annual Report for 1882, p. 22.   [6] Ibid., 1885, p. 7.
[7] Proceedings, 22nd July 1891 ; Monthly Record, December 1892.

pressure from Manchester the railway was never completed. By 1913 it had got as far as Lashio, 100 miles north-east of Mandalay; the Indian Government agreed in principle that it ought to be extended to the Chinese frontier, but the Great War checked all progress.[1] After the war, the Manchester merchants were faced with many more urgent problems than the commercial prospects of a remote province of the Chinese Empire. The railhead remains at Lashio to this day, and the famous Burma Road which carries on from there has shown no signs of becoming an important commercial highway.

[1] *Monthly Record*, December 1913; Proceedings, 10th September 1913, 11th February and 18th March 1914.

CHAPTER VIII

THE AMERICAN MARKETS

AFTER Europe, the countries of the western hemisphere were the first to free themselves from dependence on imports of British cotton goods. The United States led the way ; until 1860 its import of Lancashire goods continued to grow, but after the Civil War Lancashire's trade with the United States slowly declined, though a small trade in fine cloth was retained long after the American cotton industry had begun to supply the staple lines. The trend of trade with Brazil followed a similar course, with a time lag of thirty years. Elsewhere in South America local cotton industries had not seriously threatened Lancashire's hold on the trade before 1914; lost markets in the United States and Brazil were replaced by larger exports to other American markets, of which the Argentine was the most important. Nevertheless, the American markets, which together had been the largest single outlet for Lancashire's cloth in the middle of the nineteenth century, had fallen to third place in 1913, far behind India and some way behind the Far East.

EXPORTS TO AMERICAN MARKETS, 1856, 1880, 1913 [1]

Million yards

	1856	1880	1913
U.S.A.	207	78	44
Central and South America :	436	614	700
⌈of which Brazil	155	231	96⌉
[Argentine	28	60	199⌋
Total	643	692	744
Percentage of Total Exports	31·5	15·4	10·6

For all its importance, the trade with America rarely needed the special attention of the Manchester Chamber of Commerce. The governments of the American republics, the U.S.A.

---

[1] T. Ellison, *Handbook of the Cotton Trade* (1858), App., and *Annual Statements of the Trade of the U.K.* For Canada see below, Chapter IX.

always excepted, did not pursue the vigorously nationalist economic policies that so disturbed Manchester's relations with Europe, and consequently Manchester merchants had few complaints to put before their Chamber of Commerce.

A grievance that had long bothered Manchester merchants was the disagreement with Brazil arising from the efforts of the British Navy to suppress the trade in African slaves. Under Lord Aberdeen's Act of 1845, the British Navy claimed the right to seize any ships engaged in the slave trade.[1] By 1851, with the co-operation of the Brazilian Government, the traffic had almost disappeared, but as a precaution against its recrudescence Lord Aberdeen's Act remained in force.[2] In 1858 the Manchester Chamber of Commerce renewed its earlier agitation for the repeal of the Act, pointing to " the honourable and successful efforts " recently made by the Brazilian Government to suppress the slave trade, and the disadvantages under which British trade in Brazil laboured ; these could be removed by a commercial treaty, but Brazil would not sign one until the obnoxious Act had been repealed.[3] The Chamber raised the matter again in 1861,[4] but not until 1869 did the British Government feel that it could safely repeal the Act. Even without a commercial treaty, trade with Brazil continued to flourish.

Civil War in Mexico was a more serious hindrance to trade. In 1858 the Manchester merchants strongly protested against " the sudden imposition of what is termed a tax upon capital ", which was in effect a forced loan. Not only was it " levied for the purpose of maintaining intestine warfare ", which in itself was injurious to British residents, but it also infringed a treaty between Great Britain and Mexico. As the native Mexicans had various means of evading the tax, the burden fell chiefly on " foreign merchandise and capitalists ".[5] The Manchester merchants boldly suggested the dispatch of warships to Tampico, Vera Cruz, and Mansanillo to protect British interests ; but neither a memorial nor a deputation to Lord Malmesbury, the Foreign Secretary, could induce the British Government to act.[6] By 1861 there was " no longer any security for the lives or property of Her Majesty's

[1] A. Redford, *Manchester Merchants and Foreign Trade, 1794-1858*, p. 106.
[2] W. L. Mathieson, *Great Britain and the Slave Trade, 1839-1865* (1929), pp. 135-6.
[3] Proceedings, 22nd July 1858.   [4] *Ibid.*, 15th July 1861.
[5] *Ibid.*, 19th July 1858.   [6] *Ibid.*, 11th and 29th November 1858.

subjects " in Mexico. Anti-foreign riots, murder, looting, and a two-year stop of the Mexican Exchequer, caused the Manchester Chamber of Commerce to declare that " forbearance has reached its utmost limits ". At this point the British Government was roused to action, and with France and Spain dispatched a joint expedition to exact reparations.[1] When a naval demonstration failed to bring the Mexicans to a proper frame of mind, the French went on alone and placed Maximilian, a Habsburg prince, on the throne of Mexico. In 1867, however, he was defeated and shot, the Mexican Government repudiated its debt, and many foreigners were expelled. After the failure of its earlier attempt the British Government could take no effectual action to protect British traders and bond-holders.[2]

This was not the only dispute on which the Manchester merchants thought that British power and prestige should be brought to bear. In 1859 General Urquiza, Dictator of the Argentine Confederation, was threatening war on the Republic of Buenos Aires. At the request of an influential deputation, including representatives of the Manchester merchants, Lord John Russell agreed to appoint a mediator between the contending parties,[3] though this did not in fact avert a war. A blockade of the coast of Chile by a Spanish fleet in 1865 called forth yet another protest from the Manchester merchants, and at their instance the Foreign Office put pressure on Spain to lift the blockade.[4]

In these disputes between weaker states, Britain could hope to intervene with some success, and the Manchester Chamber of Commerce must have realised this when it asked the government to act. The American Civil War was a more formidable affair, and despite the cotton famine the Manchester Chamber of Commerce moved very cautiously. The Manchester merchants shared the very general opinion that war waged on such a scale could not last, but would speedily end with the secession of the Southern States.[5] Nevertheless, " the extreme difficulty of separating the commercial from the political part of the question had induced the Board to refrain from expressing any opinion on the subject ".[6]

[1] Proceedings, 2nd September 1861 ; Annual Report for 1861, p. 7.
[2] *Manchester Guardian*, 9th August 1867.
[3] Proceedings, 19th and 25th July 1859.
[4] *Ibid.*, 22nd November 1865 and 3rd January 1866.
[5] Annual Meeting, 30th January 1862.
[6] Annual Report for 1861, p. 15.

In 1863 the Directors of the Chamber of Commerce refused to receive a deputation from the Union and Emancipation Society " respecting the violation of neutrality by the fitting out of Confederate War Ships in British ports ".[1] Even in January 1865, the President of the Chamber could see no quick end to the war,[2] but by then the increasing supply of cotton from other sources had alleviated the worst of the distress. The settlement by arbitration of the *Alabama* dispute between Britain and the United States was for the Manchester merchants the only redeeming feature of the American Civil War. In some quarters the British Government was criticised for its weakness in allowing the dispute to go to arbitration, but at Manchester "the initiation of a wise and beneficent policy [of arbitration] was felt to be deserving the warm support of . . . trading and commercial interests ".[3]

Brazil and the United States, either through carelessness or as a matter of deliberate policy, often caused anxiety in Manchester by raising administrative as well as tariff barriers to the import of cotton goods. In 1861 the Brazilian customs authorities issued regulations demanding " vexatious and unnecessary " changes in the making out of ships' manifests ; only after the Foreign Secretary had approached the Brazilian Government was a more satisfactory arrangement devised.[4] In 1892 the Brazilian authorities began to demand certificates from exporters declaring the " names, marks, numbers, weight, kind, quality, quantity, derivation of origin . . . as well as the destination " of goods sent to Brazil. These regulations in themselves were burdensome enough, but to add insult to injury it was further provided that the certificate had to be signed by the Brazilian consul at Manchester, who happened to be a shipper of cottons himself, and would therefore have access to full details of his competitors' business. After vigorous protests, the Brazilian authorities agreed to modify the regulations.[5] Under the new regulations, the Brazilian consul at Manchester still had to sign the declaration if the goods were shipped from the port of Manchester ; this drove merchants to ship from Liverpool, thus damaging the prospects of the infant Ship Canal. The dispute dragged on for several years and was not

[1] Proceedings, 25th March 1863.   [2] Annual Meeting, 30th January.
[3] Annual Report for 1872, pp. 16-17.
[4] Proceedings, 8th April 1861 ; Annual Report for 1861, p. 10.
[5] *Monthly Record*, February ; Proceedings, 8th March and 27th April ; letter in *Manchester Guardian*, 8th March 1892.

finally settled until 1900, when it was agreed that goods could be shipped at Manchester and the documents certified by the consul at Liverpool.[1] In 1912 a further set of vexatious regulations was devised, but protests from Manchester secured first their postponement and finally their repeal.[2] Brazilian import duties had in the opinion of the Manchester Chamber of Commerce become prohibitive by the early twentieth century ; it seemed " that Brazil was more anxious to import gold than the finished commodity ",[3] although in fact a substantial trade in cotton cloth remained to Manchester until 1914.

The United States first insisted on consular certification of invoices in 1888, but without requiring the wealth of detail that made the Brazilian regulations so unpopular. Even so, the Warrington Chamber of Commerce took strong exception to the innovation, but got no support from Manchester.[4] In 1896 the United States began to follow Brazil's example in making unfair and impracticable demands ; it insisted that invoices must be certified by the consul of the district where the goods were manufactured. As Manchester had become an important warehousing centre for goods from all over Europe, merchants in some cases could not comply with this rule at all, and in other cases only at heavy cost. The U.S. Treasury eventually recognised the force of this objection, and allowed the consul at Manchester to certify the invoices of all goods dispatched thence.[5] American tariffs rarely gave Manchester merchants serious trouble before the eighteen-nineties, and even after that period they never excited the same interest and anxiety as European or Indian tariff questions. The most protectionist country in the western hemisphere was the United States, but as Manchester's trade with it had already dwindled to insignificant proportions, not even the notorious McKinley Tariff could do much harm. In Manchester the McKinley Tariff was described as " a hazardous experiment " whose chief effect might be to " educate Canada in the direction of Free Trade, an education which otherwise she would probably not have received ".[6] No doubt the Yorkshire woollen towns took a less philosophic

[1] *Monthly Record*, August 1900.
[2] Proceedings, 6th March, 17th April, and 9th October 1912.
[3] *Ibid.*, February 1907.
[4] *Ibid.*, 29th February and 30th May 1888, and 23rd February 1889.
[5] Annual Report for 1896, p. 4.
[6] *Monthly Record*, November 1890.

standpoint, since woollens and worsteds suffered much more under the new tariff than cottons.

More damaging to Manchester than high tariffs were preferential tariffs. In 1891 the United States and Brazil concluded a reciprocity treaty under which American cotton manufactures were to be admitted to Brazil at preferential rates of duty 25 per cent. below those charged on British goods. News of the treaty caused great alarm in Manchester, where it was feared

that a very large proportion of important foreign demand will be lost to the manufacturers of this country . . . unless means be taken to remove the discrimination set up by the new treaty against British goods.[1]

The British Government had needed no prompting from Manchester to protest to Brazil against denial of most-favoured-nation treatment, but its efforts were in vain.[2] In 1902 the United States concluded a similar treaty with Cuba, followed by equally fruitless protests by British traders and the Foreign Office.[3]

By 1850 the Manchester Chamber of Commerce had formulated the policy it was to follow in protecting the export trade in cotton goods over the next sixty years. This policy had nowhere been laid down as a coherent body of doctrine, but if challenged the average Manchester merchant would have summed it up in the words " Free Trade ". This was perhaps an over-simplified view of the policy, which covered not only freedom of trade in the ordinary sense of the phrase but also an insistence on low tariffs everywhere, on most-favoured-nation treatment in Europe and the Americas, and on the open door in colonial Africa and the dependent Far East. However, though Manchester merchants disliked any governmental interference with profitable business, they did not push this doctrine so far as to demand that the government should do nothing. The government might not interfere, but it should help, by providing such unprofitable services as Indian and African railways, better port installations, and firm rule over turbulent areas, without which trade could not prosper. Theorists might hold that these activities tainted the purity of free-trade dogma ; but if judged by its results

[1] *Monthly Record*, February; Proceedings, 2nd March 1891.
[2] *Monthly Record*, March 1891 ; Proceedings, 24th February 1892.
[3] *Ibid.*, 9th April 1902 ; *Monthly Record*, January 1903.

rather than by its logical coherence with Manchester's professed belief in free trade, governmental encouragement of foreign commerce paid handsome dividends. The growth of Indian demand for Lancashire cotton goods from 300 million yards in 1850 to 3,000 million yards in 1913 would hardly have taken place without government-built or government-guaranteed railways ; this fact alone is enough to explain and justify whatever inconsistencies there may have been in Manchester's policy.

CHAPTER IX

THE DEFENCE OF FREE TRADE, 1860-1914

ALTHOUGH economists had contrived an elaborate theoretical justification for the free-trade policy to which Britain turned in the first half of the nineteenth century, it does not seem likely that theory played as large a part in the development of free trade as did the practical demonstration that British industry could survive and flourish unaided by protective duties. In the same way, the argument that did most to promote the restoration of protective duties was the empirical one that particular benefits would accrue to groups that had previously suffered from unlimited foreign competition. Protectionists could advocate tariffs for widely differing purposes, though the ultimate aim remained the preservation of existing markets for British goods. The tariff could exclude foreign goods from the home market, or could be used as a bargaining counter to open markets otherwise closed to British trade ; in the hands of the imperialists it could be an economic weapon largely directed to political ends. None of these purposes appealed to Manchester merchants during the years between the Cobden Treaty and the First World War ; while the cotton trade prospered they saw no reason to alter the free-trade policy to which they believed that prosperity was largely due.

Foreign competition in the home market rarely entered the thoughts of the Lancashire manufacturers and merchants. In 1867 there was an alarm that the growth of trade unions was hampering British industry in its fight against

Belgium, France, and Germany, who were competitors with us in many manufactures ; even in regard to cotton goods, imports of some importance were made to this country from the continent.

Inquiry showed, however, that imports of cottons into Britain in 1866 had not yet reached alarming proportions ; they were valued at less than £1,000,000, which was less than 2 per cent. of the value of the export of cotton goods in the same year.[1] This was the last to be heard of foreign competition in

[1] Proceedings, 1st and 8th April 1867.

Lancashire's home market for sixty years. Clearly Manchester had no need to advocate protective duties.

Even though the home market remained a close preserve of the Lancashire cotton industry, the growth of cotton industries abroad could not be altogether disregarded. The President of the Manchester Chamber of Commerce, a juror at the Paris Exhibition of 1867, found that Swiss Turkey-red goods and French muslins were better than comparable British products, that the plain cottons from New York equalled British plain cottons, and that only in sewing cottons could Britain justly claim that she still led the world. The Exhibition showed, according to another observer, that in all questions of " taste and skill, appearance and luxury ", French and other continental manufacturers surpassed the British.[1] Trade returns showed, however, that the growth of cotton industries abroad was quite compatible with continued prosperity and expansion in Lancashire ; differences of opinion among the Manchester merchants threw more light on the temperaments of the disputants than on the real state of the cotton industry. To one man the export of textile machinery and skilled workmen to the Continent portended

an amount of competition coming against the operatives of this country which would render necessary every effort on the part of those who were advanced in intelligence, and who influenced the councils of the country, to prevent it from coming so heavily on the manufacturers and capital of this country as to destroy a great amount of them.

To another man these same facts showed that foreign cotton spinners

were obliged to come to England and, by the offer of very high wages, bribe the British workman to leave his country and go to a foreign country to superintend machinery, and teach the people how to work it. Here was proof that the foreign manufacturer had very great difficulties in working the machinery he bought in England, and that in England we had a superior class of labour at a lower price.[2]

Even when the cotton manufacture, in common with other industries, fell into an alarming decline in the later 'seventies, the Manchester Chamber of Commerce did not single out the

---

[1] *Manchester Guardian*, 3rd May 1867, and 24th January 1868.
[2] Annual Meeting, 30th January 1871.

" bugbear of foreign competition " as the prime cause of depression.   The Directors considered that

the present depressed condition of trade in Lancashire is principally due to the failure of crops at home and in India and China during late years, and to excessive production and over-trading in the past.[1]

Fluctuations in the price of raw cotton were also held to be partly responsible for the depression ; from December 1878 to September 1879 the price of middling Orleans had jumped sharply from $5\frac{1}{4}d.$ to $7d.$ a pound without a corresponding improvement in the price of yarn.[2]   The heavy burdens of taxation that the warlike governments of Europe imposed on their citizens added to the unprofitability of business.[3] In their search for particular causes of the prevailing bad trade, the Manchester merchants reached no agreed conclusions ; the Manchester Chamber of Commerce supplied documentary evidence to the Royal Commission on the Depression of Trade and Industry, but none of the Directors who submitted evidence, either individually or as a committee, particularly stressed foreign competition.[4]

During the 'nineties, the Manchester Chamber of Commerce became more sensitive to the growth of cotton industries abroad.   At the annual meeting in 1895, the President of the Chamber drew attention to the relatively slow expansion of the British industry ; in the past ten years the number of spindles had increased by 20 per cent. in Europe and America, by 70 per cent. in India, by a large but unknown percentage in Japan, but by only 5 per cent. in Britain.[5]   At this time it seemed likely that Lancashire's two most formidable competitors, Japan and the United States, would soon be entering the neutral markets of the world in full force.   As early as 1895 a Manchester spinner was arguing that as Japanese operatives were paid $5d.$ an hour for an eleven hour day, and Japanese mills ran for twenty-two hours out of every twenty-four, Britain could not afford to tighten up its factory laws without a guarantee that our competitors would follow our example.   More liberal views prevailed,[6] although the Japanese cotton industry continued to grow and was beginning

[1] Proceedings, 30th October 1878.
[2] *Manchester Guardian*, 11th September 1879.
[3] *Ibid.*, 3rd February 1880.
[4] Royal Commission on the Depression of Trade and Industry, 1886 (*Parliamentary Papers, 1886*, Vol. XXI, App. A, pp. 97-105).
[5] *Monthly Record*, February 1895.   [6] *Ibid.*, November 1895.

8

to tell on Lancashire's trade with the Far East.[1] The other
main competitor in the Far East, the United States, relied not
on low wages but on the automatic loom to oust Lancashire
from the trade in heavy goods ; by 1901 the American shipments of drills and sheetings to Shanghai were growing fast,
while Britain's shipments stagnated or even declined.[2]

The challenge from Japan and America did not develop as
quickly as the Manchester merchants seem to have expected,
and Lancashire enjoyed marked prosperity from 1900 to 1914.
But although Lancashire still held the field in overseas trade
against all other nations combined, her proportionate supremacy was declining. It seemed likely that competition for the
world's trade in cotton goods would gradually grow more
strenuous.[3] During the last years of peace Germany seemed
to have become Lancashire's chief competitor, especially in
the Middle East.[4] However, since Germany remained a
potential rather than an actual threat, the Manchester

EXPORTS OF COTTON PIECE GOODS TO THE DOMINIONS [5]

	Million yards		
	1856	1880	1913
Canada	32	37	110
Australia	26	58	170
New Zealand	—	7	43
South Africa	18	19	67
Total	76	121	390
Percentage of total exports	under 4 per cent.	under 4 per cent.	under 6 per cent.

merchants could afford to regard the progress of German
trade with friendly detachment.[6] In any case, if competition
became severe Lancashire could concentrate on the finer goods,
leaving the bulk trade to less skilful hands ;[7] after the war,
Lancashire would hear too much of this argument, but in
1913 it seemed to offer good hopes of continued prosperity.

If under free trade Manchester suffered so little in the

---

[1] *Monthly Record*, July 1898.   [2] *Ibid.*, May 1899 and July 1901.
[3] *Ibid.*, December 1908.   [4] *Ibid.*, July 1913.
[5] T. Ellison, *loc. cit.* (for 1856) ; *Annual Statements of Trade* (for 1880 and
1913).   [6] See above, Chapter V.   [7] *Monthly Record*, July 1913.

neutral markets of the world from foreign competition, the
argument for tariffs as a bargaining weapon was not likely
to carry much weight ; the imperial argument for tariffs
fared no better. Under the free-trade policy pursued by the
Indian Government, Lancashire completely dominated the
Indian trade in cotton cloth, and in our West African colonies
a smaller but still exclusively British trade was done. The
argument for imperial preference would have to rely heavily
on the advantages of closer relations with the Dominions, but
of these advantages the Manchester Chamber of Commerce
had no very high opinion. Although the export of cotton
cloth to the Dominions grew at more than the average
rate, they remained relatively small markets for Lancashire
goods.

Imperial markets would have been somewhat larger if
the Dominions had adhered to Britain's free-trade policy ;
the Manchester Chamber of Commerce considered it " an
anomaly that high and increasing rates of Import Duties
should be imposed upon our manufactures by certain of our
Colonial Governments ". It was hoped that the colonies
could be induced to abandon " a system so injurious to the
commercial interests of both countries and so diametrically
opposed to the policy of Great Britain." [1] A deputation
urged this point of view upon the Duke of Newcastle, the
Colonial Secretary ; Manchester did not object to revenue
duties, but Canada, the chief offender, had within the ten
or eleven years before 1859 increased the scale of duties
no fewer than seven times. On the chief manufactures
imported Canada now levied a duty of from 20 to 25 per cent.,
and on other articles the duty ranged from 10 to 100 per cent.,
a mode of proceeding which tended " to foster an unsound
spirit of protection to native manufacturers among the colonists ". The Duke of Newcastle had to confess, however, that
while in full agreement with the Manchester merchants, he
could exercise no stronger power over the colonists than that
of moral persuasion.[2] In 1869 the Manchester merchants
again appealed to the Colonial Office against the injustice
of Canada's protective policy, but the only satisfaction
they could get was an assurance that in future the unfilial
colonies would have to pay for the cost of their own local
defences.[3]

[1] Annual Report for 1861, p. 15.   [2] Proceedings, 13th March 1862.
[3] Ibid., 26th May 1869 ; Annual Report for 1869, p. 13.

Although arguments against free trade might seem particularly weak in Manchester, protectionist sentiment never entirely died out. At first it drew support only from those industrialists who suffered when the last trade barriers were thrown down in 1860 ; of these aggrieved industrialists only the silk manufacturers and paper makers had mills in Lancashire. The grievances of the paper makers were raised at Manchester in 1865 by Mr. Thomas Wrigley, a paper maker of Bury, who had been a Director of the Manchester Chamber of Commerce in 1858. Until 1860 Britain had levied a duty on foreign paper which offset the export tax that Continental countries levied on rags ; but the budget of 1860 swept the duty away, and the British manufacturers found themselves gravely handicapped by the high cost of their raw material. Mr. Wrigley proposed to the Manchester merchants that the British Government should either subsidise British paper makers to the extent of the foreign tax on rags, or reimpose the countervailing duty on imported paper. The Board of the Manchester Chamber of Commerce declared that the paper makers were trying to obtain a protective duty on their manufactures ; " the proposal is antagonistic to the interests of the consumer, and this Chamber decides to adhere to that Free Trade policy which it has always advocated." When Mr. Wrigley appealed from the Board to the members at large, he got even shorter shrift ; the meeting soon decided by a large majority that it would not hear Mr. Wrigley any further.[1]

At least the paper makers had been consistent ; they had recognised the danger at the time of the 1860 Budget, and had opposed the removal of the duty on foreign paper. The Manchester silk manufacturers had not even this satisfaction, for they had boasted that protective duties reflected on the efficiency of their business,[2] and had supported the repeal of the silk duties. They quickly came to regret their self-confidence, and by 1867 only two of the twenty-eight Manchester silk firms that had scorned protection remained members of the Chamber of Commerce. " Several of them have retired because we would not support them in getting back what they themselves prayed to be relieved from." [3] French competition had probably forced the rest out of business.

[1] Proceedings, 29th March and 10th May 1865 ; Annual Report for 1865, pp. 9-10.
[2] See above, Chapter I.   [3] Annual Meeting, 30th January 1868.

A third industry that suffered from Britain's free-trade policy was sugar refining, which had to compete with subsidised beet sugar imported from the Continent. As with the paper makers, the Manchester Chamber took its stand on the interests of the consumer, who obviously benefited from cheap sugar ; the Chamber recognised that the British refiners were subject to " unequal competition ", but assumed that Continental governments would " naturally take steps for the protection of their own revenue ".[1] Liverpool and not Manchester was the home of sugar refining in north-west England ; when at the end of the century the local jam and sweet manufacturers joined the Manchester Chamber of Commerce, they welcomed foreign bounty-fed sugar and were staunch free-traders.[2]

Opinion at Manchester remained so solidly in favour of free trade at the end of the 'seventies that speakers who wished to refute " persons who have never been properly converted from protection " began by apologising for the repetition of an oft-told tale. Cobden's argument that other countries would not be slow to follow Britain's example in abandoning protection was no longer heard. The President of the Manchester Chamber frankly admitted that the recent growth of the local

machine and engineering industries—in order to establish spinning and weaving concerns and print works in the chief cities and towns of the Continent—had been the means of transferring to other places the trade we had formerly enjoyed, almost exclusively, ourselves.

To prevent the export of machinery would deny " a most profitable employment to a portion of our people ". To tax our imports, on the other hand, would raise either the cost of living or the cost of industrial raw materials, thus destroying our competitive advantage in neutral markets.[3] This argument harmonised with the needs of the Lancashire cotton industry, which depended largely on the open markets of the East and of South America, and would continue to do so until the First World War ; when the protective habit spread from Europe to the rest of the world, the argument would sound less convincing, but until then it remained the stock reply of free-trade Manchester to an increasingly protectionist Britain.

[1] Annual Report for 1874, pp. 8-9.   [2] See below, pp. 108-111.
[3] Annual Meeting, 3rd February 1879.

The slow return to protectionist sentiments in Britain began with the depression of British agriculture at the end of the eighteen-seventies. By the end of the next decade, the rank and file of the Conservative party had swung back to their traditional beliefs. At the Annual Conference in 1887, the delegates overwhelmingly supported a Fair Trade resolution that called for " speedy reform in the policy of the United Kingdom as regards foreign imports and the influx of indigent foreigners " ; and the 1891 Conference voted for an Imperial Customs Union.[1] The Conservative Government, which had to conciliate its Liberal Unionist allies and to avoid a drastic change for which public opinion was unready, gave its enthusiastic followers no encouragement ; but Lord Salisbury made it clear that at the proper moment the government would feel its way back to a protective policy.[2] After the election of 1906, it appeared that two-thirds of the surviving Conservative M.P.s accepted Chamberlain's policy of Imperial Preference. Balfour thereupon admitted, at least in principle, the need for tariff reform ; and though he hedged his acceptance with ambiguous reservations, the general opinion was that from 1906 the Conservative party was committed to Protection.[3]

At about the same time the Association of British Chambers of Commerce voted by a majority against free trade. The Association had been formed in 1860 but the Manchester Chamber held aloof until nearly the end of the century, believing that the interests of its members could best be served by a local body.[4] In 1891 the Association had temporarily strayed from orthodoxy by passing a resolution in favour of Imperial Preference,[5] but it had later returned to the free-trade fold. As late as 1904, free traders could secure a majority at the Association's debates on fiscal policy ; in 1905, however, a protectionist resolution was carried by 42 votes to 21, with 39 abstentions. This was a most significant turning-point in the controversy, even though, without a two-thirds majority, the resolution could not take effect.[6] Protection continued to get a narrow majority

[1] B. H. Brown, *The Tariff Reform Movement in Great Britain, 1881-1895* (1943), pp. 69 and 78-9.   [2] *Ibid.*, pp. 78-80.
[3] E. Halévy, *A History of the English People : Epilogue*, Vol. II pp. 12-13.
[4] The decision to join was taken in December 1898.
[5] *Monthly Record*, October 1891.
[6] Proceedings, 16th March 1904 ; *Monthly Record*, March 1905.

at the annual meetings of the Association of British Chambers of Commerce ; in March 1909, for instance, the voting was 46 in favour of protection, 31 against, and 32 abstainers. The Budget of 1909 produced a sharp revulsion of feeling among business men against free trade ; at the Association's annual meeting in 1910 free trade got no more than 12 votes, protection 51, and abstentions increased to 41. The movement for Protection, in the eyes of one Lancashire business man,

amounted to a revolt of income-tax payers. . . . It was pointed out [in the Association's debates] that when they had an income tax of 1s. 2d. in the pound in times of peace, taxation would be very onerous indeed

if there were a war.[1] Tariffs were the only other likely source of revenue.

Even at Manchester the new seed did not always fall on stony ground. In 1885 a branch of the Fair Trade League, disguised under the name of the Manchester Union, was founded in the citadel of free trade ;[2] among its early members were H. F. Hibbert, a corn miller, and E. Burgis, a shipowner, both of whom became prominent advocates of the protectionist cause in the Manchester Chamber of Commerce.   For some years the Fair Traders had little success ; the fair-trade resolutions moved at the quarterly meetings of the Chamber of Commerce were consistently rejected.   Twice in 1886 the Fair Traders tested the orthodoxy of the Chamber ; on the first occasion the Chamber "recorded its unswerving confidence in the principles of free trade ", and condemned

a policy of retaliation against protectionist countries, not only on account of the reactionary nature of that policy but because it fosters the belief, which is the root of heresy—namely, that concessions made by this country are concessions which involve loss, unless they are compensated by concessions on the other side.

The Fair Traders could muster only six votes against this resolution,[3] but at a poorly attended meeting later in the year they did much better : on the motion that " Having waited in vain more than forty years for other nations to follow England's Free Trade example, this Chamber thinks the time has now arrived to reconsider its position ", the orthodox

---

[1] Proceedings, 15th February 1909, and 13th April 1910 ; *Monthly Record*, March 1910.

[2] B. H. Brown, *op. cit.*, p. 133 and note.   The Fair Trade League dated from 1881.

[3] Proceedings, 3rd May ; *Manchester Guardian*, 4th May 1886.

party won by 22 votes to 21.[1] As the Chamber of Commerce had nearly seven hundred members at the time, the Directors were quick to point out that the voting did not fairly represent the opinion of the members ; they believed that in a poll not 10 per cent. would vote for a fair-trade resolution.[2]

The Fair Traders thought otherwise ; in July 1887 Mr. Hibbert proposed the imposition of moderate duties on manufactured imports,

the abolition of all duties on tea, coffee, cocoa, chicory and dried fruit, and the imposition of revenue duties of an equal total value on imports of wheat, barley, oats, rye, peas, beans, meal and flour from protected countries.

This ingenious attempt to protect the consumer as well as the producer did not commend itself to the members, who rejected the motion by 64 votes to 33.[3] At their fourth attempt in December 1888, the Fair Traders at last secured the majority they wanted ; Mr. Hibbert moved

That in the opinion of this Chamber all goods of a nature and kind which we ourselves produce, offered for sale in the Markets of the United Kingdom, should pay that equal proportional share of the burden of Imperial and Local Taxation which they would have paid if produced or manufactured in the United Kingdom.

This was a popular form of words with protectionists for many years, and Manchester free-traders often scored debating points at its expense. In 1888, however, the resolution was carried by " a large majority " of the seventy-three members who had stayed to vote.[4] The Directors took immediate steps to reaffirm Manchester's adherence to the cause of free trade ; they declared that the vote did not represent the views of the Chamber as a whole, and conducted a poll of the members to find out the true state of feeling. Of the 1,004 members entitled to vote 621 actually voted, and the result was a considerable triumph for the free-traders ; 397 members with 556 votes approved, and 187 members with 221 votes disapproved, " the unfaltering adherence to the principles of Free Trade so often affirmed by this Chamber ".[5] Nevertheless, as the President remarked, " Mr. Cobden, if he had lived, would have been disappointed with what had taken

[1] *Manchester Guardian*, 2nd November 1886.
[2] Annual Meeting, 31st January 1887. [3] Proceedings, 27th April 1887.
[4] *Manchester Guardian*, 20th December 1888.
[5] Annual Report for 1888, pp. 24-5. Individual members had one vote ; firms had two votes. There were thirty-seven spoilt papers.

place " ;[1] for the poll showed that even in a good year like
1888 protectionists formed a considerable minority within the
Manchester Chamber of Commerce.

As no further poll on fiscal policy was held until 1916,
we cannot accurately measure the progress or otherwise of
the protectionist party at Manchester in the generation before
the First World War.   To draw a parallel from the growth of
protectionist feeling in other Chambers of Commerce might
be misleading, since the cotton trade suffered less from tariff
barriers than the woollen trade, and less from German competition, both at home and abroad, than the iron and steel,
engineering, or chemical industries.   Though Mr. Burgis
often raised the subject at Manchester, he never repeated the
fleeting triumph of 1888.   Indeed, the protectionists for some
years gave up attending the Chamber's debates on fiscal
policy ; in 1891 a protectionist resolution received only 13
votes, and in 1892 only 7 votes out of 81.[2]

There was no further test of feeling in the Manchester
Chamber of Commerce until 1903, when discussion broke out
anew in response to Joseph Chamberlain's campaign for
Imperial Preference.   The free-trade Board of Directors did
not wait to be attacked, but took the initiative in calling a
special meeting of members to consider the following resolution:

The Board of Directors, recognising that an investigation of our
Fiscal Policy is imminent, is prepared to give every assistance
to a full and fair discussion, and believes that the results of the
enquiry will be to prove that any departure from the hitherto
accepted principles of Free Trade will not only be found to operate
detrimentally to the true and fundamental interests of the United
Kingdom, but will also tend to impart into the relations of the
Mother Country with her Colonies many harassing questions
which possess the germs of future friction, conflicting interests and
ultimate disintegration.

Besides advancing the usual argument that Protection would
weaken Britain's competitive power by raising the cost of
production, the free-traders contended that the colonies
could not absorb the vast exports of British industry.   Imperial Preference might lead to a tariff war with foreign
countries that were much better customers for (say) fine
yarns than the colonies would ever be ; what guarantee would

---

[1] Annual Meeting, 4th February 1889.
[2] *Manchester Guardian*, 28th April 1891 ; *Monthly Record*, August 1892.

Britain have that the colonies would throw down their tariff barriers, giving us not merely preferential but free access to their markets ? In reply the protectionists pointed to the industries that free-trade Britain had either lost, or failed to establish, such as silks, dyes, and wheat farming ; but as the cotton trade was not one of them the arguments were not very convincing. On a vote the protectionists were defeated by 300 to 120 ; the Chamber of Commerce had at the time about 1,800 members.[1] Further debates took place in 1904, 1909, and 1910 ; on every occasion the free-traders outnumbered their opponents by three or four to one. There can, therefore, be little doubt that protectionist feeling in Manchester was no stronger in 1913 than it had been a generation before ; it may even have been a little weaker.

Throughout this generation the arguments used by the opposing parties changed little ; nor is this surprising, since the cotton industry seemed to become more prosperous as time went on. The Fair Trade movement had sprung up at a time of languishing exports ; after 1900 it appeared that the check had been only temporary, and although the heretics did not recant they made no more converts. Not only in 1913, but even in 1930, nothing seemed more natural than to refer to Manchester as " the citadel of Free Trade ".[2]

The defence of free trade in Britain was not simply a debating matter. In 1902 the Budget included a registration duty of one shilling a quarter on imported corn ; this apparent revival of the Corn Laws roused Manchester to make a spirited protest. The Directors of the Chamber of Commerce held a special meeting to denounce the tax as

an infraction of the custom and practice of free trade, and fraught with danger to the economic interest of this country ; it is likely to strengthen the cause of protection at home, in the Colonies, and in foreign nations.

The Chancellor should impose a corresponding excise duty on home-grown corn if he intended the tax for revenue only.[3] The repeal of the tax in the following year gave great satisfaction.

The fight for free trade in sugar was not to be won so easily. We have already seen that in the eighteen-seventies

---

[1] The debate is fully reported in *Monthly Record*, July 1903.
[2] *The Economist*, 7th June 1930. [3] Proceedings, 18th April 1902.

the Manchester Chamber of Commerce was indifferent to the fate of the British sugar refiners, who were carrying on an unequal struggle with subsidised refiners abroad.[1] In 1888 concern for the West Indies and for British refiners had caused the British Government to call a conference on sugar bounties, but the Convention though signed was never ratified; under it, the signatories would have penalised the import of bounty-fed sugar and prevented its re-export. The Manchester merchants rather surprisingly took no notice of this attempted interference with the free exchange of goods, but they were more alert when the question was next mooted ten years later. In 1896 Germany and Austria had doubled their already considerable bounties on exports, and France was preparing to do likewise; discussions about a new convention to end the bounties had already begun when the Indian Government precipitated action by imposing a countervailing duty on imports of bounty-fed sugar.[2] The Manchester Chamber of Commerce, always sensitive to changes in Indian fiscal policy, denounced this step

as opposed to the interests of the people of India, a dangerous precedent calculated to lead to the adoption of a similar policy in the United Kingdom, . . . and a departure from the principles of free trade.

If allowed to pass unchallenged, the policy of the Indian Government, which had the full approval of the British Government, might set a precedent for counter-measures by Britain against French, German, and American subsidies to shipping, or Canadian grants that encouraged the export of cattle and agricultural produce.[3]

In 1901, the British Government imposed a revenue duty of 4s. 2d. a hundredweight on imports of sugar whether colonial or bounty-fed. The Manufacturing Confectioners' Alliance of London asked the Manchester Chamber of Commerce to protest against the duty, but lacking expert advice from local firms engaged in the sugar trade the Chamber declined to act.[4] Manchester sugar importers, jam makers, and confectioners took the hint; by January 1904, thirty-six local firms had joined the Chamber of Commerce

---

[1] Above, p. 103.
[2] *Encyclopaedia Britannica*, 11th edn., article " Sugar ".
[3] Proceedings, 9th June 1899 ; *Monthly Record*, July 1899.
[4] Proceedings, 11th February 1902.

and formed a Sugar Trade Section. Their interests and sympathies lay with the final consumer, not with the refiner; the Sugar Trade Section consistently advocated cheap sugar from its birth in 1904 to its dissolution thirty years later.[1] Even without the advice of the sugar trade, however, the Chamber could see that the Sugar Convention of 1902 contravened free-trade principles; by it, producing countries undertook to abolish export bounties, and importing countries promised to impose a countervailing duty on bounty-fed sugar. The Chamber of Commerce opposed ratification, but in vain.[2]

When the Liberals returned to power they insisted that the Convention of 1902 should be modified if Britain was to remain a party to it. Accordingly, a supplementary Convention of 1907 relieved Britain from the obligation to impose countervailing duties on bounty-fed sugar; in return, Britain undertook to certify that exports of sugar products to signatories of the Convention did not contain bounty-fed sugar. The Manchester Chamber of Commerce would have preferred unconditional withdrawal, since

the articles of the Sugar Convention of 1902 that remain unaffected by the Protocol of 1907 will still bind us by onerous conditions, interfering with the complete freedom of trade in the commodity, which it is the wish of the sugar users to recover in its entirety;

nevertheless, the compromise of 1907 had relieved Britain from " the worst effects " of the Convention.[3]

At the same time as the Convention had been modified in Britain's favour, Russia had acceded to it, undertaking not

PRODUCTION OF SUGAR IN THE BRITISH WEST INDIES

	Tons
1887	343,000
1903	291,000
1910	221,000

to export more than 200,000 tons of sugar in each of the years 1908-9 to 1912-13. This restriction, at a time when the price of sugar was rising, provided an additional argument against the Sugar Convention. Britain had originally signed it out of consideration for the West Indies, but production

[1] Proceedings, 22nd January 1934.   [2] Monthly Record, May 1902.
[3] Ibid., December 1907 ; Annual Report of the Sugar Trade Section for 1907.

there had fallen more rapidly since 1903 than in the years when
competition from bounty-fed sugar had been at its height.
Manchester argued therefore that the cause of this decline
must be sought elsewhere, particularly since other cane-
sugar areas, including other islands in the Caribbean, were
able to prosper while the British plantations languished in
poverty.   As the Convention had not helped the West Indies,
Britain as a consuming country should consult her own
interests, which coincided with those of Russia, who wished
to export more sugar.[1] Sir Edward Grey had already
announced that if in 1912-13 Russia was not allowed to
export 500,000 tons of sugar Britain would withdraw from the
Convention, and on the 1st August 1912 Britain did announce
her intention to withdraw.[2]

The success of the agitation against the " war tax " on
sugar was less complete. The Manchester merchants at
first showed no hostility to the tax, but under the influence of
the newly-founded Sugar Trade Section they came to demand
its repeal, or at least its reduction.[3] The new section threw
itself vigorously into the fight against the tax, organising a
petition to Parliament and a deputation of sugar users to the
Chancellor of the Exchequer, Mr. Asquith.[4] The Budget of
1907 left the tax unchanged, but in 1908 Mr. Asquith sharply
reduced it to 1s 10d. a hundredweight,

which there is no doubt will be a great alleviation of the burden
which has been borne by the sugar-using industries.   They trust
that at no distant date it may be found possible entirely to remove
this duty, which was first imposed as a war tax.[5]

In 1911, 1912, and 1913, the Sugar Section repeatedly put
their case for repeal to the Chancellor, arguing that the high
cost of living, to which the tax contributed, lay at the root
of the country's industrial unrest ; but no further relief was
given.[6]

[1] *Monthly Record*, March 1912.
[2] *Ibid.*, August 1912 ; Proceedings, 4th September 1912.
[3] *Ibid.*, 10th February and 16th March 1904.
[4] *Ibid.*, 15th November 1904 ; *Monthly Record*, February 1906.
[5] *Ibid.*, June 1908.
[6] *Ibid.*, January, May, and July 1911, and March 1912 ; Proceedings,
12th February 1913.

CHAPTER X

COMMERCIAL POLICY WITHOUT TARIFFS

PROTECTIONISTS have always argued that without the power to impose tariffs Britain could not establish new industries, negotiate favourable commercial treaties, or hold her share of the world's trade ; but Manchester merchants in the nineteenth and early twentieth centuries thought that other policies could be elaborated which would maintain prosperity without jeopardising the low costs of production associated with free trade. It was considered that these other policies would supplement free trade and would make protective duties not only unsound but unnecessary.

As retaliatory tariffs were out of the question, Britain could only negotiate favourable commercial treaties by the closest co-operation between the Foreign Office and the Board of Trade. The Manchester merchants felt that this co-operation was sometimes lacking, and its absence was held responsible for the disappointing results that often followed commercial negotiations. Dissatisfaction with the work of the Foreign Office and the Board of Trade grew steadily in the years following the Cobden Treaty, when many European countries were revising their tariffs ; but when in 1862 the Leeds Chamber of Commerce proposed the transfer of the Board of Trade's commercial work to a newly-created department of the Foreign Office, the Manchester merchants demurred, although they admitted that " commercial questions generally do not receive that amount of attention from H.M. Government that their importance demands ".[1]

The matter did not come to a head until 1864, when Bradford and other towns belonging to the Association of Chambers of Commerce asked Manchester to join them in an attack on the recent conduct of commercial negotiations ; the root of the trouble was that the " interests of commerce were neglected, and its development retarded, by the double action of the Board of Trade and the Foreign Office ".[2] The Manchester Chamber of Commerce agreed with the views of

---

[1] Annual Report for 1862, pp. 5-6.
[2] Proceedings, 13th January, 10th and 17th February 1864.

the Association, but preferred to state its own case in a separate
deputation to Lord Palmerston.   The Manchester merchants
argued that it was the government's duty to open European
markets to the better qualities of Lancashire goods, as they
had begun to do by the treaty of 1860 ; but the tardiness and
inefficiency of the Board of Trade and the Foreign Office
meant that favourable opportunities were let slip.   The
French Government was much more energetic, but despite
the most-favoured-nation clause Lancashire benefited little
from this fact.

The classification and arrangement of the tariffs as settled
between France and other countries not unfrequently excludes
British manufactures . . . There are many articles of British
manufacture, nothing similar to which is produced in France,
and that country having made no provision for the admission of
such articles, no reduction of duty upon them has been obtained.

The division of authority between the Board of Trade and the
Foreign Office meant that neither felt responsible for watching
British commercial interests abroad.[1]

Lord Palmerston stoutly defended the two departments
against the charges of neglect and inefficiency, and attributed
their small succcss

to the great difficulty in inducing foreign nations to admit our goods
into their ports on more liberal terms . . . as whenever reduction
of duty on British goods is now suggested to any of them the in-
variable reply is : ' What will you give us in return ? '   And we
have nothing to offer.

If British prosperity was used as an argument the foreigner
retorted that this prosperity grew up under protection.

Lord Palmerston's defence was plausible, but was not the
whole truth ; for there can be little doubt that in particular
cases the Foreign Office and the Board of Trade showed
less zeal than might have been expected.   Mr. Beaumont,
M.P. for Newcastle, had perhaps the most telling example of
their inefficiency.   While on a holiday in Austria, he learnt
that the Austrian Government was preparing to revise the
tariff.   He wrote home to find out whether the Board of
Trade and the Foreign Office were alive to the facts ; but they
were not.   He therefore forwarded copies of the proposed new
tariff to them, and on return to England called at the Board of
Trade and Foreign Office ; but to his surprise he " found that

[1] Proceedings, 9th March 1864.

the persons in authority were unconscious of ever having received the documents in question, although after a strict search they were discovered ".[1] This and similar instances encouraged Manchester and other commercial centres to insist on an inquiry by a select committee of the House of Commons.[2]

Even before the committee had reported, the Manchester merchants had visible proof of increased activity at the offending departments ; in the second half of 1864 there was a notable increase in the number of letters and other documents received from these departments by the Manchester Chamber of Commerce.[3] But the report of the select committee, from which so much had been hoped, was disappointingly cautious ; it did no more than recommend the separation of commercial correspondence from diplomatic correspondence at the Foreign Office. The slight administrative re-arrangement which this required was soon put into effect, but was not likely to make much improvement. In a petition to the House of Commons, the Chamber of Commerce asked for legislative action to create

a separate and distinct department of State, charged with the supervision promotion and guardianship of the import and export trades, presided over by a "Secretary of State for Commerce " or other Minister invested with full authority to deal with all questions affecting our foreign, colonial, and Indian trade.[4]

This question, fitfully raised at intervals over the next fifty years as a demand for a Ministry of Commerce, was not pressed at the time. The Manchester merchants were not interested in administrative reform as such, but in vigorous and successful commercial negotiations ; whenever the Chamber of Commerce hoped for better things than the Foreign Office and the Board of Trade were willing or able to perform, the cry for a Ministry of Commerce was likely to be revived.

The upward trend of foreign tariffs from 1878 onwards provided the occasion for renewed complaints about the inefficiency of the Foreign Office, but Lord Derby gave much the same reply as Lord Palmerston had given fourteen years earlier.[5] As before, the Manchester merchants proceeded

---

[1] *Loc. cit.*   [2] *Ibid.*, 27th April 1864.
[3] Annual Report for 1864, p. 7.
[4] Proceedings, 22nd February 1865 ; Annual Report for 1865, p. 6.
[5] Proceedings, 27th March 1878.

from complaints of "the insufficient and irresponsible character of the so-called Commercial Department at the Foreign
Office" to schemes of administrative reform. One of the
most energetic Directors of the Chamber, Mr. John Slagg,
drew up a report on *Treaties of Commerce and Foreign Trade*,
which was widely circulated among Chambers of Commerce
and Members of Parliament.[1] The report complained, in
general, that the government and its departments seemed to
find political questions more interesting than commercial
questions ; a particular grievance arose from the fact that
the work of the Commercial Department of the Foreign Office
was not assigned to a special Under-Secretary of State.
Commercial functions were also scattered among many other
government departments, such as the Home, Colonial, and
India Offices, the Board of Trade, the Commissioner of
Patents, the Privy Council Office, the Science and Art
Department, and the Local Government Board. This
"scattered and powerless machinery" could not work
efficiently until it was brought under the control of a united
Ministry of Commerce.[2]

An alternative scheme for an advisory committee of business men to assist the Foreign Office was put forward at the
end of the century ; it was politely received and quietly
shelved.[3] In 1903 the demand for a Ministry of Commerce
revived, but this was to be based on the existing Board of
Trade, not a new creation ; an official committee made similar
recommendations, but the government did not adopt them.[4]
The question dragged on for some years, but when the
substance of Manchester's demands was granted—Cabinet
rank for the President of the Board of Trade, and "increased
activities in so many branches of Departmental work"—the
agitation for a Ministry of Commerce was quietly dropped.[5]

From time to time Manchester merchants criticised the
quality and quantity of commercial intelligence provided by
British consuls abroad. As early as 1835 all the stock controversies of the following eighty years were being vigorously
debated ; in that year a select committee of the House of

[1] Annual Report for 1879, p. 5.
[2] *Manchester Guardian*, 20th February 1879 ; Proceedings, 29th July
1879.
[3] *Ibid.*, 13th April 1898.
[4] *Monthly Record*, March 1903 ; Proceedings, 25th January 1905.
[5] *Ibid.*, 10th July and 4th September 1912.

9

Commons was asking whether consuls should be allowed to trade, whether the Foreign Office or the Board of Trade should supervise the consular service, and whether appointments should be confined to British subjects.[1] The Manchester Chamber of Commerce often asked the same questions, besides criticising the behaviour of particular consuls.

The consular service in Morocco aroused the interest of the Manchester merchants not only in questions of principle but also in particular cases of inefficiency. The Consul-General of Morocco lived on the coast, though the Emperor's capital was at Fez, several miles inland ; as a result, the Emperor was not kept properly advised about the folly of his economic policy, which by granting monopolies and imposing high tariffs encouraged smuggling, hindered legitimate trade, and deprived the government of revenue. The Foreign Office responded by ordering the Consul-General to proceed to Fez.[2] In 1856 the vice-consuls also came under fire ; at some of the minor ports of Morocco they were competing with the merchants they were appointed to serve, had few qualifications for their posts, and even supported the monopolies. As before, the Foreign Office quickly remedied the complaints by appointing " efficient persons, with fixed salaries, who will be restricted from engaging in mercantile pursuits ".[3]

The case of Mr. J. M. Young, a coffee planter in Costa Rica, ended less satisfactorily and showed that if the Foreign Office did not choose its consuls wisely, much mischief might be done. The misfortunes of Mr. Young began when for a short while he left his affairs in the hands of an agent ; on his return to Costa Rica he found that his agent had defrauded him, but he appeared to have overcome his difficulties when he won a lawsuit against the agent. At this point the new British vice-consul at San José in Costa Rica intervened, and persuaded the President and Prime Minister of the Republic to suspend proceedings.[4] A lengthy correspondence with the Foreign Office ensued ; the Manchester Chamber of Commerce did its best to persuade the Foreign Office to disavow the new vice-consul, but the Foreign Office was unwilling to admit that he had persuaded the Costa Rican Government to commit an injustice. Eventually the Foreign Office admitted that the

[1] Sir J. Tilley and S. Gaselee, *The Foreign Office* (Whitehall Series, 1933), pp. 231-2.
[2] Proceedings, 9th November and 27th December 1854.
[3] *Ibid.*, 24th June and 10th September 1856.
[4] *Ibid.*, 21st June 1854.

new vice-consul was in the wrong, and dismissed him from the service ;[1] but Mr. Young still had to secure justice from the Costa Rican Government, and here the Foreign Office would not help, although one of its officers was to blame for all the coffee planter's difficulties.[2] By 1861 Mr. Young had given up hope of getting the judgement enforced, and he could not afford the appeal to the Judicial Committee of the Privy Council through which he might be awarded damages from the British Government. The Manchester Chamber of Commerce therefore supported his plea that an arbitrator should assess the damages, and petitioned the Queen and the Treasury to that effect.[3] By 1863 Mr. Young had been reduced to penury, and the Chamber granted him the £20 that he had to deposit before he could even sue *in forma pauperis*.[4] At this point he and his grievance disappeared from the notice of the Chamber.

Though one consul might abuse his position, consuls as a class did useful work in promoting British overseas trade. After the Cobden Treaty had been signed, when the prospects of increased trade with France looked bright, the Manchester merchants promptly asked for the appointment of experienced consuls at Paris, Havre, Rouen, Boulogne, Dieppe, Bordeaux, and Marseilles, " it being evident that the successful working of the Treaty in all its varied details would be essentially influenced by the character and ability of the persons appointed ".[5] In 1889 they considered that the extensive capital invested at Pinos Altos in Mexico warranted the presence of a British consul ; but the Foreign Office could not agree.[6] The Chamber of Commerce had more success in 1905, when it secured the appointment of additional consuls in the French and Belgian Congos, where Manchester merchants still hoped to find large markets.[7]

As the furnishing of reports on the economic conditions of their districts was one of the consuls' most important tasks, Manchester merchants were quick to complain if these reports were inaccurate, or if their publication was too tardy to be of any use. When the consuls criticised the quality of Lancashire's exports, the Manchester Chamber of Commerce was righteously indignant ; one Director " could not conceive

---

[1] Proceedings, 6th March, 25th May, 24th June, and 23rd October 1856.
[2] *Ibid.*, 20th November 1856.   [3] *Ibid.*, 6th and 27th February 1861.
[4] *Ibid.*, 17th June and 16th December 1863.
[5] Annual Report for 1860, p. 18.
[6] Proceedings, 29th July and 27th November 1889.
[7] *Ibid.*, 25th January 1905 ; Annual Report for 1905, p. 9.

of a course more likely to injure Manchester Trade than the
publication in semi-official dispatches of remarks decrying
Lancashire goods ".[1]   In general, the Manchester merchants
regarded the reports of the United States' consuls as models
which British consuls might well copy ;

and in view of the paramount importance of commerce to this
country and the increasing closeness with which British trade is
being pressed by foreign competition, it is desirable that gentlemen
selected for this service should have adequate commercial knowledge.[2]

A commercial attaché was appointed to the Berlin embassy
in 1880,[3] and the Manchester Chamber of Commerce, when
asked to suggest improvements in the commercial service of
the Foreign Office, put as the first of its suggestions the appointment of commercial attachés at all embassies ; the attachés
should advise the ambassador on commercial questions, and
should collect and publish useful intelligence without delay.[4]
Although the number of commercial attachés did not increase
as rapidly as Manchester wished, consular reports were
published more quickly thereafter, and some were sent in
manuscript, often accompanied by samples, direct to Chambers
of Commerce ; Manchester merchants greatly appreciated this
service.[5]   Complaints of inaccuracy and delay in the publication of consular reports revived early in the twentieth
century ;[6] but the evil was not serious enough to provoke sustained demands for reform of the consular service.   As a minor
aid to efficiency and reliability, the Manchester Chamber of
Commerce recommended in 1910 that " wherever practicable ", and " at all events at the principal foreign ports ",
British consuls should be of British nationality.[7]

If the Manchester merchants were to take full advantage of
favourable economic trends, or to avoid losses in a poor market,
they needed prompt and accurate statistics of the export
trade ; on the other hand, vexatious form-filling at the behest
of the Custom House was to be avoided.   On all such
matters the Manchester Chamber of Commerce spoke with

[1] Proceedings, 28th July 1886.
[2] Letter of 24th March 1886 to the Foreign Office.
[3] Tilley and Gaselee, op. cit., p. 242.
[4] Letter of 24th March 1886 to the Foreign Office.
[5] Annual Report for 1886, pp. 11 and 45.
[6] Monthly Record, September and November 1902, September 1904,
and May 1905.
[7] Proceedings, 26th January 1910.

great authority on behalf of the export trade in Lancashire cottons. In 1861, for example, the Board of Trade applied to the Chamber for its views on a reclassification of the export statistics of cotton and other textiles. The classification which the Chamber suggested for cotton cloth—first, grey and bleached goods together, secondly, printed or dyed goods, and thirdly, mixed fabrics—was the one adopted by the Board of Trade ;[1] it remained in use until 1890, when separate returns for grey, bleached, printed, and dyed goods were called for.

In 1867 the Manchester Chamber of Commerce protested to the Board of Trade against vexatious regulations which required exporters to state the weight of woollen and worsted goods shipped. A similar regulation for cotton goods had been withdrawn already ; the Chamber contended that woollen and worsted goods should now be treated in the same way as cottons. The regulation particularly annoyed the general wholesale houses of London and Manchester ; and it was actually uncertain how far it should apply to mixture fabrics of wool and cotton, or worsted and cotton. Despite these objections, the Board of Trade refused to make any changes.[2]

Statistical documents much prized by Manchester merchants were the Bills of Entry, containing particulars of the cargo of every outward-bound ship. By a patent of the reign of Charles II, the right to publish and sell these documents had been vested in a private Bill of Entry Office, which in time came to be largely controlled by Customs officials acting in a private capacity ; the profits accrued to a life-insurance fund from which they alone benefited.[3] This anomaly aroused no protest until it became inefficient as well as illogical. In 1870 the Manchester Chamber of Commerce received complaints of wrong declarations of shipments, not corrected until long after the ship had left port ; the Bill of Entry Office rarely used its power to inflict fines for false or late returns, and consequently shippers and forwarding agents had no incentive to render prompt and true statistics. As an example of deferred entry, the Manchester Chamber cited the case of the *Blue Cross* : in the first manifest of this ship 1,000,000 yards of plain cotton cloth were declared ; but a week later additional returns were published showing that the ship was in fact carrying 5,500,000 yards of plain cloth. Such inaccuracies as these made the

[1] Proceedings, 28th October 1861 ; Annual Report for 1861, pp. 8-9.
[2] Proceedings, 4th and 27th February 1867.
[3] *Manchester Guardian*, 1st November 1870.

published Bills of Entry worthless to the merchants who bought them, whereas if properly conducted the Bill of Entry Office could produce statistics of the greatest value to merchants. The Manchester Chamber of Commerce therefore asked the Board of Trade to place the Office under a department of the Customs.[1]

The government refused to revoke the patent, however, and the delay in publication of statistics remained very serious, sometimes amounting to eighteen days after a ship had sailed ; trade with India, which was mostly carried on by weekly telegrams, was particularly embarrassed.[2] The Manchester Chamber therefore persisted in its agitation, both by memorial and deputation, for an improved service from the Bill of Entry Office. The Chancellor of the Exchequer, Robert Lowe, admitted that the existence of a private Office was an abuse, but he had no hope that Parliament would consent to vote the money necessary to end it, though the patent would not be renewed when it expired in 1879.[3] The Manchester merchants refused at first to acquiesce in so long a continuance of the abuse, but by the end of 1874 it was clear that nothing could be done until the patent expired.[4]

In 1879, after a reminder, the government refused to renew the patent and the work, after some delay, was transferred to the Statistical Department of the Customs.[5] Public control, however, did not at once ensure a more accurate and speedy service ; the Customs authorities seemed unwilling to exercise their power to fine shippers who were late in making returns. But after the Manchester Chamber of Commerce had assured the authorities that any shipper ought to be able to make his returns within five or six days from the date of sailing, the Board of Customs took heart and fined a large number of defaulters, with some show of complacency at its own rectitude.[6]

The monthly *Trade and Navigation Accounts* were also much used by merchants, and the Manchester Chamber was always ready to resist any unfavourable changes in the amount of information they conveyed. In 1876 the trade returns for

---

[1] Proceedings, 25th May and 29th June 1870.
[2] *Ibid.*, 26th April 1871 ; *Manchester Guardian*, 24th October 1871.
[3] Proceedings, 27th December 1871, 24th April and 29th May 1872.
[4] Annual Report for 1874, p. 7.   [5] *Ibid.*, 1879, p. 5, and 1881, p. 9.
[6] Letter of 26th October 1881 to the Board of Customs ; Annual Report for 1882, p. 7.

the Gambia were amalgamated with those of Sierra Leone, a change against which Manchester promptly protested.[1]   In 1908 the Chamber suggested that every country to which Great Britain exported more than £200,000 worth of cotton goods in a year should be shown separately in the monthly returns ; the annual returns already gave this information, but they were not much used by merchants.[2]   In 1909 the Board of Trade proposed to delete from the returns the details of shipments of cotton goods to the separate ports of arrival in India, but the Manchester merchants successfully challenged this decision.[3]

A decimal system of weights, coins, and measures has been under active discussion in Britain for about a hundred years ; its great advantages to commerce are evident and at Manchester have always seemed likely to outweigh the harm arising from confusion during the period of transition.   Nevertheless, the Manchester Chamber of Commerce has taken only an intermittent interest in the decimal system, and at times has given no more than lukewarm support to its advocates.   When the question was first raised in 1852, the Manchester merchants petitioned the Treasury for the immediate decimalisation of the coinage—a change which, as American experience proved, need not cause much difficulty.   The decimalisation of weights and measures would take longer, but was considered to be equally necessary.   Local weights and measures still existed in many districts, despite Acts of Parliament to the contrary ; " a fundamental change in the system would alone bring about a national conformity in weights and measures ".[4]   An agitation for the change was kept up for a while,[5] but after 1855 the question received little attention for many years.   In 1866, however, Manchester supported a plea from Liverpool for the adoption of the decimal system, and in 1868 its usefulness in trading with countries already on the metric system was for the first time advanced as a reason for adopting it in Britain ; [6] until then the argument had rested entirely on the advantages that would accrue to internal trade.

At the end of the century, when interest in the matter revived once more, national uniformity in weights and

---

[1] Proceedings, 20th December 1876.   [2] Annual Report for 1908.
[3] Proceedings, 15th February and 21st April 1909.
[4] Ibid., 25th March 1852 ; Annual Report for 1852, p. 10.
[5] Proceedings, 17th February 1853, 13th June 1855.
[6] Ibid., 4th April 1866 ; Manchester Guardian, 31st January 1868.

measures appears to have been an accomplished fact ; the sole case for decimalisation of English weights and measures, or for the adoption of the metric system, was the possible benefit to the export trade. In view of the competition of foreign countries, it was " felt to be a serious grievance that our traders and producers should be handicapped in the commercial race by the continuance of our present anti-quated system of weights and measures ". The government should make the adoption of the metric system compulsory within a stated time ; [1] the change would present little difficulty to merchants engaged in foreign trade, since " in many business houses the conversion of English into metric denominations in the invoicing of goods is a daily occurrence ".[2]

There was one branch of the export trade in which every country except France agreed to use British measures ; this was the yarn trade with its basic measure, the hank of 840 yards. Yarn exporters therefore wished to contract out of any decimal system that might be proposed ; Manchester engineers were also quite content with the existing system.[3] Opinion at Manchester accordingly veered towards a more moderate reform—the use in the cotton trade of pence and decimals instead of pence and vulgar fractions, and the use of pounds instead of tons, hundredweights and quarters. Only the home trade gave full support to a decimal system. The approval of the Chemical and Produce Sections was half-hearted ; there was definite opposition from the Africa merchants, and from the Yarn, Engineering, and Sugar Sections.[4]

A more useful antidote to foreign competition than the metric system was the improvement of technical and com-mercial education. As Manchester was a commercial rather than a manufacturing centre, and the Manchester Chamber of Commerce represented merchants rather than producers, the demand for better technical education was not voiced quite so loudly at Manchester as elsewhere ; nevertheless, as long as British technical education remained inferior to that of the United States and of our European competitors, it could well be argued that it was Britain's educational system, and not her tariff, that needed reform. Technical education first attracted

---

[1] Proceedings, 14th April 1897. [2] Annual Report for 1895.
[3] Proceedings, 9th May 1906. [4] *Ibid.*, 10th November 1909.

COMMERCIAL POLICY WITHOUT TARIFFS 123

the Manchester Chamber's attention after the Paris Exhibition
of 1867, which had shown that Britain was losing her techno-
logical superiority over her Continental rivals. In an
address to the Manchester Chamber shortly afterwards,
Professor Leone Levi, a prominent economist of the day,
argued that the weakness of the British economy lay in
technical education; he advocated the establishment of
colleges of technology, to be financed by the government's
Science and Art Department.[1] When shortly afterwards
Owens College was preparing to move from Quay Street to
its present home, it applied to the government for an annual
grant-in-aid and the Manchester Chamber of Commerce
supported the application,[2] though without any immediate
success. For the next fifteen years the Chamber hardly
concerned itself with education at all; at annual or quarterly
meetings individual members might bring to notice the well-
known superiority of German or American technical education,[3] but their words fell on deaf ears.

After about 1885 the Manchester Chamber of Commerce
took a less spasmodic interest in educational questions. In
1887, when the Victoria University made further application
for a grant from the government, the Manchester Chamber
renewed the support it had given nearly twenty years before,
this time with more success.[4] Besides its concern for higher
education in general, the Chamber made particular efforts
to stimulate the teaching of commercial subjects. In 1889 a
permanent Education Committee of the Chamber was set up

to co-operate with the leading educational authorities in Manchester with a view to raising the standard of efficiency of those
who will hereafter carry on the vast and expanding commerce of
this district.[5]

The committee and its educational advisers prepared a scheme
of commercial certificates for which Manchester youths were
invited to study; the conduct of the examinations was
entrusted to the Victoria University. The examinations
attracted a large number of candidates when they were first
held in 1891, but numbers fell so sharply in 1892 and 1893 that

[1] *Manchester Guardian*, 24th January 1868.
[2] Proceedings, 26th February 1868.
[3] E.g. Mr. J. A. Bremner at the Annual Meeting, 30th January 1871;
Mr. R. Johnson, President, 2nd November 1874; Mr. J. F. Hutton in
Manchester Guardian, 5th August 1885.
[4] Annual Report for 1887, p. 53.   [5] *Ibid.*, 1889, pp. 12-13.

the scheme was abandoned, though the Chamber's Education Committee continued in being.[1]

Having failed to establish its own system of examinations, the Chamber of Commerce gave its support to those of the University of Manchester, which in 1904 established a Faculty of Commerce. The Faculty gave instruction in modern languages, currency and banking, political economy, railway economics, commercial law, and economic history. The President of the Manchester Chamber hoped that the new degree of B.Com. would attract the sons of local business men, and save them from the unpractical education given at Oxford and Cambridge. America and Germany were making full use of a race of well educated men; British industry would have to do the same.[2] A good grounding in non-technical subjects was an essential pre-requisite of higher technical and commercial education; Manchester, through the Association of British Chambers of Commerce, pressed this view on the Board of Education which, it urged, should build more secondary schools.[3] In 1914 there was " a general feeling of dissatisfaction in commercial circles with the education provided in elementary schools "; the Chamber had already supported the government's Continuation-School Bill, believing that full-time education up to the age of fourteen, and part-time education until the age of seventeen, " would be of the highest value and importance ". Now the Chamber's Education Committee began to collate reports on the local standards of education, and proposed (if those standards were found wanting) to make its views known to the Manchester and Salford Directors of Education.[4] Unfortunately, the war brought this promising development to an abrupt end.

As the acknowledged centre of the expanding Lancashire cotton industry, Manchester could for long afford to ignore the argument that free trade was not the most favourable climate in which to rear infant industries. With the discovery of synthetic dyes, it became possible, given the right economic conditions, to establish in Britain a chemical industry which would free Lancashire from dependence on imported dyes;

[1] *Monthly Record*, March 1890; Proceedings, 29th May 1891, 26th July 1893.
[2] *Monthly Record*, December 1902. See also *ibid.*, December 1911 and July 1913.
[3] Proceedings, 12th October and 9th November 1904.
[4] *Ibid.*, 14th January and 18th July 1914.

it is notorious, however, that before the First World War Britain did not excel in the manufacture of synthetic dyes, and that their manufacture was one of the first industries to be protected when Britain moved away from her traditional free-trade policy.   At no time did the Manchester Chamber of Commerce advocate protective duties to establish the new industry ; but when chemical manufacturers and merchants joined the Chamber in large enough numbers to make their presence felt, the Chamber willingly used its influence to secure amendments of the patent laws.

Since anyone who discovers a new chemical substance or a new process may patent his discovery, and since such dis-coveries have been very numerous, the chemical industry has always been at the mercy of the patent law to a much greater extent than any other basic industry.   It has always been difficult to force a patentee to work his invention as fully as the public interest required, and while Britain pursued a free-trade policy it was difficult to make a patentee work his patent in Britain at all ; he could easily set up his works on the Continent and supply the British market from there.   Until 1883 the only remedy open to a British chemist who wished to carry on the patented process in Britain was for him to aqqly to the courts for revocation of the patent ; this was a costly business.   By the Patents, Designs and Trade Marks Act of 1883, the Board of Trade was empowered to compel patentees to grant licences when the patent was not being worked in the United Kingdom ; [1] but this innovation passed unnoticed at Manchester, where the Chamber of Commerce concerned itself almost exclusively with those parts of the Act which referred to trade-marks and designs.[2]

Interest in the patent laws strengthened with the formation in 1889 of a Chemical Section of the Manchester Chamber of Commerce, representing manufacturers, merchants, and users of chemicals.[3]   This was the first of the many sections through which most of the business of the Chamber is now conducted.   In its early years the Chemical Section was con-cerned to limit a patentee's right to amend the specifications of his patent.   Under the existing law, it was reported, a patentee

may now specify and claim almost anything that his speculative and imaginative mind may suggest, without ever having made a

---

[1] 46 and 47 Vict., c. 57, section 22.
[2] Annual Report for 1883, App., pp. 73-82, and below, Chapter XI.
[3] Proceedings, 28th January, 27th May, 6th June, and 18th July 1889.

single experiment to ascertain the possibility of the realisation of his dreams, so long as he is clever enough to make his original specification sufficiently wide and comprehensive, and to formulate it in such a manner as to permit . . . him from time to time to disclaim, correct, or explain, without in any way enlarging his claims.

The Chemical Section proposed as a remedy that patentees should specify what compounds they intended to include in a generic chemical term, and that they should deposit samples of the compounds at the Patent Office for examination and analysis ; [1] but the law remained unaltered until 1902.

Meanwhile the Chemical Section, under the chairmanship of Mr. Ivan Levinstein, had turned its attention to section 22 of the 1883 Act. For twenty years the non-working of patents by foreign patentees was to be one of the Section's chief problems. The law had from the first been almost a dead letter,[2] and in 1895 the Manchester Chamber of Commerce proposed an amendment : that the Board of Trade should grant compulsory licences if a patent had not been worked in the United Kingdom " on a scale large enough to satisfy requirements . . . within three years from the date of application ".[3] But the bill embodying this proposal never reached the statute-book.

In 1897 a firm of calico printers complained to the Chamber that it had to pay much higher prices for certain German dyes, for which patent rights were held, than were charged to consumers in other countries ; [4] German manufacturers were obviously profiting from the unsatisfactory state of British patent law. A joint deputation from Manchester and other Chambers of Commerce urged the Board of Trade to amend the Act of 1883. Mr. Levinstein, as a member of the deputation, argued that the existing law gave foreigners excessive privileges ; since section 22 was virtually a dead letter, foreign patentees had a period of fourteen years in which to exploit their inventions abroad without employing any British workmen, or contributing a penny to British rates and taxes. The Board of Trade was not convinced, however, that the law needed amendment ; it merely needed to be used more often.[5]

Not until 1902 was the patent law amended, and the Act of that year was far from satisfying Manchester. It made

---

[1] *Monthly Record*, May 1890 ; Proceedings, 13th May 1890.
[2] *Halsbury's Laws of England*, 2nd edn., Vol. 24, para. 1352, note 9.
[3] *Monthly Record*, June 1895.
[4] *Ibid.*, February 1897.   [5] *Ibid.*, April 1897.

only slight changes in the procedure by which an applicant could get a compulsory licence, and it expressly rejected the contention that a patent not worked in the United Kingdom should be either revoked or made subject to compulsory licensing :

If it is proved to the satisfaction of the Judicial Committee [of the Privy Council] that the patent is worked, or that the patented article is manufactured exclusively or mainly outside the United Kingdom, then, unless the patentee can show that the reasonable requirements of the public have been satisfied, the petitioner shall be entitled either to an order for a compulsory licence or to an order for the revocation of the patent.[1]

The new Act was, if anything, less favourable than the old to the British chemist who wished to work a patent held by a foreigner.   Under the old Act a petitioner could get a compulsory licence if the patent was not being worked in the United Kingdom ; under the new Act he could get a licence only if " the reasonable requirements of the public were not being met ", and it did not matter whether those requirements were being satisfied by British or foreign-made goods.

Not surprisingly, the Manchester Chamber of Commerce continued to agitate for reform of the patent law.   The United States and Britain were the only two countries which did not insist that patents registered there should be worked there ; in practice, however, the high tariff barriers of the United States made it necessary for the patentee to work his invention there, whereas free-trade Britain gave the patentee no such incentive.[2]   This argument came dangerously close to advocacy of Protection, and its chief protagonist in Manchester, Mr. Ivan Levinstein, was himself a protectionist, though he was also a Director of the Manchester Chamber of Commerce.[3]   The argument was attacked by the *Manchester Guardian* as an infringement of free-trade principles :

The effect of compulsory working would . . . be analogous to that of a protective tariff upon patented articles of foreign manufacture, in that it would force the establishment in this country of certain industries which are more economically carried on elsewhere. . . . The contention that compulsory working . . . would provide increased employment . . . rests upon the common

---

[1] The Patent Act, 1902 (2 Ed. VII, c. 34), sect. 3, cl. 5.
[2] *Monthly Record*, September 1904.
[3] *Ibid.*, February 1909.   Mr. Levinstein would have seconded a protectionist resolution moved by Mr. E. Burgis, but was unavoidably absent from the annual meeting.

fallacy that imports are either free gifts or are paid for with gold which somehow or other we get without working for it.[1]

Neither the Manchester Chamber of Commerce nor Lloyd George, the new President of the Board of Trade, paid any attention to this declaration. In 1907, largely owing to the insistence of the Chemical Section of the Manchester Chamber, a new Patent Act became law ; by section 27 of the Act,[2]

at any time not less than four years after the date of the patent and not less than one year after the passing of this Act, any person may apply to the comptroller for the revocation of the patent on the ground that the patented article or process is manufactured or carried on exclusively or mainly outside the United Kingdom.

In Manchester it was considered at first that the new Act was having a good effect. Under the old law we had been " hopelessly handicapping ourselves in the race for industrial supremacy " ; but under the new Act twenty factories had been built, scores of licences granted by foreign patentees to British manufacturers, and over £500,000 of foreign capital attracted to the United Kingdom. Among the new industries introduced were the manufacture of artificial indigo, office machinery, boot-making machinery, and electrical engineering goods.[3]

Satisfaction with the new Act did not last long. In 1909 the Manchester Chamber of Commerce had to oppose a reciprocal arrangement under which the working of patents in either Australia or Britain might be regarded as equivalent to working in the other. Manchester feared that as Australia was an agricultural country a Continental firm might establish a very small plant there, just large enough to satisfy Australian needs, and so " obtain a monopoly for the sale of its goods —possibly made on the Continent—in Great Britain, and thus defeat the working of the new British Patent Act ". The United States and Germany had made such an arrangement, but

similar arrangements by Great Britain, although on the first blush they may appear desirable, are not so in reality, for . . . both the United States and Germany are highly protective, whilst Great Britain is Free Trade, and matters are by no means equalised when a reciprocal arrangement has been made.[4]

---

[1] *Manchester Guardian*, 6th April 1906.
[2] Patent Act, 1907 (7 Ed. VII, c. 29).
[3] *Monthly Record*, October 1909.
[4] *Ibid.*, October 1909 ; Annual Report of the Chemical Section for 1909.

A more practical danger, though one not so quickly appreciated, arose from Mr. Justice Parker's judgement in Hatschek's case in 1909.[1] Mr. Justice Parker ruled that an applicant for revocation of a patent under section 27 of the 1907 Act must give *prima facie* evidence that a patent was being worked wholly or mainly abroad.   Not until 1913 did the Manchester Chamber of Commerce realise that the effect of this judgement had been to nullify section 27 ; it was manifestly impossible, so the Chamber held, to discover whether a patent was being sufficiently worked in the United Kingdom, without employing spies to find out what was going on in competitors' works.   In effect, the decision had " made practically inoperative the principal section of the Patent Act of 1907, namely Section 27 ".[2] The Manchester Chamber wished to make the patentee prove that his patent was being worked in Britain ; the decision in Hatschek's case put the onus of proof on the applicant. By March 1914, Manchester had persuaded the Association of British Chambers of Commerce to support its proposal for a bill reversing the decision in Hatschek's case,[3] but before any further steps could be taken, Britain was at war.   The government hurriedly passed an Act annulling the rights of enemy patent-holders, and Manchester had the gloomy satisfaction of pointing out that the Act would not have been necessary if Mr. Justice Parker's judgement had been reversed in good time.[4]

[1] *Times Law Reports*, Vol. 100, p. 809.
[2] Minutes of the Chemical Section, 28th January 1913.
[3] *Monthly Record*, September 1913 and March 1914.
[4] *Ibid.*, August 1914.

CHAPTER XI

LEGAL PROBLEMS: JUSTICE, COMMERCIAL LAW, AND TRADE MARKS

In this chapter legal technicalities will be avoided as much as possible, and attention will be concentrated upon the underlying economic conditions which led Manchester merchants to seek legal reforms. In broad outline it is easy to see what their motives were : first, they wanted cheap and ready justice from the courts ; secondly, from the legislature they wanted amendment of the law to suit the needs of commerce, and more particularly the needs of established firms in the cotton trade. At many points the law and the courts had not kept pace either with the growth of population or with changing trade customs ; Manchester wished to modernise the law.

A right which an individual cannot enforce is to him no right at all ; the dilatoriness of legal proceedings and their exorbitant cost, or the want of an easily accessible court, work greater and far more frequent injustice than the formal denial of a man's due rights.[1]

If this opinion had been available to them in the middle of the nineteenth century, Manchester merchants might have taken it for a text ; the Proceedings of the Manchester Chamber of Commerce are full of complaints of the expense and dilatoriness of the law. However, one of the most curious scandals that troubled the Manchester merchants arose not from the inherent defects of the legal system but from the personal idiosyncrasies of a judge, one of the Commissioners of the Manchester Bankruptcy Court. This gentleman appears to have modelled his life on Mr. Micawber ; he was

in the habit of contracting debts and evading their payment under circumstances inconsistent with the dignity of his office and with the due and impartial administration of justice in his Court.

---

[1] A. V. Dicey, *Law and Opinion in England* (2nd edn. 1914), pp. 205-6.

He had often been sued for the recovery of small debts, had been arrested by the Sheriff of Lancashire and only rescued by the intervention of an officer from the Bankruptcy Court. He had borrowed from the officers of his Court and from solicitors who practised in it ; he had even approached barristers with the same end in view.[1] The Manchester Chamber of Commerce and the Manchester Law Association co-operated to find a remedy for these evils, but were faced with the difficulty that judges were irremovable except after an address to the Crown from both Houses of Parliament.[2] Eventually the Chamber of Commerce took the grave step of petitioning for the judge's removal,[3] but after "private and positive assurances " that the judge would mend his ways the matter was allowed to drop.[4]

More serious were the difficulties caused by constitutional defects in the legal system. The legal business of Manchester had grown with the growth of the city, but the judges sat no more often than before ; the Manchester merchants agitated for many years before they could obtain sittings long enough for the swift hearing of lawsuits. In 1865 the Chamber of Commerce successfully joined with the Manchester Law Association in persuading the Lord Chancellor to arrange winter Assizes in Manchester for civil actions.[5] In 1872 there were loud complaints of the congestion in the Manchester Bankruptcy Court. For six months of the year the judge sat in this Court for only eight days a month ; at other times during this period he would be inaccessible to suitors. The Manchester Chamber of Commerce proposed to the Lord Chancellor that the Manchester and Salford County Courts should be amalgamated so that one judge would always be available for bankruptcy business; though the Lord Chancellor could not agree to this proposal, he met the substance of the complaints by arranging for the judge to sit more often.[6] It is unlikely that the judge was pleased with this addition to his duties, if only because the court (where he dispatched on an average thirteen cases a day) was a room no more than ten feet square.[7] Since 1867 the Chamber had been supporting

[1] Proceedings, 7th March 1859.
[2] Ibid., 12th and 28th April, and 19th July 1858.
[3] Ibid., 22nd July 1858, and 7th March 1859.
[4] Annual Report for 1859, pp. 5-6.
[5] Ibid., 1865, p. 9.
[6] Proceedings, 27th March ; Annual Report for 1872, p. 9.
[7] Proceedings, 23rd June 1873.

the judge's demand for a new Court, but not until 1873 did the Office of Works agree even to look for a site.[1]

By 1877, arrears of business at the Civil Assizes were again becoming formidable. Towards the close of an Assize often " two, three, or even four courts were sitting simultaneously for civil business " ; counsel found that they were due to conduct two cases at once, and many of the cases were " ultimately either hastily arranged or driven to arbitration ". The Chamber of Commerce prayed that as the present arrangements were " in effect a denial of justice " a fourth sitting should be held that year, and the prayer was granted.[2] However, the court continued to sit three times a year and no more, with the result that in the Queen's Bench Division of the Assize congestion was as bad as ever. The Manchester Chamber of Commerce therefore proposed that the assize system should come to an end in " large and populous commercial districts " ; in such places the High Court should sit " for fixed periods corresponding to the sittings which are now held in the metropolis ".[3] A Bill providing for continuous sittings of the High Court in provincial centres was introduced into the House of Commons every year from 1883 to 1886, but it never got further than a second reading.[4] In alliance with Liverpool, Manchester returned to the attack in 1892 ; the two Chambers of Commerce suggested that the High Court should in alternate years sit continuously at Manchester and Liverpool, but after three years' agitation the Lord Chancellor had made only minor concessions.[5] Business at the court continued to grow, and in response to fresh complaints of delay the sittings of the Civil Assize at Manchester were lengthened in 1909 from two to three weeks ; [6] but to this day only London has the benefit of continuous sittings of the High Court.

Until 1883 the Manchester Assize judges were not competent to try Chancery cases, which were always heard in London. Centralisation of justice in this way had not been a grievance when the Court of Chancery had proceeded entirely by affidavit and interrogation, but after the reforms of 1850-73

[1] Annual Reports, 1867, p. 20, 1868, p. 5 ; Proceedings, 9th July, 29th and 31st October 1873.

[2] Ibid., 25th April 1877, 30th January 1878 ; Annual Report for 1878, p. 13.

[3] Proceedings, 15th June 1883.   [4] Annual Reports, 1883-6.

[5] Proceedings, 27th July 1892, 25th January and 20th July 1893 ; Monthly Record, January 1896.

[6] Ibid., May and July 1909.

the Court often required witnesses to be present in person. Since " witness causes " were allotted only two or three days a week, a suitor might have to take his witnesses up to London week after week in readiness for the trial. It was widely held that this arrangement amounted to " a practical denial of justice in matters involving comparatively small claims ".[1] The Lord Chancellor quickly responded to complaints by appointing a Chancery judge to hear witness causes at Manchester; the Chamber of Commerce promptly asked that other Chancery cases, and cases in the Probate, Divorce and Admiralty Division, might also be heard in Manchester, but the Lord Chancellor would not go so far as that.[2]

The Manchester merchants felt that the opening of the Ship Canal in 1894 would strengthen the case for an Admiralty Court at Manchester; in 1893, when the canal was nearing completion, they accordingly memorialised the Lord Chancellor on the subject. The Liverpool County Court had Admiralty jurisdiction to within six miles of Manchester ; the Manchester and Salford courts had none. The Chamber of Commerce suggested that either or both of these courts at Manchester and Salford should " have Admiralty jurisdiction . . . from the docks at Eastham over the whole length of the canal, including the docks at Manchester, Salford, Runcorn and Ellesmere port ".[3] Though the whole of this demand was not met, the Manchester County Court did shortly become the court of first instance for Admiralty cases in the district.[4]

Slow and costly legal proceedings naturally provoked the thought that technical commercial disputes might be best settled by special tribunals staffed by men who were experts in commerce rather than law. Already in 1858 a Tribunals of Commerce Association had been established, though for some years it failed to arouse the active interest of the Manchester merchants.[5] Not until 1865 did the establishment of Tribunals of Commerce become a favourite topic of discussion at Manchester. The Secretary and President of the Manchester Chamber often acted as arbitrators in the settlement of disputes, but

to compel gentlemen to stay here day after day, to hear lawyers make long speeches and examine witnesses, was a task which no

[1] Proceedings, 8th February 1883.
[2] *Ibid.*, 7th July 1884 ; Annual Report for 1884, p. 14.
[3] *Monthly Record*, December 1893.   [4] *Ibid.*, April 1894.
[5] Proceedings, 19th July 1858 ; see also *ibid.*, 28th October 1861.

Director of the Manchester Chamber of Commerce would like to undertake.[1]

Despite this opposition, the advocates of commercial arbitration persisted with their schemes. They argued that in the ordinary courts of law commercial considerations were subordinated to legal forms, and that tribunals elected by the Chambers of Commerce would give better decisions more quickly and at less expense ; such tribunals were said to be working well in France and other countries.[2] A referendum of the Chamber's members showed, however, that interest in Tribunals of Commerce was confined to a few enthusiasts. Less than one-third of the Chamber's 437 members voted in the referendum, and the plan for tribunals secured only a narrow majority ; several Directors refused to help in setting up the tribunal, which never had a case to settle and quickly died of inanition.[3]

A glaring example of the costliness of legal proceedings provided the impetus that led to the establishment of a new tribunal in 1881. The case of Provand v. Riley had dragged on from 1876 to 1880, costing the litigants over £4,000, though the amount in dispute was less than £1,600 ; coming as it did after a long series of complaints about congestion at the Manchester Assizes, this case persuaded the Chamber of Commerce to set up what was now called a " Tribunal of Arbitration ".[4] The Board of Directors of the Manchester Chamber of Commerce were to choose a registrar and a panel of arbitrators ; parties to a dispute, having bound themselves to abide by the Tribunal's decision, were to choose one or three arbitrators to hear the case.[5] By the end of 1881 the Tribunal was in full working order, and in the course of the next year several cases were heard ; they related mainly to " questions of defective quality and length of goods, imperfect printing and dyeing and the like, questions eminently fitted for the decision of a tribunal so constituted ".[6] Such cases formed, however, only a small proportion of the disputes arising in the course of trade, and consequently the scope of the Tribunal's work

[1] Proceedings, 10th May 1865.
[2] Ibid., 18th October and 9th November 1865.
[3] Ibid., May and 24th October 1866 ; Annual Report for 1866, p. 10 ; Proceedings, 28th January 1867.
[4] Manchester Guardian, 4th May 1880.
[5] The Constitution is printed as an appendix to the Annual Report for 1880.
[6] Annual Reports, 1881, p. 8, and 1882, App. p. 85.

remained limited; even in one of its busiest years (1908) it had only ninety-one cases. The Tribunal never published reports of its decisions, or of the reasons which had led to them. It argued that publicity would limit the freedom of arbitrators, and would set precedents, whereas each case should be considered on its merits; publicity would also discourage arbitrators from serving.[1] It may well be, however, that lack of publicity discouraged business men from applying to a tribunal which worked on unknown principles and whose decisions would therefore be even less predictable than those of an ordinary law court.

The Manchester Chamber of Commerce was not only anxious to improve the administration of justice, but also to reform the law itself when the interests of trade seemed to be threatened. The Chamber's early dissatisfaction with the law of bankruptcy has been recorded elsewhere;[2] after 1860, as before, there were few years in which the Chamber did not detect some anomaly and propose some reform in this department of law.[3] As the Chamber represented successful business men it naturally pressed the claims of creditors. In 1861 it welcomed a report that the government was to introduce an amending Bill, and hoped that it would simplify procedure; the existing laws were condemned as " defective, expensive and uncertain in their administration ".[4] The Act of 1861 did not entirely meet Manchester's wishes, but met with general approval.[5] The Chamber continued to resist the abolition of imprisonment for debt; it was considered that to relieve debtors in this way would extend " a system, already carried too far, of undue sympathy with the insolvent or fraudulent trader ".[6] Reform of the bankruptcy laws should accompany any measures to relieve debtors; and this is what actually happened in 1869.[7] The Act of 1883, which provided for the appointment of an official receiver to administer the bankrupt's estate, embodied many suggestions made by the Manchester Chamber of

[1] Proceedings, 29th July 1914.
[2] A. Redford, *Manchester Merchants and Foreign Trade, 1794-1858*, especially pp. 214-15.
[3] E.g. Proceedings, 1st March 1858, 7th November 1859, and 14th November 1860.
[4] *Ibid.*, 7th January 1861.
[5] Annual Report for 1861, p. 11.
[6] Proceedings, 5th April 1865.
[7] *Ibid.*, 26th April 1869; Annual Report for 1869, p. 9.

Commerce in 1881, when a Bankruptcy Bill had been introduced but had failed to pass.[1] After 1883 the bankruptcy law in general satisfied the Manchester merchants ; on points of detail the law could still be improved, and one grievance in particular—the right of landlords to distrain for rent— caused much heart-burning.[2] In 1890, however, this preferential treatment of landlords was severely restricted. An Act of that year limited to six months the arrears of rent for which the landlord could distrain ; any further arrears would have to be met in the ordinary way by a dividend on the bankrupt's estate.

Amendment of the law of contract to suit the needs of Manchester trade was less easy. By section 17 of the Statute of Frauds (29 Car. II., c. 3), verbal contracts were not binding ; in 1864 the Huddersfield Chamber of Commerce solicited and received the support of the Manchester merchants in petitioning unsuccessfully for the repeal of the section.[3] As the Manchester Chamber explained to the House of Commons,

the mode of doing business on the Manchester Exchange, where property to the value of many hundred thousand pounds daily changes hands, is entirely at variance with the statute, orders being given and accepted without the passage of any writing whatsoever.

In 1865 and in subsequent years, therefore, the Manchester Chamber of Commerce acted independently to secure the repeal of the obnoxious section.[4] After 1869, perhaps because trade was recovering from the breakdown of 1866, the Manchester Chamber stopped agitating for this particular reform ; the law remained unchanged until 1954 although it was long regarded in Manchester " in no other light than as an inducement to fraud ".[5]

From its earliest years, the Manchester Chamber of Commerce took an active interest in partnership law, and especially in proposals to register partnerships and the names of partners. In 1858 the Chamber found itself in two minds about a Bill for the registration of partnerships bequeathed to it by the Manchester Commercial Association, which it had

---

[1] Annual Report for 1883, p. 15.
[2] E.g. Proceedings, 26th October 1885 and 29th April 1889.
[3] *Ibid.*, 13th January 1864.
[4] *Ibid.*, 3rd May 1865 and 28th April 1869 ; Annual Reports for 1868, p. 18, and 1869, p. 10.
[5] *Ibid.*, 1865, p. 13.

just absorbed.[1]   The Board of Directors was divided equally
in favour of and against registration, and among Manchester
merchants in general opinions were similarly divided.[2]   By
1865, when a Bill was introduced to extend the principle of
limited liability to partnerships, the Chamber showed that
it was moving with the times ; previously it had opposed
limited liability, but now it accepted the change, demanding
only that limited partnerships should be registered and subject
to full publicity.[3]   In 1872 the Chamber went further still,
and supported a proposal for the registration of all partnerships ; it was especially anxious that the register should
include the names and addresses of all the partners of foreign
firms operating in this country.[4]   By 1874, however, when other
Chambers of Commerce promoted a slightly more stringent
Bill, the Manchester Chamber had reverted to its original
position ; it considered that the interference of the government was undesirable, inasmuch as the names of members
of firms could be easily ascertained on inquiry, and traders
should not be relieved from a personal responsibility.   It was
already the practice of respectable firms to give full publicity
to any changes either in respect of admission or retirement of
partners ; and as the Bill would lead to the creation of a staff
of officials and the unnecessary expenditure of public money,
whilst at the same time it would be expensive to traders,
the Chamber hoped that Parliament would reject the Bill—
which it did.[5]   By the end of the century the Chamber had
again changed its mind, but several Bills for the registration of partnerships failed to pass ; unsuccessful Bills were
still being supported as late as 1914.[6]

Most business men of early Victorian times distrusted the
principle of limited liability ; the Manchester merchants
had fought hard to prevent the Bills of 1855 and 1856 from
becoming law, and experience of their working did not
remove the distrust.   According to local observation, the new
laws had not "shown that diminished pecuniary liability tends
either to increase moral responsibility, to remunerate the share-
holders, or to benefit the community ".   A Bill of 1858 which
proposed to extend limited liability to joint-stock banks was
considered " particularly inopportune, since proofs are but too
recent and glaring of great carelessness and criminality in the

---

[1] Redford, op. cit., Chapter XVII.
[2] Proceedings, 1st March, 17th May, and 7th June 1858.
[3] Ibid., 15th March 1865.   [4] Ibid., 27th March, 1872.
[5] Annual Report for 1874, p. 9.   [6] Proceedings, 8th July 1914.

conduct of some such establishments ".[1] By 1865, however, opposition had so far weakened that in principle Manchester did not object to limited partnerships.[2] The crisis of 1866 caused a revulsion of feeling. Even before the collapse of Overend, Gurney and Co., Mr. Thomas Bazley had issued a mild warning against the " enormous speculative investments " which were being undertaken in Britain : " unless we kept the investment at home within moderate bounds, he feared that some inconvenience would really be experienced." [3] After the crash, Manchester business men generally blamed the joint-stock companies ; finance companies were specially singled out for condemnation.[4] Nevertheless, opinion on the value of limited liability was too diverse at Manchester for the Chamber of Commerce to offer evidence at the inquiry into the subject in 1867.[5]

A common complaint against the early limited liability companies had been that they drew away capital into unproductive or speculative channels. Of the 339 provisional registrations in 1853 only thirty were proposals for " conducting manufactures, working patents, etc." ; the largest group was of public utilities, and insurance companies were also prominent.[6] Professor Leone Levi expressed the same complaint in 1868 when he pointed out that " money was going away from trade and manufacture to companies of all kinds ".[7] Within ten years, however, the " Oldham Limiteds " showed that the principle of limited liability could be applied quite efficiently to manufacturing industry. In 1874 some Oldham business men had wagered that by the end of February, 1875, one new limited spinning company would have been floated every week ; and by 1st February only three more companies were needed to complete the total. Mr. Hugh Mason warned the Manchester merchants that

the future of these companies was perilous. . . . The time would come, as it came in every trade, and had come in the cotton trade over and over again, when trade would be depressed and these limited liability companies would, he feared, come to grief.

The companies not only competed for scarce labour and depressed the rate of profit ; they also, by borrowing from the

[1] Proceedings, 10th May 1858.   [2] See above, p. 137.
[3] Annual Meeting, 29th January 1866.
[4] Manchester Guardian, 4th December 1866.
[5] Proceedings, 27th March 1867 ; Manchester Guardian, 3rd May 1867.
[6] J. H. Clapham, op. cit., Vol. II, p. 135.
[7] Manchester Guardian, 24th January 1868.

operatives, threatened " the hard-earned savings of a life-time ".
Very commonly half the capital resources consisted of loans, and
the dividends, which were declared on share capital only, "gave
a rather fictitious show of prosperity to the cotton trade ".[1]

Despite this warning the Manchester Chamber of Commerce did not protest against the contemporary methods
of company promotion until the depression of the cotton
trade became severe in 1885. Though the Chamber had no
definitive views to submit to the Royal Commission on the
Depression of Trade and Industry in that year, the replies
of individual Manchester merchants to the Commission's
questionnaire all agreed with this typical opinion :

There can be no doubt that much of the late overproduction is
due to the ease with which cotton mills can be built owing to
the Limited Liability Act of 1862, which certainly led to excessive
extensions in Oldham during the last ten years.[2]

From complaints about the working of the Act to demands for
a more stringent company law was not a long step. In
November 1886 the President of the Manchester Chamber
declared that there was " undoubtedly too much building of
factories " and " decided room for improving the Act ".[3]
The Chamber's proposals for amendment of the law were
therefore designed to make the flotation of companies more
difficult : 10 per cent. of the capital of every new company
should be paid on applying for shares, and a further 10 per
cent. on allotment; until 75 per cent. of the capital had been
paid up, not more than $2\frac{1}{2}$ per cent. of the capital should be
spent.[4] Early in 1887 a joint deputation from the Chamber
of Commerce and the Cotton Spinners' Association pressed
these views on the President of the Board of Trade, and made
further proposals to check the " excessive and uncalled-for
erection of cotton mills "; borrowing powers should be
restricted, and misleading accountancy punished.[5] The Manchester merchants agitated continuously for this programme of
reform during the next few years,[6] but not until 1890 was any
change in the law effected.

[1] Annual Meeting, 1st February 1875.
[2] Manchester replies to the questionnaire are printed in Appendix A of
the 1st Report (*Parliamentary Papers*, 1886, Vol. XXI, pp. 97-105).
[3] *Manchester Guardian*, 2nd November 1886.
[4] Proceedings, 5th November 1886 and 3rd March 1887.
[5] *Ibid.*, 26th January 1887 ; *Manchester Guardian*, 29th January 1887 ;
Proceedings, 9th and 17th February and 20th June 1887.
[6] Annual Reports for 1887, p. 11, and 1889, p. 15.

The Acts passed in that year did not satisfy the demands of the Manchester reformers. The only drastic change made was a clause in the Directors Liability Act that made directors liable if they negligently made false statements ; previously they had been liable only if they had intended to deceive.[1] Separate action having failed, Manchester enlisted the support of the Chambers of Commerce at Liverpool, Oldham, Blackburn, Leeds, Halifax, and Macclesfield, for its programme of reform ; but the Bill embodying its proposals never got beyond a second reading.[2] Eventually the Companies Act of 1900 met most of the Chamber's demands : by this Act, directors had to take up a certain holding of shares ; they could not proceed to allot shares until the minimum subscription fixed by the articles had been paid ; the company was to declare to the Registrar the mortgages and charges with which it was burdened.[3] The Manchester Chamber welcomed the Act as " a step towards the more effective protection and encouragement of legitimate commercial enterprise ".[4]

Though in details the Manchester Chamber of Commerce still criticised company law and wished for further protection of shareholders and creditors, its old hostility to limited liability had quite died out by the end of the century ; the Limited Partnerships Act of 1907, granting limited liability to companies with fewer than seven shareholders, was welcomed as opening " a fresh channel for the employment of capital ".[5] Manchester business men had thought very differently in 1856, and even in 1886. Their surrender to the principle of limited liability was not a triumph of logic over conservatism, but a tribute to renewed prosperity for Oldham Limiteds and private spinners alike ; it reflected a genuine improvement in the conduct of joint-stock companies and in the profits of the cotton trade.

The modern development of the law concerning trademarks began in the eighteenth century ; by the middle of the nineteenth century, the courts had fully recognised the right to property in trade-marks, but statutory recognition did not

---

[1] R. R. Formoy, *Historical Foundations of Modern Company Law* (1923), p. 3.
[2] Proceedings, 14th February and 19th May 1890, 21st January and 22nd July 1891, 27th April 1892, 26th April 1893.
[3] R. R. Formoy, *op. cit.*, pp. 141-3.
[4] Annual Report of the Home Trade Section for 1900.
[5] *Monthly Record*, October 1906.

come until after the passing of the Trade Marks Registration Act of 1875.[1] The Manchester Chamber of Commerce had been reasonably content with the protection given hitherto by the courts, and in 1873 had urged that the law should not be altered without careful consideration. The Act of 1875 set up a register of trade-marks, and provided that unregistered marks should not be protected in the courts ; this provision apparently took the Manchester merchants by surprise, for they complained in 1876 that the expense of registering the numerous marks used in the cotton trade would be very heavy, and that failure to register would deprive many merchants of marks they had owned a long time.[2] However, the protest did not develop into an attack on the principle of registration ; for the time allowed for registration was extended, a local office was established in Manchester for the preliminary registration of cotton marks, and a committee of experts, nominated by the Chamber of Commerce, was appointed by the Lord Chancellor to advise the Registrar on difficult cases.[3]

Before 1875 the Manchester Chamber had not needed to take action about trade-marks ; but thereafter trade-marks figured prominently in the Chamber's history. Many of the problems raised were too technical to be readily understood by anybody not in the trade.[4] Three of the more general problems that engaged the attention of the Chamber of Commerce concerned (a) the location of the cotton-marks register ; (b) the sort of marks that ought not to be registered ; and (c) the trade-mark law of the Empire. The first problem arose because the register was kept in London, though the trade and most of the merchants were at Manchester ; as we have already seen, the Registrar allayed complaints by setting up a subsidiary office at Manchester in 1876. This office had no power to register marks, but it did allow merchants to complete all necessary formalities at Manchester and saved them from applying in person at the London office for the registration of their marks. In 1883, however, after the passing of the Patents, Designs and Trade Marks Act, administrative changes weakened the position of the Manchester office in favour of the central register. The Manchester

---

[1] E. Jenks, *Short History of English Law* (1912), pp. 290-1 ; Sir W. S. Holdsworth, *History of English Law*, Vol. VIII, p. 430.
[2] Proceedings, 16th February 1876.   [3] Annual Report for 1876, p. 6.
[4] *Ibid.*, 1886, p. 14.

merchants reacted strongly against the tendency to centralise the work in London, arguing that as 50 per cent. of the old marks belonged to cotton firms and over 40 per cent of the new applications came from the cotton trade, the Manchester office should, like the Sheffield one, have the power to register marks.[1] On occasions too numerous to mention, the Chamber of Commerce asked that the register might be established at Manchester ; eventually this persistence was rewarded, for by the Trade Marks Act of 1905 the Manchester office was empowered to register cotton marks, subject only to the veto of the Registrar in London.[2]

When registration began in 1875 there were already 50,000 cotton marks in England,[3] and merchants needed all their ingenuity to think of new ones. They were often tempted to use words instead of pictures or symbols. The first merchant to appropriate a particular word as his own trademark might gain a considerable advantage over his competitors ; the Manchester Chamber of Commerce therefore set its face against the registration of word-marks. The Act of 1875 had prohibited the use of word-marks, but in 1883, " fancy words " became registrable ; from the first the Manchester Chamber opposed this change in the law,[4] but (despite repeated demands for an amending Bill) the use of word-marks for cotton goods was not prohibited until 1905.[5]

The idea of registering trade-marks quickly spread from Britain to other parts of the Empire ; and there was a danger that marks accepted in Britain as the property of one merchant might be registered elsewhere as the property of another. In 1879, when the Government of India was proposing to set up a trade-marks register, Manchester merchants suggested that registration in Britain should be accepted as proof of ownership in India as well, and that such marks should be registered in India for half the usual fee.[6] Nothing came of the proposed register then, or in 1903, when Manchester disputed the usefulness of setting up an Indian register for cotton marks at all, on the ground that the existing law gave adequate protection.[7] Not until 1938 was an Indian registry set up.

[1] Letter of 21st July 1883 to the Board of Trade.
[2] 5 Ed. VII, c. 15, s. 64, cl. 3-6.
[3] Annual Meeting, 31st January 1887.
[4] Petitions of 3rd March 1885 and 27th July 1888 ; *Monthly Record,* July 1890.
[5] Trade Marks Act, 1905 (5 Ed. VII, c. 15, s. 64, cl. 10).
[6] Annual Reports for 1879, p. 17 and 1880, p. 14.
[7] *Monthly Record,* April 1903.

In 1902 the Manchester merchants successfully opposed a similar project for a trade-marks register at Lagos.[1]

Commercial morality demanded that no merchant should pirate another's trade-mark; it also demanded that no merchant should falsely label the length of a roll of cloth, and that no spinner should reel and sell yarns purporting to be of a finer count than they really were. Before the eighteen-eighties, complaints about these abuses were very rare; apart from a solitary instance in 1859,[2] the records of the Manchester Chamber of Commerce do not refer to this form of fraud until 1881. This does not mean that false-folding and short-reeling were invented in 1881, but only that before then the fraud had not been so widespread as to require the attention of the Chamber of Commerce. In that year the Chambers of Commerce at Calcutta and Bombay sought the co-operation of the Manchester Chamber against the practice of giving short measure in rolls of cloth. Although English law required the use of a 36 in. yard, the custom of the trade allowed goods to be measured and folded in " yards " of 35½, 36½ or 37 inches; unscrupulous merchants could take advantage of these discrepancies to give short measure. In theory the practice was illegal, but in fact the ultimate buyer was often deceived and did not even know that he was the victim of a fraud.[3] The publication of the correspondence between the Manchester and Indian Chambers of Commerce checked the fraud for a few years, but by 1886 it had revived in a subtler form that was clearly intended to deceive, but in fact did not break the law. This feat could be performed in two ways: by omitting the word " yards " after the figure stamped on the cloths, or by folding the cloths in such a way " as to convey the impression that they are ordinary standard length, whereas in point of fact they are one, two, or more yards short of that length ".[4]

At first the Manchester Chamber of Commerce used voluntary methods to end false-folding : it drew up a declaration by which signatories undertook to mark the number of yards on the pieces of cloth they exported. All shippers trading to India were invited to sign the declaration in the

[1] Monthly Record November 1902 and April 1903
[2] Annual Report for 1859, p. 13.
[3] *Ibid.*, 1881, p. 10, and App., pp. 63-8.
[4] *Ibid.*, 1886, p. 20.

hope that, if a large majority did so, the minority would be placed in an embarrassing position. If they refused to mark the number of yards their goods would be suspect; if they did mark the number of yards but still gave short measure they would be liable to prosecution.[1] By the end of January 1887 only thirty-two shippers had signed the declaration, though it was estimated that at least a hundred Manchester firms shipped cotton goods to India.[2] The attempt to shame the fraudulent into good behaviour had therefore to be given up, and the Chamber of Commerce decided to secure an amendment of the law; two local M.P.s, Mr. Isaac Hoyle and Mr. Frank Hardcastle, succeeded in getting a clause inserted in the Merchandise Marks Act of 1887 that effectively closed the loophole.[3]

In successfully amending the English law, the Manchester merchants had won only half the battle; it remained to enforce similar penalties for false trade descriptions in India. The Indian Government quickly responded to the demand for a Merchandise Marks Act; a measure was framed that closely followed the provisions of the English Act, and "produced excellent results" from the beginning.[4] In 1893, with the hearty support of the Manchester merchants, false-folding was prohibited in the colony of Lagos; they also pressed for similar enactments in the other West African colonies, and by the end of 1894 the necessary laws had been passed.

The false-folding of piece goods had its counterpart in the yarn trade, in the fraudulent practice known as short-reeling. This consisted of reeling coarser yarns than were shown on the label, and hiding the fraud by making up hanks shorter than the usual length of 840 yards; the ultimate buyer got the weight of yarn he ordered, but of a coarser count and a shorter length than he was entitled to. Short-reeling therefore cheated the buyer in two respects at once.

For some years the Merchandise Marks Acts in England and India held short-reeling in check, but in 1901 Manchester merchants complained that up-country Indian mills were not observing the Act and were exporting short-reeled yarn to the Far East in unfair competition with legally reeled Lancashire

[1] Proceedings, 27th October 1886.
[2] Annual Meeting, 31st January 1887.
[3] Proceedings, 23rd February and 25th July 1887 ; Annual Report for 1887, p. 16 ; 50 and 51 Vict., c. 28, s. 1 and s. 3.
[4] Annual Report for 1889, p. 17.

yarns.[1] The inquiry of 1888 [2] had shown that Indian mills already had enough natural advantages in competing with Lancashire yarns in Far Eastern markets ; Manchester was determined that they should not have artificial advantages as well. It was not until 1905, however, that the Chamber of Commerce could persuade the Indian Government to enforce the Act as rigidly for exports of Indian yarn as the British Government enforced it for Lancashire yarn.[3] At the same time stricter administration of the law stopped short-reeling of Indian yarn intended for sale in India ; the Manchester merchants welcomed this stricter observance of the law : " Lancashire yarns [they considered] will no longer be met in India itself by the illicit competition of Indian mills ".[4] Indian administration of the law soon declined, however, from full vigour ; by 1913, Indian short-reeled yarns were again invading Far Eastern markets, especially the great entrepôt centre at Singapore. As Singapore was a free port and lacked even a Customs House, the Manchester Chamber of Commerce applied in vain to the authorities there for en-forcement of the law. An approach to the Siamese Govern-ment in 1918 was equally fruitless ; Siam was bound by treaty (so the Chamber was told) not to interfere with the course of trade ; and without the consent of all signatories, it could not suppress the trade in short-reeled yarns.[5]

[1] Proceedings, 27th September and 11th October 1901.
[2] *Bombay and Lancashire Cotton Spinning Inquiry* ; see above pp. 36-42.
[3] *Monthly Record*, April and December 1904, January and May 1905.
[4] Annual Report for 1906, p. 3.
[5] *Monthly Record*, 1913-18 *passim*, especially December 1917, September and November 1918, and April 1919.

CHAPTER XII

POSTAL SERVICES AND TELEGRAPHS

In the first half of the nineteenth century the slowness and cost of the inland postal services gave the Manchester merchants frequent cause for complaints ;[1] after 1850 these complaints, though not entirely stilled, were much less frequent. Overseas mails, however, remained a bone of contention between the Post Office and the Manchester merchants long after the organisation of the inland mails had been satisfactorily settled ; and the new services of telegraphs and telephones brought also new problems with them.

Complaints about inland mails, though few, could not be entirely ignored. In November 1859, the 9.15 a.m. mail train from London to Manchester was abruptly discontinued, much to the inconvenience of the shipping merchants in Manchester. Inquiry showed that it was not the Post Office but the railway company that was to blame for the alteration ; the London and North Western Railway had acted without consulting the Post Office, which would be quite glad if the mails could travel at the usual time, but would not incur the expense of a special train. Joint pressure from the Post Office and the Manchester Chamber of Commerce soon persuaded the railway company to restore and even improve the old service ; from 1st February 1860 the mail train was to leave London at 9.0 a.m. and reach Manchester by 3.15 p.m.[2]

In 1868 the Manchester merchants became aware that the local collection and delivery of mail compared very unfavourably with collection and delivery in other commercial centres. Birmingham had four deliveries a day for 50,000 letters, Glasgow five deliveries for 60,000 and Liverpool six deliveries for 65,000 ; but at Manchester there were only three deliveries for 75,000 letters. A memorial to the Postmaster General quickly brought reform. The Post Office promised to increase the number of collections from four to six ; the number

[1] A. Redford, *Manchester Merchants and Foreign Trade, 1794-1858*, pp. 188-95.
[2] Proceedings, 7th and 28th November 1859 ; Annual Report for 1859, p. 10.

of deliveries was to be increased from three to five in the busiest parts of the city, and from three to four elsewhere.[1] The authorities did not always react so promptly ; by 1875 the increase of the mails and the addition of the Telegraph and Savings Bank departments had resulted in great congestion at the Manchester Post Office. A deputation from the Manchester Chamber persuaded Sir Stafford Northcote, the Chancellor of the Exchequer, that a new Post Office ought to be built ; and by the end of 1875 the Chamber of Commerce and the Office of Works had agreed on a site. Three years later the site had been cleared, but two more years elapsed before a start was made on the new building ; the Chamber expressed its impatience at this delay, but the government was not to be hurried and Manchester's new Post Office in Spring Gardens was not finished until 1884.[2]

Overseas mail services raised many important problems which demanded the attention of the Manchester Chamber of Commerce at frequent intervals. The West Indian and South American mails formed the subject of a fairly steady agitation for more than thirty years. In the interests of speed, it was desirable that the mail packets should call at Falmouth, the most westerly port on the English Channel ; the Post Office had formerly been able to reject any such proposal on the ground that Falmouth lacked the necessary railway and docks, but by 1863 this was no longer true. The Manchester Chamber of Commerce therefore renewed its demands for the use of Falmouth as a packet station with more confidence than before : Falmouth had been a packet station as early as 1688 and as recently as 1852.[3] Nevertheless, the Post Office did not yield at all until 1867, and then only an inch. In that year Falmouth became the port of arrival for the West Indian mails ; out-going mail still went from Southampton.[4]

When the South African mail contract came up for renewal in 1868, Manchester was active in pointing out the advantages of Falmouth over Plymouth as a packet station ; to land the mail at Falmouth would save three or four hours, but apparently

---

[1] Proceedings, 24th June, 29th July, and 26th August 1868.

[2] Ibid., 24th February, 29th September, and 6th December 1875 ; 8th and 31st July 1878; Annual Reports for 1879, p. 17, for 1880, pp. 16 and 38.

[3] Ibid., for 1863, p. 12, for 1864, p. 10 ; Proceedings, 16th March and 27th April 1864.

[4] Ibid., 29th May 1867.

the Post Office did not consider this argument strong enough to justify the change.[1] Within a few years Falmouth had evidently lost even its slight hold on the West Indian mail contract, for in 1874 the government proposed to make Southampton the port for incoming as well as outgoing mail ; Manchester protested strongly against the change, which would delay mails for the North by at least twelve and sometimes twenty-four hours. The plea for the use of Falmouth was renewed ; failing that, Plymouth should continue to be the packet station. On this occasion the Post Office agreed to the compromise suggested, and the mail continued to land at Plymouth.[2] In 1891, when there appeared to be some danger that Plymouth would be displaced by Southampton as the packet station for South African mails, the Manchester Chamber of Commerce once again memorialised the Post Office against the change, on the ground that it would delay mails to the North by eight or ten hours.[3]

Plymouth was preferable to Southampton as the packet station for South American mails, but for North American mails the advantage lay with Southampton. By 1884, mail was despatched three times a week to New York by British steamers from Queenstown. The Manchester merchants believed that a fourth dispatch by the North German Lloyd line ought to be instituted ; the German steamers sailed from Southampton on Thursdays, and if they carried British mail letters posted in Manchester on Wednesday evening or Thursday morning would reach New York by Friday evening or Saturday morning of the following week, in time to be answered on Saturday. If the mail had to wait for a sailing from Queenstown, it would rarely reach New York before the Monday morning. In August 1884 the Chamber of Commerce forwarded to the Post Office a memorial signed by over fifty American houses in Manchester, praying for the dispatch of mails from Southampton as well as Queenstown. The following April the Manchester Chamber repeated its request in sharper terms :

It is difficult to make the trading class hereabouts understand why a great public department should turn its back upon those increased facilities, against which no competent financial—and, it is to be hoped, no vital departmental—arguments can be adduced.

[1] Proceedings, 24th June 1868.
[2] *Ibid.*, 24th June 1874 ; Annual Report for 1874, p. 11.
[3] Proceedings, 29th May 1891.

Actually the Chamber was mistaken, as the Post Office did send letters by the North German Lloyd line, but only if they were endorsed " *Via* Southampton " ; by the terms of the contract with the British lines, the Post Office was obliged to send letters not so endorsed *via* Queenstown.

The Manchester merchants were not convinced by this apparently reasonable explanation, and continued to press for a less casual arrangement with the German line.   In 1886, after a parliamentary inquiry, Southampton became a regular packet station for North American mails, and of the eleven vessels used (averaging 16 knots) five belonged to the North German Lloyd line.[1] At the same time the Manchester Chamber of Commerce emphasised that it was

not wanting in respect and gratitude to the great Atlantic Line Companies which have worked so splendidly the mail service *via* Queenstown ; . . . they would see with regret any diminution in the chances of efficiency of the present Liverpool and Queenstown service.[2]

A generation later, in 1909, Manchester asked that the Cunard liners sailing from Liverpool should be relieved from the duty of calling at Queenstown for mail ; but on this occasion the Post Office would not agree.[3]

The speed and frequency of the mail service to the Continent apparently gave the Manchester merchants little cause for complaint, but the Indian and Far Eastern service was less satisfactory.   In 1863, grievances about the postal service to China called for redress.   A French packet left Marseilles for China on the 19th of each month ; as the British Post Office did not prepare mail for that service, however, merchants wishing to use it had to forward correspondence to an agent at Marseilles. The Manchester merchants therefore asked that in future the Post Office should prepare mail for the French steamers ; and to this proposal the Postmaster General raised no objection.[4]   In the new contract for the Indian and China mails signed in 1868, further causes for dissatisfaction appeared. The Peninsular and Oriental Company had stipulated that Penang should be omitted from the ports of call ; the Manchester Chamber of Commerce protested that if the mail for

---

[1] Annual Reports for 1884, p. 20, for 1885, p. 13, and App., pp. 67-70, for 1886, p. 17.
[2] *Ibid.*, 1886, p. 18.
[3] Proceedings, 21st April, *Monthly Record*, May 1909.
[4] Annual Report for 1863, p. 10.

Penang were not landed there, but left at Singapore, the ensuing delay " would inflict serious injury on commercial interests in Penang, and also in the mother country ". In face of this protest the old arrangement was quickly restored.[1]

In the same year the Chamber, in the interests of speed, urged the Post Office to separate mails to India marked " *Via Brindisi* " from the other correspondence, which went by the usual route from Marseilles ; and by 1870 the Brindisi route was being used.[2] With the opening of the Suez Canal in 1869 it became possible to quicken the mails to the East ; but not until 1874 did the contracts provide for the mail to go by way of the canal. In that year the Manchester and Bombay Chambers of Commerce co-operated to secure an acceleration of the mails to India and the Far East. As a result of their efforts, the mails to Bombay, Calcutta, Shanghai, and Yokohama, reached their destination a day sooner and the subsidy was reduced by nearly £24,000 : the greater part of this saving arose from the decision to use the Suez Canal.[3] When the contracts were renewed in 1879 it was arranged by the Company that mail should arrive in London on Wednesdays during part of the year and on Fridays during the rest of the year ; previously mails had arrived on a Monday, giving ample time for a considered reply to catch the outward mail on Friday. The new arrangement, which would allow of only a hurried reply, naturally provoked criticism in Manchester ; and within a year the old system was restored.[4] One more instance of the Manchester merchants' concern for speedy delivery of the mail may be cited. On one occasion in 1890 the mail from India and China reached Calais after the packet steamer had already left for Dover, and had to wait ten hours for the next sailing ; the Manchester Chamber strongly objected to this delay, which could have been avoided if the Post Office had chartered a special steamer. To representations on this subject the Post Office merely made the formal reply that the matter was under consideration.[5]

Special facilities for sending samples and patterns through the post are an obvious convenience to business men. The

---

[1] Proceedings, 1868, p. 9.

[2] *Ibid.*, 24th June and 29th July 1868, and 28th December 1870.

[3] *Ibid.*, 19th July and 30th September 1874 ; Annual Report for 1874, p. 13.

[4] *Ibid.*, for 1879, p. 16, and for 1880, pp. 8 and 26.

[5] Proceedings, 22nd September 1890.

French Post Office pioneered cheap postage for samples and patterns, and in 1863 the Manchester Chamber of Commerce memorialised the Postmaster General, suggesting that his department should imitate the French example ; by the end of the year Britain, too, had a samples and pattern post.[1] Under the Post Office Act of 1870, the Postmaster General took powers to regulate the pattern post, and in particular to prescribe " the dimensions and maximum weights of packets ".[2] Regulations issued under the Act threatened to diminish the benefits derived from the pattern post ; in common with other associations, therefore, the Manchester Chamber of Commerce expressed " its serious and well-grounded dissatisfaction " at the restrictions.[3] This was only the first of many conflicts on the subject of pattern posts between the needs of business men and the convenience of the Post Office.

It was not, however, the British Post Office that was to blame for the most serious restriction on the pattern post ; in 1876 an International Postal Convention, against the opposition of the British delegates, had reduced the permissible weight of patterns sent by post from five pounds to eight ounces. Against this restriction the Manchester merchants waged a long war ; the Indian trade was cited as an example of the inconvenience of the new limit, on the ground that " many articles of commerce with India cannot be represented by parcels within such a limit ".[4] In 1879 the size of pattern parcels was restricted within the narrow bounds of a packet 8 in. × 4 in. × 2 in. ; as before, the British delegates had stood out for more generous treatment, but without success.[5] Bilateral negotiations later increased the permissible size of packets sent to and from France, Belgium, Greece, Luxemburg, and the United States ; but in response to further pressure from Manchester, the Post Office could only say that " the majority of the countries adhering to the Postal Union, whose views have been elicited on the subject, are hostile to any departure from the Union limits ". The Manchester merchants were especially puzzled by the opposition of the Netherlands, " having regard to its otherwise intelligent adoption

---

[1] Annual Report for 1863, p. 10.
[2] 33 and 34 Vict., c. 79, s. 9.
[3] Proceedings, 28th December 1870 ; Annual Report for 1870, p. 14.
[4] Proceedings, 19th July 1876.
[5] *Ibid.*, 30th April 1879 ; Annual Report for 1879, p. 13.

of principles calculated to afford increased facilities for the development of commerce ".[1] In 1885 the Dutch were still insisting that patterns sent to the Dutch East Indies should conform with the size and weight regulations imposed by the Convention ; the Java merchants at Manchester pointed out that these limits were

quite inadequate, as everybody in the Java trade knows by experience. . . . What is wanted is that Java and the other Dutch East India possessions should be placed on the same footing as British India, for which place packets can be sent weighing 5 lb. and measuring 24 by 12 by 12 inches, the rate of postage being one shilling per pound.

Though sympathetic, the British Post Office could not overcome the obstinacy of the Dutch.[2] Even in 1910 the question was not entirely settled, for the Manchester Chamber of Commerce was still hoping that the forthcoming Postal Conference would provide more generously for the pattern post.[3]

Postal charges were of only spasmodic concern to the Manchester Chamber of Commerce, not because the Manchester merchants did not want cheap postage, but because they had it already. In 1870, when schemes of postal reform were in the air, the Chamber expressed the opinion that the Post Office gave good value for money, and that postal rates pressed less heavily on the public than any other charge.[4] Though holding this generally favourable opinion, Manchester merchants did not uncritically accept every rate in force ; increases were always strongly resisted. In 1868, for example, the introduction of a weekly mail to India was coupled with a sharp rise in the letter rate, from 6d. to 9d. per half-ounce for mail going *via* Southampton, and from 10d. to 1s. 1d. for mail going *via* Marseilles. This change was condemned as

a retrograde policy and alike opposed to public interest and modern practice ; while a low rate of postage greatly stimulates and improves commercial intercourse, it is also more productive to the public revenue.[5]

In 1869 reductions in the rate on letters to America encouraged the hope that an Ocean Penny Postage would

[1] Annual Report for 1880, pp. 16 and 30.
[2] Annual Reports for 1885, App., pp. 71-2, and for 1889, App., pp. 49-50.
[3] Proceedings, 14th September 1910.
[4] *Ibid.*, 30th March 1870.   [5] *Ibid.*, 27th May 1868.

shortly be instituted; sharing this hope the Manchester
Chamber of Commerce memorialised the House of Commons
in favour of the project,[1] but nothing came of it for many years.
In 1890 Mr. J. Henniker Heaton, M.P., a persistent advocate
of postal reform,[2] reopened the subject and secured the
support of the Manchester merchants for an Imperial Penny
Post.[3] To convert the Postmaster General was less easy, but
even he gave way in the end; Imperial Penny Postage
(except to Australia) began in 1898, and in 1905 the
penny post was extended to Australia as well. In 1908
Anglo-American Penny Postage became a fact, almost
forty years after the Manchester Chamber of Commerce
had first advocated it.

The commercial value of the "electric telegraph" was
already well understood by the middle of the century ; oceanic
cables were still experimental. In 1856 Cyrus Field of the
Atlantic Telegraph Company addressed the Manchester
Chamber [4] in an attempt to enlist its support for his project ;
but the Chamber as such never supported private ventures,
and Mr. Field on this occasion therefore got nothing more
than an expression of the Chamber's good will. On the
1st September 1858, however, the Atlantic cable fell silent
after a month of feeble working,[5] and this untoward event
caused the Chamber to make an exception to the rule that it
would not support private ventures. The government had
itself established a precedent for public support to private
firms when, after the Indian Mutiny, it subsidised the Red
Sea and Indian Telegraph Company ; fortified by this example
the Directors of the Manchester Chamber unanimously
agreed to memorialise the Postmaster General in favour of the
Atlantic Telegraph Company. The Chamber of Commerce,
they admitted, was " as a general rule, on principle " strongly
opposed to the use of public money for private commercial
undertakings ; but the Atlantic Telegraph Company was an
exception to the rule.

It has expended (and irretrievably lost) a large amount of capital

---

[1] Proceedings, 24th February 1869.
[2] Dictionary of National Biography, 1911-1922.
[3] Proceedings, 17th December 1890 and 25th May 1892 ; Monthly
Record, November 1891 and May 1892.
[4] Redford, op. cit., p. 204.
[5] J. H. Clapham, Economic History of Modern Britain, Vol. II, p. 216.

in demonstrating the feasibility [of an Atlantic telegraph], and the public naturally hesitates to invest any more capital as a private speculation.[1]

Eventually another American company, using the *Great Eastern* as a cable-ship, successfully laid a cable from Ireland to Newfoundland ; curiously enough, this feat went unnoticed by the Manchester Chamber of Commerce.

In 1865 the telegraph service to India, the inauguration of which was " regarded as a boon of the greatest magnitude ", was the subject of frequent complaints ; many costly errors and delays had occurred, chiefly owing to the inefficient management of that part of the cable that was under Turkish control. At the end of 1866 the service remained as poor as ever, and as there seemed to be no hope of reform of the Turkish telegraph the Manchester merchants proposed the laying of an alternative cable as far as possible through British stations ; the route suggested was from " Falmouth to Gibraltar, and from Gibraltar to Malta, thence by the Red Sea to Aden and the East ".[2] The Government of India, which had already been considering an all-British telegraph cable to India, gave an assurance that India would pay half the capital cost, though it would not guarantee a dividend for private investors.[3] The British Government at first refused to contribute to the scheme, preferring to secure more exclusive control over the existing land-lines ; but it soon relented, and gave its support to the submarine cable, which was finished in 1870.[4]

By the early eighteen-eighties, the telegraph cables had linked up most of the places important in world trade. West Africa, an area in which Manchester merchants took an especial interest at the time,[5] was one of the few parts of the world not in telegraphic communication with Great Britain, and in 1884 several English companies made proposals for remedying this defect. Without committing itself to any of these plans, the Manchester Chamber of Commerce assured the government

that the commercial community of this district take considerable interest in all means which will provide this country with increased

---

[1] Proceedings, 29th November 1858.
[2] *Ibid.*, 16th August and 20th September 1865 and 19th March 1866 ; Annual Reports for 1866, p. 10, and 1867, p. 14.
[3] *Manchester Guardian*, 1st November 1867.
[4] *Ibid.*, and Proceedings, 27th March 1872.
[5] *See* above, Chapter VI.

facilities for more rapid communications in our trade with West Africa.

Six months later the government departments concerned still " had the matter under consideration ", but some slight progress had been made ; the Colonial Office was negotiating with the Portuguese Government for the right to land a cable at St. Vincent.[1]

Private and competing companies had developed Britain's inland telegraphic system, but the results were not generally considered to be satisfactory.[2] Edinburgh was the first Chamber of Commerce to propose the transfer of the inland cables to the Post Office ; in 1867 the Liverpool Chamber added its support, and asked Manchester to co-operate. The Manchester merchants accordingly asked the House of Commons for an inquiry

into the desirability of our Telegraphic System being placed under government administration with a view to an extension of telegraphic facilities, together with a reduction of rate and uniformity of system and charge.[3]

Under an Act of 1869, the Post Office took over the inland telegraphs early in 1870. The Manchester merchants had not given more than lukewarm support to the nationalisation of inland cables ; and when in 1872 the Royal Society of Arts proposed government ownership of the overseas cables as well, the Chamber of Commerce strongly opposed the suggestion.[4] In this it reflected the general opinion, and overseas cables remained in private hands until 1946.

Telegrams were a heavy item in the accounts of Manchester merchants, some of whom spent from three to six thousand pounds a year in this way.[5] Quick and accurate transmission of telegrams was essential ; but merchants also wished to have a free hand to use codes, and on this point their needs clashed with the convenience of telegraph companies and post offices all over the world. The first sign of the coming struggle was the provision in the St. Petersburg Convention of 1875, increasing charges for code words by 50 per cent. ; the Manchester merchants held this increase to be " an unjust and

---

[1] Annual Reports for 1884, App., p. 112, and for 1885, App., p. 46.
[2] J. H. Clapham, op. cit., Vol. II, pp. 207-8.
[3] Proceedings, 24th April and 26th June 1867 ; Annual Report for 1867, p. 9.
[4] Proceedings, 29th May 1872.
[5] Annual Meeting, 31st January 1876.

arbitrary exaction " [1] but were powerless to alter an international agreement. Warned by the unfavourable results of the St. Petersburg Convention, the Manchester Chamber made preparations in good time for the International Telegraph Conference held in London in 1879. A memorial to the Postmaster General urged him to resist further restrictions on the use of the telegraph ; on the contrary, he should encourage its use by extending the facilities it offered. In particular, it was hoped that, as before 1875, messages in code would be charged at the ordinary rate, and that no restrictions would be placed on the words used in compiling codes.

As compilation of codes by merchants had been attended with great expenditure of time and money, new rules of a restrictive character would render existing codes useless, and entail loss upon the senders of messages.

This plea for a free hand was in vain ; the conference at London carried further the work begun at St. Petersburg, and amongst other restrictions prohibited the use of proper names except in their natural sense, a provision that seemed likely to make every existing code useless. [2]

In 1890 a conference at Paris still further restricted the use of code telegrams by insisting that codes should use an official vocabulary drawn from eight languages ; the vocabulary would include about 240,000 words. Though opposed to the change on principle, the Manchester merchants accepted it without too much fuss because the number of words allowed seemed fairly generous. [3] Towards the end of 1894 the official vocabulary was published and was soon found to be inadequate. Disappointed with the vocabulary, the Chamber of Commerce thereupon resumed its root-and-branch opposition to compulsory vocabularies in general ; it circularised every Chamber of Commerce in Europe, urging that

each should spread abroad the knowledge of the danger threatening the freedom of merchants in all parts of the world, and call attention . . . to the great importance of preventing the compulsory and exclusive application of this or any other vocabulary.

Among 102 replies, not one disagreed with Manchester's

---

[1] Proceedings, 1st and 22nd December 1875 ; Annual Report for 1875, p. 11.

[2] Proceedings, 28th May and 25th June 1879 ; Annual Report for 1879, pp. 14-15. One merchant had to spend " not less than £2,000 " to have his code recast. (*Monthly Record*, May 1890.)

[3] Proceedings, 7th May 1890 ; *Monthly Record*, December 1893.

opinion of the official vocabulary, though several Chambers of Commerce were ready to accept some restrictions on the use of code words.[1] The opposition of the organised merchants caused the authorities first to postpone the enforcement of the official vocabulary, and eventually to abandon it.[2]

[1] *Monthly Record*, February, March and May 1895, and January 1896.
[2] Proceedings, 22nd July 1903 ; Annual Report for 1903, p. 3.

CHAPTER XIII

RAILWAYS, CANALS AND SHIPPING

By 1860 Britain's main-line railways had nearly reached their modern form.   In earlier years the Manchester Chamber of Commerce had taken a keen interest in the growth of the railways,[1] but after 1860 there were few opportunities to consider new developments.   One of the last major additions to the network of railways serving Manchester was the line to Derby, which opened a direct route to the East Midlands. The London and North Western Railway already provided good communication with the West Midlands, but to Derby, Nottingham, and Leicester there were only the circuitous routes by way of Sheffield or Birmingham.   In 1862 the Midland Railway promoted a Bill to remedy this defect, and asked the Manchester Chamber of Commerce to petition Parliament in its favour.   Owing to the rule that the Chamber should not support " any specific joint-stock undertaking ", the Manchester merchants did not feel able to comply with this request, but they did petition in general terms for a more direct route to the Midlands.   As the Midland Railway's Bill was the only scheme before Parliament that would achieve this object, the Manchester petition was tantamount to support for that particular project ; the Bill passed, and by 1867 the Midland Railway had reached Manchester.[2]

The services given by the railways were sometimes, though not often, criticised by Manchester merchants.   In 1867 the Manchester and Macclesfield Chambers of Commerce urged Parliament to make railways liable for damage to silk goods in transit ; in 1865 an amendment to the Carriers' Act had somewhat extended the carriers' liability, and it was felt that the continued lack of protection to silk goods was unjustifiable.[3]   In November 1870 a serious accident to the Liverpool express at Harrow, the latest of a long series of railway disasters, provoked the Manchester merchants to

[1] A. Redford, *Manchester Merchants and Foreign Trade, 1794-1858*, pp. 178-80.
[2] Proceedings, 12th March 1862 ; Annual Report for 1862, p. 8 ; J. H. Clapham, *op. cit.*, Vol. II. p. 182.
[3] *Ibid.*, 1867, p. 13.

criticise " the defective control and management " of the railways ; in a memorial to the Board of Trade, they " urged the necessity of interference for the better security of the lives of those who travel ".[1] Serious defects were by no means common, however, and railway services (as distinct from railway charges) gave little cause for complaint until 1913. In that boom year, merchants and manufacturers complained bitterly of delay in the delivery of goods by rail. In March the Chamber of Commerce instanced 123 cases of delay, ranging from three days to ten weeks ; in June twenty engineering firms supplied another 111 instances. It would be rash, however, to put all the blame on the railway companies, for firms often dispatched goods with no indication of address beyond the consignee's name ; when this happened, delay was inevitable.[2]

In 1871 the London and North Western Railway and the Lancashire and Yorkshire Railway announced their hope of early amalgamation ; the announcement revived the discussions on monopoly and state ownership that had been dormant since the 'forties. The Manchester merchants did not go unheard in the renewed debates ; they " viewed with disfavour, on economic and political grounds, the project of the purchase and working of the Railways by the State ".[3] In this they agreed with Sir Edward Watkin, the Chairman of the Manchester, Sheffield and Lincolnshire Railway ; in 1872 he said that

he should be sorry to see a democratic Government, or any Government, obtaining patronage which would be connected with the employment of half a million people, from the office boy at five shillings a week to the general manager at £5,000 a year.[4]

On railway amalgamations the Manchester merchants had less decided views : the furthest they would go was to express the opinion " that it is essentially necessary to preserve the principle of competition, which has done so much for the general interests of the country." [5]

The failure of the amalgamation movement of the early 'seventies killed all interest in the question, for railways and traders, during the next generation. But as prices rose after

[1] *Annual Register*, 1870, p. 132 ; Proceedings, 30th November 1870.
[2] *Monthly Record*, March and June 1913.
[3] Proceedings, 13th May 1872.
[4] Annual Meeting, 29th January 1872.
[5] Proceedings, 13th May 1872.

1896 the railways, unable without great difficulty to raise their charges, looked once more to amalgamation for the economies necessary to keep them solvent.[1] The first fruit of the new amalgamation movement was the proposed union of the Great Northern, Great Central, and Great Eastern Railways. This time the Manchester Chamber of Commerce did not oppose amalgamation, but asked the President of the Board of Trade " to secure for traders a reasonable portion of the savings effected ".[2] This moderate attitude contrasted with the more hostile opinions of other Chambers of Commerce which " viewed with the greatest alarm " every increase in railway charges, however justifiable, and every proposed amalgamation or working union ; the Manchester merchants agreed that every amalgamation and agreement should receive parliamentary sanction,[3] but they did not show consistent hostility to every proposal made by the railway companies.

Amalgamation in itself would not have alarmed the Manchester merchants ; it was the fear of high charges and monopoly profits after amalgamation that aroused their suspicions. At Manchester, current railway charges were not often criticised before the 'eighties ; the Chamber of Commerce sought rather to amend legislation affecting future freight rates. In 1866 when the railway companies hoped to get parliamentary recognition of their terminal charges, the Manchester merchants opposed the passage of the Bill as it then stood ; eventually it was withdrawn, because the railway companies could not agree to the safeguards proposed by the Chambers of Commerce.[4] In general, the Manchester merchants welcomed the Railway and Canal Traffic Act of 1873, which set up a Railway Commission to hear and remedy complaints of excessive charges ; the measure was in their opinion " calculated to provide an equitable control over a powerful interest which has a tendency towards the creation of a monopoly injurious to the public ". Regrettably, Parliament had not compelled the companies by law " to adopt as between themselves and the public the Clearing House classification " ; such a provision would have been

a step towards the publication and general knowledge of actual rates, the Companies at present having the power arbitrarily

[1] J. H. Clapham, op. cit., Vol. III, p. 361.
[2] Monthly Record, April 1909.   [3] Proceedings, 30th July 1913.
[4] Ibid., 4th April 1866 ; J. H. Clapham, op. cit., Vol. II, p. 195.

to place in one class or another, or to remove from class to class, the many unenumerated goods.[1]

Though the Railway Commission proved ineffective, Manchester merchants remained unperturbed at the level of railway charges. In 1881 a select committee of the House of Commons was appointed to consider railway rates and fares. The Manchester Chamber of Commerce invited local business men to provide evidence of excessive charges, to be collated for submission to the select committee ; but so few and trivial were the complaints, that the Chamber decided not to give evidence, a decision that the spokesman of the railways did not fail to bring to the committee's notice.[2] In 1884 the question of railway rates became important enough to warrant the appointment of a special committee of the Chamber ; and in 1885 the Chamber protested against further attempts by the railway companies to get their terminal charges recognised and increased.[3] Not until 1888 was the Act of 1873 amended. The Act of 1888 provided for a new classification of goods and new maximum rates ; the companies were to draw up new schedules, to which traders could then object before a government commission.[4] In the North West, the Chambers of Commerce joined together to form the Lancashire and Cheshire Conference on Railway Rates, whose task was to scrutinise the schedules when the companies published them. By the end of 1888 the Manchester Chamber, partly alone and partly in association with the Conference, had produced " a carefully prepared list of objections " for the consideration of the Board of Trade.[5] The special commissioners appointed by the Board of Trade duly considered the objections, but revised the schedules upwards rather than downwards ; the Chamber of Commerce would perhaps have felt less alarmed if they had realised that the schedules provided not for actual but for maximum rates. When on the 1st January 1893 the new classification and rates came into effect, however, the worst fears of the merchants were realised, for the companies proceeded to act as if they too regarded actual and maximum rates as synonymous. Profiteering on this scale could not go unchallenged. The Lancashire and Cheshire

[1] Annual Report for 1873, p. 9.
[2] Proceedings, 24th May 1881 ; Select Committee on Railway Rates and Fares (*Parliamentary Papers*, 1881, XIII) qq. 15,139 and 15,140.
[3] Annual Report for 1884, p. 12 ; Proceedings, 4th March 1885.
[4] J. H. Clapham, *op. cit.*, Vol. III, pp. 356-9.
[5] Annual Report for 1889, pp. 10-11.

Conference sent a deputation to represent to the Prime Minister " the serious and widespread injury which would be inflicted upon British industry and commerce if the advanced rates should be insisted upon " ; the Manchester Chamber expressed " its strong disapproval of the serious increase in railway rates . . . and earnestly hoped that the railway companies would immediately return to the rates in force prior to January 1893 ".[1] By the end of the year, the railway companies were admitting that they had acted too hastily, and guaranteed to refund all overcharges when their new working rates had come into force. Nevertheless, an Act of 1894 severely curtailed the companies' right to increase their charges ; before they could do so, they would have to prove their case before the Railway and Canal Commission, whereas previously the burden of proof had rested on traders.

The upheaval of 1888-93 was not the only reason why the Manchester Chamber of Commerce began to take a keener interest in railway rates. As the Chamber's membership grew, and sections were formed to represent special interests, different classes of traders came to use the prestige of the Chamber in their efforts to reduce railway rates. Even in 1889 the newly-formed Chemical Section had put forward many objections to the railways' proposed new rates for chemicals.[2] Later, it was the chemical manufacturers and merchants, with their need for cheap transport for bulky goods, who led the agitation for the revival of canals as a spur to the railways.[3] Another group formerly without much representation in the Chamber comprised the produce merchants, who formed themselves into the Produce Section in 1894.[4] Manchester was fast becoming an important food distributing centre, but the growth of this trade was hindered by the differential railway rates favouring Liverpool. The railway companies defended this discrimination by asserting that consignments from Liverpool were on the whole larger, and could therefore be carried more cheaply ; but the Manchester produce merchants denied that this was true, or alternatively asserted that it would not long remain true if Manchester received equal treatment. By November 1901 the combined efforts of the Manchester merchants and the Coventry Trade Association had forced

---

[1] Proceedings, 25th January and 22nd February 1893.
[2] Annual Report for 1889, p. 11.
[3] See below, pp. 165-6. [4] Proceedings, 9th May 1894.

the railway to equalise the Liverpool-Coventry and the Manchester-Coventry rates.[1]

This victory merely whetted the appetite of the Produce Section :

The inquiry into differential rates from Manchester and Liverpool to Coventry has raised a far wider question.   If the carriage of produce to and from Manchester is a few shillings higher than the rate to rival commercial centres, an unjust condition is imposed on Manchester trade which it cannot and ought not to bear. . . . It is possible that there will be long and protracted proceedings before anything is done, but no effort will be spared to bring the railway companies to reason, even if it necessitates application to the Board of Trade.[2]

The railway companies gave way without forcing the merchants to have recourse to the Board of Trade.   Throughout 1902, 1903, and 1904, the produce merchants were kept busy negotiating new and lower rates between the ports of the north-east and north-west coast and Manchester ; on butter, cheese, and bacon, the railways reduced the rates by between 15 and 25 per cent.[3]   In 1906 the Produce Section turned its attention to the differential rates from London ; to Liverpool the rate on produce was 2s. 6d. per ton less than to Manchester. The Railway Clearing House at first refused to make any concessions, but later agreed to the mediation of the Railway Department of the Board of Trade ;   eventually the parties compromised on a London to Manchester rate of 26s. 6d. per ton, which was a reduction of 1s.[4]

In 1909 the Chemical Section, which had come to realise the difficulties facing a revival of the canals, returned to the question of railway rates.   The classification of chemicals and drugs in the railways' schedules dated from 1870, and was clearly obsolete ; moreover since 1870, and in particular during the past fifteen years, there had been " a general depreciation in the value of Drugs and Chemicals ", a depreciation not reflected in the railways' freight charges.   In association with the London Chamber of Commerce, the Chemical Section therefore submitted a claim for lower freight charges on drugs

---

[1] Proceedings, 14th November 1900 and 17th April 1901 ; Annual Report of the Produce Section for 1901.

[2] Annual Report of the Produce Section for 1901.

[3] Annual Reports for 1902, 1903, 1904, and 1905 ; *Monthly Record*, March and June 1903.

[4] *Ibid.*, July, August, and November 1906, and February 1907.

12

and chemicals.[1] The times were not opportune, however, and the claim was unsuccessful. Prices had been rising since 1896, though railway rates had altered little, thanks to the Act of 1894; the railway strike of 1911 resulted in an increase of wages that made higher railway rates inevitable. The government had to pass an Act allowing the railways to raise their charges ; and Manchester, unlike some other Chambers of Commerce, accepted the Act without complaint.[2]

Apart from government supervision, the only way to keep down railway rates was to encourage competition, either by forbidding amalgamation or by preserving the independence of the canals. Amalgamations after 1872 were rare, but agreements which fell short of union might serve the same purpose almost as well. Canals, after the Railway and Canal Traffic Act of 1873, could no longer be absorbed by the railways, but independence was not a guarantee of survival, and for many years the Manchester Chamber of Commerce did not pay much attention to the independent but largely derelict waterways. Canals threatened with railway control received more sympathetic consideration in Manchester. The Act of 1873 had come too late to save the Bridgewater Canal, which had been sold to the railways the year before, much to the alarm of Manchester merchants to whom the sale suggested " the probable raising of rates for the carriage of goods ". The Chamber of Commerce told the President of the Board of Trade that " the transfer of the Canal between Manchester and Liverpool to certain Railway Directors is adverse to the commercial interests of the two towns ".[3] But since the law did not forbid such a transfer, nothing could be done. In 1882 several railway companies promoted Bills that would empower them to gain control of independent canals. The Manchester merchants were quick to protest at this attempt to evade the Railway and Canal Traffic Act of 1873 :

Water carriage [they declared] is an economical, as it is often the most convenient means of conveyance, particularly of heavy goods and articles in which the element of cost of carriage is of vital consideration. Railway companies have already in various ways succeeded in obtaining a considerable power in the control of canals and waterways, and by raising the rates or tolls have

---

[1] Proceedings, 10th November 1909.
[2] Ibid., 11th December 1912 and 30th July 1913.
[3] Ibid., 25th September 1872.

prejudicially interfered with the use of canals in competition with railway rates, and have thus to a large extent deprived the public of the less costly mode of carriage by water.[1]

The railways did not get the powers they asked for.

The Manchester Chamber did not begin to advocate more active measures for the revival of canal traffic until the Chemical Section took the matter up in 1896.   The chemical manufacturers and merchants, being concerned with the transport of cheap bulky goods, stood to gain more from the use of waterways than shippers of the comparatively light and expensive textiles to which transport charges were less burdensome.   At first the Chemical Section confined itself to research into the condition of inland water transport ; surprisingly enough, it was discovered that most of the canals had never been absorbed by the railways, and that statistics of the capacity, capital, revenue, expenditure, and profits of the canals were far from adequate.[2]   Such facts as were available convinced the Chemical Section of the great potential value of British canals, but the section was not prepared to support the drastic proposal of the Bristol Chamber of Commerce that the canals should be made more serviceable by being nationalised.[3]   The less ambitious request for a Royal Commission met with approval at Manchester, and indeed at every large commercial centre in Britain ; the Association of Chambers of Commerce organised a strong deputation to the Board of Trade to support this request, but had no success.[4]

Though the President of the Board of Trade refused the demand for a Royal Commission, he promised to " consider carefully " any canal Bill that the mercantile interests might promote.   In 1902 the Bristol Chamber of Commerce sponsored a Bill which would have empowered local authorities, with the consent of the Board of Trade, to help public trusts formed to take over and improve the canals.   The Manchester Chamber welcomed this proposal and asked local M.P.s to support it,[5] but the Bill did not pass.   Interest did not wane at Manchester, despite this setback.   By 1904 the Chemical Section, led by Mr. I. Levinstein, had come to the conclusion that a permissive measure would not be enough : What

---

[1] Annual Report for 1882, p. 13 and App., p. 77.
[2] Proceedings, 30th September and 9th December 1896.
[3] Ibid., 21st February 1900.
[4] Monthly Record, September and December 1900.
[5] Proceedings, 18th April 1902.

interest, it asked, could the Buckinghamshire County Council have in the improvement of the Grand Junction Canal ? The canal passed through Buckinghamshire, but its more efficient use would benefit no one except midland manufacturers and London merchants. Only government action could revive the use of the canals.[1] Manchester proposed that the government should take over and work the canals in the public interest, or that they should be vested in a public trust " with government guarantee, supervision and control ".[2] Early in 1906 the new Liberal Government so far recognised the potential importance of the canals as to appoint a Royal Commission ; it reported in 1909 in favour of Manchester's public trust, and of a scheme to develop a " cross " of waterways centred on Birmingham.

To improve the canals as the Commission recommended would cost £17½ million. The Chemical Section welcomed the report, but did not favour the construction of a ship canal at the expense of the national exchequer. On the other hand, the Board of Directors, which had hitherto allowed the Chemical Section to develop its own policy, did not approve of a large national expenditure on canals.[3] From being the champion of state action, Manchester now became the advocate of local finance for local canals ; it was argued that as Manchester had financed its own Ship Canal so Birmingham should finance its own projects, and should not expect the national treasury to spend money on what were essentially local schemes.[4] The Manchester merchants steadfastly maintained this attitude until 1914, when the outbreak of war ruined what slender chances there had ever been of carrying the Royal Commission's Report into effect.

Long before Manchester's own Ship Canal was cut, Manchester merchants were led to take a lively interest in the working of the Suez Canal. This interest, however, was relatively slow in emerging. De Lesseps had addressed the Manchester Chamber in 1857, and later sent a complimentary copy of a book he had written, but without evoking much enthusiasm.[5] During the Cotton Famine, indifference turned to hostility because the Viceroy of Egypt conscribed

[1] Proceedings, 9th December 1903 ; *Monthly Record*, January 1904.
[2] *Ibid.*, September 1904.
[3] Proceedings of the Chemical Section, 7th and 21st February 1911.
[4] *Monthly Record*, March and May 1911 ; Proceedings, 4th September 1912, 30th July 1913, and 14th January 1914.
[5] Redford, *op. cit.*, p. 204 ; Proceedings, 19th March 1860.

60,000 fellaheen for labour on the canal at a time when
Lancashire needed every bale of Egyptian cotton it could get ;
the Manchester merchants so strongly resented this action
that they asked the Foreign Office to use its best endeavours
to end the system of forced labour.[1]   Nevertheless, the President of the Manchester Chamber, Hugh Mason, attended the
opening of the canal in 1869 ; the shorter route, he believed,
would reduce freight rates very considerably, though the gain
would not be England's alone :

It might be that English merchants would have to meet greater
competition to India . . . because the ports on the Mediterranean
would be brought much nearer to India than they were formerly.

However, as England did four-fifths of the trade, she should
still be able to hold her own.[2]
    By 1878 Manchester merchants fully appreciated the value
of the Suez Canal.   When the British Government brought
troops through it from India to Malta, the Manchester
Chamber was much alarmed, and resolved :

That means should be adopted by all governments to ensure the
strict neutrality of the canal in time of war, so that the trade and
commerce of the world may never be endangered in the use of it.[3]

In 1883 the British Government was negotiating an agreement
with the Suez Canal Company, which was to lower its tolls and
improve the canal in return for a loan at a low rate of interest.
The Manchester merchants, sensible though they were
of " the benefits which M. de Lesseps' great work had con-
ferred on the civilised world ", were very critical of the proposed
agreement ; in view of the company's high profits and of the
favourable terms of the proposed loan, the reductions in the
" excessive dues and pilotage now levied " were considered
altogether inadequate.   Moreover Britain, with only three
of the twenty-four seats, would be badly under-represented
on the Board of Directors.[4]   In 1889, the Manchester Chamber
suggested that a vacancy on the company's board should
be filled by a Lancashire shipping merchant ;   shipowners
already had enough representatives, but the cotton trade had
none.[5]

[1] Proceedings, 25th January, 17th February, and 9th March 1864.
[2] Annual Meeting, 31st January 1870.
[3] Proceedings, 6th and 29th May 1878 ; and see above, p. 85.
[4] Annual Report for 1883, pp. 17-18.
[5] Proceedings, 29th May 1889.

From the earliest years of the railway system, Manchester merchants had feared the power of the railway companies to exact monopoly profits from traders ; the conference system, by which shipowners combined to regulate competition on the world's shipping routes, excited similar hostility at Manchester. The first conferences of shipping rings grew up in the later eighteen-seventies,[1] but it was not until 1886 that their activities roused Manchester merchants to resistance. In recent years, it was declared, shipowners had

gradually protected themselves by exceptions in their bill of lading against every risk of liability for damage to the goods they carry, until the bill of lading contains fifty or sixty lines of closely-printed conditions and exceptions, and there appears to be no duty imposed on the fortunate shipowner but that of receiving the freight.[2]

Without their conferences, shipowners could not have reached this privileged position ; and without counter-combination shippers could not hope to redress the balance. Accordingly, the Manchester Chamber began negotiations with the Calcutta and Bombay Steam Trade Conferences for a more equitable bill of lading.[3] Fifteen months protracted discussion followed, but eventually agreement was reached on a new bill of lading.[4] In 1893, however, the Conference altered the terms of the bill of lading in the shipowners' favour ; they declined to negotiate further with the merchants' representatives, " and the Chamber can only content itself with protesting against any deviation from the document which was accepted by each side ".[5]

At the end of the century the Manchester merchants came into more serious conflict with the shipping rings. The rings had from the first fixed freight charges, and by a system of deferred rebates had obliged merchants to use conference steamers only, on pain of losing the rebate. The conferences often also discriminated against British ports ; the freight from New York to Shanghai was considerably lower than that on the much shorter haul from Liverpool to Shanghai, and on the Java route Dutch goods were carried at a lower rate than British ones. The British shipping rings thus appeared to

[1] J. H. Clapham, op. cit., Vol. III, p. 314.
[2] T. E. Scrutton, The Contract of Affreightment (1886), quoted in Annual Report for 1887, App. p. 68.
[3] Proceedings, 26th March and 5th April 1886.
[4] The report of the Chamber's delegates to the negotiations is given on pp. 68-70 of the Appendix to the Annual Report for 1887.
[5] Proceedings, 10th May 1893 ; Monthly Record, March 1894.

be deliberately fostering foreign competitors of British industry.[1] The Manchester Chamber of Commerce formally expressed its disapproval of the system of deferred rebates, and in 1901 carried a resolution to the same effect at the autumn meeting of the Association of British Chambers of Commerce.[2] Having thus given notice of their frame of mind, the Manchester merchants proceeded to organise themselves for negotiations with the shipping rings. In 1902 the President and some other Directors of the Chamber of Commerce met Alfred Holt, the representative of the China Conference, and secured considerable reductions in freight charges. Mr. Holt conceded a specially low rate for drills and sheetings, a line of goods in which United States manufacturers were rapidly ousting the British ; the new rates put Lancashire on equal terms with America.[3] Nevertheless, Manchester had not been able to get rid of the deferred rebates.

Apart from their success in the negotiations with the China Conference, Manchester merchants were unsuccessful in their attempts to bring down freight rates. In evidence before the Royal Commission on Shipping Rings in 1907, the Chamber's President, Mr. E. H. Langdon, admitted that the Conferences provided fixed freights, a good class of steamer, and regular sailings ; but he would not agree that these services gave shipowners the right to insist on the deferred rebate.[4] The Royal Commission's remedy against the danger of monopoly was combination among merchants to negotiate with the shipowners. Mr. Langdon had protested in evidence that "It is utterly impossible for any body of merchants in the cotton textile trade in England to combine . . ." ;[5] and the Manchester Chamber of Commerce made no special efforts to carry out the recommendations of the Royal Commission. Actually, the history of both earlier and later negotiations showed that it was quite possible for the merchants to combine, if the incentive was strong enough. In 1908 the Manchester Association of Importers and Exporters was set up with the special object of negotiating with shipowners ;[6] but in fact it did not represent the cotton trade as such, but rather the

---

[1] Proceedings, 13th April and 8th June 1898 ; *Monthly Record*, October 1901.

[2] Proceedings, 12th December 1900 ; *Monthly Record*, November 1901.

[3] Proceedings, 9th and 16th April, and 11th June 1902 ; *Manchester Guardian*, 27th May 1902.

[4] Written memorandum ; and qq. 855 and 1000.

[5] *Ibid.*, q. 713.   [6] Annual Report for 1909.

general exporters. In time the Chamber's export trade committees (which were raised to the status of sections in 1916) came to negotiate with the shipowners regularly and on equal terms. Other Chambers of Commerce were less enterprising ; even in 1928 many had failed to organise their members for negotiations with the shipping rings—a procedure which by then had long been standard practice at Manchester.[1]

When the Manchester Chamber of Commerce urged that the neutrality of the Suez Canal should be respected in time of war, it was showing more concern for the rights of the individual merchant than for Britain's strategic interests ; it was hoping that in any future war business would go on as usual. In the wars of the eighteenth century this had often been possible, and when the French adopted harsher rules during the Revolutionary Wars, Manchester merchants deplored the change.[2] For over a hundred years Manchester merchants consistently strove to limit the impact of war on commerce. Their concern for the neutrality of the Suez Canal is but one example of this policy ; another is their attitude to questions of contraband and commercial blockade.

After the Crimean War, the Powers agreed to certain modifications in the international law of contraband and blockade ; privateering was abolished, paper blockades were declared unlawful, and enemy goods other than contraband were to be immune from capture at sea if carried in neutral vessels. In 1859 the United States proposed to extend this last doctrine so that all non-contraband private property, enemy or neutral, should be immune from capture at sea, as it was on land ; the United States also wished to narrow the definition of contraband. The Manchester Chamber of Commerce wholeheartedly supported the American views ; it urged " upon Her Majesty's Government the justice and expediency of all merchant ships and cargoes at sea, in wartime, being placed on a like footing with private property on land ". Lord John Russell declined, however, to commit himself to an opinion on " this important subject ".[3]

After the outbreak of the American Civil War, the question

---

[1] Proceedings, 7th March 1923, 10th October and 14th November 1927, and 14th May 1928.

[2] Redford, *op. cit.*, pp. 37-41.

[3] Proceedings, 7th and 28th November 1859, 4th and 23rd January 1860. Manuscript letter of 18th November 1859, from the Foreign Office.

became of immediate practical importance. If all private property at sea in wartime had been immune from capture (as the Americans had themselves proposed in 1859) the North would have had no legal right to prevent the export of cotton from the Confederate states ; there might have been no cotton famine. Richard Cobden made this the theme of an address he gave to a special meeting of the Manchester Chamber of Commerce in October 1862 : [1]

There is no doubt [he declared] that if in 1859 the English Government, followed as it would have been by the other Governments of Europe, had accepted cordially and eagerly, as it was our interest to have accepted it, the proposal or suggestion of the American Government, it would have been possible to avoid all that is now happening in Lancashire ; and trade, as far as cotton is concerned, would have been free between Liverpool and New Orleans. . . . There can be no doubt that in that case the American Government would have been obliged to carry on the war with the Southern States without imposing a commercial blockade ; or if they had attempted to impose such a blockade in violation of their international engagements, they would have involved themselves in hostilities with the rest of the world—a policy which, of course, no rational Government would ever dream of entering upon.

Whether the governments of the world would have rallied to the cause of international law as quickly as Cobden hoped, may be doubted ; but the speech was received with enthusiasm. It was later printed as a pamphlet called *Maritime Law and Belligerent Rights*, and was issued as a supplement to the Annual Report of the Chamber of Commerce.

In 1869 the Birmingham Chamber of Commerce revived the question and resolved that " the private property on the ocean, of belligerents as well as of neutrals, should be exempt from capture, unless contraband of war or breaking a blockade ". The Manchester merchants rightly refused to support this resolution as it stood ; they considered that it would have made very little difference to existing law. As Cobden had said in 1862 : " If you exempt private property from capture at sea during war, you must also consent to give up the system of commercial blockades." Manchester merchants were quite willing to do this, but apparently those of Birmingham were not.[2]

In 1903 the government appointed a Royal Commission on the Supply of Food and Raw Material in Time of War.

[1] Proceedings, 25th October 1862.   [2] *Ibid.*, 10th February 1869.

For over thirty years the Manchester Chamber of Commerce had not had occasion to reconsider its views on contraband and commercial blockade ; its evidence to the Royal Commission showed that Manchester still had faith in international agreements as a means of mitigating the disastrous commercial effects of war. Mr. Elijah Helm, Secretary of the Chamber, considered that the abolition of commercial blockades by international agreement was "the most important point that could be contemplated or considered by this Commission", and added : "I think solemn agreements of that kind have been generally observed." When asked "Would you be prepared to stake your cotton industry on the belief that this would be observed ?", Mr. Helm replied : "I think so."[1] The Commission was less sanguine, however, and declared :

We cannot but think that belligerents may sometimes be tempted to disregard the rules of International Law in cases where they consider themselves to be in a position to do so with impunity.[2]

Moreover, even if other countries were sure to observe the law it would not have been in the interests of so great a naval power as Britain to surrender the right of blockade, which was one of her strongest weapons.

It was this conflict between naval and commercial interests that stultified the Declaration of London. At the second Hague Conference in 1907, a committee had set to work to revise the law of contraband and blockade ; in 1909 the labours of this committee resulted in the Declaration of London, which the Powers were invited to ratify. The Declaration contained the first attempt to define (and restrict) contraband ; it accepted the old-established British distinction between absolute and conditional contraband.[3] Absolute contraband was restricted within the narrow limits of munitions of war ; conditional contraband (that is, articles that could be seized if intended for the use of military forces) included food ; raw materials and household products were put on the free list, and were therefore to be exempt from capture in all circumstances. Though the Declaration restricted contraband within such narrow limits, it did not satisfy the Chambers of Commerce. Glasgow took the lead in opposing ratification,

---

[1] Evidence of E. Helm : written memorandum and qq. 4640 and 4605-7.
[2] Majority Report, para. 112.
[3] L. Oppenheim, *International Law* (3rd edn., 1921), pp. 547 ff. ; A. Pearce Higgins in *Cambridge History of the British Empire*, Vol. II, p. 867.

and was quickly supported by London, Leeds, Liverpool, Bradford, and Manchester. They contended that to make food conditional contraband gave European powers an unfair advantage over Britain ; Continental powers could import food through neutrals, and the British Navy could not prove that the ultimate destination was an enemy country. Britain had no neutral neighbours, however, and all her ports were connected with military bases ; it could there-fore be argued that all her food imports were contraband and liable to seizure.[1] The Declaration was never ratified.

In readiness for the third Hague Conference, the Manchester Chamber of Commerce reiterated, early in 1914, its uncompromising hostility to the seizure of private property at sea :

This Board adheres to the opinion, which the Chamber placed before the Government of the day as far back as 1859, that . . . private property other than contraband should be exempt from capture or confiscation at sea in time of war, as is the case with private property on land.[2]

On the 29th July the Board considered the agenda for the autumn meeting of the Association of British Chambers of Commerce ; the meeting had evidently been arranged before the international crisis had become acute. Nevertheless, the London Chamber had tabled a motion advocating a govern-ment insurance scheme for shipping and naval protection for food ships if war broke out. Consistent to the last, the Manchester merchants decided to oppose this resolution ; but Austrian shells were already falling on Belgrade, and for the next four years the world had little time to spare for the niceties of international law.

[1] Proceedings, 14th September and 14th December 1910.
[2] Ibid., 14th January 1914.

CHAPTER XIV

THE DOCK BOARD AND THE SHIP CANAL

BEFORE 1860, Manchester had reason for complaint in that
the Corporation of Liverpool exacted town dues from the trade
of the Mersey and applied them to the improvement of the
town.[1]   But in 1860 this long-standing grievance was removed;
in the negotiations that had preceded the establishment of the
Mersey Docks and Harbour Board in 1857, it had been agreed
that Liverpool should transfer the right to levy town dues
to the Dock Board, receiving the compensation of £1,500,000.
As a non-profit-making body, the Dock Board would have
applied any profits accruing from the transaction either to the
reduction of dock charges, or to the improvement of its
estate ; but the Manchester Chamber of Commerce wished
the dues levied on goods carried up the Mersey beyond Liverpool to be applied to other purposes, and in particular to the
conservancy of the Upper Mersey.   In a petition to Parliament, the Manchester Chamber recited that

There is large and convenient dock accommodation at Garston,
Widnes, Runcorn situated on the Upper Mersey, and the Upper
Mersey is directly connected with Manchester by Rivers, Canals and
Railways and a very large amount of traffic passes by means of
such Rivers, Canals and Railways.

It was only reasonable, therefore, that the dues collected on
this traffic should be used for the conservancy of the Upper
Mersey and not for the benefit of the Liverpool Docks.[2]
Parliament recognised the force of this argument, and the
Upper Mersey Dues Act of 1860 transferred the revenue to
the Conservancy Board.

For the next twenty years, the Manchester merchants
remained well satisfied with the Mersey Docks and Harbour
Board.   It is true that in 1864 the Chamber of Commerce
objected to a Wallasey Embankment Bill on the ground that

the payment of the interest on the moneys borrowed would form a

[1] A. Redford, *Manchester Merchants and Foreign Trade, 1794-1858*,
p. 186.
[2] Proceedings, 20th February 1860.

permanent charge on merchandise entering or leaving the river Mersey, and thereby increase a burden already sufficiently onerous ; [1]

but with this exception Manchester had nothing ill to say either of the dock charges or of the development schemes.   On the contrary, the Chamber supported the Dock Board's plans, and helped it to resist the pressure put on it by the Corporation of Liverpool.   In 1867, the Dock Board sought and secured the agreement of the Manchester merchants to a Bill it was promoting to add to its borrowing powers and to provide for the purchase of land near the Queen's Dock and Coburg Dock.[2]   In 1871, when the Dock Board again applied to Parliament, the Liverpool and Birkenhead Corporations sought to make the Dock Board pay for better services on the Liverpool-Birkenhead ferry and for improvements to the river approaches ;   in resisting these demands the Dock Board turned for support to the Manchester Chamber of Commerce, which was naturally unwilling to see the trade of the Mersey burdened with "extravagant expenditure" on behalf of local interests.[3]   Two years later the trade of Liverpool was outgrowing the dock accommodation, and the Dock Board again applied to Parliament for power to build new works on the Liverpool side of the river.   Recognising that the trade of Lancashire and Yorkshire was "to a very large extent dependent on conditions . . . at the port of Liverpool ", the Manchester merchants supported the Dock Board's Bill, which eventually passed.[4]

The only serious grievance disturbing the harmony of that generation was quickly removed.   Of the twenty-eight members of the Dock Board, twenty-four were elected by dock-ratepayers (almost entirely from among the Liverpool merchants [5]), and four were the nominees of the Mersey Conservancy Board.   The commercial interests of other parts of Lancashire were not directly represented ; in 1871 the Manchester merchants therefore asked that as one of the representatives of the Conservancy Board had retired the Admiralty should appoint a representative of Lancashire commerce to fill his place.   After some hesitation, the Admiralty complied with

---

[1] Proceedings, 27th April 1864 ;   Annual Report for 1864, p. 10.

[2] Proceedings, 25th and 27th March 1867 ;   Annual Report for 1867, p. 8.

[3] Proceedings, 29th March, 9th and 28th June 1871 ;   Annual Report for 1871, p. 8.

[4] Proceedings, 23rd May 1873 ;   Annual Report for 1873, p. 8.

[5] B. D. White, *The Corporation of Liverpool, 1835-1914* (1951), p. 76.

this request and appointed Mr. Hugh Mason, President of the Manchester Chamber, as a representative of the Conservancy on the Dock Board.[1] With this concession Manchester was well satisfied at the time ; but the predominance of Liverpool merchants on the Dock Board was later felt to be a serious grievance, and did much to exacerbate relations between the Board and the Manchester Chamber in the 'eighties, during the controversy about the authorisation and construction of the Manchester Ship Canal.

Ill feeling between the Dock Board and the Manchester Chamber of Commerce, however, was not a cause but a result of the Ship Canal project. At no time did the Manchester Chamber accuse the Dock Board of extravagance or of partiality to Liverpool interests ; and not until they had accepted the Ship Canal as a practicable scheme did the Manchester merchants launch their attack on the constitution of the Dock Board. This attack was prompted by the Manchester City Council, which early in 1883 had already given the Ship Canal project its blessing.[2] Acting on the Council's suggestion, the Chamber appointed a committee to study the constitution of the Dock Board ; it reported in June 1884 [3] that the Dock Board was almost wholly dominated by Liverpool business men. Anyone who paid £10 a year in dock rates was entitled to vote for the 24 elective members of the Dock Board ; but in fact there were only 2,400 names on the register. Nearly 2,200 of these were from Liverpool and district, and only 20 from Manchester. Because proxy voting was not allowed, business men living at a distance from Liverpool would rarely be able to vote even if their names were put on the register, and in any case they would have to vote for Liverpool men, since persons living more than ten miles from Liverpool were not eligible for election to the Dock Board. "The present system", the committee concluded,

is practically one of local representation only, and does not provide for a sufficient control over expenditure with regard to the interests of payers of dues at the port, and on this ground it is desirable that the voting for the Dock Board should be extended over a wider area. It is evident that any injudicious outlay must proportionately increase the dock charges, which fall directly on the mercantile and

[1] Proceedings, 27th December 1871, and 28th February 1872.
[2] A. Redford, *The History of Local Government in Manchester*, Vol. II, p. 361.
[3] Annual Report for 1883, p. 22 ; Proceedings, 25th June 1884.

manufacturing classes, and to this extent they are an aggravation of the difficulty of competition in foreign markets.

The Manchester Chamber of Commerce did not make any complaint against the general policy of the Dock Board. It may secretly have hoped, by capturing control of the Dock Board, to circumvent opposition to the Ship Canal ; but this motive, if it existed, does not appear in the records. The Chamber did not assert that the Dock Board was extravagant, only that it might become so. To this the Dock Board justly replied that " dock electors residing at Liverpool have just as much interest in preventing unnecessary expenditure as parties residing at a distance ". The Board was not prepared to agree to proxy voting, but it was willing to abolish the residential qualifications for members of the Board, if members living at a distance would make regular attendance at the frequent meet- ings of the Board and its committees.[1] In effect, this reserva- tion amounted to a refusal to end the residential qualification.

For five years Manchester sought, with the co-operation of other Lancashire Chambers of Commerce, to remedy this state of affairs. In 1887 it forced the Dock Board to withdraw a Bill which did not redress the grievances complained of,[2] but this was the Chamber's only success in these years. In 1889, when the Dock Board promoted another Bill, Man- chester tried unsuccessfully to get clauses inserted allowing proxy voting and extending the residential qualification to a radius of fifty miles from Liverpool. Parliament's refusal to accept these clauses ended Manchester's attempt to secure such constitutional reforms ;[3] thereafter the Dock Board was left in peace. Only when Manchester and Liverpool merchants agreed in their criticisms of the Dock Board did their efforts have any result. In 1886 Mr. T. H. Ismay, a Liverpool shipowner, criticised the Dock Board's failure to increase the depth of water over the Mersey Bar. The Dock Board saw no reason to engage in such a costly operation so long as ships could enter and leave the port on every tide, but under joint pressure from Manchester and Liverpool it eventually agreed to take action. Beginning in 1889, dredgers increased the depth at low-water spring tides from 11 to 28 feet.[4]

[1] Annual Report for 1884, App., pp. 115-19.
[2] Proceedings, 21st January and 3rd February 1887.
[3] Annual Report for 1889, p. 19.
[4] Proceedings, 26th November 1886 ; Annual Report for 1886, App., pp. 40-2 ; J. H. Clapham, op. cit., Vol. III, p. 368.

A forgotten pioneer, if not of the Ship Canal at least of the port of Manchester, was Mr. William Gibb, a wine merchant and a Director of the Manchester Chamber of Commerce. In 1860 Mr. Gladstone introduced a Bill relieving inland towns from the expense of maintaining the local Customs House, but he proposed to lessen the benefits of his new measure by levying a special charge on goods taken from bond. At Mr. Gibb's instance, the Manchester Chamber of Commerce memorialised the Chancellor of the Exchequer against the proposed levy, which would " operate as a preferential duty in favour of ports of import as against inland towns ". As a result, the inland bonding charges were considerably reduced,[1] but inland towns with bonded warehouses still paid £900 a year to the Exchequer as a badge of their inferiority to the seaports ; of this sum Manchester contributed £600. In 1867 the Chamber again protested at this invidious distinction, but it was not until 1869 that inland towns were put on an equality with the seaports.[2]

This was not Mr. Gibb's only service to the trade of Manchester. In 1861 he called attention

to the possibility of . . . importing foreign products direct to Manchester. He would not alarm them by proposing a ship canal or a deepening of the river Irwell—questions which in their day had been keenly discussed ; but he believed that the practice, which was adopted on the Thames and other rivers, might be adopted in the Mersey, namely : transhipping foreign produce into properly constructed lighters. . . . If they could only get the goods past Liverpool, the people of Liverpool would have no right to complain.

The Chamber of Commerce took the suggestion up without delay and memorialised the Lords of the Treasury. Under the existing system goods destined for Manchester had to be landed at Liverpool, " thereby incurring a large expenditure for landing charges, cartages, Porterages, Cooperages, forwarding Commissions, and Dock rates " ; transhipment on the Mersey would avoid all these charges, and lighters of fifty or seventy tons could easily reach Manchester up the Mersey and Irwell. To make this possible it was only necessary to declare Manchester a port, or a sub-port of Liverpool or Runcorn, and in November 1861 the customs authorities

---

[1] Proceedings, 13th and 20th February 1860 ; Annual Report for 1860, p. 6.
[2] Annual Meeting, 30th January 1868 ; Annual Report for 1869, p. 12.

agreed to this request ; lighters could now proceed unexamined up the river to Manchester.[1]

Manchester was now technically a port ; but a port without open access to the sea is a port only in name. In its first year, " large quantities of goods were brought direct to Manchester, including Madders, and wines and spirits " ; and in 1863, 2,884 packages were imported direct to Manchester.[2] At no time, however, before the opening of the Ship Canal did the traffic of the port of Manchester warrant separate enumeration in the *Annual Statements of Trade.*

In the early history of the Manchester Ship Canal, the Chamber of Commerce played no very conspicuous part. The very idea of a ship canal had long been dormant, and when it was revived in 1876 the moving spirit was Mr. George Hicks,[3] who was not even a member of the Chamber of Commerce. He realised, however, the importance of gaining the support of the organised merchants at an early stage, and in 1877 promoted a petition asking the Chamber to inquire into the cost and profitability of making Manchester a port open to the largest steamers. At the time the proposal was for a tidal navigation, that is, for canalising the Mersey. The Directors of the Chamber cautiously declined to take the responsibility for making such an inquiry, contenting themselves with the opinion that " the Scheme, if successfully carried out, would, there is no doubt, be of the greatest service to the interests and trade of the District ".[4]

The Directors maintained this reserved attitude throughout the early struggles to get parliamentary sanction for the canal. In July 1882, when the tidal navigation scheme was still being discussed, the Directors again declared that in principle they favoured it, and this attitude was " cordially approved " by the ordinary members at the next quarterly meeting of the Chamber.[5] Early in 1883 the Directors took another small step towards approval of the Ship Canal, though with evident reluctance ; the tidal navigation scheme had by then been abandoned, and a Canal Bill presented to the House of Commons where the examiner of private Bills had refused to allow it to proceed. At the annual meeting of the Chamber

[1] *Manchester Guardian*, 22nd January 1861 ; Proceedings, 17th June and 28th October 1861 ; Annual Report for 1861, p. 7.
[2] Annual Meetings, 26th January 1863 and 25th January 1864.
[3] Sir B. T. Leech, *History of the Manchester Ship Canal*, Vol. I, p. 73.
[4] Proceedings, 28th February and 25th April 1877.
[5] *Ibid.*, 26th July and 13th November 1882.

of Commerce, a resolution was passed in favour of asking the House of Commons to waive Standing Orders and allow the Canal Bill to proceed. The Directors as a body did not oppose the resolution, though two of them spoke against it ; it was nevertheless carried by a handsome majority, and the President's signature was added to the petition that the City Council had already agreed to send.[1]

Later in 1883, the provisional committee for the Ship Canal invited the Directors of the Chamber of Commerce to a conference " to consider the future steps to be taken in the promotion of the Manchester Ship Canal " ; but the Directors were still cool. They declined the invitation, giving as their reason that they did not feel themselves authorised to appoint a delegate.[2] As the Chamber had not formally declared itself in favour of the Ship Canal, this made a plausible excuse, though the real reason was that the Directors were adhering closely to the rule that the Chamber should not support private enterprises. At the annual meeting early in 1884, the members at large demonstrated that they did not share these reservations, when they carried by an overwhelming majority the following resolutions :

That it is essential in the interests of the increasing commerce and population of this district to adopt cheaper means than at present exist for the transport and handling of merchandise, minerals, etc., between Manchester and surrounding towns and the sea coast and places beyond.
That in the opinion of this Chamber the project known as the Manchester Ship Canal affords the best means of giving effect to these objects, and this Chamber heartily approves of the application now before Parliament for powers to carry out the work.[3]

It was a corollary of this resolution that delegates from the Chamber of Commerce should give evidence before the Private Bill committees of both Houses of Parliament; but although the Chamber's delegates were thus committed to support the Bill, the Directors still hesitated. After the engineer and some of the promotors of the canal scheme had interviewed the Directors, the President of the Chamber cautiously remarked that the project was " a subject of deep interest to the locality, but it was at the same time one which required careful examina-

[1] Annual Meeting, 5th February 1883 ; A. Redford, *The History of Local Government in Manchester*, Vol. II, p. 361.
[2] Proceedings, 26th September 1883.
[3] Annual Meeting, 4th February 1884.

tion and close study ".[1] Even when in 1885 the Bill became
law, the Directors showed no warmth of feeling, baldly re-
marking in their annual report that the Chamber had given
evidence in favour of the Bill, and that its chief promoter,
Daniel Adamson, was a Director of the Chamber.[2]

The opening of the Ship Canal in 1894 aroused warm
enthusiasm among the ordinary members of the Chamber of
Commerce, and the Board of Directors took the first opportunity

to record its satisfaction that the Manchester Ship Canal has been
completed and opened for the navigation of sea-going vessels, and
heartily to congratulate the Directors of the Canal on the accom-
plishment of their great engineering enterprise after encountering
the most formidable difficulties.[3]

The Chamber appointed a Shipping Committee consisting of
Directors, merchants, and shipowners ; its purpose was " to
consider business arising from the opening of the Ship Canal
and the establishment of the Port of Manchester ".[4]

The most urgent business of the Shipping Committee was
to attract more trade to the new port.   In 1893 the Agent-
General of New South Wales had written to the Chamber
suggesting direct shipments of Australian produce to Manchester ; the direct route would have " many advantages over
the existing practice of shipping to London ".   The Chief
Dairy Commissioner of New Zealand later addressed the
Chamber to the same effect ; and in 1895 direct shipment of
dairy produce from Australia to Manchester began.[5] The
produce merchants also made valiant efforts to induce
shipowners to deliver Danish dairy produce to the Manchester docks, and for thirteen years they approached one
company after another, without success.   The usual route
(Copenhagen-Hull or Copenhagen-Newcastle) with its heavy
railway charges from the north-east coast to Manchester, was
declared to be altogether too expensive ; but the shipping
companies, Danish and English alike, thought that the journey
round the north of Scotland would be more expensive still.
Only if the Forth and Clyde Canal were open to sea-going
vessels would direct shipments to Manchester pay.[6]

[1] Proceedings, 12th February 1884.   [2] Annual Report for 1885, p. 5.
[3] Proceedings, 10th January 1894.   [4] Ibid., 14th March 1894.
[5] Ibid., 10th May 1893 ; Monthly Record, October 1893, March 1894,
and July 1895.
[6] Ibid., July and December 1896, and April 1897 ; Annual Reports
for 1897, 1904 and 1908 ; Monthly Record, June 1909.

Produce merchants were not alone in seeking to increase the trade of the port. The Chamber of Commerce often appealed to shipping merchants to make better use of the canal ; but the merchants were not well organised, and could not compel shipowners to use the port of Manchester. The only instance of a large-scale diversion of the piece-goods trade from Liverpool to Manchester owed nothing to the organised

THE TRADE OF THE PORT OF MANCHESTER, 1894-1913 [1]

	Merchandise Imports and Exports (000 tons)	Receipts (£000)
1894	926	98
5	1359	137
6	1826	182
7	2066	205
8	2596	236
9	2778	265
1900	3061	291
1	2942	310
2	3418	358
3	3847	397
4	3918	418
5	4253	449
6	4700	499
7	5211	536
8	4582	507
9	4563	534
1910	4937	556
1	5218	581
2	5340	605
1913	5780	656

action of Manchester merchants ; the credit was due entirely to the Ship Canal Company and the Bombay Native Piece Goods Merchants' Association, who agreed in 1894 to ship direct from Manchester to Bombay.[2] The West Africa merchants tried to make Messrs. Elder, Dempster and Co. follow this example. They complained of the primitive loading facilities at Liverpool, where bales of cotton goods were thrown from carts on to the quay and dragged about with

[1] Annual Report of the Manchester Chamber of Commerce for 1913, p. 9.
[2] Sir B. T. Leech, op. cit., Vol. II, pp. 229-31.

hooks. Manchester docks, in contrast, were fully equipped with the latest machinery ; but the shipowners persevered with Liverpool.[1]

The Directors of the Ship Canal Company had estimated that in its first year the canal would handle 3 million tons of merchandise, and that by the seventh year the traffic would have grown to well over 9 million tons.[2] These estimates were too optimistic ; a traffic of 3 million tons was not reached until 1900 (the seventh year), and in no year before the outbreak of war in 1914 did the traffic reach 6 million tons. Nevertheless, trade grew steadily (with the merest check in 1901) until 1906-7, when there was a sharp rise in the tonnage handled. In 1907 there were heavy shipments of Yorkshire coal and heavy imports of iron ore—a temporary trade that fell off in 1908 ; but the better class trade " was well maintained on the whole ".[3] By 1910 the level of 1906 had been passed, though 1907 remained the peak year ; but in the last three years of peace the record of 1907 was beaten, and beaten almost entirely by shipments and imports of the better class of goods. In 1894 Manchester was only the sixteenth port in the kingdom ; by 1900 it had risen to sixth place, and by 1913 to fourth—just ahead of Glasgow and Southampton, well behind Hull, and far behind London and Liverpool, the two giants who handled well over half of Britain's foreign trade.

Though the port of Manchester served an area that depended very largely on exports, the trade of the port more closely resembled that of London, where imports were larger than exports, than that of Liverpool, where the value of imports and exports roughly balanced. In 1913 the port of Manchester (including Ellesmere, Partington, Runcorn, and Warrington) imported goods worth £35,000,000 but exported goods worth only £21,000,000.[4] The imports consisted largely of wheat, maize, and cotton, though there was also a considerable trade in lard, fruit, refined sugar, and dairy produce ; Manchester was already the second oil port in the country, though oil had not then the prominent place in world trade that it has since acquired. Imports of raw cotton by weight were less than a quarter of Liverpool's, though by value the

[1] *Monthly Record*, October 1913.
[2] Sir B. T. Leech, *op. cit.*, Vol. II, p. 282.   [3] Annual Report for 1908.
[4] These paragraphs, except when otherwise stated, are based on the *Annual Statement of Trade of the U.K.* for 1913.

proportion was higher, since over half the Egyptian cotton came direct to Manchester ; but the trade in raw cotton, large as it had become, was not (in the opinion of Manchester men) " so great as could be desired, or might have been expected ".[1]

Manchester had captured an even smaller proportion of the export trade in cotton yarn and piece goods. In yarn alone, Manchester had obtained nearly half the trade, though the finer and more valuable cargoes still went from Liverpool. In the much more important piece-goods trade, Manchester's exports, by value and volume alike, amounted to only one-sixth of those of Liverpool. Even so, cotton yarn and piece goods accounted for over 60 per cent. by value of the goods shipped from the port of Manchester. The woollen trade had remained almost entirely in the hands of Liverpool ; hardly any of the woollen yarn exports and only 5 per cent. of the woollen piece goods were shipped from Manchester.

If we compare the achievements of the Ship Canal with the high hopes of its promoters, then the canal was anything but a success, but by any less optimistic standards it had clearly succeeded ; to have surpassed in twenty years the trade of Southampton and Glasgow, and of such a famous and ancient port as Bristol, was no mean achievement. Failure to attract the vast trade forecast in the canal's early days did mean, however, that whoever else benefited, the share-holders did not. The Ship Canal always covered its working expenses,[2] but until 1907 it had never paid in full the interest on its debenture debt to the Corporation of Manchester. Until 1913 no dividend was declared on the Corporation's pre-preference shares ; and it was only in 1916 that small first dividends of $1\frac{1}{2}$ and $\frac{3}{4}$ per cent. were declared on the preference and ordinary shares respectively.[3]

When Manchester became a port it began to develop the trades and industries characteristic of ports. It had long been the market for cotton yarn and piece goods ; it now began in a small way to rival the Liverpool Cotton Exchange in the trade in raw cotton. The heavy imports of Irish dairy produce, especially cheap butter, made Manchester one of the largest centres in England for distributing provisions ; the area served extended as far as the Potteries in one direction,

[1] J. S. McConechy, " The Economic Value of the Ship Canal to Manchester and District " (*Trans. Manchester Statistical Society*, 1912-13).
[2] Sir B. Leech, *op. cit.*, Vol. II, p. 256.
[3] *Monthly Record*, August 1910 ; *The Economist*, 19th February 1916.

and Sunderland in another.[1] The cheap transport provided
by the canal also made it possible to establish at Manchester
food-processing industries that relied on imported materials ;
flour milling, oil-seed crushing, and lard refining became
important Manchester industries. But the most spectacular
industrial development that followed the opening of the Ship
Canal was the growth of a large engineering industry. The
great trading estate in Trafford Park was established in 1896,
and quickly attracted a wide variety of industries, because
of its proximity to the docks and its good railway communications.[2] Much of Manchester's food-processing industry was
to be found there, but engineering easily took first place.
The rateable value of Trafford Park grew from £3,000 in
1897 to £100,000 in 1912. By then ninety-seven firms,
large and small, had works established in Trafford Park ;
in 1929 the estate carried 200 industrial undertakings employing 30,000 workers ; [3] by 1952 the numbers employed
there had risen to more than 50,000. Daniel Adamson and
Bosdin Leech had prophesied truly when they declared that
the Ship Canal would attract the heavy trades to Manchester
and save it from the fate of towns that put all their trust in a
single industry.

[1] *Monthly Record*, June 1901 and July 1909.
[2] Sir B. T. Leech, *op. cit.*, Vol. II, pp. 249-51, has a list of the sixty
firms established in Trafford Park by 1906.
[3] *Monthly Record*, March 1914 ; H. Clay and K. R. Brady (ed.),
Manchester at Work (1929), p. 36.

PART II

WAR, DEPRESSION, AND NEW PROBLEMS

CHAPTER XV

MANCHESTER TRADE IN WARTIME, 1914-1918

THE Manchester Chamber of Commerce had always been hostile to the system of commercial blockades by which peaceable merchants were prevented from carrying on their business as usual in time of war. This hostility did not extend to the British Navy, which was recognised to be an indispensable bulwark against foreigners who tried to hinder the maintenance of British trade. It is true that the Manchester Chamber did not support an unlimited extension of British naval power, as some Chambers of Commerce appeared to do ; in 1911, for instance, Manchester declined to be represented in a deputation that the London Chamber of Commerce was organising

in order to impress upon His Majesty's Government the need of adequate provision being made for strengthening the Navy and to assure them of the support of the commercial community in such financial measures as may be necessary.[1]

Nevertheless, all reasonable steps to maintain Britain's naval power received full support at Manchester. In 1910, for instance, the Chamber of Commerce joined with similar bodies from all over the country in urging the Admiralty to build dry docks capable of repairing a Dreadnought on the Tyne and Humber ; at the time no such dock existed at any point on the east coast between the north of Scotland and Portsmouth. The Admiralty was able to assure the deputation that suitable docks were already being built.[2]

On military questions, the Manchester Chamber took up an equally moderate position. It gave unreserved support to the East Lancashire Territorials ; [3] but it was opposed to anything resembling conscription. Other Chambers of Commerce, including those of London and Leeds, were prepared for more drastic measures, but when the Association of British Chambers debated the subject in 1913, Manchester supported

---

[1] Proceedings, 15th February 1911.
[2] *Monthly Record*, March 1910 ; Proceedings, 20th July 1910.
[3] *Ibid.*, 13th November 1912.

the most lukewarm of the six resolutions on the agenda; it agreed

that the youth of the Empire should universally undergo such a course of training in discipline and arms as, without undue interference with industrial employment, will fit them to take their part as citizens for the purpose of the Empire's defence.[1]

It was wholly consistent with this attitude that the Manchester merchants should try to stop the armaments race. The lead came from Oldham at the end of 1913; Manchester responded with a long resolution deploring the burden of armaments and urging the government to seek international agreement for a reduction. At the half-yearly meeting on the 22nd July 1914 the President, Mr. R. N. (later Sir Noton) Barclay, summed up Manchester's attitude :

We give place to no one in the desire, nay the determination, that no expense should be spared in securing our safety as a nation. . . . We are anxious not only that we ourselves shall not be guilty of setting the pace, but that no opportunity shall be lost of bringing about by mutual agreement among the Powers a saner and more reasonable expenditure of the resources of the nations.[2]

Manchester therefore met the international crisis in a pacific though not a pacifist mood. On the 1st August 1914, when Austria and Serbia were already at war, when Russia had mobilised and Germany had sent ultimatums to both Russia and France (but not as yet to Belgium), the President of the Manchester Chamber of Commerce sent the following telegram to the Prime Minister :

Mercantile community Manchester strongly favour everything possible being done in order to preserve British neutrality.

I would also urge enormous advantages both Imperial and Commercial of England remaining in this crisis the predominant neutral Power of Europe.

On the morning of Tuesday the 4th August the Board of Directors held a special meeting at which they " heartily approved " of the telegram the President had sent. In the meantime, however, it had become known that Germany would not respect Belgian neutrality ; and Sir Edward Grey had declared in the House of Commons on the 3rd August that

---

[1] Proceedings, 5th February 1913. See also ibid., 26th January 1910.
[2] Monthly Record, January 1913 ; Proceedings, 10th December 1913 ; Monthly Record, July 1914.

Britain could not stand aside when Belgian independence was at stake.   In these circumstances the Board cancelled the special general meeting of members that had been called for the afternoon of the 4th August.

When the Board next met, on the 6th August, uncertainty had ended, and for the next four years Manchester merchants were struggling with new problems to which old policies could not be applied.   From the very beginning of the war, the Board of Directors was surprisingly willing to support unorthodox policies.   It expressed its satisfaction with the government's financial emergency measures—a prolonged bank holiday, and a moratorium—and it urged the government " to fix by Proclamation the prices at which the staple articles of food should be sold both by wholesale and retail traders ".[1]   As the most influential voice of the business community of Lancashire, the Board gave a lead to business opinion in the early days of the war : it appealed to employers to keep their workpeople employed as far as possible ; it urged buyers to pay at least as much of their accounts as would allow their suppliers to pay wages ; it suggested that the delivery of goods under contract should be spread out, and that consignments should be paid for in full.   Local newspapers printed these resolutions, which were designed to steady opinion and maintain employment [2] in what everyone imagined was an economic crisis.   The alarm did not subside at once, for even in September the Chamber was urging that the moratorium should be extended for another month from the 4th October, the date on which it was due to expire.[3]

Though in peace the Chamber had opposed commercial blockades and the capture of private property at sea, in war it immediately fell in with the government's prohibition of trading with the enemy.   It urged shippers to report any attempts that the enemy might make to trade with Britain through neutral countries, and gladly passed on to the authorities any information received about such attempts.[4] In the China market the position was particularly complex : a proclamation of the 23rd December 1914 had prohibited trade with enemy firms in China if their headquarters were in Europe ; but trade with firms domiciled in China, though undesirable, remained lawful.   By May 1915 absolute

[1] Proceedings, 6th August 1914.
[2] Ibid., 6th, 7th, and 8th August 1914.
[3] Ibid., 11th September 1914.   [4] Monthly Record, October 1914.

prohibition of trade with enemy firms in China was being discussed ; a large minority of the China merchants at Manchester
favoured continuance of the trade, but the majority recommended prohibition, provided that existing contracts remained
valid. The prohibition should extend to the Treaty Ports, even
if Japan did not follow the British lead. This unbending view
became official policy, and trading with the enemy in China was
forbidden from the 26th July 1915.[1]

In most other neutral markets, trading with the enemy was
permissible if the goods were to be consumed locally and the
enemy firms had no connections with a parent firm in Europe.
As the government could not reasonably expect traders to
find out for themselves if a particular firm fulfilled both these
conditions, the War Trade Department compiled a black list
of firms with which trade was not allowed. At first the department refused to let the list leave its possession, but after
a while a copy was deposited at the Chamber of Commerce,
where merchants could see it confidentially.[2] When the
United States entered the war, it compiled its own black list ;
its list of South American firms did not entirely coincide with
the British one, however, and as a result Manchester goods
that were being shipped to South America by way of the United
States were impounded when the United States black-listed
firms to which the British Government had no objection.
The United States consul in Manchester was therefore asked to
supply a copy of his government's black list ; but the precaution was unnecessary, as his government agreed to issue
licences for the transhipment of goods through the United
States to Central and South America if the firms were on the
black list of the United States, but not on that of Britain.[3]

The outbreak of war interrupted the large trade between
Manchester and Germany, leaving many merchants without
hope of recovering the debts due to them, except from overseas subsidiaries of their German customers. Fortunately
several of the German firms in question had West African
branches, whose assets might be used to pay the debts of the
parent firm. The Colonial Office decided, however, that claims
on a German head office could not be met from the assets of
its West African subsidiary ; and only after persistent pressure

[1] *Monthly Record*, December 1914 and July 1915 ; Proceedings, 12th
May and 9th June 1915.
[2] *Ibid.*, 8th December 1915 and 16th February 1916.
[3] *Ibid.*, 12th December 1917, and 13th February and 13th March 1918.

for a whole year did the Manchester merchants persuade the authorities to reverse their decision.[1]

The successful liquidation of pre-war contracts and the severing of trade connections with enemy firms were comparatively petty problems.   Much more serious were the restrictions that government control and the inevitable shortages of the war years placed on the export of cotton goods and yarn.   From the beginning of the war, the government used export licences to prevent goods reaching Germany through neutral countries ; and by October 1914 the Manchester Chamber was complaining of delay in the issue of licences, which should be dispatched to the merchant by return of post, if possible.[2]   There was a special reason for restricting the export of cotton goods, namely the danger that Germany might use fine cloth for the manufacture of aircraft and airships.   In November 1914 the Board of Trade, through the Manchester Chamber, asked merchants to abstain from the export of silk piece goods to Scandinavia, whence the silk might find its way on to Zeppelins.   On 3rd May 1915 the government suddenly imposed an embargo on the export of bleached cottons, but promptly withdrew this measure when the Manchester merchants protested that " the trades concerned should be consulted before such new regulations are promulgated ". [3]

By August the government, in consultation with the Chamber of Commerce, had devised a complicated scheme by which it was hoped to prevent cloth suitable for aircraft from being exported to Germany.   No cloth weighing between $2\frac{1}{2}$ and 10 oz. per square yard, and with 72 or more threads per square inch, could be exported unless the Testing House of the Manchester Chamber certified that the cloth was below a specific strength of " 6 " ; cloth with a higher strength would be suitable for aircraft, and would therefore need an export licence from the War Trade Department.   The scheme took little account of the complexity of the cotton export trade ; with 900 firms engaged in a trade that was " so large and so much of a retail character ", and that was distinguished by the " variety and smallness of individual consignments ", it was estimated that the Testing House would have to make 15,900 tests every day, which was impracticable.   The

[1] *Monthly Record*, October 1914, July 1915, and July 1916.
[2] *Ibid.*, October 1914 ; Proceedings, 11th November 1914.
[3] *Ibid.*, 12th May 1915.

Manchester merchants therefore asked for certain modifications in the scheme; the government should exclude from it exports to India, the Dominions, the Crown Colonies, and (if possible) allied countries, and there should be narrower limits to the types of cloth that would need testing. If the government would make these concessions, the scheme would be workable, though very inconvenient.[1] At the last moment, however, the government changed its mind and replaced its scheme of certification by a straightforward licensing system; it prohibited the export of cotton and cotton products to neutral Europe (except the Iberian peninsula), and to all Mediterranean and Black Sea ports, except under licence. The Manchester merchants welcomed this simple solution of a difficult problem.[2]

The government's imperfect knowledge of the yarn export trade led to further difficulties for Manchester merchants; in July 1915 the export of yarn (except under licence) was prohibited, and foreign merchants had to sign a declaration that the yarn would be woven in their own factories and not sold to the enemy. The Manchester Chamber of Commerce quickly pointed out that if this declaration were required of Balkan importers, the export of yarns to that market would cease, because yarns sold to the Balkans (chiefly of counts 8 to 24) were woven not in factories but on the peasants' handlooms. At first the government refused to modify the declaration, but in the end it was made to see reason, and when the export of cotton goods to Europe was prohibited, except under licence, a satisfactory form of words came into use at the same time.[3]

Apart from direct control to prevent cotton goods reaching the enemy, the government intervened very little with the ordinary course of business until shortages became acute in the last eighteen months of the war; indirectly, however, the war had greatly interfered with business long before the government started to ration raw cotton and shipping. The railways quickly became clogged with goods that they could not move, and even Manchester's traditional Whitweek holiday had to be abandoned in order to give the railway companies a chance to reduce the arrears of work. In July 1915 the Cham-

[1] Proceedings, 11th August 1915.

[2] Monthly Record, November 1915; Annual Report for 1915.

[3] Monthly Record, July and August 1915; Proceedings, 10th November 1915.

ber of Commerce urged the Board of Trade to insist on " the complete interchange, where practicable ", of railway waggons, but its suggestions had been anticipated.[1] Pooling of waggons must have been more apparent than real, however, for at the end of the year serious congestion at the port of Manchester led to the suggestion

that the shortage of railway waggons might be relieved by abrogating all rules tending to hinder the complete interchangeability of waggons . . . without regard to the ultimate ownership of the waggons.

Soldiers and prisoners of war should also be used to move goods from congested railway yards.[2]

The war quickened the development of motor transport, and by 1917 merchants were looking with envy at the War Office's fleet of lorries. The Manchester Chamber suggested that drivers might carry goods to the docks while undergoing training, but the War Office declared that there were no lorries to spare : the Army was already providing transport for the Road Board, the Post Office, the railways, and the Ministry of Munitions.[3]

It was not only the British transport system that was working under great strain ; French ports and railways were equally congested, and in a life-and-death struggle the French Government was little disposed to help the transit trade from Britain across France. By October 1915 they had forbidden the use of the large French ports for the Anglo-Swiss transit trade, which they confined to the little port of Cette, a hundred miles west of Marseilles. Prompted by the British Chamber of Commerce at Paris, Manchester protested against this restriction of the trade to Cette; if it was too much to ask for Marseilles or Bordeaux, merchants would be satisfied if they could ship through La Pallice.[4] There is no evidence that the French authorities took any action to remove this grievance.

Transport was probably the weakest link in the economic chain, but it was closely followed by manpower. By the end of 1915 Manchester merchants were beginning to feel that the recruiting movement was hampering the maintenance of exports. The Chamber of Commerce urged the Reserved Occupations Committee to place indispensable men in the

---

[1] Proceedings, 12th May and 14th July 1915.
[2] Ibid., 8th December 1915, and 12th January 1916.
[3] Ibid., 14th February 1917.
[4] Ibid., 14th April and 8th October 1915.

14

export trade in Group D; this would make their attestation unnecessary. In the Chamber's opinion, indispensable men would include heads of departments, principal clerks, and expert assistants. The government, on the other hand, did not believe that the conventional terminology was a reliable guide to an employee's duties; the case of every clerk would have to be considered on its merits.[1] By February 1917 the call-up of shipping clerks had seriously interfered with the export trade; the government replied to warnings with the non-committal remark that " it recognised the importance of the work carried on by firms engaged in the export trade. . . . No apprehensions need therefore be entertained."[2] A reply couched in such terms might mean much or little; but the Manchester Chamber did not renew its complaints.

It may be, however, that the volume of exports was by then falling faster than the number of clerks in the merchants' offices. From the middle of 1916 supplies of all kinds were becoming increasingly scarce. In July the Board of Trade restricted the export of goods in jute bags, despite protests from Manchester. By October the government was preparing to requisition all supplies of chlorine in the country, regardless of the effect on the cotton trade; the government suggested that the bleachers should import bleaching powder from the United States, and ignored the counter-proposal that the government should get its chlorine abroad and leave supplies in Britain for the bleachers. In the end the Director of Trench Warfare bluntly told Manchester that the cotton trade would have to use less bleaching powder until new plant for the production of chlorine had been built.[3]

Early in the war the cotton industry learnt that there would be few war contracts except for spinners of coarse counts and manufacturers of heavy goods.[4] Though cotton was not an essential industry, the government made no deliberate attempt to restrict its output, which shrank only as men and materials grew scarcer in the ordinary course of events. This contraction was in itself serious enough, however, and by February 1917 shippers to the East were alarmed at the declining volume of exports. Two hundred and fifty of the shipping firms took concerted action to secure the issue of an Order-

---

[1] *Monthly Record*, 8th December 1915 and 12th January 1916.
[2] *Ibid.*, 14th February and 10th May 1917; *ibid.*, March 1917.
[3] Proceedings, 11th October, 8th November and 13th December 1916.
[4] *Monthly Record*, December 1914.

in-Council compelling manufacturers, dyers, bleachers, and finishers to give preference to orders for export after government orders had been met. The Chamber of Commerce refused to aid this movement, and declared : " The Chamber is much more than an Association of Eastern Shipping Merchants, and it is manifestly impossible " for it to disregard the interests of other sections of its membership.[1] Though the Chamber refused to initiate any plan for putting the industry's production to the most efficient use, some such plan had soon to be devised, however, for stocks of raw cotton had fallen very low and heavy shipping losses also threatened to make it impossible to export the goods manufactured. The government met the emergency by appointing the Cotton Control Board in June 1917 to regulate the output of yarn, especially in the American section. Mr. (later Sir) Edwin Stockton represented the Chamber of Commerce on the Cotton Control Board, most of whose members were industrial employers or operatives.[2]

The shortage of ships was to prove a more troublesome problem, which increased in gravity as the war became more critical. Insurance problems apart, shipping questions remained in the background until early in 1916, when the exorbitant freight rates then ruling prompted the mercantile interests to take vigorous action. At that time government control of shipping was haphazard and incomplete. Tramp shipping was requisitioned as and when it was needed to carry war supplies and sugar ; the rest of the country's imports and exports were handled by private merchants, who chartered such tramp steamers as were available, and still had the use of Conference liners, which remained unrequisitioned until early in 1917.[3] If the government was content with this situation, the Manchester merchants were not ; the enormous rise in freight rates was increasing the cost of living and of raw materials, and constituted " a serious handicap for our industries in competition with such a country as the United States of America ", where at the time cotton was 2d. a lb. cheaper than in Lancashire. The Manchester merchants urged the government " to grapple with the situation either by taking over control of all British shipping or in some other

---

[1] Proceedings, 14th February 1917.
[2] H. D. (later Sir Hubert) Henderson, *The Cotton Control Board* (1922), pp. 7-8.
[3] A. Salter, *Allied Shipping Control*, pp. 59-60, 70-2.

adequate manner ".[1] Nevertheless, it was not until a year later, when losses from submarines had become dangerously high, that the government overcame its reluctance to control every ship sailing under the British flag.

In the meantime, the failure to match shipping resources against the goods to be carried led to some curious anomalies. For example, in November 1916 the Manchester Chamber protested that the government had provided no ships to carry goods to Greece, though it had issued export licences on the strength of which the goods had already been manufactured.[2] Even after the government had formally assumed control over all British shipping, merchants could not regulate their trade successfully because they still did not know how much shipping space would be allocated to them. By April 1917 it had been agreed that merchants in the Eastern piece-goods trade should notify the Shipping Controller of their probable requirements ; but the Minister of Shipping would not guarantee that those requirements would be met.[3] As long as the merchants did not know how much shipping space they would be allotted, they were tempted to ask for more than they expected to get. In July 1917 they pressed for more shipping for the North African trade, and for a resumption of sailings to Greece ; but in neither case did the Minister of Shipping meet their wishes.[4] It was not until March 1918 that the government set up a Textile Exports Shipping Committee under the chairmanship of Mr. (later Sir) Edward Rhodes ; the committee consisted of shippers from the various textile centres, and its job was to allocate shipping space among textile exporters. This work of rationing was successfully carried out until the committee was dissolved in December 1918 ; if the committee had been appointed earlier, the government might have avoided much of the friction caused by its own handling of the cotton trade's shipping problems.

The shortages of men, ships, cotton, bleaching powder, dyes, and packing materials combined to reduce the exports of cotton yarn and piece goods year by year, until in 1918 and 1919 they had fallen to only about half the record volumes of 1913.

[1] Proceedings, 31st January 1916 ; *Monthly Record*, February 1916.
[2] Proceedings, 8th November 1916.
[3] *Monthly Record*, April 1917.
[4] Proceedings, 17th July and 3rd September 1917.

EXPORTS OF COTTON YARN AND PIECE GOODS, 1913-20 [1]

	Yarn		Cloth	
	Mill. lb.	£ mill.	Mill. linear yd.	£ mill.
1913	210	15	7076	98
1914	179	12	5736	79
1915	188	10	4749	65
1916	172	13	5256	89
1917	133	17	4979	113
1918	102	21	3696	139
1919	163	34	3529	179
1920	148	48	4437	316

In value, however, thanks largely to the higher price of raw cotton, exports had by 1917 risen above the pre-war level ; but the sharpest rise came in the last year of the war, and after it had ended.   Cotton growers were not alone in profiting from the rise of prices ; spinners' and manufacterers' margins grew so much wider that very large profits were made on a greatly reduced output.   As the President of the Manchester Chamber of Commerce remarked at the half-yearly meeting of members in July 1918 : " More money has been made in the Lancashire cotton spinning trade this year than in any similar half-year in the history of the industry." [2]

The war not only reduced the volume of exports ; it largely altered their direction.   France, unimportant as a buyer of cotton goods before the war, took large quantities of piece goods and yarn to replace the production of her own mills, which the Germans had overrun.   In 1918 France was importing nearly 200 million yards of cloth and 60 million lb. of yarn from Lancashire.   French colonies, too, relied on Lancashire for their wartime supplies, and some of the Manchester merchants wished to use this opportunity to secure equal treatment for British and French cotton goods in French colonies ; but the Board of Directors of the Manchester Chamber of Commerce resolutely refused, both during and after the war, to take advantage of France's difficulties in this way.[3]   The South American trade stood up to wartime strains fairly well, though some ground was lost to local

[1] H. D. Henderson, op. cit., App. C.
[2] Monthly Record, August 1918.
[3] Proceedings, 9th September 1914, 10th March and 12th May 1915, 12th April 1916, 11th December 1918, and 8th January 1919.

industries (especially in Brazil) and to the United States. The greater part of the wartime decline in exports occurred, however, in the Eastern trade. In 1913 India, China, and the Dutch East Indies had imported 4,000 million yards of Lancashire cloth ; in 1918 they took only 1,300 million yards. This decline accounted for three-quarters of Lancashire's wartime losses ; [1] and the failure to recover more than a fraction of this trade in the 'twenties was largely responsible for the post-war depression in the cotton industry.

Because the volume of trade had contracted so sharply, high wartime profits did not encourage complacency. Early in 1915 the Chamber of Commerce was watching Japanese policy with a suspicious eye, fearing that Japan might take advantage of the European war to secure special privileges in China ; the Foreign Office was able, however, to reassure Manchester merchants on this point.[2] Even without the aid of political pressure, Lancashire's competitors had a golden opportunity to develop their trade. Although in 1916 Lancashire was still doing " a great trade ", the Chamber found it

significant that the trend of our business lately has been to finishing goods and away from sized greys ; the large output lately from the Indian mills suggests that progress has been made by a very obvious competitor.[3]

The natural conclusion was that " Lancashire will have to keep its place by stimulating the demand for the better and more elaborate classes of goods " ; [4] this was an old argument, but (as was later to be shown) not a good one. Japan, like India, was an obvious competitor who had " strained every nerve to supply the deficiency [of Lancashire's wartime cotton exports] at comparatively low prices ".[5] In February 1918 the President of the Manchester Chamber of Commerce had expressed his personal view that Japan was the greatest danger to Lancashire's prosperity :

German competition . . . I do not fear so much as that of certain other nations ; are we going to allow free access at home and in our Dominions to the products of those nations who command labour at a tithe of the wages prevalent in our country ? [6]

[1] *Annual Statement of Trade* for 1918.
[2] *Monthly Record*, March 1915 ; Proceedings, 14th April 1915.
[3] *Monthly Record*, February and June 1916. [4] *Ibid.*, October 1916.
[5] *Ibid.*, December 1918. [6] *Ibid.*, March 1918.

CHAPTER XVI

"TRADE AFTER THE WAR": WARTIME PLANS FOR POST-WAR RECONSTRUCTION

IN the early days of the war the slogans " Business as Usual " and " Capture German Trade " vied with each other in popularity. By the 27th August 1914 the Board of Trade had prepared and published bulletins on eighteen classes of goods that enemy firms had previously sold in colonial and neutral markets; "a large number of other bulletins " was being prepared.[1] In October the British Imperial Council of Commerce, the executive organ of the Association of Chambers of Commerce of the British Empire, invited Manchester " to indicate the best methods of supplanting the enemy trade by an Imperial interchange of commodities ".[2] By November a third slogan, " Continuity of Trade after the War " had appeared as the logical corollary of the attempt to capture German trade. If manufacturers and merchants were to invest capital in new business wrested from the Germans, they would want a guarantee that after the war they would be able to hold the positions they had won.[3]

Continuity of trade after the war implied protection, which most Chambers of Commerce would have welcomed ; but Manchester was not yet converted. Even the acute shortage of the aniline dyes that were so important to the cotton trade did not at first move Manchester from strict adherence to the doctrines of free trade. The dyestuffs industry was the most glaring example of the extent to which Britain had depended before the war on German supplies, and the government and most business men early decided that it was essential to " liberate British trade from the domination of Germany in the provision of these necessary supplies ". The Directors of the Manchester Chamber met specially to consider proposals for government assistance to industries started during the war, and resolved " to oppose proposals for any form of financial assistance from the Government to Industries ". The aniline dye industry came specially under discussion, and the Board

---

[1] *Monthly Record*, August 1914.
[2] Proceedings, 14th October 1914.   [3] *Ibid.*, 11th November 1914.

recorded its opinion " that any questions as to the extension of Aniline Dye manufacture in this country are matters for consideration between producers and consumers in the trade ".[1] But the Directors quickly retreated from this extreme position ; in December Lord Moulton, an eminent lawyer whom the government had put at the head of the Explosives Supply Department, spoke at Manchester in favour of state assistance to the dyestuffs industry. His words carried conviction, and the Directors rescinded their resolution as far as it related to dyestuffs, " while adhering to their opposition to the general principle of state assistance to industries . . .".[2]

Though " in the exceptional circumstances " financial assistance was warranted, the Manchester Chamber of Commerce would not support even temporary protective duties on dyestuffs.[3] The President emphasised this point in his address to the annual meeting of members :

In our endeavours to meet what are after all temporary difficulties . . . we must avoid as far as possible such action as would tend to continue those evils indefinitely after the war is over, and which might end in artificial bolstering up of industries.[4]

It is not surprising that, holding these views, Manchester did not welcome proposals for a Royal Commission on tariff policy, and was not particularly anxious that the government should declare its policy for continuity of trade after the war.[5] Nevertheless, just as the shortage of dyestuffs had caused one breach in Manchester's policy, so the government's undeniable need for revenue and the shortage of foreign exchange caused another. The Budget of September 1915 imposed a 33⅓ per cent. duty on imported motor cars and cycles, films, watches, clocks, and musical instruments ; these were the famous McKenna Duties, which the Manchester Chamber " abstained from criticising . . . from a desire not to embarrass the Government in the extraordinary circumstances of the time ". As was well known, the Chamber was most anxious that nothing should be done which might prove to be permanently at variance with, or hereafter endanger, Free Trade principles.[6] The government's needs brooked no delay, but long-term policy was a different matter ; hasty action by the Association of Chambers was to be deprecated, owing to " the difficulty

[1] Proceedings, 2nd November 1914.   [2] Ibid., 15th December 1914.
[3] Ibid., 21st January and 24th February 1915.
[4] Monthly Record, February 1915.
[5] Proceedings, 24th February 1915.   [6] Monthly Record, October 1915.

under existing abnormal conditions of taking an altogether dispassionate view as to the wisest commercial policy to be adopted " after the war.[1]

Early in 1916, however, the Directors of the Manchester Chamber so far yielded to the current fashion as to appoint a special committee on the question of trade after the war ; without delay the committee prepared a memorandum embodying the policy that the Directors proposed to put before the Association of Chambers of Commerce. The memorandum contained a reaffirmation of belief in Free Trade, some proposals for reforms (none of them very substantial), and a statement of policy towards " key " industries hitherto dominated by Germany. The memorandum put forward few proposals that had not been acceptable to the Manchester merchants before the war ; it had not much anti-German bias, and it was a very full restatement of Manchester's continued devotion to economic liberalism.

The Manchester Chamber of Commerce [declared the memorandum] adheres to the policy of Free Trade—not a doctrinaire Free Trade, but Free Trade for the purpose of admitting imports at the lowest possible cost, especially raw materials and semi-manufactured articles, which are practically the raw materials of various trades, and resists proposals for Protective Tariffs, seeing that these tend to bolster up artificially inefficient industries at the expense of the community.

Britain's past commercial greatness had been due to free-trade policies ; and protection would not be any more necessary in the future, since we should emerge from the war relatively stronger than the enemy.

Only two of the Directors' proposed reforms would have penalised Germany alone ; these were measures to prevent German financial penetration of British business, and to prevent Germany from regaining her pre-war monopoly of the supply of such raw materials as spelter. Unfair advantages to German shipping, such as the right to anchor off Southampton and pick up passengers without paying harbour dues, should be eliminated ; and there was room for further reforms of the patent law. Though cast in an anti-German mould, these suggestions might have been applied equally well to allied and neutral countries. Nor would the Directors admit that British dependence on Germany for certain strategic materials warranted either tariff protection or state

[1] Proceedings, 8th December 1915.

aid to key industries. A minority of the Directors would have approved " some measure of Government assistance for limited periods and carefully safeguarded so as not to discourage private enterprise " ; but an amendment to this effect was lost.[1]

The Directors submitted their memorandum to the annual meeting of members on the 14th February 1916. In his presidential speech Mr. R. N. Barclay stressed the danger of succumbing to anti-German feeling ; many proposals for trade after the war, he said,

are not economic considerations at all, they are in the nature of reprisals. . . . In talking of trade after the war, we are discussing not war but peace conditions, and it is absolutely essential, if our judgments are to be wise judgments, that we should endeavour to take a dispassionate view.

This appeal to reason fell on deaf ears ; opponents of the memorandum roundly declared that " they wanted definite action to keep out enemy traders ", and on a vote the memorandum was referred back by a large majority of the 600 members present. A poll of the membership at large was equally decisive : 988 votes were cast against the Directors' policy, and only 527 in favour ; individuals and firms with 975 votes did not express any opinion.

All but three of the Directors thereupon resigned : only five of the elected Directors who had resigned stood for re-election, but seven of the eight Directors who held office as chairmen of sections were re-appointed ; the eighth did not stand.[2] The new Board was enlarged by the addition of five new sectional Directors. Formerly the oversight of the export trade to particular markets had been entrusted to committees appointed by the Board ; these committees were now replaced by sectional committees. Under the new arrangement shipping merchants had a better opportunity to influence the course of events ; they themselves could now choose the chairmen and other officers of the export trade committees.[3] Thus the new Board of Directors, thirty-eight strong, included few of the men whose policy the members had rejected ; only fourteen of the new Directors had had seats on the old

---

[1] Proceedings, 31st January 1916 ; the text of the memorandum is reprinted in *Monthly Record*, January 1916.
[2] *Ibid.*, February and March 1916 ; Proceedings, 14th, 16th, 22nd and 23rd February 1916.
[3] *Ibid.*, 12th April 1916.

Board and three of them had refused to resign, presumably because they agreed with the members at large in opposing the free-trade, non-discriminatory policy of their fellow Directors. At most, therefore, eleven Directors remained of those who had approved the ill-fated memorandum.

The new men were not slow in producing a revised plan for trade after the war. It began with a recital of various minor reforms, such as better technical education, amendment of the patent laws, extension of the system of Trade Commissioners, and other measures to which all business men would agree. The remainder of the new statement of policy struck a more ominous note :

Exceeding in urgency any of these desirable reforms, this Chamber considers it to be essential that after the war the same facilities for trading with the British Empire shall not be allowed to our enemies as those granted to our Allies and to Neutral nations, and particularly that steps shall be taken not only to render dumping and a return to pre-war conditions impossible, but also effectually to eliminate enemy influences so actively in operation prior to the war. This Chamber also urges that immediate consideration be given by H.M. Government to the desirability of preferential reciprocal trading relations between all parts of the British Empire and as far as possible with our Allies.[1]

The members endorsed this statement by 932 votes to 234 ; over half the members abstained.[2]

Whether this result committed the Manchester Chamber of Commerce to support of Imperial Preference was open to doubt. The new President, Mr. R. B. Stoker, declared that he himself supported Imperial Preference, but that " this phase of the question has not yet been considered in detail by the Board ".[3] Nevertheless, many contemporary observers were confident that the citadel of free trade had at last capitulated. The Prime Minister of Australia, Mr. W. M. Hughes, said that

In Manchester, the Mecca of *laissez-faire*, the Chamber of Commerce has by an overwhelming majority declared that the economic policy which for over three-quarters of a century has been regarded with almost religious veneration by the people of Britain is inadequate to serve them in this great crisis.[4]

[1] *Monthly Record*, May 1916.
[2] Proceedings, 10th May and 7th June 1916.
[3] *Monthly Record*, August 1916.
[4] *Ibid.*, June 1916 ; see also *ibid.*, March 1917, and *Annual Register*, 1916, p. 65.

The new Board had already broken with the rigid free-trade policy of its predecessor. In March 1916, at the instance of the Chemical Section, it had urged the government

to foster and encourage such of the chemical industries as are vital to our national welfare by means of import duties to be levied on the products of the corresponding industries, for an adequate period after the war.[1]

Nevertheless, this was hardly a decisive abandonment of free-trade policy because in fact, though not in form, the proposal was as much an anti-German as a protectionist measure. In July the Chamber welcomed the conclusions reached at the Paris Economic Conference of the Allies, including the proposed post-war boycott of enemy raw materials and manufactured goods.[2] Taxation was a third economic weapon that might be turned against Germany. In May 1916 the Manchester Chamber suggested that after the war enemy firms trading in Britain should pay a special turnover tax, and that enemy commercial travellers should also be taxed. Later this suggestion became more general, and the Chamber supported a comprehensive scheme for the taxation of all foreign firms trading in Britain. They should all pay a turnover tax ; enemy firms should be allowed to trade here only under licence and on payment of specially heavy imposts.[3] Finally it was proposed that the German mercantile marine should be limited after the war until Allied shipping losses from the submarine campaign had been made good.[4]

The events of 1916 had left it uncertain whether the Manchester merchants had forsaken their traditional free-trade policy altogether, or only as far as Germany was concerned. The publication in September 1918 of the Balfour Committee's *Report on Commercial and Industrial Policy after the War* allowed a further test of opinion in Manchester to be made. The majority report, on which Britain's fiscal policy was to rest until 1932, recommended a limited measure of protection for key industries, by subsidy, tariff, or other suitable method. Special measures were recommended against dumping and sweated goods, but other industries were not to be protected

---

[1] *Monthly Record*, April 1916 ; Annual Report for 1916.
[2] Proceedings, 24th July 1916.
[3] *Monthly Record*, June and November 1916 ; Proceedings, 25th January 1917.
[4] *Ibid.*, 18th March 1918.

except "for reasons of national safety" or to help a major industry assailed by foreign competition; where duties were imposed, Empire goods should receive preferential treatment. The minority report simply proposed a 10 per cent. duty on all wholly or mainly manufactured imports. The Board of the Manchester Chamber conducted a poll of the members on these two reports; but fewer than 700 votes out of a possible 3,000 were cast. The figures show that a decided majority of those sufficiently interested to vote favoured protection in one form or another: only 193 votes (under 30 per cent.) were cast against both reports, presumably by die-hard free-traders; the majority report secured 303 votes, well over 40 per cent. of the total, and the minority report attracted 165 votes; 26 votes were cast in favour of both reports.[1] A moderate form of protectionism was evidently gaining ground at Manchester, though free-traders still outnumbered thorough-going protectionists.

Wartime plans for reconstruction did not begin and end with fiscal questions; the Manchester Chamber of Commerce, like other organisations, took the opportunity to scrutinise many of the institutions on whose efficiency post-war prosperity would depend. The scrutiny did not expose any glaring weaknesses in the British economy; there was need for improvement, but not on a revolutionary scale.

The railways did not entirely escape criticism, though the Manchester Chamber had no drastic reforms to propose. One Director, Mr. Marshall Stevens,[2] chairman of Trafford Park Estates Ltd., put before the Board a far-reaching scheme for railway reform. He argued that high railway charges were due to the excessive warehouse accommodation provided by the companies; if the companies merely carried goods from station to station, leaving traders to make their own arrangements for warehousing and carting, a saving of 25 per cent. would result. In effect he was proposing abolition of the railways' terminal services and of the terminal charges that went with them; this was the system which prevailed on the Continent, and it accounted for the lower railway rates there. Mr. Marshall Stevens also urged a more thorough pooling of rolling stock. These proposals never became the

[1] Proceedings, 30th September and 9th October 1918.
[2] *The Dictionary of National Biography, 1931-40* has a brief account of his career.

official policy of the Chamber of Commerce, though when the
scheme was first propounded the Board urged the government to make

such arrangements with the Railway Companies as will enable
them to extend to our Manufacturers and our other Producers
similar conditions of favourable treatment to those which prevail
abroad—to the great advantage of Producers abroad.[1]

In 1918, however, the Directors declined to base their evidence
to a select committee on transport on Mr. Marshall Stevens's
plan, because to do so would only confuse the issue and
jeopardise other plans that had already been put forward.
The principle on which the Chamber took its stand was that
the railways should freely co-operate with each other as much
as possible ; failing that, Manchester " did not object to
purchase of the Railways by the State, but it did not favour
Government control ".[2]

Traditionally, the Manchester Chamber of Commerce had
been a staunch champion of financial orthodoxy.   Manchester
merchants had resisted with equal firmness the blandishments
of the Birmingham inflationists and of the Liverpool bimetallists.[3]   When British banking came under review towards
the end of the war, much of the old orthodoxy still survived ;
the chief difference between the Victorian Manchester
merchants and their successors was that by 1918 business
men no longer had confidence in their own judgements on
banking.   In the middle of the nineteenth century the leading
members of the Manchester Chamber of Commerce, merchants
and spinners as well as bankers, had confidently discussed the
working of the Bank Charter Act of 1844 ; but during the
First World War the Manchester Chamber of Commerce took
its banking policy at second-hand from the banks or from
academic economists.   Interest in banking policy was stimulated by the appointment of the Cunliffe Committee on
Currency and Foreign Exchanges in January 1918.   Shortly
afterwards, the Manchester Chamber appointed a special
committee to study the working of the Bank Charter Act of
1844 ;   and with the assistance of leading local bankers it
produced a memorandum on banking policy in the following

---

[1] *Proceedings*, 24th July 1916.
[2] *Ibid.*, 25th September, 13th November, and 11th December 1918.
[3] A. Redford, *Manchester Merchants and Foreign Trade, 1794-1858*,
pp. 158-60, 163-8 ; above, pp. 34-40.

July.[1] The most important point considered was the relation of the bullion reserve to the note issue. The Board considered that the Bank Charter Act of 1844 should be amended to allow an increase of the note issue ; in addition to the fully-covered issue of notes against bullion, the Bank should be allowed to issue notes against securities to an amount equal to one-and-a-half times the value of the bullion held. The Board maintained that a bullion reserve of $33\frac{1}{3}$ per cent. was "hardly sufficient", and that a reserve of 40 per cent. would not be too high. On the other hand, in times of crisis it was considered impracticable to delay the suspension of the Bank Charter Act until the bank rate had reached 10 per cent. ; with the permission of the Treasury, and subject to a graduated tax, the Bank should be empowered to issue more notes whenever the situation required such action. These were the main points ; but the Manchester Chamber also recommended that the Bank should issue £1 and 10s. notes and publish half-yearly balance sheets, and that the government should appoint two of the Directors of the Bank ; the issue and banking departments should remain separate, and the Bank should not compete with other banks.

The war had disrupted the organisation of Britain's overseas trade, which had been financed to a considerable extent by German firms. Anti-German feeling made British merchants look for other sources of credit, and proposals to establish trade banks became popular. At Manchester, Mr. Marshall Stevens devised a scheme "to assist British Traders to sell upon credit terms and so help to make the best use of the manufacturing advantages of this country in the coming International Trade Competition". He proposed the establishment of trade banks with a minimum capital of £100,000 subscribed by firms in the trade. The trade banks would issue notes to the supplier of goods, who could have the notes discounted at an ordinary bank ; this would be possible because the notes would have a Treasury guarantee, though a severely restricted one. Under this system traders could sell on credit terms without increasing their working capital.[2] The committee appointed by the Board of Trade to advise on financial facilities for trade after the war made less sweeping proposals. It suggested the establishment of one large bank with a royal charter and an eventual capital

---

[1] Proceedings, 13th February ; *Monthly Record*, July and August 1918.
[2] Proceedings, 25th September 1916.

of £10,000,000, privately subscribed. The purpose of the bank would be to provide credit for export contracts on which ordinary banks would not advance money. The Manchester Chamber of Commerce gave general approval to the report, but criticised it as not being sufficiently far-reaching : " it does not adequately provide for the requirements of traders, since the capital and credit are insufficient adequately to replace enemy firms and organisations in neutral countries." [1]

Schemes for a decimal coinage and a metric system of weights and measures had been in abeyance at Manchester in the years immediately before the war, but reform of the British system of weights, measures, and coinage came to be looked at in a more favourable light when so many other plans for reconstruction were in the air. As early as 1915 the old Board of Directors of the Chamber of Commerce had given its blessing to proposals for adopting the metric system, though it would not support its enforcement by law. The new Board elected in March 1916 appointed a special committee to study the question ; it reported against decimal weights and measures but in favour of a decimal coinage. The particular scheme that Manchester championed was one based on the pound sterling, with the florin and a new coin worth one-tenth of a florin for small change.[2] A Bill incorporating this scheme was actually introduced into the House of Lords, but without success.

[1] Proceedings, 11th October 1916.
[2] *Monthly Record*, September 1916 ; Proceedings, 24th February 1915, 10th May 1916 and 10th October 1917.

CHAPTER XVII

THE FIRST DECADE OF DEPRESSION, 1920-1930

THE post-war boom was short. In some of the Lancashire cotton towns trade was still very bad in March 1919; at Burnley only 30 per cent. of the looms were at work. In April more orders came in and prices began to rise ; and by August resurgent confidence had touched off speculation in the purchase of cotton mills.[1] Within a year, however, unmistakable signs of depression were appearing. Early in February 1920 the Board of Trade gave warning that a business crisis threatened at Constantinople, where excessive stocks of textile goods had accumulated. In April business was dull on the Manchester Royal Exchange, and the speculation in cotton mills was dying down ; in May new business was " rather slack " ; June was a month of " comparative depression " ; and in July came the first of a long series of cancellations of orders already booked.[2] By the end of the year the cotton industry was severely depressed ; " the great disasters " had begun.

EXPORTS OF COTTON PIECE GOODS AND YARN, 1919-29

	Piece Goods Mill. sq. yd.	Yarn Mill. lb.		Piece Goods Mill. sq. yd.	Yarn Mill. lb.
1919	3,529 [3]	163	1925	4,434	190
1920	4,437	148	1926	3,834	169
1921	2,903	147	1927	4,117	200
1922	4,184	203	1928	3,867	169
1923	4,140	145	1929	3,672	167
1924	4,444	163			

The volume of cloth exports was lower in 1919 than in 1918, though in value there was a sharp rise ; the yarn trade

[1] *Monthly Record*, March, April, and August 1919.
[2] Proceedings, 2nd February 1920 ; *Monthly Record*, April, May, June, and July 1920.
[3] Million linear yards. In 1920 the quantities are given in square yards for the first time. After that date all the statistics used in this work are in square yards, unless the contrary is stated. The cloths varied in width, but the average width was about a yard.

recovered more quickly from the effects of the war, and during the 'twenties was fairly well maintained. It was in the export of cloth that Lancashire failed to recover the trade lost during the war. Nobody expected to see the record total of 7,000 million yards equalled in the post-war years,[1] since in 1919 hours of work in the mills had been reduced from $55\frac{1}{2}$ to 48 per week ; but the fall to an average export in the middle 'twenties of about 4,200 million square yards of cloth meant that the world was not even taking up Lancashire's reduced output. Calculation showed that after making allowances for the better average quality of Lancashire's post-war exports, their real value had declined to just over 70 per cent. of the pre-war value ; Lancashire's share in the international trade in cotton piece goods and yarn had fallen from 73 per cent. in 1909-13 to 57 per cent. in 1921-5.[2] In the later 'twenties Lancashire's exports fell again after a period of relative stability between 1922 and 1927.

On its interpretation of this alarming trend of trade would depend the policy of the Manchester Chamber of Commerce. At first, the Chamber expected the depression to be no more than a temporary setback ; the President declared in July 1920, and was to repeat several times afterwards : " Lancashire goods are an economic necessity, and the markets of the world cannot afford to delay their purchases for any length of time." In August the considered opinion of the Chamber was : " There is every indication of recovery in the near future. . . . Prices will not decline to any great extent." The *Manchester Guardian* thought that this opinion would be endorsed " by all who have watched cotton trade questions closely ".[3] Manchester merchants based their confidence on the absence of foreign competitors for the international trade in cotton goods. The wartime fear of Japan had quite disappeared. In February 1920, before the boom had broken, the President declared that the Japanese had made little use of their wartime opportunities,

for instead of doing themselves credit, they have done their trade enormous injury . . . by failing to deliver the standard quality

[1] *Monthly Record*, March 1920.
[2] G. W. Daniels and J. Jewkes, " The Comparative Position of the Lancashire Cotton Industry and Trade ", pp. 91-2 (*Transactions of the Manchester Statistical Society*, 1926-7).
[3] *Monthly Record*, July and August 1920.

for which they had contracted. . . . The sweated condition of labour in Japan is not a real advantage to them.[1]

Even after the depression had set in, Manchester merchants did not openly fear foreign competition. They admitted that in some lines Lancashire and Japan might come into conflict, but declared that there was room for both in world markets ; all Lancashire's potential competitors—Japan, Germany, the United States, and India—had very large home markets and little to spare for export.[2]

Optimism soon gave way to depression among business men,[3] but though continued unemployment forced the Manchester Chamber to take a more serious view of Lancashire's prospects, no novel or untried remedies were as yet proposed. The fullest statement of local opinion about the causes of the depression is to be found in evidence submitted at the end of 1924 to the Balfour Committee on Industry and Trade. In form the evidence represented the views of the shipping merchants only ; but in fact, as the separate evidence of the spinners and manufacturers shows, the whole of the cotton trade was united in its diagnosis of the causes of the depression, as they were understood at the end of 1924. The shipping merchants attributed the decline in Lancashire's exports to foreign competition, to high costs of production and reduced purchasing power, and to some causes of a more general nature.

Twenty-five years ago [they declared] Lancashire occupied such a position in the markets of the world that the question of competition scarcely presented itself at all. That is not the case today. In many directions Lancashire's position has been quite clearly and definitely assailed ; in a few it is seriously threatened.

In the Indian market the chief competitors were the protected Indian industry, Japan, and Italy. In China, Japan was the chief competitor, followed by China herself. In South America, Lancashire had to contend with native industries, especially in Brazil, and with competition from the United States and Italy. Increased customs tariffs could be blamed for only a small part of the loss of trade.

In India the last increase to 11 per cent. is almost lost sight of in the seriousness of the general situation. . . . Neither in China nor Egypt have customs duties entered into the position. As far as the

---

[1] *Monthly Record*, February 1920.
[2] *Ibid.*, December 1920 and December 1921.   [3] *Ibid.*, October 1921.

past is concerned, therefore, customs duties are not important, but they must be watched in the future. We must at least have most-favoured-nation treatment everywhere.

The shipping merchants gave more weight to the " combined effects of our high prices and our customers' reduced purchasing power " than to foreign competition, higher tariffs, or indeed any other cause of the depression. They argued that the price of raw cotton had risen far more than prices in general, and that as a result cotton goods were relatively much dearer than before the war. Unfortunately, Lancashire's best customers were primary producers in India, the Far East, and South America, whose goods bought a smaller quantity of manufactures than before the war. It was this change in the terms of trade, together with the exceptionally high price of cotton goods, that the Manchester merchants in 1924 blamed for the greater part of their post-war losses. Political disturbances in India and China, and fraudulent practices such as false-folding of cloth and short-reeling of yarn, were also briefly mentioned ; but given better supplies of raw cotton and lower costs of production Manchester merchants believed that they could recover much of the ground lost since 1913.[1] Even in 1928, when the cotton trade was as depressed as ever, the Manchester Chamber of Commerce continued to hope for better times. It pointed out that only in the American section of the industry had losses occurred ; the yarn trade was almost as large as it had been before the war, and the finer trade using Egyptian cotton was prosperous enough. As the world's demand for cotton goods was steadily rising, Lancashire had some ground for hoping that prosperity might return.[2]

The Manchester Chamber's wartime conversion to a moderate form of protection did not last long. In June 1919 the Chamber welcomed the faint beginnings of Imperial Preference in British policy when the Budget of that year gave preferences to Empire wines, dried fruits, sugar, and tobacco.[3] Thereafter, however, Manchester quickly renewed its allegiance to free trade, though with some loss of unanimity. Several Directors and a large minority of the members now

[1] Committee on Industry and Trade, Minutes of Evidence, 1924-7, Vol. I, pp. 94-122.
[2] Monthly Record, July 1928 ; Manchester Chamber of Commerce Handbook, 1928-29, pp. 13-19.
[3] Monthly Record, June 1919.

held views that prevented the Chamber from crusading against protection with the fervour traditional since the days of the Corn Laws. Manchester now opposed only those measures that affected its own trade, and even there opposition was not carried to extremes ; when the government insisted on fresh tariffs, the Chamber of Commerce acquiesced in the change of policy and directed its efforts to mitigating the worst results of the change.

During the war, Manchester merchants had urged the need to develop a British dyestuffs industry with the aid of protective tariffs. By 1920, when the government was formulating its policy for dyestuffs, Manchester was less certain. The Import and Export Regulation Bill presented to Parliament early in 1920 proposed to safeguard key industries by protective duties ; the Manchester Chamber objected that the Bill would not meet the requirements of national safety and would be detrimental to research and the development of industry.

The Chamber has concentrated particularly on the dye situation and considers that the only satisfactory way of permanently establishing the dye industry in this country is for that industry to be subsidised by the State.

Tariff protection gave no guarantee that the necessary manufacturing plant would be kept in commission ; moreover, " tariffs are against the interests of the consumers of dyes ".[1] The Bill was withdrawn, but later in the year the Dyestuffs (Import Regulation) Act was passed, prohibiting the import of dyestuffs except under licence ; the Manchester Chamber acquiesced in this solution of the problem.

The government proposed to treat other key industries differently. The Safeguarding of Industries Bill of 1921 provided for import duties on goods whose manufacture in Britain it was desired to encourage. By the narrow majority of 12 to 11 the Board of Directors of the Manchester Chamber of Commerce resolved :

That . . . the Safeguarding of Industries Bill is likely to prove injurious to the trade and commerce of the country. While they agree that it is necessary for some time to protect certain industries for the defence of the country, they believe that this could best be done by subsidy, granted by a competent authority and subject to a time limit and financial conditions. They therefore urge the Government to amend the bill accordingly.

[1] *Monthly Record*, February 1920.

Matters had, however, gone too far to make this possible ; the government would not agree to subsidies, and as the Chamber was divided in its opinion it did not persist in its opposition to the Bill. Nevertheless, it is clear that Manchester had lost its wartime fondness for tariff barriers.[1] Nor was the change confined to the cotton trade ; the Engineering Section of the Chamber also opposed tariff protection for key industries, though it supported Part II of the Safeguarding of Industries Act, which was designed to prevent dumping.[2]

Oddly enough, it was this part of the Act that really stirred the Manchester Chamber of Commerce to active protest. Late in 1921 the Board of Trade made an order imposing heavy duties on imports of fabric gloves from Germany ; this was done under the section of the Act providing for duties on goods artificially cheapened by exchange depreciation. This order, which closely affected the cotton trade, provoked much more strenuous opposition than the Act as a whole had done. The Manchester merchants argued that the duty would do serious damage to the export trade in yarn ; 90 per cent. of the yarn used in the Saxon glove industry was spun in Bolton, and this trade would be endangered if the government antagonised the German manufacturers. Moreover, Britain did not produce more than one-fifth of the gloves she needed, and would lose the valuable re-export trade in German gloves ; the government was therefore urged to exclude fabric gloves from the list of dutiable articles.[3]

This vigorous opposition did not move the government, but it did harden Manchester's attitude to protectionist measures in general. At the end of 1922 it was decided to hold a plebiscite of members of the Chamber of Commerce on the question whether they were in favour of the repeal of the Dyestuffs Act of 1920 and the Safeguarding of Industries Act of 1921. The results of the voting showed a decisive swing away from protectionist doctrines ; 1,600 out of a possible 3,800 votes were cast, and only 300 favoured continuance of the Acts, as against 1,300 for their repeal. The government was therefore urged to repeal the Acts " at the earliest possible moment. . . . In so far as safeguarding of certain industries may be essential for national safety, such end may best be

---

[1] Proceedings, 11th and 27th July 1921 ; *Monthly Record*, August 1921 ; *Economist*, 27th August 1921.

[2] Annual Report for 1921.

[3] Proceedings, 14th November 1921, 8th May and 24th July 1922.

secured by means of subsidy." [1]   The *Economist* noted with satisfaction :

The decision indicates very clearly that after a trial Manchester traders are sick and tired of government intervention in trade matters, and it is safe to say that commercial Lancashire is stronger on the Free Trade issue today than ever before.[2]

In this the *Economist* had sadly exaggerated, for the Chamber contented itself with a formal denunciation of the Dyestuffs and Safeguarding Acts, and took no steps to agitate for their repeal.   It did not wax enthusiastic over the lapsing of the McKenna duties in the Labour government's Budget of 1924, and declined to take part in the " political " discussion on the subject at the meeting of the Association of British Chambers of Commerce : " it was not a Manchester commercial question, and it would be best to leave it for the members to deal with individually." [3]   In the nineteenth century such an objection would not have deterred the Manchester merchants from strongly approving the fall of yet another tariff barrier.   Even the taxation of rayon in the Budget of 1925, which touched the cotton trade more nearly, evoked only mild protests from the Manchester Chamber of Commerce. Mr. Churchill's proposals were for import and excise duties mitigated by a drawback on exports ; and from the first the Directors of the Manchester Chamber concerned themselves with the administrative details rather than with opposition to the principle of the taxation of artificial silk,

which is a raw material of growing importance to the cotton trade. Unless the difficulties of a system of rebate of duties to the merchant exporter can be satisfactorily solved, the result of the tax will undoubtedly be most disadvantageous to a branch of the Lancashire export trade that is of increasing importance and promise.

In the end the administrative difficulties were overcome, and though the members at large pressed the Directors to oppose any tax on artificial silk, the Chamber's policy remained unaltered.[4]   Similarly, in 1926 Manchester refused to join the Blackburn Chamber of Commerce in agitating for the repeal of the Dyestuffs Act; and in 1927 the Manchester Chamber did not comment on the new import duties included

[1] Proceedings, 11th December 1922 and 8th January 1923.
[2] *Economist*, 13th January 1923.   [3] Proceedings, 12th May 1924.
[4] *Ibid.*, 11th May, 15th June, 13th July, 14th September, and 12th October 1925.

in the Budget, giving the usual reason that " the commodities affected do not include any upon which Manchester can speak with special authority ".[1] Though Manchester was unwilling to engage in a struggle with the government on fiscal questions, it was still prepared to resist proposals made in other quarters for more protection. In 1928 the Birmingham Chamber of Commerce proposed that a simplified procedure should be used in hearing applications for protection under the Safeguarding of Industries Act. With a flicker of the old fire Manchester objected that the Birmingham proposal was no more than a device by which industries " that had failed to pass the examination should have an easier one ".[2]

The only group of Manchester business men who vigorously attacked every manifestation of the protectionist spirit were the importers and users of sugar, who had long been militant free-traders.[3] Even during the war the Sugar Section of the Manchester Chamber of Commerce had persisted in its opposition to preferences for Empire-grown sugar,[4] an opposition which it maintained thereafter.[5] It opposed with equal vigour, but with as little success, the government subsidies to the beet-sugar factory at Kelham.[6] In 1924 the sugar users, whose considerable export trade in confectionery was prejudiced by the high price of sugar, renewed their efforts to free the trade from arbitrary restrictions ; but realising that it would be too much to hope for complete freedom of trade in sugar, they suggested that the imperial preference should be replaced by a grant-in-aid to the sugar-growing colonies ; the grant should be based on the tonnage of sugar exported from the colony to Britain. The beet-sugar factories at Kelham and Cantley should receive subsidies calculated in the same way, not block grants as before. This last suggestion was carried into effect by the British Sugar (Subsidy) Act of 1925, but the subsidies were so generous that the change could hardly be regarded as a step towards free trade ; nor did the opposition of sugar users prevent a safeguarding duty being put on wrapping and packing paper.[7]

In other fields of economic policy, the Manchester Chamber

---

[1] Proceedings, 14th April 1926 ; *Monthly Record*, April 1927.
[2] *Ibid.*, October 1928.   [3] See above, pp. 103, 108-111.
[4] Annual Report of the Sugar Section for 1916.
[5] Proceedings, 2nd June 1919 ; *Monthly Record*, March 1922.
[6] Annual Reports for 1919 and 1921.
[7] Proceedings, 12th October 1925 ; Annual Report of the Sugar Section for 1925.

of Commerce was equally unadventurous during the 'twenties. The business world accepted as a matter of course the need to return to the gold standard ; the disastrous fall of the rupee in 1920 convinced those who otherwise might have toyed with the idea of free exchange rates.[1] The crucial question of the level at which to stabilise the pound was almost entirely ignored by the business men, who left the Treasury and the banks to settle it among themselves ; as the President of the Manchester Chamber freely admitted, it was a question not properly understood by the man in the street.[2]

In an endeavour to get European trade moving again, the government had decided to grant credits to exporters whose business was reasonably sound but not sound enough to be financed by ordinary banks. The Manchester Chamber of Commerce did not object to the export credits scheme in this form, because it was clearly a necessary step to recovery in Europe ; but when the government decided to extend the scheme from Europe to the Commonwealth and Empire, Manchester merchants became seriously alarmed. They considered that the scheme should not go beyond its original purpose ; in particular the India and China merchants declared that in their trade existing financial facilities were " amply sufficient ". Because of this opposition, India and British possessions in the Far East were excluded from the extended scheme.[3] Throughout the 'twenties the India and China merchants resolutely maintained this attitude, although by 1928 there was a growing feeling that " times had so changed as to make it a wise policy for firms to obtain cover against apparently sound business as well as that of a problematical nature ".[4] Manchester's refusal to support the export credits scheme recalls memories of earlier opposition to the principle of limited liability. Just as limited liability had caused over-investment in cotton spinning after 1875, so export credits might encourage the growth of " unsound " business in eastern markets, and might divert trade from the established houses to new firms unfairly subsidised by the state. " This diversion would not represent a net gain to the country." [5]

[1] Proceedings, 10th January 1921.   [2] Monthly Record, February 1925.
[3] Ibid., May 1921 ; Proceedings, 9th May and 14th November 1921.
[4] Monthly Record, July 1924 ; Proceedings, 12th October 1925, 24th July 1928, and 8th April 1929.
[5] Committee on Industry and Trade, Minutes of Evidence, 1924-7, Vol. I, p. 104.

If export credits could not generate demand for cotton goods, neither could exhibitions. The Chamber of Commerce did not object to its members advertising their goods at exhibitions if they so desired; but it did not itself actively support them. For instance, it declined to share in any arrangements for a cotton section at the Wembley exhibition in 1925 ;[1] and even in 1928 Manchester merchants still declined to exhibit at the British Industries Fair, on the ground that no orders resulted.[2] When the spinners suggested a cotton exhibition at Manchester, they met with the same reply as the Department of Overseas Trade, which sponsored the British Industries Fair. Group advertising for Lancashire cotton goods was also condemned.[3] Trade in 1929 was rather worse than it had been in 1928 ; this further deterioration exhausted the patience of the Manchester merchants, and tended to change their attitude to exhibitions as to other aspects of policy. They decided that " The time had certainly arrived when the cotton trade should try to push itself a little more vigorously ". In 1930 the Chamber decided that it would support the British Industries Fair of 1931, and to prove that its change of heart was genuine guaranteed up to £1,500 to cover losses on the cotton section of the Fair.[4]

Throughout the calamitous nineteen-twenties, the old and tried policy of reducing costs remained the Lancashire cotton trade's chief hope. Because they believed that the exceptionally high price of raw cotton after the war was the most important single cause of the depression, the Manchester merchants put much emphasis on the need to stimulate cotton growing. Africa appeared to be the most promising source for extra supplies, but without government help little could be done. In 1923 the President of the Manchester Chamber estimated that the government should aim to produce a million bales of Empire cotton within two or three years ; [5] and in the evidence submitted to the Committee on Industry and Trade at the end of 1924 the Manchester merchants emphasised the importance " of getting increasing supplies of raw cotton from the British Empire in particular and from other countries in general ". Before the output

---

[1] Proceedings, 9th March 1925.   [2] Ibid., 14th May and 13th June 1928.
[3] Ibid., 10th September and 12th November 1928.
[4] Ibid., 9th December 1929 and 15th September 1930.
[5] Monthly Record, September 1923.

of cotton could be increased, however, the government
would have to develop colonial railways ; this was a task not
likely to attract private investors.[1]

High taxation was another serious obstacle to trade, in
that it raised the cost of goods and thus restricted demand.
For several years after the war, the Manchester Chamber of
Commerce waged an incessant campaign for economy in
national and local expenditure. Manchester merchants
had more than one reason for disliking high taxation ; but
when the slump set in, their already vigorous opposition to
heavy taxes grew stronger than ever. The Manchester
Chamber had in May 1920 reluctantly accepted the increase
in the Excess Profits Duty from 40 to 60 per cent., because
it appeared to be the only alternative to a capital levy.[2]
By the end of the year, when the boom had already broken,
the Chamber was calling for a drastic curtailment of national
expenditure, and " viewing with alarm the ever-increasing
local rates not only in Manchester but throughout the
country ".[3] The economies suggested in the Geddes Report,
which was published early in 1922, met with full approval
at Manchester ; expenditure ought to be reduced, it was
considered, by an amount " certainly not less in total than is
suggested in the Report ".[4] So urgent did the need for
economy appear that the Chamber appointed a special
National Finance Committee, which carefully scrutinised
every Budget from 1922 to 1925. In 1926 the committee was
not reappointed ; this may have been a sign that the national
economy drive had exhausted its impetus.[5] Local taxation
was still too high, partly because of extravagant estimates
for current services but more particularly because of the ever-
increasing debt charges ; and what made matters worse was
that local rates had to be paid whether firms made a profit
or not, whereas income tax was payable only on profits. " At
the present time ", the Chamber asserted,

in more than one industry in the City price is the all important
factor in securing orders. Our industries are meeting with fiercer
competition than ever before from foreign countries. Tariff
barriers . . . in many cases are *ad valorem*, so that the effect of the

---

[1] Minutes of Evidence, 1924-7, Vol. I, p. 101.
[2] Proceedings, 26th April 1920.
[3] *Ibid.*, 29th November and 8th December 1920.
[4] *Ibid.*, 20th February 1922.
[5] *Ibid.*, 21st June 1922 and 17th February 1926.

tariffs upon the ability of consumers to buy our goods is all the more severe inasmuch as the duty is calculated on our selling prices, which include the cost of taxation.[1]

A further element in the high cost of cotton goods was the inflated charges made by the finishing trades—bleachers, dyers, and printers—and by shipowners. When the profits of other sections of the cotton industry had sadly dwindled, the well-organised finishers were still paying large dividends ; and in 1923 the Manchester Chamber of Commerce decided to negotiate on behalf of merchants for reduced finishing charges. The dyers would agree to reduce their charges only if a graded discount scheme was accepted at the same time; merchants who did all their business with firms in the Dyers' Federation would get a 5 per cent. discount, and smaller discounts would be allowed to merchants who had some of their goods dyed by firms outside the Federation.[2] The merchants reluctantly accepted these terms, which at least made some concessions to the need for lower prices ; other sections of the finishing trade declared that price reductions were not immediately possible. In evidence before the Committee on Industry and Trade, the shipping merchants again attacked the price policy of the finishers, though without advocating government action to prevent abuse of the finishers' monopolistic position.[3] The merchants also acquiesced in the system of deferred rebates by which shipping rings prevented merchants from taking their custom to independent shipping lines.[4] Nevertheless, though the Chamber thought that the benefits of fixed freights and regular sailings outweighed the disadvantages of the deferred rebate and the absence of competition, it was always ready to negotiate with the Conferences for lower freight rates. For example, in 1922 the India merchants were notably successful in such negotiations. The Bombay and Karachi Steam Trade Conferences were persuaded to lower their rates by more than a third, and the Calcutta rate also was reduced.[5] A further small reduction in the freight rate to Calcutta was secured in 1928, and at the same time the India merchants

[1] Proceedings, 8th November 1926.
[2] Ibid., 8th January, 14th February, 8th October, and 10th December 1923.
[3] Minutes of Evidence, 1924-7, Vol. I, pp. 101-3.
[4] Ibid., q. 1945.
[5] Minutes of the India Section, 5th and 12th October 1922, and 7th July 1923.

managed to prevent an increase in the Bombay rate, which the Chairman of the India Section described as " the cheapest outward rate in piece goods to any part of the world ".[1]

[1] Minutes of the India Section, 30th November 1928 and 9th January 1929.

CHAPTER XVIII

THE STRUGGLE FOR FREER WORLD TRADE,
1919-1929

MOST of the wartime restrictions on the export of goods did
not long outlast the war itself. The most serious restriction
on the export of cotton goods—the allocation of shipping
space by an official committee—came to an end in December
1918.[1] To the great dissatisfaction of the Manchester
Chamber of Commerce, the blockade of neutral and enemy
Europe persisted well into 1919, since it was agreed among
the Allies that the blockade should not be lifted until Germany
had signed a treaty of peace. At the end of April 1919 the
blockade of Switzerland and northern Europe was relaxed,
subject to guarantees against re-export,[2] but Germany remained a closed market until the end of June. It was largely
as a result of vigorous protests by the Manchester merchants
that the black list of 2,000 South American firms was scrapped
as early as April.[3]

After the war, Manchester picked up the threads of its
traditional policy of low tariffs and most-favoured-nation
clauses where they had been dropped in 1914; as before,
the British Government could offer other countries nothing
in return for fiscal concessions, and year by year tariff barriers
rose against British goods. The most ruthless exponents of
economic nationalism were European countries, and it was
with the tariff barriers of Europe that the Manchester Chamber
of Commerce concerned itself most busily during the nineteen-
twenties. In 1921 France raised her tariff on some classes of
cotton goods to what the Manchester Chamber called a prohibitive level.[4] In 1922 the French, Italian, and Danish
tariffs were all raised, and the Manchester Chamber could
report no considerable success in resisting the increases.
The higher Danish tariff smacked of ingratitude, in view of
" the amount of foodstuffs which this country regularly
purchases from Denmark and which of course enter this

---

[1] Monthly Record, January 1919.
[2] Proceedings, 12th March, 9th April, and 14th May 1919.
[3] Ibid., 9th April 1919.   [4] Monthly Record, February 1921.

country free of duty ".   Manchester merchants felt that this
fact constituted " a fair and reasonable argument for pressure
to be applied ",[1] though such fair and reasonable arguments
were not likely to cause any change in the tariff policy of
Denmark ; nor would the Danes heed the further argument
that their own mills did not manufacture the fine goods that
were to be subject to heavier duties.[2]

Under the Treaty of Versailles the cotton manufactures of
Alsace-Lorraine were to be admitted to Germany duty-free
until the end of 1924.   As that day approached, the Lancashire cotton industry became anxious that this discrimination
in favour of Alsace-Lorraine should not be continued.   A
deputation from the whole trade waited on the Prime Minister,
Mr. Ramsay Macdonald, and received a reassuring reply.
Shortly afterwards an Anglo-German commercial treaty was
signed, providing for most-favoured-nation treatment and
for the suspension of the German import licence system.[3]
This was especially welcome because Manchester merchants
feared import prohibitions and licences even more than high
tariffs.[4]

The Manchester Chamber sounded a more belligerent note
in its attitude to the tariff policies of Spain and Portugal,
whose need to sell their wine on the British market had made
them susceptible to pressure at least since the eighteen-eighties.
In 1926 Spain increased her duties on steel, copper, machinery,
and yarns by a sixth or a quarter without giving shippers due
warning.   The existing commercial treaty, Manchester merchants complained, was in effect a useless scrap of paper ;
Great Britain ought to denounce the treaty when it expired in
April 1927, and seek a new agreement.   Shortly afterwards
the government announced that this was the course it intended
to pursue ; [5] but the new treaty, signed before the end of 1927,
was of no benefit to the cotton trade : " in many cases the
duties were entirely prohibitive ".[6] Portuguese policy left
at least as much to be desired.   In 1926 the duties on cotton
goods, " a very large proportion " of British exports to

[1] *Monthly Record*, February 1922 ; Annual Report of the Europe and
United States Section for 1922.

[2] *Monthly Record*, April 1923.

[3] Proceedings, 8th September and 8th December 1924 ;   *Monthly
Record*, October 1924.

[4] Committee on Industry and Trade, Minutes of Evidence, 1924-7,
Vol. I, qq. 2101-6.

[5] Proceedings, 11th October 1926 ;   *Monthly Record*, October 1926.

[6] Annual Report of the Europe and United States Section for 1927.

Portugal, had almost doubled ; the only benefit Britain had from the existing commercial treaty was most-favoured-nation treatment, though even this concession did not apply to the important Portuguese markets of Spain and Brazil. The Portuguese advantage from the treaty was disproportionately large, for Britain forbad wines other than those from Portugal or Madeira to be described as " port " or " Madeira " ; this was a very valuable concession. The Manchester Chamber urged the government to denounce this treaty also, and to negotiate a more equitable one in its place, using the facilities granted to Portuguese wines as a bargaining counter.[1]

As in the nineteenth century, the problems of trading in American markets caused little discussion, because American governments pursued a policy that was comparatively benevolent to Lancashire. During the war, exports of cotton goods to the Americas fell off sharply, and never recovered. Latin America, which in 1913 had taken 700 million yards of Lancashire's cloth, took only 420 million yards in 1920 ; during the 'twenties exports stagnated and in 1929 were a little below 400 million yards. Exports to the United States were more erratic ; in 1920 at 100 million yards they were more than double the pre-war figure, but the increase depended on a complete miscalculation by American importers of what the market would bear, and many orders were cancelled when the boom broke. From 1923 to 1925 imports of Lancashire cloth were again very large, rising above 150 million yards ; this too was only a temporary increase that was due to " a quite exceptional shortage in America of certain qualities of textiles ".[2] By 1929 exports had fallen back to below the 1913 level.[3] On the whole, however, Lancashire had less cause to complain of its American markets than of some others.

Nevertheless, the wholesale cancellation of orders from the United States was a serious problem, for to allow the repudiation of contracts to go unchallenged would have struck at the root of trade. The Manchester merchants agreed to refuse all requests for cancellation, and insisted that American importers should abide by their pledged word.[4] The American consular service provided facilities for the removal of " trade

[1] Proceedings, 11th October 1926 ; Monthly Record, November 1926.
[2] Proceedings, 13th December 1937.
[3] Annual Statement of the Trade of the United Kingdom.
[4] Monthly Record, November 1920.

misunderstandings ", which the Manchester merchants were invited to use. In most cases, however, they preferred the good offices of the New York Chamber of Commerce, whose arbitration led to many settlements satisfactory to the Manchester exporters ; by the middle of 1922 many of the disputes had been ended.[1] Manchester merchants did not fare nearly so well in somewhat similar negotiations, for the recovery of pre-war debts, with many eastern European firms : Austrian and Bulgarian debts remained unpaid until at least 1922 ; Rumanian firms did not come to a settlement until 1925 ; [2] and negotiations with Yugoslavia dragged on until 1930, when creditors received a dividend of some seven shillings in the pound.[3]

Few tariff questions caused trouble in the markets of the western hemisphere during the 'twenties. In 1920 Brazil concluded a commercial agreement with the United States by which each party allowed certain preferential tariff rates to the other. True to its traditional policy, the Manchester Chamber of Commerce deprecated this unequal treatment of Britain in the Brazilian market, and urged the Board of Trade and the Foreign Office to secure most-favoured-nation treatment for Britain ; but in the absence of a commercial treaty with Brazil nothing could be done.[4] Cuba was amenable to pressure. The British Budget of 1920 had put a 50 per cent. *ad valorem* surtax on imported cigars, and this heavy duty together with the depression greatly diminished the consumption of, and the revenue from, cigars ; in the year 1920 the cigar duty brought in only £325,000 whereas the estimated revenue had been £1,300,000. Cuba suffered serious injury from the reduced export to Britain, and the Cuban consul at Liverpool declared that " as a direct result " Cuba was thinking of retaliatory duties on British exports ; he urged the Manchester Chamber to put pressure on the Treasury for a lower duty on cigars. This was done : in a letter to the Chancellor of the Exchequer the Chamber pointed out that Cuba was a valuable market for English textiles, and that members of the Chamber were greatly concerned at the possibility of a tariff being raised against their goods as a

---

[1] Proceedings, 8th November 1920, 11th July 1921 and 24th July 1922.
[2] *Ibid.*, 10th April and 18th September 1922, and 6th April 1925.
[3] *Ibid.*, 12th May 1924, 16th April 1928, 15th September and 10th November 1930.
[4] *Ibid.*, 5th July 1920 ; Annual Report of the Central and South American Section for 1920.

16

counter-measure to the British tobacco duty.[1] Whether
the danger to British exports influenced the Chancellor as
much as the loss of revenue it is impossible to say ; however
that may be, the Budget of 1921 removed the obnoxious
surtax on Cuban cigars.

Before the war Manchester merchants had often complained
about the illiberal policies followed in the French colonial
empire. The war did nothing to alter French policy, and when
peace was restored Manchester merchants had once more to
contend with the unfair treatment meted out to them in the
much enlarged French colonial empire. Despite France's illiberal record, the Chamber of Commerce had not opposed
French annexations of former enemy territory. Early in 1919
the Chamber had been urged to resist on strategic grounds the
government's intention to hand over Alexandretta and Aleppo
to the French ; but the Chamber declined to meddle in " High
Politics ". The French, who were already in possession of
Beirut, had lost no time in promoting their own trade with
the Lebanon ; and the Manchester merchants protested to the
Minister of Blockade that the French were issuing import
licences only to their own nationals.[2] After the war, in their
determination to restrict the colonial carrying trade to their
own ships, the French tightened up the long-standing restrictions on the use of British and other foreign ships. Formerly
it had been permissible to carry goods for Cochin-China
as far as Singapore in British ships ; but in 1920 the French,
despite protests from Manchester, laid it down that the goods
would have to be transferred to a French ship at a French
port.[3] In North Africa, too, the Manchester merchants had
reason to complain of the " quite extraordinary lengths "
to which the French authorities went in fostering the import
of French cotton goods.[4]

It was hostility to France rather than any love for
Egyptian nationalism that prompted the Manchester Chamber
to support the ending of the Capitulations in Egypt. In
1914 Britain had proclaimed Egypt a protectorate, thus
ending Turkish suzerainty, but without making English the
official language or English law the law of the Egyptian
courts ; in these matters French influence remained supreme.

[1] Proceedings, 14th March 1921 ; Monthly Record, March 1921.
[2] Proceedings, 8th January 1919.   [3] Ibid., 5th May 1920.
[4] Committee on Industry and Trade, Evidence, 1924-7, Vol. I, qq.
1969-77.

Not until 1917 did the Manchester Chamber realise how anomalous it was that French should be the official language and that French law should be the law applied in the courts of a British Protectorate; and even after this date, wartime attempts to remedy the situation were unavailing. Finally, in 1921, the Manchester Chamber took the opportunity afforded by the Anglo-Egyptian negotiations to recommend the ending of the Capitulations, under which French law and language held their privileged position.[1] Manchester's attitude to the problem of the Sudan reinforces the view that the Chamber of Commerce had not supported the ending of the Capitulations merely out of regard for Egyptian nationalism. In 1924 and again in 1930 the Chamber urged the government not to yield too much to Egyptian pressure : " As cotton-growing increased the population and wealth of the Sudan, its importance as a market for Lancashire goods would be enhanced." [2]

In China, too, the growth of anti-foreign feeling created problems for the Manchester merchants. The Chinese import of Lancashire cotton goods even in 1920 amounted to only 64 per cent. of the 1913 figure, which had reached the enormous total of 700 million yards. By 1925 China was taking only 170 million yards of Lancashire cloth, and trade remained at or near this level until a further sharp decline took place in 1930.[3] The Manchester Chamber of Commerce realised that trade might well decline still faster if the special privileges of the foreign trading community in China were abrogated, and in common with other business organisations did its best to minimise the concessions that the British Government felt obliged to make to Chinese nationalism. The needs of business did not, however, receive as much consideration as they should have done. In 1925, in preparation for the Peking Tariff Conference which was to be held in the autumn, the Manchester merchants drew up a full statement of the policy they wished the British Government to follow; deputations saw the Foreign Secretary, Austen Chamberlain, and the leader of the Opposition, Ramsay Macdonald. The Manchester Chamber opposed the suggested reclassification of the Chinese tariff on cotton

---

[1] *Monthly Record*, December 1917, January and April 1918, April 1921.
[2] Proceedings, 7th July 1924, 14th April and 12th May 1930.
[3] *Annual Statements of the Trade of the United Kingdom*. Exports to Hongkong are included.

goods ; if, as the Chinese wished, the tariff were to be calculated on the number of threads per square of 5 millimetres, British trade would be injured. In order to pay the lowest possible duty, merchants would have to abandon many old and favoured kinds and qualities of cloth, and so lose the goodwill attached to them.[1]

Broader questions soon arose, and at the request of the Foreign Office the Manchester Chamber formulated its views on the problems of tariff autonomy, extra-territoriality, and the local government of Shanghai. The Chamber made few concessions to the Chinese feeling against the " unequal Treaties ", arguing that China might well turn the weapon of tariff autonomy against British trade.

On the other hand, if a stable representative government on western lines eventuated in China, it would not be right to permanently withhold tariff autonomy. As and when that condition was fulfilled a gradual series of limited concessions might be made, but at the present time the condition was not fulfilled and tentative steps could not be conceded.

The Chamber extended the same uncompromising resistance to the Chinese demand for the abolition of extra-territoriality, but was prepared for (say) a third of the members of Shanghai Municipal Council to be Chinese.[2] The British Government yielded much more than this ; the Peking Conference broke up when the Chinese Government fell before Chiang Kai-Shek's armies, but the Powers had already conceded the justice of China's claim for tariff autonomy, and in 1929 the new tariff came into force.

Tariff autonomy was not the only point at which Britain yielded ground before the rising tide of Chinese nationalism. In 1927 Britain abandoned her Concession at Hankow; according to merchants, this conciliatory gesture lowered British prestige and was definitely harmful to trade. The China Committee, which represented all sections of British commerce in China, including Manchester shippers, felt that :

Until Chinese nationalism is able to furnish more evidence of constructive and administrative capacity than it has so far given, the safeguards under which British trade has been conducted ought not to be further weakened.

[1] Minutes of the China and Far East Section, 3rd July 1925 ; Proceedings, 13th July 1925.
[2] Minutes of the China and Far East Section, 9th September 1925.

In particular, Britain should not surrender any more Concessions, or allow extra-territorial privileges and foreign administration of the Chinese Customs to be ended. " An abandonment of these safeguards would be more dangerous to our trade than boycott, dangerous as that has proved to be." It was with some reluctance that the Manchester Chamber agreed to the publication of these views in *The Times*, sweetened though the views were by an admission that the Chinese tariff might justly be raised.[1] If the Foreign Office had disapproved of the letter, no Manchester signatures would have appeared on it, for the Chamber took great care not to differ from the Foreign Office in public.[2]

The Persian market for Manchester goods, which had been quite considerable before the war, dwindled after it to much less than half its former size ; in 1913 Persia had taken 40 million yards of Lancashire cloth ; in the 'twenties the figure never rose above 20 million, and sometimes fell below 10 million. Nevertheless, Manchester merchants were unwilling to see any part of the trade that remained to them jeopardised by hasty concessions to Persian nationalism. When, therefore, in 1927 the Persian Government gave notice that it intended to abolish the Capitulations in the following year, the Manchester Chamber of Commerce urged the British Government to resist the change. As a correspondent wrote from Persia, it would be impossible to secure justice in the Persian courts, and the foreign merchant would be liable to fantastic claims and taxes, if the foreign community in Persia lost its extra-territorial privileges.[3] The British Government did not take this die-hard view. It agreed to the ending of the Capitulation as from May 1928, and in return Persia guaranteed fair treatment of foreigners ; they were not to be kept in prison for more than twenty-four hours without appearing before a magistrate, and in all commercial cases involving foreigners, only written evidence would be admissible.[4]

As exports to foreign countries, to India, and to British colonies in the Far East went on declining throughout the nineteen-twenties, the relatively stable markets in British West Africa and the Dominions became increasingly important to Lancashire. Canada was an exception to this rule, for by

[1] *The Times*, 14th November 1927.
[2] Proceedings, 14th November 1927.
[3] Minutes of the Egypt, Greece and Levant Section, 13th June 1927.
[4] *Annual Register*, 1928, p. 200.

1929 her import of cotton cloth from Lancashire had fallen to 38 million square yards, which was only a third of the 1913 amount. Australia, New Zealand, the Union of South Africa, and British West Africa, which had imported 425 million yards of Lancashire cloth in 1913, still took 400 million yards in 1929 when the rest of Lancashire's trade had shrunk to just over half its pre-war volume. On the whole the Dominions treated Lancashire's cotton goods very fairly. Tariffs were usually low, and with a preference over foreign competitors, though with the growth of local industries, particularly in Australia, a disturbing tendency to rising tariffs became apparent. Not all cotton goods suffered from these tariff increases, which at any one time usually applied only to special lines. For instance, in 1925 Australia imposed a duty of 1s. per square yard plus 30 per cent. *ad valorem* on cotton tweed, which was a " prohibitive " rate of duty ; the Manchester Chamber admitted that the great bulk of the trade and most firms would be unaffected by the tariff, " but for the particular firms the matter was one of the utmost gravity ".[1] By 1927 Australia had grown into the habit of making frequent increases in the tariff without due warning : the latest increase, Manchester complained, would double the price the Australian importer would have to pay for khaki drills, which had formerly been on the free list ; the Chamber therefore sent a deputation to the Australian High Commissioner to protest against the trend of Australian policy.[2] Whether the protest had any effect does not appear, but 1928 was free from alarms about the Australian tariff. Late in 1929, however, there was renewed cause for anxiety. Recent tariff increases had affected cotton yarns and made-up goods "of great importance to the Lancashire trade " ; the Manchester Chamber of Commerce, which had hitherto been reluctant to criticise Australia openly, now entered a solemn protest against the recently announced increases in the Australian tariff, which raised the duties on several commodities to prohibitive levels and would therefore gravely impede the further development of Anglo-Australian trade.[3]

Though largely concerned with contesting particular threats to the free interchange of goods, the Manchester Chamber of Commerce also supported general movements for

---

[1] Proceedings, 14th September 1925.
[2] *Ibid.*, 12th September and 10th October 1927.
[3] *Ibid.*, 9th December 1929.

the easing of trade restrictions. These movements usually centred round the newly-formed League of Nations, and were international in scope ; international conferences were frequent. An International Chamber of Commerce was founded in 1920. Before the war occasional congresses of Chambers of Commerce had been held, but there had been no continuing organisation ; the Manchester Chamber welcomed the new body and became an enthusiastic member of it.[1] In its early days the International Chamber of Commerce gave much attention to the problems of international commercial arbitration, which were of great interest to Manchester, especially after the wholesale repudiation of contracts in the second half of 1920. Manchester submitted to the International Chamber a memorandum on the subject, and was gratified to find that the proposals it contained had received general support.[2] By 1923 the work for international commercial arbitration had passed from the hands of the International Chamber to the League of Nations itself ; the League drafted a protocol that bound signatories to enforce the awards made under arbitration, and the British Government signed it without delay.[3] Other conferences and international movements also received the enthusiastic support of the Manchester merchants. The Genoa Conference in 1922, which was expected to assist the recovery of trade by restoring good relations with Russia, aroused high hopes at Manchester ; the Chamber of Commerce gave its hearty approval to the British Government's effort " to restore the European commercial and financial situation to a more stable basis through mutual co-operation ".[4]

The most serious threats to the free exchange of goods came, as always, from the fiscal policies of other nations. In 1924, in evidence before the Committee on Industry and Trade, Manchester merchants had not emphasised the adverse effect of tariffs ; but they had given a warning that customs duties " must be watched in the future ".[5] By 1927 the constantly rising tariffs, especially in Europe, were causing considerable anxiety.[6] In these circumstances, the Chamber of Commerce attached great importance to the World Economic Conference held at Geneva in May 1927 ; it hoped that the

---

[1] Proceedings, 11th October 1920 ; Annual Report for 1920.
[2] Proceedings, 10th April 1922.
[3] Ibid., 11th June and 10th September 1923.   [4] Ibid., 10th April 1922.
[5] See above, pp. 213-4.   [6] Proceedings, 11th April 1927.

Conference would stimulate the movement for the removal
of trade barriers, " which was the all-important policy for this
country ", and the Conference did in fact make proposals
" to diminish the severity of the obstacles to trade recovery
in the form of excessive Trade Barriers ".[1] The International
Chamber of Commerce shortly afterwards held its own
congress at Stockholm, where it called upon all countries
to reduce trade barriers, and especially tariffs ; the President
of the Manchester Chamber played a prominent part in the
deliberations of the congress, being appointed chairman of the
English Committee on trade barriers.[2] Nevertheless, Manchester merchants, and particularly those trading with Europe
and the United States, were well aware of the difference
between words and deeds. A high official of the Board of
Trade had privately warned the Chamber of the government's
powerlessness to prevent tariff increases ; all that the government could do was to " act as a kind of Post Office in the
matter ". Members of the Europe and United States
Section of the Chamber could draw little comfort from this
view. They asserted that " The inevitable result of a continuance of present tendencies will be a permanent diminution
in the export of Manchester goods " ; and they asked the
government whether it had explored " every possible means of
dissuading other countries from imposing increased tariffs
on our goods ". The Board of Trade returned an evasive
and unsatisfactory reply, which provoked the section into
advocating a mild form of retaliation ; it was suggested that
the imposition of import duties on luxury articles not produced in Britain might have some effect on countries that
seemed to be paying no more than lip-service to the principles
enunciated at the Geneva Conference. Mild as this suggestion
was, the Directors of the Chamber would not allow the section
to put it before the Board of Trade ; while Manchester was
exhorting others to reduce their tariff barriers, it could not well
advocate an increase in the number of British customs duties.[3]

As well as the general conferences, there were in these
years two important international meetings to discuss particular obstacles to trade. In October 1927 a conference

[1] *Monthly Record*, February 1927 ; Proceedings, 30th May 1927.
[2] *Ibid.*, 15th June and 11th July 1927.
[3] *Ibid.*, 12th September, 10th October, and 12th December 1927 ;
Minutes of the Europe and United States Section, 27th September and
10th November 1927.

opened at Geneva on non-tariff trade barriers. The Manchester Chamber held that these barriers, where they existed, were " perhaps more fatal to trade than customs walls " ; the conference was " but one step in a series of practical measures which must be undertaken if the trade barriers at present existing are to be reduced ".[1] The other conference was to discuss customs nomenclature and tariff classifications. The Manchester Chamber considered that *ad valorem* tariffs were the fairest and should be kept where, as in India, honest administration could be guaranteed ; specific duties on named varieties of cloth it condemned as " the worst of all possible systems ". There remained the " scientific " tariffs, first adopted in France and becoming increasingly popular ; these raised very technical questions, according to whether the specific duties were to be levied simply by weight, or whether consideration was also to be given to the number of threads in a given area. Either of these systems had some advantages for Lancashire : her " infinitely diversified " cotton industry could more easily take advantage of the more complicated system than could other cotton industries specialising in mass-produced goods. On the other hand, the simpler system of levying duties by weight might also favour Lancashire, whose goods were of a higher quality, weighed less, and would pay less duty than those of her competitors. It seemed to the Manchester Chamber that Lancashire's advantage in flexibility would probably outlast her advantage in quality ; but Lancashire could only use her diversified, flexible industry to the best advantage if highly complex tariffs persisted, and as it seemed likely that the conference would recommend a uniform tariff classification, highly complex tariffs might well disappear. On these grounds, Manchester urged the British Government to support specific duties by weight only, in the hope that in the short run the higher quality of Lancashire goods would bring the industry some advantage ; in public, the government would be able to argue that specific duties by weight only would be simple to calculate and administer, and would lead to fewer disputes.[2]

From the labyrinth of tariff classification the Manchester Chamber returned to consider less speculative matters. Early in 1929 the Europe and United States Section noted

[1] Proceedings, 10th October 1927.   [2] *Ibid.*, 10th September 1928.

" the failure of most countries to bring into operation the sentiments expressed at the World Economic Conference at Geneva in May 1927 " ; and remarked that " the policy hitherto pursued by this country has not resulted in any improvement in the prospects of the British textile export trade ".[1]   In 1929 tariff changes were fewer than in 1928, but what changes there were put fresh obstacles in the path of trade ; in the annual report for 1929 the Directors of the Manchester Chamber noted the growing feeling in Britain that other countries were determined not to lower trade barriers, and that in these circumstances it would be unwise for Great Britain to tie its own hands.   Though the Chamber as a whole might still hesitate to abandon its traditional policy, the merchants trading to Europe were fully convinced of the need for change.   Early in 1930 they considered the " Tariff Truce " proposals that were to be put before an international conference at Geneva.   The League had failed to reduce trade barriers, but if it could persuade the nations to observe a tariff truce, trade barriers would at least rise no higher.   The Europe and United States Section viewed this prospect with anxiety ; the truce would tie Britain's hands, and subject the country to a flood of imports at a time when the export trade was dwindling.   Instead of observing a tariff truce, Britain ought to impose duties on all manufactured goods imported into the country ; in 1929 £77,000,000 worth of textiles had been imported, which if manufactured here would have relieved unemployment, lessened the burden of unemployment relief, and lowered costs of production.[2] When even Manchester merchants began to argue in this fashion the end of free trade could not long be delayed.

[1] Annual Report of the Europe and United States Section for 1928.
[2] Proceedings, 5th February 1930.

CHAPTER XIX

THE FALL OF FREE TRADE, 1929-1932

By 1929 many influential business men in Manchester had become convinced that their old policy of free trade had failed, and that the adoption of some form of protection was inevitable. Early in 1929 a group of cotton manufacturers headed by Mr. (later Sir) Robert Waddington, who was himself a spinner and manufacturer and a Conservative M.P., had set on foot an agitation for a change in Britain's fiscal policy. They had begun by approaching the Directors of the Manchester Chamber of Commerce, " the only organisation which could speak with any weight for the whole of the cotton trade " ; but the Directors had shown little sympathy with the movement, not only because they were themselves staunch free-traders, but also because they feared that so explosive a question might provoke a constitutional crisis in the Chamber, as it had done in 1916. The General Election in the spring of 1929 averted this danger because the cotton manufacturers had to drop their agitation for the time being, though not before they had discovered a surprising volume of support for their idea. " From a simple resolution to the Chamber it was becoming a similar movement to the Anti-Corn-Law League." The movement had become national in character and large subscriptions had been promised.[1] In the autumn the Association of Chambers of Commerce took up the cry : only the Blackburn Chamber of Commerce openly opposed a protectionist resolution moved at the Association's half-yearly meeting ; the Manchester delegates maintained a discreet silence.[2]

While the business world was drifting towards protection as an antidote to the prolonged and now deepening depression of British industry, the new Labour government was con-templating repeal of the few protective duties that had been imposed during the past fourteen years. Among the duties that might be repealed were those on artificial silk, first imposed in the Budget of 1925. As soon as it began to

[1] Proceedings, 18th February and 8th April 1929.
[2] Monthly Record, October 1929.

be rumoured that Mr. Snowden might remove the duties, trade in artificial silk was hampered by uncertainty as to the future course of prices ; until the government assured traders that it would give a rebate on stocks that had already paid duty, orders were not being accepted for delivery later than March 1930. Under pressure, Mr. Snowden at length gave the required assurance that if the duties were repealed in 1930 holders of stocks would not suffer any loss.[1] Sugar users, whose business was affected by uncertainty about the sugar duties, received a similar assurance.[2]

No sooner had the question of rebates on duty-paid stock been settled, than the Manchester Chamber raised the more important question whether the time was opportune to repeal any duties at all. At the beginning of 1929 Lancashire business men had considered that there was " quite a good chance of a moderate revival occurring soon ". These hopes had quickly been dashed : in the first half of the year trade had not been unsatisfactory by post-war standards, but in July " yarn and cloth business was exceedingly dull " ; in August there was a three weeks' strike in the industry ; in September demand from India fell off noticeably ; October ended with the Wall Street crash ; and the last two months of the year brought only small orders to the trade. The trade returns for 1929 had already reflected the falling demand for cotton goods. The export of piece goods fell short of the 1928 total by nearly 200 million square yards ; though yarn exports did not show the same marked decline, the total value of cotton yarn and manufactures exported fell by nearly £10,000,000 from 20 to 18·5 per cent. of the total exports. At the beginning of 1930, therefore, the cotton trade faced the future with less confidence than it had felt twelve months before ; [3] and since confidence was low, industry did not want the burden of direct taxation to be raised, as it would have to be in order to cover the loss of revenue if import duties were repealed. This was the argument advanced by Manchester merchants in support of a resolution urging the government to exercise rigid economy, to impose no further direct taxes, and to repeal no import duties. To allow the Safeguarding and McKenna Duties to lapse, as the Labour govern-

---

[1] Proceedings, 17th June and 14th October 1929 and 13th January 1930.
[2] Ibid., 9th December 1929.
[3] Monthly Record, January to December 1929, and January 1930 ; Annual Statement of Trade of the United Kingdom.

ment proposed, would cost twenty or thirty million pounds, and in the existing depression of industry it could do nothing but harm to raise this sum by direct taxes. By a two to one majority, the Directors of the Manchester Chamber of Commerce accepted this argument and passed the resolution.[1] Nevertheless, though they were opposed to any immediate repeal of import duties, the Directors had not committed themselves to a new fiscal policy. This was made clear in the following month when they considered the resolution of the Europe and United States Section against the proposals for a tariff truce. The Directors allowed the Section to approach the government separately, without committing the Chamber as a whole to its views ; in this way they hoped to avoid re-enacting the unfortunate events of 1916.[2] To clarify the situation, however, the Directors decided to hold a referendum on fiscal policy ; and the voting upon a series of carefully phrased questions showed how quickly the climate of commercial opinion was changing. Out of 3,941 possible votes, 2,343 valid votes were cast, which was roughly a 60 per cent. poll as in 1888 and 1916 ; in 1923 only 40 per cent. of the possible votes had been cast. The poll showed that the opinions most commonly held in 1923 had been quite overthrown during the following seven years :

In favour of	Votes
Free Trade	607
Safeguarding	986
General Protection	232
Protection except of raw materials	196
Protection except of foodstuffs	27
Protection except of foodstuffs and raw materials	295

In accordance with the precedent established in 1923, the Directors formally notified the government of the result of the poll, but made no attempt to agitate for a change of policy such as the members would desire.[3] In any case, as Liberal journals were quick to point out,[4] the Chamber of Commerce

[1] Proceedings, 13th January 1930.   [2] Ibid., 5th February 1930.
[3] Ibid., 14th April and 23rd June 1930.
[4] The Monthly Record for June reprints leading articles from the Liberal Manchester Guardian and Manchester Guardian Commercial, and from the Protectionist Daily Dispatch. See also The Economist, 7th June 1930.

had not voted decisively one way or another. If free-traders were in a minority, so too were advocates of general protection; the only policy which could claim to have secured an absolute majority of votes was that of safeguarding, for all protectionists would surely support safeguarding measures, although these fell short of complete protection. This being so, the Directors of the Chamber would have had difficulty in finding a policy to fit the members' wishes, except the one already adopted of opposition to the abandonment of the Safeguarding and McKenna Duties.

In September 1930 the Manchester Chamber urged the government to retain all the import duties : " the country could not afford to spend more than it earned". At this time very few of the Directors would have acquiesced in the repeal of the duties ;[1] free-trade beliefs were dying fast at Manchester. The decisive break with the traditional policy came in October : the Canadian Government had offered to increase the preference by raising duties on non-British goods if Britain would grant a preference to Canadian primary products ; if the British Government accepted the offer, details would be worked out subsequently at a conference at Ottawa. The Manchester Chamber of Commerce welcomed this offer by formal resolution :

The Board of Directors of the Manchester Chamber of Commerce express the hope that the Imperial Conference now in session will investigate thoroughly the proposals put before it by the Prime Minister of Canada.

In view of the opinions recorded by the members of the Chamber in a recent referendum on fiscal policy, the Board have no reason to suppose that a majority of their members would be opposed in principle to variations in Great Britain's fiscal policy as part of an Empire-wide plan designed to ensure an all-round encouragement of inter-Empire trade.

The Board wish to point out, however, that any such plan must be based on real equality of contribution as between the different countries in the British Commonwealth of Nations. The Canadian proposals seem to the Board to call for sacrifices by Great Britain out of all proportion to the contributions proposed by Canada.[2]

In their annual report, the Directors enlarged upon their new policy : " The Board believes that the members of the Chamber now have a perfectly open mind on matters formerly subject to rigidly held theoretical beliefs " ; but if Britain was to give

[1] Proceedings, 15th September 1930.   [2]Ibid., 13th October 1930.

a preference to the Commonwealth's primary products, she would expect in return "a genuine *quid pro quo*", which might mean checking to some extent the industrialisation of the Dominions.

At the same time, the whole of the influence of the Manchester Chamber of Commerce was thrown against the enforcement of the tariff truce. In the previous February only the Europe and United States Section of the Chamber had opposed the truce ; now the whole body of Directors "without dissent" urged the government to move for postponement. Apart from Britain, no first-class Power had ratified the truce, the other signatories being a group of small European states—Belgium, Denmark, Finland, Latvia, Norway, Sweden, and Switzerland. As the Directors very reasonably argued,

Apart altogether from the principles involved, the small number of States . . . which have ratified the Tariff Truce . . . renders it inimical to the best interests of this country that the Convention should become legally operative.[1]

Shortly afterwards, representatives of the signatory states met at Geneva and agreed to postpone the enforcement of the truce.

The year 1930 must be considered to have been an important turning point in the history of the Manchester Chamber of Commerce. In that year the Chamber had supported imperial preference and, by implication, the protective tariffs already in existence ; it had opposed the tariff truce which would have prevented further action ; but it had not, as yet, called for a general tariff. Such a course could hardly be considered practical politics while the Labour government remained in office, convinced for the most part of the virtues of free trade, and in any case dependent on the votes of the Liberals. Not until the National Government took office in the last week of August 1931 did the Manchester Chamber advance further on the road to protection. The Chamber, while disclaiming any intention to intervene in politics, supported the new government and accepted the new taxes imposed in the emergency Budget introduced early in September ; it also welcomed the decision to retain the Sinking Fund, which demonstrated the government's adherence "to sound financial principles". The Chamber

[1] Proceedings, 10th November 1930.

noted, however, that the Budget contained no provision for redressing the adverse balance of trade, a defect which might be remedied by restrictions on " certain classes of imports " if the introduction of a general tariff were considered too controversial.[1] Very soon the Chamber's attitude became bolder ; on the 14th September the Directors urged the government to persist in seeking to balance the Budget and redress the balance of trade.   By 17 votes to 5 the Directors resolved that :

> The Board of the Chamber believes that the only immediately practicable and effective method of achieving this end is the imposition of a system of tariffs, and earnestly hopes that such a system will be introduced as soon as possible.[2]

For fear of offending any remaining free-traders among the members, this resolution committed only the Directors and not the Chamber of Commerce as such ; but the precaution was unnecessary, for only two members wrote to protest that the country could overcome the crisis without the aid of a tariff.[3]

An even more effective way of stemming the drain on the country's gold reserves was to abandon the gold standard. This step was not considered practicable by the Manchester Chamber of Commerce, for only seven months earlier Mr. Montagu Norman and his advisers had privately assured a deputation from Manchester that " British industry must put itself right by the stern method of reduced costs ", and that to expand the fiduciary issue (as the Chamber was then suggesting) would cause inflation, ruin London's prestige as the world's banker, and " reduce this country at once to the level of a second-rate power ".[4]   How much more damaging to London's prestige if Britain were to abandon the gold standard! Yet when the National Government decided to leave the gold standard after all, the Manchester Chamber of Commerce accepted the change quietly and issued a statement approving the government's decision.[5]

On 20th November the royal assent was given to the Abnormal Importations (Customs Duties) Act of 1931, which empowered the Board of Trade to impose temporary duties of up to 100 per cent. *ad valorem* on wholly or mainly manu-

---

[1] *Monthly Record*, September 1931.
[2] Proceedings, 14th September 1931.   [3] *Ibid.*, 22nd September 1931.
[4] *Ibid.*, 24th February 1931.   [5] *Ibid.*, 22nd September 1931.

factured imports. The question at once arose whether, and if so which, cotton yarns and goods should be dutiable; at first the Chamber suggested to the Board of Trade that all imports of cotton goods should be dutiable, " conditionally upon some system of exemption being possible in regard to imports proved to be composed of Lancashire yarns or Lancashire grey cloth, and with re-export facilities from bond ".[1] If the Board of Trade had followed this suggestion, it would have been favouring spinners as against manufacturers, and both as against finishers : for whereas the Chamber favoured a duty on foreign yarn, it opposed duties on foreign grey cloth woven from Lancashire yarn and on goods finished abroad from Lancashire grey cloth. The finishers naturally took " very strong exception " to this discrimination, and in face of their protests the Chamber withdrew its earlier request for the exemption from duty of Lancashire cloth reimported after finishing abroad.[2] Nevertheless, the Customs authorities proceeded to exempt Lancashire cloth finished abroad from the 50 per cent. duty that had been imposed on textiles, though at the same time foreign cloth imported for finishing in Britain was subjected to duty. At the instance of the finishers, the Chamber asked for this anomaly to be removed ;[3] but even then the policy of the Chamber had not been finally clarified. Within a few weeks the balance of opinion among the Directors had once more turned against the manufacturers and finishers ; in March 1932 the Chamber urged the Import Duties Advisory Committee to give preferential treatment to imports containing British raw materials or British semi-manufactured components, and the letter conveying this recommendation to the Committee mentioned goods made from Lancashire yarn as a case in point.[4]

The Imperial Conference of October 1930 had agreed that a further conference—on Empire trade—should be held in Ottawa twelve months later, but owing to the financial crisis in Britain and the change of government it was not until July 1932 that this further conference began. In preparation for it, the Manchester Chamber asked the government to appoint an expert from the cotton trade as an official adviser to the British delegation ; to this the government would not

---

[1] Minutes of the Executive Committee, 7th December 1931.
[2] Proceedings, 14th December 1931.
[3] *Ibid.*, 11th January 1932.   [4] *Ibid.*, 14th March 1932.

agree, however, and the Chamber had to be content with the
right to send unofficial advisers. Mr. J. H. Rodier was chosen
to lead the Manchester delegation because he had the three
essential qualifications : he had the confidence of the cotton
trade, he was a merchant, and an India merchant at that.
Though the conference aroused high hopes, the Manchester
Chamber did not forget that Britain could not live by Empire
trade alone, and warned the government that :

The arrangements made at Ottawa should be such as will afford
every opportunity for foreign countries who will deal on a satisfactory basis with Great Britain or the Empire to be allowed or
encouraged to do so.[1]

Similarly, though this was not proclaimed from the house-tops,
the Directors of the Chamber were " definitely of the opinion
that duties on food and raw materials are undesirable ".[2]

As the acknowledged spokesman for the cotton trade, the
Chamber prepared a printed memorandum entitled " The
Ottawa Conference 1932 and the British Cotton Export
Trade to the Dominions (Including Artificial Silk) ". The
memorandum contained a full account of the principles and
policy that, in the opinion of the Chamber, ought to be followed
by the British delegation when dealing with the cotton trade.
It began with a recital of general principles. Between Great
Britain and any of the Dominions

the best interests of both can be served by one allowing to the other
an acknowledged supremacy in certain fields of economic activity
in return for similar concessions in other fields.

Lancashire had " unrivalled equipment for producing cotton
goods ", and from this fact certain consequences flowed :

In cotton goods the rule should be free entry (or revenue tariffs
only) throughout the Empire ; where protective tariffs are raised
at all, they should still allow an acknowledged predominance to
the Lancashire Cotton Trade in some at least of the numerous
varieties of cotton goods. This predominance must be admitted
over the local industry and not merely over the competing foreign
industries. Otherwise the whole principle of genuine economic
co-operation becomes quite worthless to the Lancashire Cotton
Trade.

In applying these principles to the Dominions one by one,
the Manchester Chamber of Commerce made much less

[1] Proceedings, 9th May 1932.   [2] Ibid., 11th July 1932.

sweeping demands than might have been expected; it rejected any attempt to negotiate a uniform scale of tariffs on cotton goods with all the self-governing Dominions. Where much trade had already been lost by Lancashire to the local industry or to foreign competitors, Manchester asked for large concessions. Canada had been trying to build up a complete cotton industry of her own; the Chamber recommended that Canada should restrict the tariff to certain lines, and there grant Lancashire a 25 per cent. preference over her foreign (especially United States) competitors. From Australia, the Chamber asked for a wider preference on artificial silk goods and on cotton yarns; and from South Africa, where there was virtually no preference, Manchester asked for a preference of 20 per cent. From New Zealand Manchester asked nothing, for Lancashire still dominated the trade in cotton goods in that " most loyal of markets ".[1]

The concessions won at Ottawa bore little relation to those asked for by the Manchester Chamber of Commerce. As the Chamber's delegation reported on its return,

Although the dominating note of the conference was a cry for help from the primary industries of the Dominions, the better organised forces of Dominion secondary industries were still able to hold their own.

Nevertheless, half a loaf was better than no bread.

Measured by the standard of what might have been done, the Ottawa Conference may have disappointed many hopes. Measured by what was practicable and immediately possible, we believe it achieved something appreciable and likely to benefit our industry.[2]

Even this cautious statement proved to be too optimistic. A recovery of ground lost in the Indian market would have done more than anything else to lift depression from the Lancashire cotton industry, but no firm agreement on the treatment of Lancashire goods in India was arrived at in Ottawa; preferences were recommended for Lancashire, but before they could become effective the Government of India would have to secure the approval of the Legislative Assembly and the expert advice of the Indian Tariff Board. Neither of these procedures was likely to be quick. The Canadian agreement provided for a number of minor tariff changes, " which fell far short of those which the textile industry in

[1] Proceedings, 9th May 1932 ; *Monthly Record*, October 1932.
[2] *Ibid.*, September 1932.

this country had claimed to be justifiable"; further concessions would depend on the Canadian Tariff Board.[1] In public, the Chamber lost no time in asking the government to negotiate a more favourable agreement with Canada : in particular Canada should remove the exchange-dumping duty and other additional taxes, and replace her complicated tariff by a single straightforward rate of duty; the few tariff reductions already made should be extended to more and wider classes of goods ; and in due course the British Government should take steps to put Lancashire's case for further concessions before the Canadian Tariff Board. In private, members of the Chamber commented that the agreement with Canada was one that provided protection by Canada to her own industries and help to Canadian agriculturists by Britain.[2] Australia, like Canada, was not very generous to Lancashire at the Ottawa Conference. There were no tariff changes on cotton goods as such, though recalculation of preference margins might help to some extent ; genuine reductions would depend on the findings of the Tariff Board. South Africa and New Zealand, where Lancashire had few competitors, could afford to be more generous ; the cotton industries of these two Dominions were not powerful enough to resist unfavourable tariff changes. South Africa granted a definite preference on cheap cotton goods ; and New Zealand made some tariff reductions that would, it was hoped, " render still more secure the dominant position already enjoyed by British goods ".[3]

Though the Ottawa Agreements benefited the Lancashire cotton industry relatively little, they and the already existing preferences helped to save the export trade in cotton goods from the very steep decline so noticeable in other markets during the depression. In 1935, when the total export of cotton goods was little more than half what it had been in 1929, the Dominions imported rather more than in 1929. On the other hand, the Dominions markets had not collapsed so completely as some others in 1931, which was the worst year of the depression ; Ottawa therefore cannot take all the credit for the good results of later years.

Whatever the merits and effects of Ottawa, the Manchester

---

[1] *Monthly Record*, October 1932.
[2] Minutes of the Home and Overseas Dominions Section, 2nd November 1932 ; Proceedings, 14th November 1932.
[3] *Monthly Record*, October 1932.

merchants were now thoroughly weaned from the free-trade ideas to which they had clung so long. Even the preference for Empire food and raw materials went unchallenged, though before the Ottawa Conference had begun the Manchester Chamber had, privately at least, registered its opposition to duties on food and raw materials. Belief in the need for protection went along with an awareness of its dangers. Thus the Manchester Chamber of Commerce rejected Lord Beaverbrook's ideal of a closed imperial trading system; it could hardly do otherwise when nearly half the cotton goods exported went to non-Empire markets. Similarly, where protection led to a monopoly harmful to the cotton industry, the Manchester Chamber could still, for tactical reasons, advocate

EXPORTS OF COTTON PIECE GOODS, 1929-35

(million square yards)

	1929	*1931*	*1932*	*1935*
TOTAL	3,672	1,716	2,198	1,949
The Dominions	309	229	267	333
Australia	170	122	152	118
New Zealand	34	28	41	36
Canada	38	28	27	60
South Africa	67	51	47	119

free trade. In 1932 a deputation representing the whole of the cotton trade urged the Import Duties Advisory Committee to recommend the withdrawal of protection from the dyestuffs industry: one effect of the Dyestuffs Act was to make dye-users pay for research that ought to be financed by taxpayers generally; another was that the dyestuffs industry had become strong enough to conclude with its foreign competitors an agreement that " had resulted in an increase in prices . . . and the withdrawal of competition ". Despite this protest, the Dyestuffs Act remained on the statute book: the only concession the Import Duties Advisory Committee would make was to withdraw the (non-protective) duties on imported dyes; import licensing continued.[1] The dyestuffs industry was an extreme case of a fairly general danger: that the export trade would be neglected in the general desire to protect the home market. The President

[1] Annual Reports of the Finishing and Allied Trades Section for 1932 and 1933.

of the Chamber, Mr. (later Sir) Thomas Barlow, pointed out in July 1932 that for the cotton trade protection of the home market was scarcely needed ; so far as cotton was concerned, tariffs should be used for bargaining rather than protection.[1]

To use tariffs for bargaining did not necessarily mean the abandonment of either the open door or the most-favoured-nation clause.   Before 1914 Germany had successfully combined a tariff with the most-favoured-nation clause and with the open door for all who wished to trade with her colonies. In 1930 and 1931 this was in effect the policy that the Manchester Chamber of Commerce urged on the British Government ; but, as Japanese competition became more intense, this relatively mild policy gave way to a more exclusive one. In the extremity of catastrophic depression the Manchester Chamber of Commerce made haste to denounce both the open door and the most-favoured-nation clause ; these cherished beliefs were shattered with surprising ease and abandoned with little apparent regret.

[1] *Monthly Record*, July 1932.

CHAPTER XX

JAPANESE COMPETITION IN THE COLONIES AND DOMINIONS

In 1872 a Japanese embassy visited Britain for the first time. Eager to widen the bounds of commerce, the Manchester Chamber entertained the mission at a banquet, and expressed the hope that commercial relations between the two countries might be maintained and extended. " Every assistance was afforded to aid the members of the Mission in their enquiries respecting our local institutions and manufactures." Mr. Hugh Birley, M.P., expressed a feeling common at the time when he declared :

Those who had the honour of receiving invitations from the President, or who met the Embassy elsewhere, must have been very much impressed with the apparent receptiveness of these gentlemen to European, or English, feelings and habits. There may be as mighty a change effected in the great empire of Japan as the world has hitherto seen, or as has ever been recorded. The imitative faculties and the great intelligence of that people may cause a change in the system of commerce in the East which our descendants may compare, perhaps, to the opening of the trade of the East in the time of Vasco da Gama, or that of the West by Columbus.[1]

The calamitous way in which this prophecy was to be fulfilled did not become apparent for many years ; the Japanese challenge to Lancashire's supremacy in the international trade in cotton yarn and piece goods developed very slowly. Alarms in the eighteen-nineties and again during the First World War later proved to have exaggerated the immediate danger. In the early years of the twentieth century, it was the Indian cotton industry that suffered at the hands of Japan; Japanese spinners quickly wrested the Chinese yarn trade from the Indian mills,[2] which had themselves ousted Lancashire yarns in the eighteen-eighties. Before 1918 Japan had been primarily a yarn exporter ; in that year her yarn exports totalled 170 million lb., but her exports of piece goods

[1] Annual Report for 1872, p. 15.
[2] V. Anstey, The Economic Development of India (1936), p. 262.

(chiefly grey cloth) amounted to only 657 million yards, against 455 million yards in 1914.[1] During the 'twenties Japan's cloth exports steadily increased. By 1925, three-quarters by volume and two-thirds by value of China's import of cotton goods came from Japan ; Lancashire's share in the trade had fallen away correspondingly.[2] In East Africa, Japanese competition began to make itself felt in 1923 ; in 1924 it had become serious ; and by 1926 Britain's share of the trade had fallen to 30 per cent., though part of the loss was due to Indian competition as well.[3] In India itself, and in the Dutch East Indies, Japan was also strengthening her position. By 1929 Japan was exporting nearly 1,800 million square yards of cotton cloth—almost half as much as Lancashire. In the ensuing depression her exports fell much less markedly than Lancashire's ; in 1932 they rose sharply to record levels.

EXPORTS OF COTTON PIECE GOODS : UNITED KINGDOM
AND JAPAN 1929-32 [4]

Million square yards

	1929	1930	1931	1932
United Kingdom	3,672	2,407	1,716	2,198
Japan	1,791	1,572	1,414	2,032
Japanese Exports as percentage of World Exports of Cotton Piece Goods	23	27	29	36

Until 1931 the Manchester Chamber of Commerce did not try to obstruct Japanese expansion. In the 'twenties Manchester merchants had hoped, but not pressed, for a preference in India against Japan ; but elsewhere they had relied on the ordinary processes of competition to keep the Japanese at bay. Early in 1931, however, the Africa merchants resolved to take more decisive action ; they asked the Manchester Chamber to seek a preferential tariff for British textiles in British Somaliland. Before agreeing to press the

[1] K. Yamasaki and G. Ogawa, *The Effect of the War on the Commerce and Industry of Japan* (Carnegie Endowment for International Peace, 1929), pp. 114 and 320.

[2] B. Ellinger, " Lancashire's Declining Trade with China " (*Transactions of the Manchester Statistical Society*, 1927-8), pp. 5-7.

[3] Annual Report for 1923 ; *Monthly Record*, April 1924 ; Lord Hailey, *An African Survey* (1938), p. 1336.

[4] G. E. Hubbard, *Eastern Industrialisation and its Effect on the West* (1935), p. 5.

demand, the Directors of the Chamber called for a legal and statistical survey of the problem ; but in principle they did not object to ending the rule of the open door.[1] The report was ready by the end of the year, but in the most material respect it was out of date before it was drawn up, for the trade statistics it contained were those of 1929. It was not for this reason, however, but because the Ottawa Conference was pending, that the Directors decided to postpone action on the report. Being based on old statistics, the report found that there were few colonies where a preference would do good. In British West Africa, only harm could result from denunciation of the Anglo-French Convention of 1898, which guaranteed the open door in Nigeria, the Gold Coast, the Ivory Coast, and Dahomey ; for Lancashire would gain less in the British than it would lose in the French colonies, by denouncing the Convention. Similarly in East Africa, though Japanese competition was severe, Lancashire would lose trade in Belgian and Portuguese territories by denouncing the Congo Basin Treaties ; and Tanganyika would have to be excluded from any preferential system under the terms of the League of Nations Mandate. In Ceylon, the largest competitor was the Indian cotton industry, which could hardly be excluded from the benefits of an imperial preference. Only in Malaya (admittedly an important exception) and in Jamaica, where the United States was the chief competitor, would Lancashire get a definite advantage from preferential tariffs.[2]

The growing pressure of Japanese competition soon persuaded the Manchester Chamber of Commerce that it would be unwise to delay action until after the Ottawa Conference. In March 1932 the Directors unanimously resolved :

That preferential duties are desirable in the Crown Colonies. . . . The interests of the populations of the Crown Colonies can be best served by embracing them within the schemes of Imperial economic co-operation to which [the Dominions] have already agreed in principle. . . . His Majesty's Government should immediately take steps to free themselves from all treaty restrictions on their future course of action.

The Directors argued that this step would be fully justified in view of the economic crisis, Britain's changed fiscal policy, the probability of imperial preference, and " the emergence of much more drastic competition from certain industrial

[1] Proceedings, 9th March and 11th April 1931.
[2] Ibid., 14th December 1931.

countries with lower standards of life ". The London and Liverpool Chambers of Commerce, formerly less liberal in their views than Manchester, were not so easily moved from their adherence to the principle of the open door ; and without their agreement the government would not denounce the treaties that prevented the imposition of preferential tariffs in the African colonies.[1] By the autumn of 1932 Japanese goods were penetrating markets where they had never been seen before ; they were flooding the Ceylon market at prices with which Lancashire could not hope to compete, and in Australia Japanese prices were so low that under the 25 per cent. *ad valorem* tariff their goods paid only twice as much duty as Lancashire goods admitted at the preferential rate of 5 per cent. Hitherto, the Manchester Chamber of Commerce had not asked for special measures against Japan alone, but had been content to ask for a preference against all competitors. Now, however, the Chamber took the much more serious step of asking the government to discriminate against Japan alone ; in West Africa this could be done only by denouncing, so far as Japan was concerned, the treaties binding Britain to maintain the open door.[2] Moreover, Japanese goods were so cheap that *ad valorem* tariffs were not stringent enough to exclude them ; specific duties would certainly be needed, and perhaps only a system of quotas would be strong enough to stem the tide.[3] The Directors strengthened their hand in fighting for this policy by calling a special general meeting of members, at which it was unanimously resolved that throughout the Empire, and wherever Britain granted foreign products favourable terms for entry into the British market, British cotton goods ought to have preferential treatment " against the competition of countries with lower standards of living and depreciated exchanges ".[4]

Towards the end of 1932 the demand for colonial preferences began to bear fruit. In Ceylon and Malaya 10 per cent. preferences were granted to British cotton goods ; this was a very small gain, but it served as a basis for further concessions. In March 1933 the Manchester Chamber declared that the 10 per cent. preference in Malaya was not large enough to restrain Japanese competition ; the Chamber called upon the government to take " adequate measures ", without specifying

[1] Proceedings, 14th March and 9th May 1932. [2] *Ibid.*, 10th October 1932.
[3] *Ibid.*, 14th November and 12th December 1932.
[4] *Monthly Record*, December 1932.

what those measures should be.[1] By April the lines of policy had become clearer. A deputation to the President of the Board of Trade, Mr. Runciman, and to the Colonial Secretary, Sir Philip Cunliffe-Lister, put three suggestions before the government. The first was for discrimination against Japanese goods throughout the colonial empire ; but though the government promised to threaten action in Malaya, Ceylon, and the West Indies, it would only guarantee to take action in West Africa. This action took the form of giving a year's notice to exclude West Africa from the scope of the Anglo-Japanese commercial treaty. The Manchester merchants' other proposals were more tentative ; they asked for a division of markets with Japan, and for subsidies on the export of cotton goods. The government discreetly ignored the proposal for a subsidy, but agreed that a division of markets would help.[2]

The Japanese were not unwilling to negotiate for a division of markets. In June 1933 they suggested conversations, and by October these had begun.[3] By the middle of March 1934 the talks had broken down, and it rested with the government to decide what action should be taken in defence of Lancashire's trade. In 1933 Japan had gained a little more ground at Lancashire's expense, and for the first time the volume of Japanese exports of cotton goods slightly exceeded Lancashire's ; even in British West Africa, where in 1932 Lancashire had had 90 per cent. by volume of the trade in piece goods and Japan only 3 per cent., there were signs of coming disaster in 1933, for Japan increased her share of the trade to 11 per cent. ; in Ceylon, Malaya, and British East Africa, Japan had already taken more than half the trade by 1932.[4] In these circumstances the British Government came to a momentous decision, and on 7th May 1934 Mr. Runciman announced in the House of Commons that the import of cotton and rayon goods into the colonies would be subject to quotas. Except in West Africa, where only Japan would be affected, the quotas would apply to all foreign imports ; the government had chosen the years 1927 to 1931 as the base period " with a view to reinstating this country in the position in those markets which she held before the present abnormal period ". The quotas, which would be introduced without delay, would apply

[1] *Monthly Record*, March 1933.   [2] Proceedings, 10th April 1933.
[3] *Ibid.*, 19th June and 9th October 1933.
[4] G. E. Hubbard, *op. cit.*, p. 38.

retrospectively to 7th May 1934. The markets principally affected were British West Africa, the West Indies, Ceylon, and Malaya ; Hongkong was excluded.[1]

The unofficial members of colonial legislatures, especially in Ceylon and Malaya, strongly resisted the imposition of quotas, which (as the Manchester merchants themselves realised) would deny to the colonial peoples the right to buy their cloth in the cheapest market. This resistance to quotas, Manchester argued, was a mistaken policy. Europe, and especially Great Britain, bought the greater part of the colonies' exports ; if Britain was impoverished by losing her export markets, she would be unable to buy colonial produce, and if this happened the colonies would suffer.[2] The argument convinced few people outside Lancashire, and had to be buttressed in various ways. In 1936 a group of economists, writing under the joint auspices of the Carnegie Endowment for International Peace and of the International Chamber of Commerce, advocated the abolition of quotas. Manchester opposed the suggestion and declared that from motives of self-preservation it would continue to do so " as long as Japanese goods continue to intrude in world markets at price levels which involve sudden and complete destruction of British trade ". Instead, Manchester suggested, the nations should agree to abide by the principle that they would not enter world markets on " conditions calculated to disturb world trade ". Japan, not Manchester, was to blame for the proliferation of trade barriers ; she had neglected " her responsibilities to world trade by depriving it of stability ".[3] Manchester did not, however, go so far as to propose that trade should be frozen in its existing channels ; the quota system was by no means inflexible, and as advocated by Lancashire would allow a percentage of the total trade to be set aside to meet unforeseen changes in demand, or to provide for newcomers.[4]

However shaky the theory might be, the practical benefits to Lancashire from the colonial quotas were substantial enough. In 1933 the " quota colonies " had taken 170 million square yards of Lancashire cloth ; in 1935, the first full year in which the system of quotas was in operation, these colonies took 275 million square yards, and in 1936 and 1937 just over 300 million

[1] Hansard, 5th series, Vol. 289, col. 716 ff. : H.C., 7th May 1934. Proceedings, 11th June 1934.
[2] Monthly Record, July 1934. [3] Proceedings, 14th September 1936.
[4] Monthly Record, August 1938.

square yards *per annum*.[1] There can be little doubt that but for quotas the Japanese would have taken this extra trade. Having secured the quotas in 1934, the Manchester Chamber of Commerce took care that they should be maintained and strengthened thereafter. In 1936, when the French denounced the Convention of 1898, it became possible to impose quotas on textile imports from all countries into British West Africa ; this was expected to eliminate " the Chinese menace ".[2] In 1937 the Chamber tried to get the Japanese quota in Malaya reduced ; the entrepôt trade of Singapore made it difficult to administer a quota system for retained imports only. When the quotas were fixed in 1934 it had been assumed that Britain and Japan re-exported an equal proportion of their deliveries in Malaya ; but later statistics had shown that Japan had a more than proportionate share of the re-export trade. On this ground Manchester tried to get the Japanese quota reduced from 34·7 to 23·3 million yards.[3] Manchester further protested that Japan's puppet state of Manchukuo had been granted a textile quota in Jamaica ; this quota was withdrawn.[4] With less success Manchester opposed a change in the quota system in Ceylon. In order to get Ceylon to agree to imperial preference, the government had withdrawn grey goods from the quota system and had increased the quotas for other piece goods by 50 per cent. ; these changes were much to Japan's advantage. There was some alarm at Manchester until an assurance was given that Ceylon was a special case, and that the government had no intention of abandoning quotas generally.[5]

British colonies were not the only ones that felt the effects of Japanese competition. Before the war and even in the 'twenties, the Dutch East Indies and the French possessions in Africa had bought heavily from Lancashire. The largest market was the Dutch East Indies, which as recently as 1929 had taken 120 million square yards of cloth from Lancashire ; by 1932 the figure had fallen to 44 million square yards. Only by the imposition of quotas could Lancashire hope to recover her lost trade. In April 1933 the British and Dutch cotton industries held a conference at which it was agreed that quotas should be imposed in the Dutch East Indies to restore the

[1] *Working Party Report : Cotton* (1946), p. 120.
[2] Proceedings, 14th December 1936.
[3] *Ibid.*, 8th March 1937. [4] *Ibid.*, 13th September 1937.
[5] *Ibid.*, 13th September and 11th October 1937 ; *Monthly Record*, September 1937.

trade to its 1928-29 position; this would add nearly 100 million yards to Lancashire's exports. The Dutch in return wished to revive their exports to Britain; they had been severely damaged by the adoption of tariffs in 1932. On balance, every section of the Lancashire cotton industry would have benefited from the agreement except the yarn dyers, and in the general interest they were ready to be sacrificed.[1] Sir Leonard (later Lord) Lyle helped to gain the necessary consent of the Java sugar producers by undertaking to buy a definite quantity of Javanese sugar at world prices for a period of five years. However, the Board of Trade did not act quickly enough, with the result that the Dutch Government imposed quotas to suit the Dutch textile industry only; 60 per cent. of the trade was reserved to the Dutch and the rest was left to be competed for by Japan and Lancashire. In practice this meant that 40 per cent. of the trade fell to Japan.[2] Not until July 1935, after a conference at the Hague with representatives of the Lancashire cotton industry, did the Dutch agree to revise the quotas. As a result of this agreement, it was hoped that Lancashire would have much better prospects for trading in the Dutch East Indies; but the quotas announced in November 1936 did much to dash this optimism. The " global " quotas, which gave Japan all the trade not specifically reserved for the Dutch, were kept for the main classes of cotton goods; where "national" quotas had been arranged, Lancashire's share, especially in bleached, printed, and fancy goods, was disappointingly small; only the quota for dyed goods was satisfactory.[3] Despite these grievances, trade greatly improved in 1937. In 1935 Lancashire's trade with the Dutch East Indies had dwindled to 10 million yards; it rose to 60 million yards in 1937. This was still only half the total of 1929, but was a better result than had been obtained in 1932, and a vast improvement on 1935.

French possessions in Africa raised fewer commercial problems. In West and Equatorial Africa, Japanese competition never became serious, and Lancashire's moderate trade went on unhindered. Morocco, a somewhat larger market, was almost as good a customer to Lancashire in 1932 as it had been in the record year of 1913. But this was too good to last; Japanese competition became severe in 1933, and at

---

[1] Proceedings, 8th May 1933.   [2] Ibid., 12th March 1934.
[3] Ibid., 9th September 1935 and 13th January 1936.

the end of the year joint consultations took place between French and British textile interests. Nothing resulted, however, because France was bound under the international agreement made at Algeciras in 1906 to preserve the open door in Morocco, and the United States would not agree to the abrogation of its rights under the treaty. Fresh negotiations in 1935 broke down for the same reason.[1] The Congo Basin Treaties had an equally cramping effect in British East Africa. In the confident days of the later nineteenth century, Manchester had rejoiced that so large an area of the world's surface would be permanently open to economic penetration; but now Japanese competition threatened to wipe out Britain's trade with East Africa. In 1934, and again in 1936, the Manchester Chamber of Commerce made tentative approaches to the Board of Trade and the Colonial Office;[2] but the government shrank from denunciation of the Congo Basin Treaties and they remained in force. However, under the peace treaty of 1951 Japan waived her rights to equal access to the markets covered by the Congo Basin Treaties, and Manchester at last gained satisfaction on this legal point.

It has already been shown that the Ottawa Agreements fell short of the hopes at one time entertained in Lancashire. By the end of 1932 Manchester merchants were referring to the " disastrous effects of Japanese competition " in the Australian market, for Japanese prices were less than half those of Lancashire.[3] Since the Australian tariff was *ad valorem*, this meant that despite the preference the Japanese could easily undercut Lancashire's prices; during 1933 and 1934 the Manchester Chamber of Commerce accordingly argued that only if Australia changed from *ad valorem* to specific duties could Lancashire hold her own. Moreover, it was maintained, Australia should enforce section 9 of the Australian Customs (Industries Preservation) Act, which provided for the imposition of dumping duties.[4] Instead of helping, however, Australia seemed bent on hindering Lancashire's trade, for in August 1934 increased duties were imposed on some classes of goods. The Manchester merchants argued that these duties infringed the Ottawa Agreement, and were " gravely concerned by the application

---

[1] Proceedings, 18th December 1933, and 8th July 1935.
[2] *Ibid.*, 8th October 1934, 9th December 1935, and 15th June 1936; Annual Report for 1935.   [3] Proceedings, 14th November 1932.
[4] *Ibid.*, 8th May 1933 ; *Monthly Record*, February 1934.

of protective duties to goods which have not previously been made in Australia ".[1]

To some extent this outcry was premature. Exports of cotton piece goods to Australia had reached a very high level in 1932 and had not fallen very far in the following two years. In 1935, however, the situation decidedly changed for the worse, and by May the Manchester merchants were asking the Board of Trade to suggest to the Australian Government that only quotas could now save Lancashire's trade. They asked too, for a ruling on the interpretation of the Ottawa Agreement to allow British industries to compete with Australian industries on fairer terms. The government sympathised with Lancashire's predicament ; so did the Australian Prime Minister when he was interviewed a few months later, but he could not promise any tariff reductions.[2] In these circumstances, the Manchester Chamber of Commerce decided to send a mission to Australia to gain support for the policy of quotas ; the controversial but less important question of the tariff rates on Lancashire goods would not be raised. The Chamber recognised that as Japan was a heavy buyer of Australian wool the Australian Government would have to move cautiously ; on the other hand, Lancashire was also an important market for Australian products, and " Manchester, which was formerly opposed to a policy of Imperial preference, is now prepared to wield an outstanding influence in the production of true reciprocity in Empire markets ".[3] The mission spent two months in Australia, and before it had returned to England the Australian Government announced changes in policy that appeared to be friendly to Lancashire. The request for quotas was not met, but Lancashire's earlier policy—a change from *ad valorem* to specific duties—was unreservedly accepted ; the new duties gave Lancashire a preference of $7\frac{1}{2}d.$ per linear yard on rayon, and of $2\frac{1}{2}d.$ to $3d.$ per linear yard on cotton piece goods. The Manchester Chamber of Commerce did not claim the credit for this welcome change of policy, however, because it seemed likely that the Australian Government had made up its mind on the question before the Chamber's mission arrived.[4]

Events soon proved that Australia had not imposed specific

[1] *Monthly Record*, September 1934.
[2] Proceedings, 13th May and 8th July 1935.
[3] *Ibid.*, 14th October and 9th December 1935.
[4] *Ibid.*, 12th June 1936.

duties because of any special tenderness for Lancashire. At the end of 1936 Japan and Australia concluded an agreement that largely nullified Lancashire's gains. Under the agreement, which was to run for eighteen months, Australia allowed Japan a quota of 120 million square yards of cloth : 17·5 million yards of calico for bag-making would be admitted duty free, and 102·5 million yards of textile fabrics, divided equally between cotton and rayon, would be admitted on payment of duties at only half the rate of those previously in force. In return Japan agreed to buy 800,000 bales of Australian wool during the next eighteen months. This agreement bitterly disappointed the Manchester Chamber of Commerce, for the quotas allowed Japan to consolidate most of the gains made since 1932, when she had exported only 44 million yards of cloth to Australia. Nevertheless, the Chamber was unwilling to dissipate goodwill by hastily criticising Australia's behaviour ; some agreement with Japan Australia had to make, for both political and economic reasons. Manchester put the blame for the unfortunate turn of events upon the Board of Trade, which had failed to use its influence to get better terms for Lancashire. The British Government was declared to be showing " callous indifference " ; " we are not getting proper assistance under the Government policy of trade treaties ; they will not use either their influence or bargaining power in favour of Lancashire textiles ".[1] Despite this setback, Lancashire's exports to Australia in the last two full years of peace remained well above the low levels of 1935 ; but the level of 1932 was not regained.

The restrictions placed on the Japanese cotton trade from 1934 onwards prevented any general expansion in Japan's exports and in some markets actually caused a decline ; but Japan's exports when diverted from one course rushed into another, with the result that Lancashire had no sooner filled one breach than another was opened. Thus in 1936 the South African and New Zealand markets, hitherto free from Japanese competition, began to be affected. In South Africa certain piece goods used in industrial processes were admitted duty free and the trade began to fall into Japanese hands. In New Zealand, too, Japanese competition had assumed " serious proportions " by the end of 1936.[2] Egypt had been a large market for Lancashire goods in the 'twenties, and

[1] Proceedings, 11th January 1937.
[2] Ibid., 13th July and 9th November 1936.

18

despite the growth of a local industry still took 80 million yards of cotton cloth in 1932. Thereafter Japanese competition reduced Lancashire's trade with Egypt still further, and by 1935 the Manchester Chamber of Commerce was asking for the imposition of quotas, in return for which Lancashire would guarantee to buy substantial quantities of Egyptian cotton. An Egyptian economic mission that visited Britain in 1935 reported against the idea of quotas,[1] and the matter dropped until 1937. By then Lancashire's trade with Egypt had dwindled to 50 million yards, and in an endeavour to recover lost ground the Manchester Chamber dispatched a mission to Egypt with the object of securing quotas. It returned empty-handed, however, and the Egyptians preferred to meet the dangers of Japanese competition (which affected the local industry as well as Lancashire) by imposing heavy duties. A second mission was dispatched from Manchester to Egypt, and successfully arranged for the imposition of quotas based on purchases of Egyptian cotton over the past three years ; on this basis Lancashire would be allotted nearly one-third of the quota, which would stabilise her trade at a level slightly lower than that of 1937.[2]

The various arrangements by which a fixed share in a market was reserved to British textiles raised the question " What are British textiles ? " Clearly the raw cotton would not be British ; but what would be the status of British grey cloth finished in Switzerland ? Or (more important) the status of Japanese grey cloth finished in Britain ? Should these goods of mixed origin be allowed to enter foreign markets as part of the British quota ? Before the war and during the 'twenties, those Dominions that had granted preferences to British textiles had usually stipulated that a certain percentage of the value of the goods—25, 33, or 50 per cent.—should have been derived from Empire sources. Though sometimes dissatisfied with the percentage fixed, Manchester merchants accepted the principle that goods should be called " British " if their Empire content reached an agreed percentage. The severe depression that afflicted the cotton industry after 1929 caused Manchester merchants to retreat from this position to a less liberal one. In September

---

[1] *Monthly Record*, August 1935.
[2] Proceedings, 13th December 1937; *Monthly Record*, January, May, October and December 1938.

1934, only a few months after the government had decided to impose textile quotas in the colonies, the Manchester Chamber of Commerce began to demand a revised definition of British origin. In a memorandum submitted to the Board of Trade, the Chamber pointed out that during 1934 British imports of Japanese grey cloth had been increasing, and that if the cloth were re-exported as British in fulfilment of a quota, British spinners and manufacturers would suffer. The Chamber suggested a new definition of British origin, namely, that all the main manufacturing processes—spinning, weaving, and finishing—should have been carried out in Britain; and it urged the Board of Trade to press colonies, Dominions, and foreign countries to adopt the new definition together with safeguards, such as certificates of origin issued by Chambers of Commerce.[1]

The " spun, woven, and finished " formula was favourably looked upon by the Board of Trade, which promised to press for its inclusion in future trade agreements. The colonies and several of the smaller European countries—Lithuania, Latvia, and Finland—raised no objection to Manchester's definition.[2] Logically, the new definition ought to apply to all exports of cloth from Britain, and a case soon arose when the Chamber had to decide whether logic or expediency should triumph. In Guatemala, British textiles had a preference over Japan but not over any other country; in these circumstances, the finishers argued, to apply the " spun, woven, and finished " formula would lose business for the finishers without bringing any to the spinners and manufacturers; the whole trade would go to Lancashire's European competitors. Eventually the Chamber adopted this view, which it appeared to share with the Board of Trade; maximum business for the Lancashire cotton industry, or for any section of it, was preferred to an insistence on strict logic.[3] If the Chamber wished to be quite logical, it ought (so it was argued) to press for the exclusion of Japanese grey cloth from Britain either by fixing quotas, or by raising tariffs and refusing a drawback on re-export; but the Chamber hesitated to go so far, knowing that imports of cotton cloth were in any case equal to only 1 per cent. of Lancashire's output.[4] Before

[1] Proceedings, 10th September 1934.　　　[2] Ibid., 11th March 1935.
[3] Ibid., 13th January, 9th March and 11th May 1936; Hansard, 5th series, Vol. 311, col. 1499 : H.C., 5th May, 1936.
[4] Proceedings, 13th July and 9th November 1936; Annual Report for 1938.

1935 imports of Japanese grey cloth for finishing in Britain never reached a million yards ; in 1935 they rose to 8 million yards, and to just under 20 million yards *per annum* in the years 1936 to 1938. From these figures it may appear that the importance attached to the problem in the nineteen-thirties was out of proportion to its size, and that the controversy was significant mainly as a symptom of Lancashire's state of mind at that time. More recent events and developments might suggest, however, that Lancashire manufacturers and merchants had some cause to be alarmed at the persistent growth of Japanese competition in the home market.

CHAPTER XXI

BILATERAL BARGAINING AND THE COTTON TRADE, 1932-1939

AT the same time as the Manchester Chamber of Commerce abandoned its earlier belief in the policy of the open door, it came to look with increasing disfavour on the working of the most-favoured-nation clause. The two devices had essentially the same effect in preventing discrimination on behalf of one country at the expense of another; but whereas the open door applied to colonial and semi-colonial markets, especially in Africa and the Far East, the most-favoured-nation clause was embodied in commercial treaties between equal and sovereign states. It was especially applicable in Europe and America.

The debate on the most-favoured-nation clause began in Manchester in the autumn of 1932 when the government was preparing to negotiate a series of commercial treaties, using Britain's new tariff as a bargaining weapon. The negotiations with the Argentine, a large market for Lancashire textiles, led the Manchester Chamber of Commerce to draw up a memorandum which it submitted to its members and to the government. The memorandum discussed the disadvantages of the most-favoured-nation clause, the chief disadvantage being that concessions negotiated by one country might in the end benefit another instead. To guard against this danger, the Chamber tentatively suggested that import duties should be related to the proportion of a country's exports taken by other countries; for instance, if Britain bought more Argentine beef than Germany, British goods ought to be admitted to the Argentine at lower rates of duty than German goods. Though the Chamber realised how risky it might be to apply this doctrine to the Far East, where Japan was a large buyer, nobody objected to its application to the Argentine, where the predominant buyer was Britain. The Directors of the Manchester Chamber urged the government to apply this discriminatory policy to the Argentine negotiations, and sought the co-operation of the Federation of British Industries and the Association of British

264 MANCHESTER MERCHANTS AND FOREIGN TRADE

Chambers of Commerce to this end. The decision to abandon the long-standing belief in the value of most-favoured-nation treatment was quite explicit and deliberate. In the Chamber's own words :

Believing that no material advantages are obtainable by tariff negotiations with the Argentine based only on a reclassification of existing tariffs, which will be applicable equally to all competing countries, the Manchester Chamber of Commerce urges H.M. Government not to give concessions in the British market except in return for some arrangement whereby the restrictive effect of the most-favoured-nation clause may be avoided and British exporters may secure a benefit fairly apportioned to the share Great Britain takes of Argentine exports.[1]

The Manchester Chamber persuaded the Association of British Chambers of Commerce that, while there was no need to eliminate the most-favoured-nation clause entirely, it ought at least to be modified to " permit of genuine reciprocal trade arrangements ". The government should convene a meeting with industrial and commercial leaders to discuss future policy.[2] This was the more necessary because the Ottawa Agreements had already infringed the most-favoured-nation clause to which Britain professed to adhere.[3] The official view, however, was that the Ottawa Agreements did not infringe most-favoured-nation treatment, and the government had no intention of using them as a precedent to demand special favours from other countries. Throughout 1933 the Manchester Chamber protested against the government's refusal to demand special treatment in the Argentine, for this question had become the touchstone of the principles on which Britain's commercial policy should rest ; but as neither the Board of Trade nor the Argentine was willing to depart from most-favoured-nation treatment, Manchester's protests were of no avail.[4] As the Board of Trade explained, the question of modifying or deleting the most-favoured-nation clause was one to be decided on its merits in each particular case ; with some countries the mere threat to denounce the clause had produced benefits for British trade, whereas with others different tactics might be necessary.[5]

[1] Proceedings, 12th September 1932.
[2] Ibid., 10th October and 14th November 1932.
[3] Annual Report for 1932.
[4] Proceedings, 13th March, 8th May, 17th July, 11th September and 18th December 1933.
[5] Ibid., 8th and 25th January 1934.

Stimulated by the continuing pressure of foreign (and especially Japanese) competition, the Manchester Chamber quickly produced a more practical policy for submission to the government. It argued that the development of secondary industries in formerly agricultural countries and the competition of countries with very low standards of living had invalidated the most-favoured-nation clause, for only very high tariffs could exclude Japanese goods, and such tariffs would cripple the trade of other countries as well. On the other hand, a general denunciation of the most-favoured-nation clause would not help ; what was needed was a series of devices for evading its ill effects in particular cases. A good example was the Indo-Japanese trade agreement, which had fixed minimum and maximum imports of Japanese cotton goods ; the actual figures would depend on the quantity of Indian cotton taken by Japan. Some other suggested devices did not seem so promising to the Manchester merchants. Tariff specialisation gave only temporary benefits, because competing countries would soon adjust their output to take advantage of the lowest rates of duty. Purchasing agreements might benefit the coal industry, which could negotiate bulk sales, but they were inappropriate to such industries as cotton. Exchange control could also be manipulated to evade the most-favoured-nation clause, but exchange control did not outlast the financial crisis that made it necessary. From this analysis of the situation the Manchester Chamber of Commerce could draw relatively little comfort. General abandonment of the most-favoured-nation clause, and tariff specialisation, were definitely ruled out ; and the Chamber had to fall back on " large and increasing use of the methods of quotas, exchange control, and purchasing agreements, unless and until greater freedom is secured as regards tariffs ".[1] These were not original conclusions, for the government had already secured benefits for British trade by means of purchasing agreements and exchange control, and had promised to impose textile quotas in the colonies ; after careful consideration, the Manchester Chamber of Commerce had agreed that the government's piecemeal methods were the best way of using Britain's bargaining power in the interests of the export trades.

It did not follow that the Manchester Chamber of Commerce was satisfied with the results of the government's policy. It

[1] Proceedings, 14th May 1934.

was one thing to hit upon the right method of restoring the export trade in cotton goods, and another to apply it; as usually happened when trade agreements were not bringing the expected benefits, Manchester merchants began to doubt the efficiency of the government's machinery for conducting commercial negotiations. Even in 1934, the Directors of the Manchester Chamber were wondering whether the Board of Trade was adequately staffed to deal with the many commercial treaties which were being negotiated; Britain had been a tariff country for more than two years, but the cotton trade had still to benefit from the country's recovery of bargaining power.[1] Not until 1936, however, did Manchester become acutely dissatisfied with the conduct of commercial negotiations. Behind the discontent lay the failure to raise the volume of exports above the level of 1932 ; but the immediate occasion of the Chamber's criticism of the Board of Trade was the trade agreement between Peru and Japan, concluded early in 1936. The Board of Trade had had eighteen months in which to persuade Peru to regulate the import of cotton goods by quota ; the favourable opportunity had been let slip, and now, thanks to the Board of Trade's inaction, Japan would overrun yet another Lancashire market. The cotton trade would continue to suffer as long as the Board of Trade was overworked and understaffed.[2]

The Australian-Japanese agreement signed at the end of 1936, after the Board of Trade had added to its staff, convinced the Manchester Chamber of Commerce that more radical measures were needed than administrative reform. The " callous indifference " of the government to the interests of the Lancashire cotton trade could be met only by political activity, and the Chamber determined

to bring insistent pressure on the Prime Minister himself . . . urging that it should be a Cabinet decision that the export trade in cotton and rayon goods should be effectively protected in future negotiations.[3]

A parliamentary debate on conditions in Lancashire offered a good opportunity to educate public opinion and to convince the government that the question was important. A fairly thin House resolved to urge " the Government to give the fullest consideration to the needs of Lancashire industries

[1] Proceedings, 9th April 1934.   [2] Ibid., 13th January and 6th April 1936.
[3] Annual Report for 1936 ; Proceedings, 11th January 1937.

in formulating their future course of action, more particularly in the matter of obtaining favourable and secure conditions in overseas markets ".[1]   The Chamber followed up this parliamentary success by preparing a memorandum which set out in some detail the volume of exports the government should try to secure for Lancashire in particular markets. The memorandum was submitted to the government and in July a deputation waited on Mr. Oliver Stanley, the new President of the Board of Trade, to discuss it.   His reply was not encouraging to the cotton trade : the Chamber had admitted that in the colonies and the home market Lancashire's interests had not been neglected, and this showed that in " the only two instances where the Government had been able to arrive at clear-cut decisions on their own account " the cotton trade had no reasonable grounds for complaint. Mr. Stanley reminded the delegation that elsewhere—in India, the Dominions, or foreign countries—" there were always two parties to a negotiation ".   It would be unwise to overrate the strength of Britain's bargaining position; we had to import raw materials and foodstuffs, and could not therefore do just as we liked in asking for concessions in (say) the Dutch East Indies or Egypt.   Moreover, in many countries tariffs were not merely protective weapons but an essential source of revenue ; and in some countries unfortunate political reactions might follow as a direct result of commercial negotiations.[2]

Though the cotton trade could not hope for any dramatic improvement in its prospects from more vigorous commercial negotiations, it could at least resist attempts to remove the defences already built up.   The movement to reduce trade barriers, in which Manchester had been so active between 1927 and 1929, had come to a sorry end in the depression ; but with the devaluation of the franc and a Democratic administration in Washington, talk of freeing world trade from vexatious restrictions revived in the autumn of 1936.   At first the Manchester Chamber of Commerce declined to comment on the new movement,[3] but by the middle of 1937 it had become so popular a topic of discussion that the Chamber felt obliged to intervene before it was too late. Economic and military disarmament, it pointed out,

---

[1] *Hansard*, 5th series, Vol. 319, col. 1683 ff. : H.C., 3rd February 1937.
[2] Minutes of the Executive Committee, 7th July 1937.
[3] *Monthly Record*, October 1936.

were not unlike ; any change in British commercial policy " should . . . afford the major export trades of the country reasonable prospects of stable and secure outlets for their products ". In the opinion of the Chamber the United Kingdom was " already making a greater contribution than any other country to the expansion [of world trade]. . . . This is fully evidenced by the mounting figures of imports ". The Chamber was satisfied that

it would be a grave error to relinquish any of the reciprocal guarantees or advantages so far obtained for exports of British manufactured goods, or diminish the efforts to secure additional benefits by further negotiations, the more so as the maintenance of the purchasing power of these islands, which constitute the world's greatest single import market, is as vital to the world at large as to our own people.

At its autumn meeting the Association of British Chambers of Commerce unanimously endorsed Manchester's views, and in 1938 and 1939, far from supporting the movement to free world trade, proposed a three-column tariff that would confine trade still more closely to its bilateral channels.[1] Empire goods would pay low rates of duty ; foreign countries that treated British exports fairly would pay somewhat higher rates ; and countries not treating British exports fairly would be subject to a penal rate of duty until they came to their senses.   The Association of Chambers would also have forbidden overseas investment, except by the government, and would have stipulated that loans to foreign countries should be spent in Britain.   This was a dusty answer to return to the American assault on trade barriers ; but neither then nor since has British industry felt strong enough to return any other.

For the sake of clarity, it is convenient to separate the general account of Manchester's new policy on the most-favoured-nation clause from applications of it to particular trade agreements ; but this divorce of principle from practice is quite unreal.   Manchester merchants did not evolve a policy and then look round for opportunities to apply it ; on the contrary, policy grew out of the needs of the moment. The Manchester Chamber of Commerce had first questioned the value of the most-favoured-nation clause when an Anglo-Argentine trade agreement was being negotiated.   This was

[1] Proceedings, 14th June 1937 ; *Monthly Record*, October 1937, November 1938, and January 1939.

natural enough, for by 1932 Argentina was Lancashire's best foreign customer. Under the trade agreement signed in May 1933, the Argentine Government promised Britain a share of foreign exchange proportionate to British purchases of Argentine products ; thus, as long as exchange control lasted, Lancashire had a reasonably secure foothold in the Argentine market. Manchester merchants feared, however, that exchange control would not last long, and that when it came to an end Japanese competition would become severe. A rumour current at the end of 1933 that Argentina was about to lift her exchange controls caused great alarm at Manchester, and the Chamber of Commerce renewed its demand for a direct tariff preference ; [1] the rumour was unfounded, however, and favourable treatment of British imports continued. Argentina gave fresh guarantees about the supply of foreign exchange when the trade agreement was renewed in 1936.

Other South American countries were not so obliging. Early in 1935 Peru had suggested to the Board of Trade that Peruvian imports of cotton goods from the various manufacturing countries should be regulated by quotas based on those countries' respective imports of Peruvian cotton ; on this basis Lancashire would get 68 per cent. of the trade and administer a severe check to Japanese encroachment in the Peruvian market. The Manchester Chamber of Commerce could not make up its mind whether, in general, quotas based on takings of raw cotton would benefit Lancashire ; in Peru they certainly would, but if India were to regulate imports on that basis Lancashire would suffer. The Chamber therefore left it to the Board of Trade to decide whether to accept Peru's offer, and long negotiations ensued ; before they had been completed, Peru came to an agreement with Japan under which quota restrictions on Japanese imports were removed. The Manchester Chamber of Commerce at first blamed the Board of Trade for this unfortunate result ; [2] though it might have been avoided if Manchester had advised the Board of Trade to accept quotas based on imports of Peruvian cotton. On second thoughts, the Chamber admitted that Britain had no right to interfere, though it still thought that the British Government should be " as awkward as possible " :

[1] Proceedings, 8th May and 18th December 1933.
[2] Ibid., 14th January and 11th November 1935, and 13th January 1936.

it was obviously to the British interest to have the restrictions on Japanese goods as rigid as possible and fixed as definitely as could be done for the longest time that could be arranged.[1]

Nevertheless, where the balance of trade was heavily in favour of Britain, the Manchester merchants recognised that it would be unreasonable to press for concessions. San Salvador, for instance, sold little of her chief export, coffee, to Britain, though she was a heavy importer of British goods ; if Britain promised to buy more coffee from San Salvador, other coffee-growing countries would be offended, but unless San Salvador could increase her exports to Britain it would be difficult to press British claims.[2]   Colombia, Lancashire's second largest foreign market, used the same argument in 1938 when imposing restrictions on British imports, half of which were cotton textiles. All that the Manchester Chamber of Commerce could do was to send a deputation to the Board of Trade, hoping that something would turn up ; on its own principles of reciprocal trade, Manchester could not complain of unfair treatment.[3]

Canada and the United States offered more scope to the Lancashire cotton trade.   The Ottawa agreement with Canada had greatly disappointed the Manchester Chamber of Commerce, which could only hope that the Canadian Tariff Board would recommend further concessions. It was generally agreed in Lancashire that to ask for sweeping reductions of the tariff on all classes of cotton goods would be risking a rebuff. Instead, a Lancashire delegation submitted proposals for lower duties on particular classes of goods ; unless duties were lowered it was feared that Lancashire would lose ground to its United States competitors.[4]   The Canadian Government faithfully carried out the recommendations of the Tariff Board, which were for lower duties, especially on rayon and mixture fabrics.[5]   Shortly afterwards negotiations began for a revision of the Anglo-Canadian Ottawa Agreement ; much to the Chamber's relief, the new agreement contained specific concessions for cotton goods and did not refer Lancashire to a Tariff Board, which might or might not be friendly. However, the new agreement was not thought likely to lead to " any substantially increased

[1] Proceedings, 9th March 1936.   [2] Ibid., 8th April 1935.
[3] Monthly Record, March and May 1938.
[4] Proceedings, 12th November 1934 and 13th January 1936.
[5] Monthly Record, May 1936.

volume of trade ", and the Manchester Chamber of Commerce decided to content itself with an expression of " restrained appreciation ".[1]

From a trade agreement with the United States, the advocate of freer world trade, the Manchester Chamber of Commerce could hope for little. In preparation for the discussions, Manchester had asked the Board of Trade to secure from the United States a quota for British textile exports, together with low tariffs on the stipulated volume of trade. The quota was needed because since 1929 exports of cotton cloth to the United States had shrunk to an average of about 10 million yards a year; whereas in 1936 Japanese exports, hitherto insignificant, had shot up to 80 million yards. Apart from particular cotton trade questions, the Manchester merchants showed little enthusiasm at the prospect of a trade agreement with the United States. They considered that any modification of the American attitude towards tariff problems should be welcomed, but they emphasised " the indispensable nature of many of the present safeguards to British and Empire trade ".[2] The agreement eventually concluded reduced the American tariff on cotton goods by amounts varying from 20 to 33 per cent. ; the Manchester Chamber " heartily welcomed " the reductions, though at the same time it pointed out that the American tariff was one of the highest in the world, and that it would be unwise to prophesy how much Lancashire would benefit. However, the agreement was encouraging enough for the Chamber to dispatch a mission to the United States, and to establish a United States Market Committee ;[3] the post-war dollar drive was casting its shadow before.

Though exports of piece goods to Europe had fallen by more than a third between 1929 and 1932, European markets took proportionately more of Lancashire's exports in the 'thirties than the 'twenties, other markets having shrunk on the average to little more than half their earlier size ; the treatment of cotton goods in trade negotiations with European countries was therefore a matter of no small importance to the Manchester merchants. As in America, Manchester sought from the European countries direct tariff preferences, and if possible quota arrangements for cotton goods, but with only

[1] Proceedings, 8th March 1937.
[2] Ibid., 13th December 1937.
[3] Monthly Record, November 1938 and July 1939.

limited success. The Anglo-Danish agreement signed in April 1933 was a case in point. Danish importers of coal, jute, iron and steel were well enough organised to guarantee that they would buy certain quantities of British goods ; but neither the Danish importers nor the Manchester shippers of textiles had the necessary organisation to arrange such semi-official quotas. Nor would the Danes reduce their tariffs to any considerable extent ; though, as the Chamber pointed out, Lancashire might not benefit much from tariff reductions so long as Denmark granted them impartially to Lancashire and her competitors.[1] Somewhat to the surprise of the Manchester Chamber, the Anglo-Finnish trade agreement signed in September 1933 gave " considerable benefits " to British textiles ; because the local cotton industry supplied 80 per cent. of Finnish needs Manchester had not expected a reduction in the tariff on cotton goods, but for once the Chamber's hopes were more than fulfilled.[2] The Lancashire cotton trade also benefited from trade agreements made in 1934 with Lithuania, Latvia, and Estonia ; these little Baltic states relied heavily on the British market for the disposal of their agricultural surplus, and the Board of Trade took advantage of this fact to get concessions for cotton as well as for the other staple industries. Latvia and Estonia fixed maximum rates of duty on British cotton goods, and Lithuania introduced quantitative control of textile imports ; at the time, the Manchester Chamber of Commerce was well pleased with the results of these negotiations.[3] By 1938, however, it was clear that Latvia, at least, was not abiding by the spirit of the agreement. British exports to Latvia had been stationary for several years, and in 1937 had actually declined ; Latvian exports to Britain had risen substantially, thus increasing still further Britain's adverse balance of trade with Latvia. The Manchester Chamber put these facts before the Board of Trade, with the suggestions that Latvia might well be induced to increase her imports from Britain, particularly her imports of cotton goods.[4]

The Manchester Chamber of Commerce based its demands for fair treatment of the Lancashire cotton trade on the argu-

[1] *Monthly Record*, May 1933.
[2] Proceedings, 13th March and 20th November 1933.
[3] *Ibid.*, 16th July and 10th September 1934.
[4] *Monthly Record*, May 1938.

ment that Britain was contributing to world prosperity by her huge imports of food and raw materials, but could not afford to go on buying unless she was also allowed to sell. At the same time the Manchester Chamber had tacitly accepted a policy of protection for British agriculture, though this policy would inevitably limit the British demand for foreign and Empire food. How, if at all, were these seemingly contradictory policies to be reconciled ? At first the problem seemed to be ignored. The Manchester Chamber made no comment on the agricultural clauses of the Ottawa Agreements, which bound the government to tax foreign wheat in order to give a preference to Empire wheat ; neither the Chamber nor the Manchester produce merchants openly opposed the duties on dairy products under the Import Duties Act of 1932.[1] It was not long, however, before the protection of British agriculture came under fire from Manchester. The earliest attacks were not made by shipping merchants anxious about their markets overseas, but by the produce merchants whose import business was affected by protection and especially by the bacon quota. It was only later that some sections of the cotton trade awoke to the contradiction between trade agreements and agricultural protection.

Quantitative restriction of bacon imports began in November 1932, and was opposed by Manchester produce merchants from the start. They argued that an import duty whose proceeds " could have been applied to assisting British producers until such time as they could stand on their own feet " would have been preferable. But an import duty was only the lesser of two evils ; produce merchants favoured neither.[2] By 1934 the quota had reduced bacon imports very sharply and raised the price per hundredweight from fifty-three shillings in 1932 to eighty shillings ; home production of bacon had by no means filled the gap left by the reduction of imports, and the produce merchants again pointed out that an import duty would have been preferable to the quota.[3] In an attempt to end such an unsatisfactory state of affairs, the Produce Section of the Manchester Chamber prepared a detailed memorandum setting out the case for a moderate specific duty on bacon imports ; this memorandum they submitted, with the approval of the Board of Directors, to the government. However, in committing itself to opposing

[1] Annual Report of the Produce Section for 1932.
[2] Ibid.   [3] Ibid., 1934.

the bacon quota, the Manchester Chamber made it quite clear that it was not abandoning its belief " in the efficacy of quota systems in coping with the difficulties arising in the Lancashire export trade ".[1] In any case, the government declined to follow Manchester's lead, and continued to regulate bacon imports by means of the quota.

In the meantime some sections of the shipping merchants were becoming alarmed at the possible effects of agricultural protection. In 1934 the Europe and United States Section of the Manchester Chamber became alarmed at the effect of the bacon quota on trade with Denmark. They recognised the importance of " the great basic industry of agriculture " and declared that they would support " any reasonable policy " designed to assist it. On the other hand, it was difficult to foster agriculture and the export trade at the same time ; the Section's very moderate proposal was that the Ministry of Agriculture and the Board of Trade should co-operate to find a " middle course ". The Produce Section supported this proposal, but the Directors of the Chamber were unwilling to take action on so controversial a subject.[2] At the same time, British and Empire farmers were agitating for a reduction in the quota of foreign meat imported into Britain. The Central and South American Section of the Chamber, which had viewed the Ottawa conference without enthusiasm, [3] was much alarmed at the threatened restriction on beef imports from the Argentine. The South American shippers were convinced that

it would be contrary to the interests of this country to prolong and much more to extend the scope of the Ottawa agreements, or to place any further restrictions on Argentine imports.

As before, the Board of Directors refused to be drawn into a discussion of agricultural policy, which could wait (they thought) until the Anglo-Argentine agreement came up for renewal in 1936 ; the only satisfaction for South American shippers was that the Board of Trade learnt in general terms of their views.[4] This did not prevent the Argentine meat quota from being reduced. In 1935, when it appeared that the Argentine quota might be still further whittled away, the

[1] *Monthly Record,* April and May 1935.
[2] Minutes of the Europe and United States Section, 6th February 1934 ; Minutes of the Produce Section, 31st May 1934 ; Proceedings, 11th June 1934. [3] Minutes of the Section, 1st April 1932.
[4] *Ibid.,* 18th June ; Proceedings, 16th July 1934.

Chamber agreed with the South American shippers that a stand must be made ; the Board of Trade was reminded that Argentina was Lancashire's most valuable foreign market and that imports of Argentine meat ought not to be allowed to fall below the existing level.[1] In 1936, however, when the Anglo-Argentine agreement came up for renewal, the Manchester Chamber of Commerce could not maintain this position. It was clear that Argentina and Australia could not both have the British beef trade, and Manchester had to decide which to support. Several Directors felt very strongly that imperial sentiment and self-interest should encourage Britain to consider Australia in preference to Argentina ; but while negotiations with Argentina were proceeding in London, this could not be openly said. Manchester therefore issued a statement that denied any clash of interest between Australian and Argentine meat producers;[2] but whether this deceived anybody may be doubted.

Preference for Empire meat producers endangered Lancashire's South American markets ; protection for the British dairy farmer endangered the European markets for cotton goods. In 1934 the produce importers and the European shippers had collaborated in protest against the bacon quota ; in 1935 they renewed the alliance when it was rumoured that the duty on imported butter might be raised, and on this occasion the Directors put the whole weight of the Chamber's authority behind the protest.[3] In 1937, however, when a demand arose for much higher duties on imported eggs, the produce importers and the European shippers found themselves in a minority. The produce importers strongly opposed either higher duties on, or quantitative control of, egg imports ; but the Directors would neither associate the Chamber with the protest against higher duties, nor allow the Produce Section to make separate representations to the government. The Import Duties Advisory Committee was less tender to the poultry farmers, and their application for higher duties was turned down.[4]

[1] Proceedings, 8th April 1935.
[2] Ibid., 15th June 1936 ; Monthly Record, June 1936.
[3] Proceedings, 9th September 1935 ; Annual Report of the Produce Section for 1935.
[4] Minutes of the Produce Section, 3rd and 24th March, 21st April, and 31st May 1937; Minutes of the Europe and United States Section, 28th April 1937 ; Proceedings, 8th March, 12th April, 10th May, and 14th June 1937 ; Annual Report of the Produce Section for 1937.

19

Though the Manchester Chamber of Commerce had found itself in logical difficulties when advancing reciprocal-trade theories at the same time as it acquiesced in protection for British and imperial agriculture, it was lucky enough to get the best of both worlds ; for the illogical combination of trade agreements with agricultural protection did bring some benefits to Lancashire trade. Between 1933 and 1937, when exports to other foreign countries fell from 684 to 537 million square yards of cotton cloth, exports to " trade-agreement countries " fell by less than 30 million yards—from 306 to 278 million yards. Again in 1938 and 1939, when the export trade in cotton goods collapsed for the third time in twenty years, the " trade-agreement countries " and the Dominions were the only markets that withstood the depression at all well.[1] Nevertheless, some sections of the Lancashire cotton trade, especially the spinners and manufacturers, were critical of the Manchester Chamber's attitude to trade agreements. In 1933 and 1934, in particular, it was widely believed that the Manchester Chamber had not pressed the claims of the cotton trade with all possible energy, and the members passed a resolution calling for the " initiation by the Board of Directors of a commercial policy of a more active character ".[2] These criticisms of the Directors were quite unjustified ; the Chamber was always alert to the interests of the cotton trade, but against high tariffs and increasing Japanese competition there was little that any merchant or body of merchants could do to preserve Lancashire's export trade. By the end of the 'thirties there was fairly general agreement in Lancashire that the decline of the cotton export trade was " perhaps historically inevitable ".[3] Trade agreements did something to check the decline, but there was no satisfactory trade agreement with Lancashire's largest market, India. Whatever Lancashire gained by colonial quotas, by the Ottawa agreements, and by commercial treaties with foreign countries, was offset by the steady and inexorable decline of the Indian trade.

---

[1] *Working Party Report : Cotton* (1946), p. 119.
[2] Proceedings, 29th January 1934 ; *Monthly Record*, February 1934.
[3] *Ibid.*, February 1938.

CHAPTER XXII

THE LOSS OF THE INDIAN MARKET

In 1913, a record year, India [1] imported over 3,000 million linear yards of cotton cloth from Lancashire, valued at £35,000,000; in 1938 India imported less than 300 million square yards of cotton cloth from Lancashire, valued at £4,500,000. This drop represented almost exactly half of Lancashire's losses in overseas markets measured by volume, and rather less than half measured by value because the quality of the cotton goods exported to India was slightly below the average quality of Lancashire's exports. By 1938, though still the largest importer of Lancashire cottons measured by volume, India had sunk to third place in the list, behind Australia and South Africa, when values are being considered. Thus, the shrinkage of the Indian market accounts for about half the decline in Lancashire's exports of cotton goods; the story of Manchester's relations with India sums up the changes in the policy of the Manchester Chamber of Commerce and of the cotton trade as a whole in the years 1914 to 1939.

Even if war had not broken out in 1914, there would have been at least a temporary reduction in the export of cotton goods from Lancashire to India. In October 1913, transactions in cloth and yarn were meagre on the Manchester Royal Exchange : " India ", it was reported, " does at last begin to show some signs of the glut that has so long been predicted ". In November prices were declining and Manchester's markets were well stocked. By July 1914 the cotton trade was doing very badly and production had been considerably reduced.[2] Exports to India in 1914, measured by volume, were 13 per cent. lower than in 1913. A further and sharper fall took place in 1915, when shortages were beginning to affect the output of the cotton trade ; from 1915 to 1917 exports to India were fairly steady at the low level of 1,900 million yards ; but in 1918 they fell again to 900 million yards. At the same time Indian factory production was growing, and in particular the output of plain greys had largely

---

[1] Throughout the book, unless otherwise stated, India includes Burma.
[2] *Monthly Record*, October and November 1913, and July 1914.

increased;[1] in 1913 grey cloth had accounted for nearly half Lancashire's exports to India.

These developments might not have caused great alarm in Lancashire by themselves; but in March 1917, after a long twenty-year truce, the struggle over the Indian import duties on cotton goods broke out again. Since 1895 there had been a 3½ per cent. customs duty on imported cotton goods and a countervailing excise duty on Indian production; the Indian Budget of March 1917 raised the import duty from 3½ to 7½ per cent., but did not alter the excise. In the House of Commons, Austen Chamberlain, the Secretary of State for India, declared that the gift of £100,000,000 that India was making to the cost of the war would not have been made if the home government had insisted that the excise be raised as well as the import duty.[2] This did not deter Lancashire from opposing with the utmost vigour the protection that was being given to the Indian cotton industry, which they feared more than any other. On the same day that Mr. Chamberlain made his announcement in the Commons, the Directors of the Manchester Chamber of Commerce unanimously resolved that they must

strongly protest against the proposed increase of the import duty on cotton goods from 3½ to 7½ per cent. WITHOUT A CORRESPONDING INCREASE IN THE COUNTERVAILING EXCISE DUTY ON COTTON GOODS MANUFACTURED IN INDIA.

Representatives of the Blackburn, Bolton, Burnley, Bury, Oldham, and Preston Chambers of Commerce, and a crowded meeting on the floor of the Manchester Royal Exchange, endorsed the resolution, which undoubtedly expressed the general feeling of the Lancashire cotton industry, including the operatives as well as the manufacturers and merchants. A deputation from the whole industry met Mr. Chamberlain a week later, only to be told that for twenty years the excise duty had been " an open sore in India ", and that there was " complete unanimity among all classes and both races " against the countervailing excise. The British Government could not " hold out any hope whatever " to Lancashire that the excise would be raised. In the face of this forthright

[1] *Monthly Record*, June 1916;   V. Anstey, *Economic Development of India* (3rd edn., 1936), p. 531.
[2] *Hansard*, 5th series, Vol. III, cols. 3-4 : H.C., 3rd March 1917.

refusal to meet Lancashire's demands, there was little more
that the Manchester Chamber of Commerce could do for the
time being ; it could only console itself with the government's
promise to review the fiscal relations of the various parts of
the Empire after the war.[1] When the Oldham Chamber of
Commerce hoped that all Lancashire Chambers would urge
candidates at the General Election in 1918 to support the
abolition of the protective duties, Manchester declined to do
so, on the ground that " It is contrary to the practice of the
Board to intervene in a political contest ".[2]

The Indian Budget of 1921 set the seal on the work of
1917. It raised the import duty on cotton goods to 11 per
cent., but again left the excise unchanged, giving the Indian
mills a protective duty of $7\frac{1}{2}$ per cent.   On this occasion there
was no joint protest from the whole of Lancashire : in 1917
the spinners and manufacturers had used forcible language
in opposing the higher duties and had, so the Manchester
Chamber believed, overstated their case.   In 1921, therefore,
the Manchester Chamber made its separate protest on behalf
of the merchant community ; it argued, on lines familiar to
successive governments, that Lancashire was only asking for
fair treatment.   " If we have equal opportunity, in spite of
our tremendous handicaps we shall not complain at all."
The new duties should be postponed until the conference on
imperial fiscal problems, promised in 1917, had taken place.
As in 1917, the Secretary of State for India denied that Lancashire had any real cause for alarm ; only over a limited range
of counts did the Indian and Lancashire industries compete,
and by concentrating on the finer qualities Lancashire could
easily hold her own.   He ended with the fateful words :
" I cannot recede from the position that India is to be permitted to devise her tariffs in her own interests." [3]   Lancashire could counter this argument only by an appeal to
free-trade doctrine : " Lancashire ", the President of the
Manchester Chamber declared,

of all places in the world seems to have been created for the manufacture of cotton goods. Agriculture is the natural sphere of
India and the Indians. It can never be in the interests of our great
Empire to endeavour to counter the arrangements of nature by
ill-omened legislation.[4]

[1] Proceedings, 5th and 19th March 1917 ; Monthly Record, March
1917.   [2] Proceedings, 11th December 1918.
[3] Monthly Record, March and April 1921.   [4] Ibid., July 1921.

This was not a point of view likely to appeal to Indians, and the Manchester Chamber was probably well-advised to refrain from giving evidence before the Indian Fiscal Commission appointed in 1921.[1]

The Commission reported in 1922 in favour of moderate protection for selected industries, and recommended the establishment of a Tariff Board to hear and report on the merits of particular demands for protection. As the British Government had already conceded fiscal autonomy to India in fact, if not in form, the Manchester Chamber of Commerce now had to abandon its long campaign for free trade in India. In 1924 the Chamber admitted (in private) to the Committee on Industry and Trade that : " The fixing of the duty and the excise has now passed from this country to the Indian Government." [2] At the end of 1925, when the Government of India suspended the excise duty with a view to its abolition in the next Budget, the Manchester Chamber joined with the spinners and manufacturers in a public statement that accepted the change without dispute. Lancashire still hoped, however, that the import duty would be reduced when Indian finances permitted, and that Lancashire would be left to concentrate on the finer goods, leaving the coarser qualities to Indian mills.[3] By 1925 Indian millowners feared competition from Japan more than from Lancashire. India and Lancashire had a common interest in resisting encroachments from the Far East ; and in accepting the abolition of the excise duty, the Manchester Chamber hoped to win the goodwill of the Bombay millowners. In return for benevolent neutrality over the excise, and support for measures against Japan, Bombay would (so Manchester hoped) " exert its influence . . . to ensure that . . . the position of Lancashire goods will not in any event be further prejudiced." [4] The Manchester Chamber was also beginning to hanker after a preference in India over Japanese goods, but this remained only a faint and private hope for some years.

In the later 'twenties Lancashire's position in the Indian market was not worsened by any further tariff changes. This was not for want of trying on the part of the Indian cotton industry, which was naturally anxious to exclude both

[1] Proceedings, 14th November and 12th December 1921 ; *Monthly Record*, July 1923.
[2] Minutes of Evidence 1924-7, Vol. I, qq. 2076-77.
[3] *Monthly Record*, December 1925.
[4] Proceedings, 12th October and 9th November 1925.

Lancashire and Japan from the Indian market. In 1926, at the request of the Bombay Millowners' Association, the Indian Tariff Board considered a proposal to raise the import duty on cotton goods from 11 to 28½ per cent. Though deeply alarmed at the prospect, the Manchester Chamber of Commerce took no public action ; the most it could do was to consult with other Lancashire organisations and with the Board of Trade. The Tariff Board recommended an increase in the import duty from 11 to 15 per cent. for three years, but the Government of India refused to accept the recommendation.[1] Hardly less dangerous to Lancashire than higher import duties would be a change from *ad valorem* to specific duties, for which the Bombay millowners began to agitate in 1929 ; having failed to get increased protection by direct methods, they hoped to achieve the same end indirectly. As in 1926, the Manchester Chamber organised a joint deputation to the Board of Trade to protest against abandonment of the *ad valorem* principle ; it also submitted a memorandum to Mr. Hardy, the Collector of Customs at Calcutta, whom the Indian Government had appointed to inquire into the matter. He reported against specific duties ; but no sooner had this danger been averted than, with the onset of the general depression, Manchester had to face once more the possibility that Indian import duties would be raised again.[2]

Despite the increase in the import duty from 7½ to 11 per cent. in 1921, and the abolition of the 3½ per cent. excise in 1925, Lancashire's post-war trade with India, though much smaller than in the pre-war years, had remained until 1929 fairly stable at from 1,400 million to 1,650 million square yards of cloth a year. The best post-war years were 1924, 1926, and 1927 ; no marked downward trend could be detected before 1929, when exports to India fell below 1,400 million square yards for the first time since 1921, the blackest year of the post-war depression. The finances of the Government of India, like the Lancashire cotton trade, suffered in 1929 from the beginning of general depression, and in his Budget speech at the end of February 1930 the Finance Minister announced that import duties on cotton goods would be raised to 15 per cent. with an additional 5 per cent. on foreign

<hr>

[1] Proceedings, 12th July and 11th October 1926 ; V. Anstey, *op. cit.*, pp. 263, 277-8.

[2] Proceedings, 22nd July, 9th September, 14th October and 9th December 1929.

goods. The Manchester Chamber of Commerce did not protest against the increased duties, for it feared that a hostile
attitude might endanger the 5 per cent. preference, which
though small might form the basis for a wider preference
later. The Chamber persuaded the Joint Committee of
Cotton Trade Organisations, a body in which producers had
the largest voice, to issue a conciliatory statement to the Press.
It expressed " profound dismay " at the increased duties ;
but on the other hand it welcomed the friendly feeling shown
in the granting of the 5 per cent. preference.[1]

Despite the preference, Lancashire's trade with India
rapidly declined ; in part this was due to the general depression, but in part also to the boycott of British goods, organised
in April 1930 by the Indian National Congress under Mahatma
Gandhi. The Indians hoped that the boycott would induce the
Manchester Chamber to put pressure on the British Government and to support India's demands for constitutional
reform. But the India merchants refused to be intimidated ;
they denounced the boycott and declared that they would
insist on the sanctity of contracts.[2] By September 1930 the
Indian trade had reached a state of " grave crisis " ; shipments had fallen to a quarter of what they had been in the
corresponding period of 1929, and direct sailings from Manchester to Bombay and Karachi were being withdrawn.
Nevertheless, the Manchester Chamber persisted a little
longer in its policy of non-intervention in politics, " because
of the fear that any public action might be wrongly interpreted
in India ".[3] When the Round Table Conference met in
November to discuss Indian constitutional reform, however,
Manchester broke silence ; experience of the boycott, as one
Director of the Chamber said, made it clear that " if complete
fiscal autonomy were granted to India it was doubtful whether
trade could continue to survive ". The Board of Directors
therefore called upon the British Government

in planning India's constitutional reforms to uphold the supreme
necessity of guarding the mutual trade between Great Britain and
India against injury or suppression by penal tariffs and fiscal
enactments.

As was carefully explained, the resolution did not specifically

[1] Proceedings, 10th March 1930 ; *Monthly Record*, March 1930.
[2] Proceedings, 16th May 1930.
[3] *Ibid.*, 15th September and 13th October 1930.

deny India's right to fiscal autonomy. The Chamber would not quarrel over mere phrases, but would be content with any solution that worked in practice ; " reciprocal undertakings, for instance, may be compatible with technical fiscal autonomy ".[1]

In March 1931 an agreement between the Viceroy and Mahatma Gandhi formally ended the political boycott of British goods ; but in fact the boycott continued, and while Lancashire's exports declined still further it was learnt that six new mills were to be built at Ahmedabad. In these circumstances, feeling at Manchester hardened not only against Indian constitutional reform but against the British Labour Government. When the Viceroy certified the Finance Bill, which the Indian Legislative Assembly had rejected, the Manchester Chamber pointed out that : " This is additional proof, if such were needed, that the Fiscal Autonomy Convention . . . does not give India, as is frequently stated, fiscal independence." In a letter to the President of the Board of Trade, the President of the Manchester Chamber remarked :

I feel it is my duty to inform you that feeling in Lancashire is becoming intensely bitter against our Government in what is believed to be its complete disregard for our interests, which it cannot be too often and repeatedly stressed, are not antagonistic to the interests of India as a whole. The weak replies in Parliament by the Secretary of State for India are making a painful impression on us.

Behind this letter lies the fact that in 1931 exports to India were running at a rate of less than 400 million yards a year, only a quarter of the average in the better years of the nineteen-twenties. " Disaster was staring Lancashire in the face " ; if the government did not crush the boycott, the ruin of Lancashire's trade was inevitable.[2] The harsher treatment dealt out to the Indian nationalists by the British National Government therefore found a ready response in Manchester, which " endorsed the policy of enforcing the law and proceeding cautiously with the reforms ".[3]

In March and September 1931 the Government of India had raised the import duties on cotton goods until they stood at 25 per cent. on British, and 31¼ per cent. on foreign cloth.

---

[1] Proceedings, 10th November 1930; Monthly Record, November 1930.
[2] Proceedings, 13th April and 13th July 1931.
[3] Ibid., 11th January 1932.

Undoubtedly, these high rates of duty contributed to the steep decline of Lancashire's exports to India in 1931 ; when preparing for the Ottawa Conference, reduction of the Indian import duties was the point on which the Manchester Chamber of Commerce laid the greatest stress. Policy towards the Dominions was laid down in a memorandum on " The Ottawa Conference, 1932, and the British Cotton Export Trade to the Dominions " ;[1] but Lancashire depended so heavily on the Indian market that the Manchester Chamber of Commerce prepared a separate statement of its policy towards India. "The Ottawa Policy and the Lancashire Cotton Goods Export Trade to India " was a lengthy document that had the approval of the whole of the Lancashire cotton trade, though it had been drafted entirely by the India Section of the Manchester Chamber of Commerce. The memorandum began with the assertion that " the future of Lancashire is definitely dependent upon a recovery of at least a substantial proportion of the India trade ". It argued that there were four causes (apart from the world-wide depression) of the decline in Lancashire's trade : increases in the Indian import duty, Japanese competition, the competition of the Indian cotton factories, and the political situation in India. It admitted that no tariff bargain could entirely eliminate the competition of the Indian cotton industry ; "but the Japanese competition can be materially influenced by means of preferential tariffs ". An agreement might have the further good effect of removing the cotton trade from " the arena of political faction " and so ending the use of the boycott. Translated into practical terms, Manchester's policy was simple and precise : when Indian finances permitted, the government should reduce the duty on piece goods to 11 or 15 per cent. and on yarns to not more than 5 per cent. ; the minimum preference should be 20 per cent. on cloth and 10 per cent. on yarns, " bearing in mind the standards of labour and living that have to be encountered ".The memorandum was rather vague as to what India would get in return ; it drew attention to the Indian products, notably tea, that already enjoyed a preference in the British market, and in general terms it suggested that these preferences might well be increased. The possibility that Lancashire might use more Indian cotton was not even mentioned in the memorandum.[2]

[1] See above, pp. 244-5.
[2] Minutes of the India Section, 10th May 1932.

This development was suggested by the Indian delegation to Ottawa, with whom the representatives of the Lancashire cotton trade had preliminary talks in London ; without glossing over the difficulty of persuading people to use more Indian cotton, the Lancashire representatives promised to look into the matter.[1]

At Ottawa, the Lancashire delegation and the British Government entered into a more definite commitment to encourage the use of Indian cotton.[2] To this end the government later set up an Indian Cotton Enquiry Committee under the chairmanship of Sir Richard Jackson, and experiments were conducted to see how Lancashire could best use Indian cotton.[3] The Manchester Chamber, representing the merchants, gave full support to these efforts : " The whole question had a great bearing on our prospects in the Indian market, and it would be very helpful in improving the political atmosphere." Extended use of Indian cotton was not without its difficulties ; chief of these was that the Indian and Japanese industries took the best quality cotton and Lancashire had to be content with the short and medium staples. Some firms, though willing to buy Indian cotton, had difficulty in getting supplies, and all found that Indian dealers did not want goods made from Indian cotton to be marked as such. Thus the propaganda value of Lancashire's efforts was diminished.[4] Nevertheless, Lancashire persevered, and not unsuccessfully. By 1937, 12 per cent. by weight of Lancashire's raw cotton came from India ; this was double the proportion which had been taken in 1930.[5]

In the last resort, it was the spinners who had to decide whether to use Indian cotton ; but on the vexed question of Indian constitutional reform it was the Manchester Chamber of Commerce which took the lead in shaping the policy of the Lancashire cotton trade. The Chamber could claim that : " Throughout the post-war years it has successfully exercised a moderating influence in Lancashire. . . ." ;[6] but during the first half of 1933 it seemed likely that the Chamber would abandon its moderate attitude and argue for some limitation on India's fiscal autonomy. In December 1932 a Joint

---

[1] Minutes of the India Section, 27th June 1932.
[2] Monthly Record, September 1932.
[3] Proceedings, 10th and 17th July 1933.
[4] Ibid., 10th July and 11th September 1933, and 14th January 1935.
[5] Working Party Report : Cotton (1946), p. 24.
[6] Proceedings, 9th January 1933.

Select Committee of both Houses of Parliament had been set up to examine the British Government's White Paper, which contained proposals for the new Indian constitution but did not include any safeguards for Lancashire's trade. Three courses were open to the Manchester Chamber of Commerce at this juncture : it could try to procure the defeat of any Government of India Bill which might be promoted ; it could propose a limitation on India's fiscal autonomy in order to keep the cotton duties within reasonable bounds ; or it could seek a trade agreement with India modelled on the Ottawa agreements. The Chamber did not favour rejection of such a Bill, nor did it find the prospect of a trade agreement very attractive ; the India merchants wished to limit India's fiscal autonomy and the Chamber told Sir Samuel Hoare, the Secretary of State for India, that it would almost certainly give evidence in this sense.[1] Despite a warning from Sir Samuel that to limit India's fiscal autonomy would be politically and economically impossible, and that " the only true line of advance is that the two Governments in concert should devise trade arrangements to their mutual advantage ", the Manchester Chamber with the full support of the spinners and manufacturers proceeded to draw up written evidence in favour of limitations on India's fiscal freedom.[2] At the same time Lancashire was preparing to send a mission to India under Sir William Clare Lees to discuss cotton trade problems with the Indian millowners ; Sir Samuel Hoare and Lord Derby advised the Manchester Chamber of Commerce that the mission would fail if the evidence to be submitted to the Joint Select Committee were not drastically amended. Even more important, the mission itself telegraphed from India that if the original evidence were submitted there would be no agreement with the Indian millowners. Under this severe pressure, the Manchester Chamber of Commerce preferred not to endanger the success of the mission ; though the evidence had already been printed, it was withdrawn before copies of it had reached the members of the Joint Select Committee. Those parts of the evidence that advocated the limitation of Indian fiscal autonomy were deleted,[3] leaving (in Mr. Churchill's words) "a

[1] Proceedings, 10th April 1933.
[2] *Ibid.*, 8th and 19th May 1933 ; Minutes of the Executive Committee of the Board, 23rd June 1933.
[3] Proceedings, 17th July, 11th September and 20th November 1933 ; Minutes of the India Section, 26th October 1933.

ghost of the original evidence, a poor, shrunken, emasculated thing ".[1]

Mr. Churchill, the bitterest opponent of the Government of India Bill, raised the whole incident in the House of Commons on the 16th April 1934. He suggested that Sir Samuel Hoare and Lord Derby, both of them members of the Joint Select Committee, had committed a breach of privilege in persuading the Manchester Chamber of Commerce to alter its evidence. The matter was referred to the Committee of Privileges, which held that no breach of privilege had in fact occurred, a view accepted by the House of Commons without a division.[2] The unwelcome publicity that Mr. Churchill had given to the whole affair led to a demand for a special meeting of members of the Chamber ; it was held in July 1934 and (at the instance of the Board of Directors) a resolution was passed that appeared to renew the demand for constitutional safeguards against further damage to the Lancashire cotton trade. However, the Directors did nothing to rouse further apprehensions in India, and accepted the report of the Joint Select Committee when it appeared at the end of the year ; but they maintained that the conclusion of an Anglo-Indian trade agreement was an " essential preliminary to the granting of a new constitution ".[3]

By refusing to advocate the limitation of India's fiscal autonomy, and by encouraging the use of Indian cotton, the Manchester Chamber of Commerce had done all in its power to conciliate Indian opinion and prepare the way for a favourable trade agreement ; but its efforts were of no avail. The Anglo-Indian Ottawa agreement had not provided for any change in the cotton duties, because an Indian Tariff Board was then considering them. The Clare Lees Mission to India a year later was rather more successful ; it secured an agreement with the Bombay millowners and with all the up-country millowners except those at Ahmedabad. Lancashire recognised that : " The Indian Cotton Textile Industry is entitled for its progressive development to a reasonable measure of protection against the imports of United Kingdom yarns and piece goods." Lancashire further agreed to use more Indian cotton, and to let the Indian cotton industry

---

[1] *Hansard*, 5th series, Vol. 288, col. 717 : H.C., 16th April 1934
[2] *Ibid.*, Vol. 288, col. 714 ff., and Vol. 290, col. 1711 ff. : H.C., 16th April and 13th July 1934.
[3] Proceedings, 10th September and 10th December 1934 ; " Lancashire and India "," Indian Constitutional Reform ", two supplements to *Monthly Record*, August and November 1934.

share the benefit of preferences and quotas secured in Empire
and overseas markets. In return, the Indian millowners
promised not to oppose the removal of the 25 per cent. surtax
on piece-goods imports ; this change would reduce the duty
to 20 per cent. Duties on Lancashire yarns would not exceed
5 per cent. *ad valorem* plus 1¼ annas per lb.[1] Because the
reduction of duties had to wait for an improvement in the
finances of the Government of India, Lancashire did not gain
any tangible advantage from the agreement ; the Manchester
Chamber believed, however, that but for the Clare Lees
Mission the situation would have deteriorated still further,
for India might have imposed specific duties on a sliding
scale.[2] The agreement with the Bombay millowners was not
incorporated into an official trade agreement between the
two countries until the beginning of 1935 ; this trade agreement the Manchester Chamber of Commerce regarded as
" in many ways the coping stone of the work of the past
two or three years ".[3] The coping stone was more ornamental
than useful. It gave Lancashire the right to submit evidence
to the Indian Tariff Board, whose duty it would be " to equate
prices of imported goods to fair selling prices for similar goods
produced in India " ; and it promised an eventual reduction of
the duties on piece goods to 20 per cent. (or 3½ annas per lb.
on plain greys), though for revenue purposes the Indian
Government might raise the duty above 20 per cent. In any
case there would be " no immediate reduction in the duty
and no immediate prospect of increased trade ".[4] In fact,
though Manchester pressed for speedy action and prepared
an elaborate case for the Indian Tariff Board, the duties were
not reduced to 20 per cent. until June 1936 ; and from this
small concession prints, yarns, and rayon piece goods were
excluded.[5]

The Manchester Chamber of Commerce found the reduction
" extremely disappointing ". As the following table shows,
exports to India, after a slight recovery from 1932 to 1935,
fell again in 1936 almost to the calamitous level of 1931. Early
in 1937, the chairman of the India Section of the Chamber
of Commerce admitted that the policy recently followed must
be considered a failure. Since the Indo-Japanese trade

[1] *Monthly Record*, November 1933.   [2] Proceedings, 20th November 1933.
[3] Annual Report for 1934.   [4] *Monthly Record*, January 1935.
[5] Proceedings, 11th February, 8th April and 14th October 1935, and
20th January 1936 ; *Monthly Record*, July 1936.

EXPORTS OF COTTON PIECE GOODS TO INDIA

(million square yards)

1930	778
1931	389
1932	599
1933	486
1934	583
1935	543
1936	416

agreement, signed in 1934, Japanese competition in the Indian market had been strictly limited by quotas ; it was now " abundantly clear that the decline in our trade is due to excessive protection of the Indian cotton industry rather than to Japanese competition ".[1] This accounted for no more than a sixth of Lancashire's losses in the Indian market; elsewhere, Japan had captured more than a third of the trade that Lancashire had lost since 1913.[2]

Nevertheless, the Manchester Chamber of Commerce refused to accept defeat. When negotiations for a new trade agreement began at the end of 1936, it advised the government to press the claims of Lancashire with all possible vigour ; the rapidly growing consumption of Indian cotton would provide a useful bargaining weapon.[3] The Chamber also loyally kept that part of the agreement made with the Bombay millowners in 1933 which allowed India to share the benefits of preferences and quotas ; in 1937 Indian competition in Nigeria and Guatemala provoked complaints, but the Manchester Chamber took no action, because any proposal to check Indian exports " would cut right across the proposition of an agreement with India ".[4] In November 1937 the negotiations for a new agreement broke down, and it was felt that " judged by the standards of the past, even if a new arrangement were made, the future outlook for Lancashire trade in India is anything but bright ".[5] Yet one more effort was made. A Lancashire delegation went to India to hold talks with the Indian cotton industry in the hope of breaking the deadlock; but it could not succeed where the official negotiators had failed, and in the end the two governments

[1] *Monthly Record*, January 1937.   [2] *Ibid.*, June 1937.
[3] Proceedings, 14th December 1936.   [4] *Ibid.*, 11th October 1937.
[5] Annual Report of the India Section for 1937.

had once more to take charge of the negotiations.[1] Eventually, a new agreement was signed in March 1939. It related the Indian import duties to Lancashire's purchases of Indian raw cotton. The higher Lancashire's consumption of Indian cotton the lower the duties would be ; provided Lancashire took the stipulated amount of raw cotton the duties would not rise above $17\frac{1}{2}$ per cent. for prints, and 15 per cent. for other cloths, which represented a considerable reduction from the prevailing rates. The duties could be increased, however, if Lancashire exported more than 500 million yards of cloth to India ; and they could be reduced if Lancashire's exports fell below 350 million yards. The negotiators had clearly taken the Indo-Japanese agreement of 1934 as their model ; and the quantitative restriction of Lancashire's exports to India dealt the final blow to any lingering hopes that the trade could be fully recovered. On paper, however, the agreement was

a considerable advantage to Lancashire when compared with the present situation. . . . It is fairly clear that without an agreement the Lancashire export of piece goods to India would have continued its rapid decline.[2]

The course of trade in 1939 shows that even without a war Lancashire would have continued to lose ground, despite the new agreement. Every year from 1935 onwards the volume of trade shrank, until in 1939 it did not reach 220 million yards.

Thus, successive Manchester policies had failed to prevent the loss of the Indian market. The growth of Indian nationalism had forced Manchester to abandon its stand for free trade in India ; but the conciliatory policy followed between 1925 and 1935 was equally unsuccessful in preventing further losses. When to conciliation Manchester added practical inducements, such as a larger consumption of Indian cotton and the sharing of benefits from textile quotas and preferences, it did secure a reduction of the duties ; but even then the Lancashire cotton industry was not able to surmount the still considerable tariff barriers.

[1] *Monthly Record*, April and June 1938. [2] *Ibid.*, March 1939.

CHAPTER XXIII

THE END OF *LAISSEZ-FAIRE*

IN general terms, it is true to say that the Manchester Chamber of Commerce abandoned its earlier belief in the virtues of *laissez-faire* during the nineteen-thirties. At no time had the Manchester Chamber denied the usefulness of collective action either by the state or by the business men. The very existence of a Chamber of Commerce was incompatible with rigid adherence to extreme individualist doctrines ; and the chief function of the Manchester Chamber has always been to put pressure on the government to do something that would benefit the business community of Manchester and the trade of Lancashire. Nevertheless, in the nineteenth and early twentieth centuries, the larger part of economic life was left to individual decisions and private enterprise. What happened in the nineteen-thirties was that collective action either by the state or by business men became much commoner than before, and that the Manchester Chamber of Commerce either welcomed, or admitted the need for, this widening of the sphere of collective action.

Collective action by the cotton trade has never been easy to arrange, but its advocates found more support after the beginning of general depression in 1929. Even in the nineteen-twenties, the Manchester Chamber had organised a Statistical Bureau with the approval and financial support of the whole cotton trade ; but not until 1930 did the Chamber decide that the time had come for the cotton trade " to push itself a little more vigorously ".[1] This new spirit found expression in the organisation of a " National Cotton Week " in May 1930, a brief but intensive propaganda campaign that would, it was hoped, stimulate the home demand for cotton goods.[2] In 1935 the Chamber appointed a Special Commissioner to manage its newly established Department for the Promotion of Export Trade.[3] And in 1936 the Chamber entered the field

[1] See above, p. 220.
[2] Proceedings, 10th May and 23rd June 1930 ; *Monthly Record*, May 1930.
[3] Proceedings, 14th October 1935.

of group advertising for the first time when it sponsored a Manchester stand at the Johannesburg Exhibition of 1936-37.[1] Nor did the Chamber limit its activities to the stimulation of the cotton trade, for in 1938 it set up an Export Development Register to foster non-textile exports by bringing together merchants and manufacturers.[2] These were ventures that the Chamber would not have seriously considered ten years earlier.

It was clearly recognised that the efforts of business organisations would need to be supplemented by government action. As Mr. (later Sir) Thomas Barlow remarked in his presidential address early in 1933 :

I certainly subscribe as freely as anybody to the abstract doctrine that governmental interference with trade is an evil to be avoided, and that if industry is dependent on governmental aid it cannot be in a sound condition. If times were normal, I would be the first to advocate that Government should interfere as little as possible. . . . The fact is, however, that times are far from being normal, and that no industry either in this country or in any other can hope to plan wisely or progress satisfactorily so long as the fundamental machinery of world trade is all at sixes and sevens. It is beyond the power of industry and trade to put the machinery in working order again because all the vital issues lie with the governments of different countries to determine. Until they are satisfactorily restored, trade and industry are helpless to help themselves.[3]

Prominent among the subjects requiring government intervention were currency and foreign exchange. The Manchester Chamber of Commerce had acquiesced in the restoration of the gold standard in 1925 ; but it was not prepared in the nineteen-thirties to allow the automatic working of any gold standard to ruin the prospects of the cotton trade. Early in 1934, when the International Chamber of Commerce called for the speedy stabilisation of exchange rates, the Manchester Chamber, with Japanese competition in mind, resolved :

The Board is opposed to the stabilisation of the pound sterling under existing world conditions, but in any future consideration of the problem . . . the Board urges that the comparative external and internal values of the British pound and the Japanese yen should be regarded as factors of primary importance.[4]

As long as the danger of Japanese exchange depreciation

---

[1] Proceedings, 15th June and 14th September 1936.
[2] Monthly Record, November 1938.   [3] Ibid., February 1933.
[4] Proceedings, 12th March 1934.

persisted, Lancashire could hardly ignore the dangers of a premature return to the gold standard. On the other hand, the Manchester Chamber approved the use of the Exchange Equalisation Fund to keep sterling rates as steady as possible ; but it felt that to take the further step of fixing an unalterable rate would be going too far.[1]

The decline of the export trade in cotton piece goods left the cotton industry with a vast surplus capacity that had to be eliminated before the industry could be successfully re-organised. At first the work of disposing of surplus capacity was left to various combines, notably the Lancashire Cotton Corporation, acting with the help of the banks but not of the government. In the 'twenties, every suggestion that the plight of the industry demanded government aid was fiercely resented. In 1927 even a proposal for a government inquiry called forth the indignant retort that " Lancashire is surely not so dead yet " as to require government interference.[2] In 1929, when the second Labour government appointed a committee of inquiry into the state of the cotton industry, it did so in the teeth of strong protests from the Manchester Chamber of Commerce which declared :

If we believed in the methods of Mr. Mussolini, it might do very well for the government to have an inquiry and then say what must be done. In this country that is impossible. Improvement in Lancashire's position can only be effected by the voluntary action of the individuals in the trade, who must first be convinced that the changes are necessary.[3]

This attitude did not survive the depression, but it was not until 1936 that the Lancashire cotton industry could agree on any steps that the government could usefully take. In that year the Cotton Spinning Industry Act established a Spindles Board with power to buy and scrap redundant spindles ; the matter was one primarily for the spinners, and officially the Manchester Chamber of Commerce made no comment. Some members strongly opposed, however, the "defeatist" character of the measure, and the President of the Chamber made arrangements for a debate. A resolution opposing the Bill was defeated by 104 votes to 67 ; [4] among those who supported the Bill was Sir Thomas Barlow, who was later to lead the opposition to the more drastic Cotton Industry

[1] *Monthly Record*, July 1937.   [2] *Ibid.*, February 1927.
[3] *Ibid.*, July 1929.   [4] *Ibid.*, February 1936.
20*

(Reorganisation) Bill, which embodied the proposals first outlined in *Lancashire's Remedy*.

Lancashire's Remedy was the work of the Joint Committee of Cotton Trade Organisations. Published towards the end of 1937, it proposed an enabling Bill that would establish a Cotton Industry Board with power to administer redundancy and price schemes submitted to it by the various sections of the industry. In principle, the Manchester Chamber of Commerce did not object to forcible reorganisation of the cotton industry under an Act of Parliament, and it resolved to support the approach to the government for an enabling Bill. On the other hand, as the sole representative body for the export merchants, who opposed *Lancashire's Remedy*, the Chamber insisted that :

Legislation should contain adequate safeguards for the protection of export trade interests and for defence against misuse of monopolistic powers ; unless satisfied with the provisions of the Bill in these and other respects, the Chamber shall be free without breach of faith to oppose it.[1]

Not until the middle of 1938 did the government agree to sponsor an enabling Bill ; and until full details of the proposed Bill had been made known, the Manchester Chamber of Commerce would not commit itself further, though opposition within the industry had already been organised under the leadership of Sir Thomas Barlow and Sir Kenneth Lee. Early in 1939 a special meeting of members of the Manchester Chamber rejected by a narrow majority a resolution in favour of the enabling Bill. At the same time it was decided to form a separate body to represent merchants only, working outside the Chamber but in close co-operation with it ; and by the end of March over five hundred merchants had joined the new Cotton Trade Merchants' Association, on whose committee sat four Directors of the Manchester Chamber of Commerce. A ballot of the members of the Chamber had shown how necessary it was to form a separate merchants' association to oppose the enabling Bill, for whereas the merchants within the Chamber opposed the Bill by a majority of three to one, the large body of producers who belonged to the Chamber supported the Bill almost as heartily as the merchants opposed it; in these circumstances the Manchester Chamber of Commerce had to remain neutral.[2] Nevertheless, however little the Chamber

[1] Proceedings, 29th November 1937 ; *Monthly Record*, December 1937.
[2] *Ibid.*, March and July 1939.

or a large part of its members liked the particular Bill, none disputed the need for collective action of some sort to rescue the cotton trade. Demarcation disputes with the woollen and rayon industries showed that industries which had not suffered in the depression to the same extent as cotton would not tolerate the rigid controls to which the cotton industry was willing to submit. The post-war attitudes of the cotton and woollen industries to the Cotton Board and to the proposed Woollen Industry Development Council respectively, suggested that the individualist tradition had stronger roots in Yorkshire than in Lancashire.

Reorganisation of the cotton industry was one of the two major problems facing Lancashire in the nineteen-thirties ; the other was to attract new industries, which would give employment to displaced cotton operatives and to unemployed coalminers and Merseyside dockers. By the end of 1930 the Manchester Chamber of Commerce, like other representative Lancashire bodies, had recognised that " the contraction of certain staple industries, such as cotton and coal, was likely to prove permanent " ; but the industries that should be replacing cotton and coal were moving steadily southward, to the Midlands and the Greater London area.[1] In an attempt to reverse the trend, the Lancashire Chambers of Commerce agreed to form the Lancashire Industrial Development Council, which the Manchester Chamber would run on their behalf ; Manchester promised £500 a year to the new organisation.[2] In general, the Manchester Chamber of Commerce left the Industrial Development Council to act independently, and took little direct part in the attempt to bring new industries to Lancashire. In 1933, for instance, it was the Industrial Development Council, not the Manchester Chamber, that protested against the government's refusal to control the location of industry ;[3] though everybody knew that behind the Industrial Development Council there lay the organisation and influence of the Manchester Chamber of Commerce. When the rearmament drive began in 1936, the Chamber of Commerce took a more active part ; its Engineering Section co-operated with the Industrial Development Council to attract defence orders to Lancashire, and the Chamber urged Lancashire M.P.s to keep the county's interests

[1] Proceedings, 8th December 1930.
[2] *Ibid.*, 26th January, 13th April and 11th May 1931.
[3] *Monthly Record*, May 1933.

prominently before the government.   At first it did not appear
that many contracts would be placed in Lancashire ; but
early in 1937 all the distressed areas joined in a chorus of
protest when the government announced that it was to
build a new aircraft factory near Maidenhead.   The Manchester Chamber lent its voice to the outcry, and the government, hastily changing its mind, agreed to establish the new
factory at Speke, near Liverpool.[1]

The " special areas " legislation, by which the government
hoped to reduce unemployment in the districts that had
suffered most from the depression, was not particularly
effective during the nineteen-thirties ; but on the principle
that every little helps, the Manchester Chamber and the
Industrial Development Council wished to see the Wigan coal
district and the weaving belt north-east of Blackburn and
Darwen classified as special areas.   The Special Areas
(Amendment) Act of 1937 did not meet this demand, but it
did allow the Commissioner for Special Areas to make grants
to companies that wished to develop trading estates in areas
of heavy unemployment outside those classified as "special".
Lancashire lost no time in taking advantage of this law, and
by the beginning of 1938 the Lancashire Industrial Sites
Company had been formed.[2]

During the nineteen-twenties, Manchester merchants had
resolutely opposed the export credits scheme, on the ground
that it would foster nothing but " unsound " business.[3]
The depression, and the continued growth of the Manchester
engineering industry, caused a change of outlook ; and by
1933 the Chamber was urging the government to extend the
scope of the export credits scheme.[4]   In 1935, when a careful
investigation was made of prospects in the China market,
little hope could be seen for Lancashire's traditional export
trade in cotton piece goods ; on the other hand, China was
increasing her purchases of textile machinery, locomotives,
prime movers, and heavy chemicals, all goods that Lancashire
was well fitted to supply.   Given " credit on a scale unusual
in normal trade relations ", credit that only the British
Government could provide, China might well become a

[1] Proceedings, 9th March and 15th June 1936 and 25th January 1937 ;
Hansard, 5th series, Vol. 319, cols. 481-90, 753-54 : H.C., 21st and 26th
January 1937.
[2] Proceedings, 14th December 1936 ; Monthly Record, January 1938.
[3] See above, p. 219.   [4] Proceedings, 15th May 1933.

very satisfactory customer of the Lancashire engineering and chemical industries.[1]

Though this particular hope was never fulfilled, Lancashire continued its recovery from the depression. Early in 1938 Sir Edward Rhodes had expressed the hope that the decline in cotton goods exports was now over, and that " our present levels represent rock-bottom ".[2] This hope also was disappointed ; actually, the years 1938 and 1939 were anything but prosperous years for the cotton trade. Nevertheless, Lancashire could face the future with some confidence ; the engineering and chemical industries were prospering, and newer industries were making " excellent progress ".[3] On the eve of the Second World War, the Manchester Chamber of Commerce could fairly claim that Lancashire had made the adjustment

rendered necessary by the changed position of its staple industries, coal and cotton ; it has brought in new industries to fill the gaps and is today as vitally powerful a division of the economic forces that this country commands as ever it was.[4]

Much has happened since 1938 to test the vitality and resilience of Manchester and of Lancashire ; the story is not yet ended, but the spirit of the city and the county remains as stubborn and as staunch as ever.

[1] Proceedings, 8th July 1935.   [2] *Monthly Record*, February 1938.
[3] *Ibid.*, January 1938.   [4] Annual Report for 1938.

APPENDIX

THE MEMBERS OF THE MANCHESTER CHAMBER OF COMMERCE

FROM its establishment in 1820, the Manchester Chamber of Commerce was looked upon as the mouthpiece of the Lancashire cotton trade, though in fact it did not always have enough members to be a truly representative body. In 1825, when the first printed list appeared, the Chamber had 229 members ; by 1845 the number had risen to rather more than 300, but when the protectionists seceded to form the Manchester Commercial Association the membership of the Chamber declined and stood little higher in 1853 than it had done in 1825.[1] The reunion of the Commercial Association and the Chamber of Commerce in 1858 added more than 100 members,[2] and a canvass of local firms had by 1860 raised the number of subscribers to nearly 500.[3] No further increase in numbers took place until the end of the eighteen-eighties, when in the space of a few years a vigorous recruiting drive raised the membership from 550 to 1,000.[4] Not until the twentieth century did numbers begin to rise again, but by 1911 the Chamber had more than 1,500 members.[5] Numbers continued to grow and by 1927 had reached 2,600. From that time, as the depression in the cotton trade deepened, the trend was reversed and for the next five years members fell away, especially among textile exporters.[6] Matters improved in 1933 and the succeeding years, but even in 1935 the Chamber still had fewer than 2,300 members.[7]

The table given below analyses the membership of the Manchester Chamber of Commerce in the years 1825, 1860, 1900, and 1935. No special significance attaches to these dates, which were chosen for convenience only : in 1825 appeared the first printed list of members ; and in 1935 we have the Chamber's own handbook with details of its members' businesses ; 1860 and 1900 were convenient intermediate points. Local directories,[8] supplemented in 1900 by the Chamber's own records, give the required information for most of the members, but it has not been possible to trace all the names. In 1935, when

---

[1] Annual Reports for 1825, 1845 and 1853.
[2] *Manchester Guardian*, 27th January 1859.
[3] Annual Report for 1860.
[4] Proceedings, 27th January 1887 ; Annual Report for 1889.
[5] *Monthly Record*, February 1912.
[6] Proceedings, 12th December 1932.
[7] *Manchester Chamber of Commerce Handbook*, 1935-6.
[8] Pigot's *Directory of Northern England*, 1816-17, and *Manchester Directory*, 1832 ; Slater's *Directory of the Northern Counties*, 1848 and 1858 ; Whelan's *Manchester Directory*, 1853; the *Manchester Directory*, 1854-5, published by the *Manchester Examiner and Times* ; *Manchester Royal Exchange Directory*, 1899-1900 ; Edward's *Manchester and Salford Directory*, 1906.

the official handbook is available, the number of members who cannot be assigned to one category or another is very small.

THE MEMBERS OF THE MANCHESTER CHAMBER OF COMMERCE, 1825-1935

	1825	1860	1900	1935
Total	229	484	1,108	2,249
(1) Cotton	150	352	674	1,192
Spinners and Doublers	14	30	78	78
Manufacturers	32	42	94	330
Spinners and Manufacturers	16	41	16	43
Finishers	33	30	64	136
Merchant-Producers	4	11	22	96
Merchants	34	159	323	400
Others	17	39	77	109
(2) Other Trades, etc.	56	104	352	1,044
Engineering	4	13	47	196
Chemicals	7	7	67	108
Food	20	13	61	87
Clothing		not known		125
Transport	1	7	12	47
Banking	4	10	14	30
Miscellaneous	20	54	151	451
(3) Untraced	23	28	82	13

Some explanation of the terms used in the table is perhaps necessary. In the cotton section the " merchant-producers " are mostly manufacturers and merchants, though large integrated firms like Rylands and Sons and Tootal Broadhurst Lee also come into this category ; " merchants " include " shippers " and yarn merchants ; " others " is a miscellaneous group comprising importers of raw cotton, yarn agents, grey cloth agents, packers, and ware-housemen. The engineering, chemical, and food sections include merchants as well as manufacturers ; indeed, in 1825 importers and dealers in food were a relatively large group, but food processors or manufacturers did not join the Manchester Chamber in any numbers until the end of the century. The " miscellaneous " group (which has grown steadily in relative importance as the Chamber has become more fully representative of Manchester's business life) comprises a wide variety of activities : advertising agents, chartered account-ants, solicitors, insurance companies, forwarding agents, general merchants, stock-brokers, printers, and manufacturers of many different products.

The table shows that even in 1935 the cotton industry directly provided over half the members of the Manchester Chamber of Commerce, and indirectly many more ; and in earlier years the predominance of cotton interests had been greater still. Within the cotton trade, merchants were naturally the largest group, but producers belonged to the Chamber in much larger numbers than

might have been expected. In 1825 they outnumbered the merchants, though perhaps not so much as the figures suggest : the
finishers were mostly described in the directories as " calico printers
and warehousemen " and this may mean that they were in process of
becoming merchant converters. The sharp decline after 1860 in
the number of firms that combined spinning and manufacturing
is an interesting reflection of a well-known trend ; what is more
surprising is that in 1860 combined spinning and weaving firms were
relatively more numerous than they had been thirty-five years before.

The Board of Directors of the Manchester Chamber of Commerce
was similarly dominated by the cotton trade.

THE DIRECTORS OF THE MANCHESTER CHAMBER OF COMMERCE,
1825-1935

	1825	1860	1900	1935
Total	24	24	28	42
(1) Cotton	19	19	22	33
Spinners	6	2	2	3
Manufacturers	4	—	3	4
Spinners and Manufacturers	—	4	2	2
Finishers	2	1	—	3
Merchant-Producers	—	1	4	5
Merchants	6	9	9	14
Others	1	2	2	2
(2) Other Trades, etc.	3	5	6	9
Engineering	1	—	—	2
Chemicals	—	—	3	—
Food	—	1	1	2
Banking	—	2	—	—
Transport	—	1	1	2
Miscellaneous	2	1	1	3
(3) Untraced	2	—	—	—

Because the Chamber concerned itself with the commercial rather
than the industrial problems of the cotton trade, merchants formed
the largest group of Directors ; but, as in the membership at large,
producers did not go unrepresented. Apart from the cotton trade,
the only other interest that regularly had a seat on the Board of
Directors was the Bridgewater Trust and its successor, the Manchester
Ship Canal Company. The sectional system, by which small trades
could be assured of a seat on the Board of Directors, did little before
1939 to diminish the predominance of cotton interests ; until 1939
there were never more than six non-cotton sections, and one of those
(the Chemical Section) was often represented on the Board of Directors by a finisher, not a chemical manufacturer. The President of
the Chamber was usually chosen from the cotton trade ; only rarely
was an ironmaster, an engineer, or a chemical manufacturer elected
to this distinguished office.

INDEX

HALIFAX, 140.
Hallé, Charles, xix.
Hamburg, 58.
Hart, Sir Robert, 82.
Haydon, Benjamin, xix.
Heaton, J. Henniker, 153.
Helm, Elijah, 172.
Henderson, W. O., 16 n., 17 n., 18 n.
Hibbert, H. F., 105, 106.
Hoare, Sir Samuel, 286-8.
Holland, 47, 62, 84, 151.
Hongkong, 80 n., 81, 254.
Hubbard, G. E., 250 n., 253 n.
Huddersfield, 88.

IBADAN, 74.
Imperial preference : 201, 205, 214, 240-1, 247 ; action against Japan, 250 ff., 257-9 ; relations with India, 280-2, 284, 288-9 ; arguments against, 101, 107-8 ; preferences on foodstuffs, 274-6 ; Ottawa agreements, 241-6, 251, 257, 264, 273-4.
Import Duties Advisory Committee, 243, 247, 275.
India : constitution, 15, 23, 26-7, 285-7 ; cotton industry, 28-9, 36-8, 41, 46, 99, 145, 200, 249, 251, 277-8, 283, 287 ; currency and finance, 13, 16-17, 23-4, 26, 29, 31, 33, 34, 39-40 ; export credits, 219 ; factory acts, 41-2 ; fiscal autonomy, 279, 280, 282-3, 285-7 ; import duties, 13, 23-6, 27-31, 34, 40-1, 43, 109, 213, 245, 250, 278 ff.; excise duties, 41, 43, 278-80 ; Japanese competition, 280, 284, 289 ; law, 13-16, 45 ; nationalism, 45-6, 282-3, 284, 290 ; public works, 13, 14 ; railways, 13, 32-4 ; cotton growing and supply, 13-20, 77, 284-5, 289 ; telegraph, 154 ; trade agreements, 265, 267, 284 ff.; trade-marks, 142. See also Cotton goods, export of.
Industry, location of, 295-6.
International Association of the Congo, 64.
International Chamber of Commerce, 233.
Irwell, River, 178.
Ismay, T. H., 177.
Ispahan, 86.
Italy, 48-9, 213, 224.
Ivory Coast, 251.

JACKSON, Sir Richard, 285.
Japan : cotton industry, 99-100, 200 ; exchange depreciation, 292 ; export of cotton goods, 212-3, 248 ff., 280, 289 ; extra-territoriality, 83 ; import of cotton goods, 80, 83, 263 ; import of yarn, 36-8 ; supplier of raw materials, 83 ; tariff, 83-4 ; trade agreements, 265, 266, 269.
Jewkes, J., 212 n.
Joint Committee of Cotton Trade Organisations, 282, 294.
Justice, administration of, 130-4.

KANO, 77.
Karachi, 33, 222, 282.
Kianghung, 88.
Kumasi, 72.

LAGOS, 60-2, 66, 70, 72-3, 75, 143.
Laing, Hon. S., 14.
Laird, McGregor, 60.
Langdon, E. H., 169.
Lashio, 89.
Latvia, 241, 261, 272.
Law : of bankruptcy, 135-6 ; of contract, 136 ; international, 85, 167, 170-3, 191 ; of partnership, 45, 136-7, 140 ; of patents, 125-9, 205. See also Company Law, Justice.
League of Nations, 233.
Leech, Sir Bosdin T., 179 n., 182 n., 183 n., 184 n., 185.
Leeds, 112, 140, 173.
Lees, Sir William Clare, 286-8.
Leicester, 158.
Leopold II of Belgium, 62, 64, 65, 68.
Levi, Leone, 138.
Levinstein, Ivan, 126-7.
Liberia, 58.
Li Hung Chang, 81.
Likin. See China, internal tolls.
Linen industry, xx.
Lithuania, 261, 272.
Liverpool : and Africa, 66, 70, 252 ; and bimetallism, 35 ; and Burma, 88 ; and the cotton famine, 13ⁿ; and the Manchester Ship Canal, 93, 182-3 ; import of raw cotton, 59 ; Mersey Docks and Harbour Board, 174-7 ; sugar refiners, 103 ; town dues, 174-5 ; miscellaneous references, 132, 140, 146, 155, 163, 170, 183.